Dictionary of
Behavior Therapy
Techniques

(PGPS-132)

Pergamon Titles of Related Interest

Barlow/Hersen SINGLE CASE EXPERIMENTAL DESIGNS: Strategies
for Studying Behavior Change, Second Edition
Bellack/Hersen RESEARCH METHODS IN CLINICAL PSYCHOLOGY
Goldstein/Hersen HANDBOOK OF PSYCHOLOGICAL ASSESSMENT
Hersen/Bellack BEHAVIORAL ASSESSMENT: A Practical Handbook,
Second Edition
Papajohn INTENSIVE BEHAVIOR THERAPY: The Behavioral
Treatment of Complex Emotional Disorders
Wolpe THE PRACTICE OF BEHAVIOR THERAPY, Third Edition

Related Journals*

ADVANCES IN BEHAVIOUR RESEARCH AND THERAPY
BEHAVIOUR RESEARCH AND THERAPY
CLINICAL PSYCHOLOGY REVIEW
JOURNAL OF BEHAVIOR THERAPY AND EXPERIMENTAL
PSYCHIATRY

*Free sample copies available upon request

PERGAMON GENERAL PSYCHOLOGY SERIES

EDITORS

Arnold P. Goldstein, *Syracuse University*
Leonard Krasner, *SUNY at Stony Brook*

Dictionary of Behavior Therapy Techniques

Edited by

Alan S. Bellack

*Medical College of Pennsylvania
at Eastern Pennsylvania Psychiatric Institute*

Michel Hersen

*University of Pittsburgh
School of Medicine*

PERGAMON PRESS

New York   Oxford   Toronto   Sydney   Paris   Frankfurt

Pergamon Press Offices:

U.S.A.   Pergamon Press Inc., Maxwell House, Fairview Park,
                Elmsford, New York 10523, U.S.A.

U.K.   Pergamon Press Ltd., Headington Hill Hall,
                Oxford OX3 0BW, England

CANADA   Pergamon Press Canada Ltd., Suite 104, 150 Consumers Road,
                Willowdale, Ontario M2J 1P9, Canada

AUSTRALIA   Pergamon Press (Aust.) Pty. Ltd., P.O. Box 544,
                Potts Point, NSW 2011, Australia

FRANCE   Pergamon Press SARL, 24 rue des Ecoles,
                75240 Paris, Cedex 05, France

FEDERAL REPUBLIC   Pergamon Press GmbH, Hammerweg 6,
OF GERMANY   D-6242 Kronberg-Taunus, Federal Republic of Germany

Copyright © 1985 Pergamon Press Inc.

Library of Congress Cataloging in Publication Data
Main entry under title:

Dictionary of behavior therapy techniques.

  (Pergamon general psychology series ; 132)
  Bibliography: p.
  Includes index.
  1. Behavior therapy--Dictionaries. 2. Behavior
modification--Dictionaries. I. Hersen, Michel.
II. Series.
RC489.B4D54   1984   616.89′142   84-14801
ISBN 0-08-030168-1
ISBN 0-08-030167-3 (pbk.)

Printed in the United States of America

CONTENTS

PREFACE

Twenty years ago behavior therapy consisted of only a handful of distinguishable treatment procedures: systematic desensitization, implosion, token economies, various operant procedures, and so on. Even with this small number of techniques there were terminological arguments and areas of confusion. For example, was flooding synonomous with implosion or were they only partially overlapping? However, it was easy for the 1960s behavior therapist to provide a (generally) accurate description of every available technique. Even the beginning student could quickly develop name recognition for the entire behavioral armamentarium. As is obvious to every current behavior therapist and student, this situation has changed dramatically in the last two decades. The field has expanded at a dizzying rate. Behavioral technology has been applied to a host of new problems and populations. Our theoretical perspective has become more diverse, leading to alternative and competing "behavioral" conceptualizations of many disorders. The behavioral database has expanded geometrically, stimulating the development of scores of new procedures and the modification of existing strategies.

This tremendous development has made it impossible for anyone to be expert on the entire field. We have entered an era of specialization: behavioral medicine, cognitive behavior therapy, applied behavior analysis, depression, and so on. Each area has its own increasingly large, technical, and arcane literature. Not only has it become impossible for anyone to be conversant with all of the specific treatment procedures employed, but even sophisticated readers regularly come across terms and procedures that they cannot readily define. The neophyte regularly becomes lost in the terminological morass. There are as many separable treatments for some individual problems (e.g., phobias, noncompliant behavior) as existed for *all* disorders 20 years ago. Furthermore, many treatments have numerous sub-components or variations which further complicate the matter. For example: systematic desensitization, self-control desensitization, in vivo desensitization, covert rehearsal, and contact desensitization are all related variations of Wolpe's original procedure. Until now, there have been two courses of action one could take upon encountering a new or confusing term: ask a colleague or go through the often laborious procedure of referring to a basic source on the topic. Neither of these solutions is convenient or apt to provide reliable information. The former tends to yield opinion more than fact, while the latter generally provides data rather than a brief overview of clinical issues. We have felt the need for a single source book which concisely defines and describes the full range of behavioral treatment techniques; a resource which provides an accurate but brief overview for the casual reader rather than the in-depth review required by the expert. This volume is designed to meet that need.

We have ventured to catalog every identifiable behavioral technique. We generated an initial list by culling through our own behavioral libraries. We then circulated this list among a large number of colleagues, requesting additions and changes. This expanded list was then reviewed by the contributors to this volume. Each technique was classified as major, secondary, or minor as a function of its overall significance or breadth of application. This classification was reviewed by all contributors, and determined the amount of coverage accorded to each procedure. Contributors were requested to submit 5–10 pages for major techniques, 3–5 for secondary, and one-half-page for minor entries. Major and secondary techniques are first defined, and clinical applications are then described and evaluated. Differential diagnostic guidelines for use, side effects, contraindications, and expected outcomes are presented when justified by the literature. Finally, references for more detailed reports are provided. Minor techniques and component elements of major or secondary techniques are simply defined and cross-referred to the parent entry. For the most part, we have avoided the typical use of in-text citations to support conclusions and identify specific research studies. Our interest was to provide a clinically oriented overview, rather than empirically based reviews and critical evaluations. Our goal was to produce a ready reference source from which the student, clinician, or scientist could quickly and easily learn what a technique is, how it is applied, and to what other procedures it is related.

We would like to express our appreciation to the many contributors to this volume, whose cooperation and knowledge were essential. We would also like to thank Florence Levito and Mary Newell for their heroic secretarial and administrative assistance. Finally, we would like to thank Jerry Frank for his support on this and other projects.

Alan S. Bellack, Ph.D.
Michel Hersen, Ph.D.

Dictionary of Behavior Therapy Techniques

(PGPS-132)

ALTERNATIVE INCOMPATIBLE BEHAVIOR
Patricia Wisocki

In eliminating problem behavior it is advisable at the same time to reinforce alternative behavior which is incompatible with the problem behavior. Inclusion of the strategy in a treatment program avoids the potentially harmful side effects of punishment and enhances the opportunity for positive gain. Change agents should be careful to select incompatible behavior which will be reinforced in the natural environment after the treatment program is discontinued.

See: Differential Reinforcement of Other Behavior

ANGER CONTROL THERAPY
Raymond W. Novaco

This treatment method for problems of anger and aggression is a cognitive-behavioral intervention that follows a more general therapeutic model known as "stress inoculation." The stress inoculation approach is a coping skills therapy that aims to provide the client with the cognitive and behavioral resources for dealing with stressful situations and for regulating personal stress reactions.

Anger problems are understood in terms of human stress because anger can be prompted by exposure to environmental demands that are ambient as well as acute and that are temporally distant as well as proximate. This derives from a conception of anger as an emotional state defined by the presence of physiologcal arousal and antagonistic cognitions. Exposure to environmental demands, which may be elements of physical, social, or biological fields, can induce physiological arousal and influence cognitive structures that determine the perception and interpretation of events. A second reason for the stress framework is that anger as a recurrent problem has consequences considerably beyond a transient emotional upset. Anger reactions can be part of a learned style of coping with life demands, such as work pressures or family problems. Anger activates aggressive behavior and harm-doing actions, but even less intense antagonistic responses increase the stressful components of one's life. Moreover, anger has been linked to various stress-related disorders, particularly cardiovascular problems such as coronary artery disease and hypertension. The stress framework, therefore, informs us about the range of circumstances that can engender anger and about the adverse consequences of anger proneness.

The stress inoculation procedures are a coping skills therapy, and the therapeutic process hypothetically works by first developing coping skills and then exposing the client to manageable doses of a stressor; doses that arouse, but do not overwhelm, the client's defenses. The procedures are designed to help the client learn to cope with stressful events having a high probability of occurrence. Additionally, in learning how to regulate thoughts, emotions, and behavior and to optimize environmental conditions so as to reduce exposure to stressors, anger management is achieved by preventive means as well as by coping activities.

As a cognitive-behavioral intervention, the treatment is based on theoretical principles of cognitive mediation of emotion and behavior. The anger control procedures are based on the view that emotional arousal and the course of action that such arousal instigates are determined by one's cognitive structuring of the situation—specifically by expectations and appraisals. Further, the therapeutic procedures are predicated on the proposition that behavior is reciprocally related to internal emotional state. Therefore, one's actions influence the occurrence of anger and accompanying cognitions.

The stress inoculation approach to anger control aims to impart coping skills that are of three basic kinds: (a) preventive, (b) regulatory, and (c) executional. The general goals are to prevent anger from occurring when it is maladaptive, to enable the client to regulate arousal when it does occur, and to provide the performance skills needed to manage the provocation experience.

CLINICAL PROCEDURES

The treatment approach involves three basic steps or phases: (1) cognitive preparation, (2) skill acquisition, and (3) application training.

The cognitive preparation phase educates clients about the functions of anger and about their personal anger patterns. It also provides a shared language system between client and therapist and introduces the rationale of treatment. An instructional manual for clients is used to facilitate these tasks. Clients are also asked to maintain a self-monitoring record or diary that serves as a database for discussion of therapeutic principles and goals. The anger control components of the cognitive preparation phase consist of (a) identifying the persons and situations that trigger anger, (b) distinguishing anger from aggression, (c) understanding the multiple determinants of anger, (d) understanding provocation in terms of interaction sequences, and (e) introducing the anger management techniques as coping strategies to handle conflict and stress.

The skill acquisition phase teaches cognitive arousal reduction and behavioral coping skills which follow from the model of anger. At the cognitive level, the client

is taught to alternatively view provocation circumstances and to modify the exaggerated importance often attached to events. A basic goal is to promote flexibility in one's cognitive structuring. In this regard, expectations and appraisals linked with anger arousal are targets for modification. Particular attention is paid to inordinately high expectations of others' behavior and to the appraisal of events as personal affronts or ego threats. The ability to "not take things personally" is a fundamental skill. This is accomplished by fostering a task orientation to provocation, which involves a focus on desired outcomes and the implementation of a behavioral strategy to produce those outcomes. The cognitive modification goals are facilitated by the use of self-instructions in the form of coping self-statements designed for specific provocation events. Applied to various stages of a provocation sequence, these self-statements serve as instructional cues that guide the client's thoughts, feelings, and behavior toward effective coping.

For arousal reduction, the client is taught relaxation skills and is also encouraged to begin a personally suited program that is explicitly directed at reducing arousal monitored by the client and therapist. This may involve continued use of the deep-muscle relaxation techniques and/or alternative strategies such as hypnosis, meditation, yoga, Tai Chi, aerobic exercise, or aesthetic enjoyment. An imporant cognitive element to arousal reduction is the attenuation of the angry client's preoccupation/rumination tendencies. By dwelling on provocation experiences, arousal is prolonged or revivified. Through self-monitoring and self-instructions this self-defeating cycle can be short-circuited.

The behavioral coping skills concern the effective communication of feelings, assertiveness, and the implementation of task-oriented, problem-solving action. The client is helped to maximize the adaptive functions of anger and to minimize its maladaptive functions. When arousal is activated, the client is taught to recognize anger on the basis of internal and external cues and to then communicate that anger in a non-hostile form or use it to energize problem-solving action, keeping the arousal at moderate levels of intensity. The task-oriented response set gears the person to engage in behavior that is instrumental to producing desired outcomes. Anger becomes a signal that problem-solving strategies are to be implemented, which requires a focus on issues and objectives. This prevents the accumulation of anger and prevents aggressive over-reaction by imposing thought between impulse and action. The client is also taught how to optimize environmental domains in which they routinely function (e.g., home, work, transportation, recreation) so as to minimize exposure to stressors and maximize environmental reinforcers.

The various coping skills are modeled by the therapist who then gives the client the opportunity to practice them in the application training phase. The anger control procedures are designed to build personal competence and, therefore, the client's proficiency must be tested. The practice is conducted by means of imaginal and role play inductions of anger. The context of these simulated provocations is constructed in collaboration with the client. They are presented in a hierarchical sequence, as in systematic desensitization. The scenarios involve anger situations that the client is likely to encounter in real life. The coping skills that have been rehearsed with the therapist are then applied to these simulated provocations beginning with the mildest and progressing to the most anger-arousing. This process continues throughout the course of treatment and enables both client and therapist to gauge the client's proficiency.

The stress inoculation approach to anger control is a particular kind of cognitive-behavioral therapy that emphasizes coping skills for handling stressful events and regulating disturbing emotions. This approach differs from other cognitive-behavioral therapies with regard to the explicit attention given to the environmental/contextual determinants of problem conditions and its three-phased structure, including the explicit exposure to graduated dosages of problem-relevant stimuli. The cognitive and behavioral coping skills are designed to control negative, self-defeating ideation, to divert attention from anger-engendering stimulation, to promote alternative constructions of provocation events, to regulate physiological arousal, and to implement problem-solving behavior.

EXPECTED OUTCOMES

The treatment method is designed for 8 to 15 sessions. The success of therapy can be gauged according to several dimensions linked to the model of anger. Self-report, physiological, and behavioral measures are ideally used as evaluative indices. Because of the importance of physiological arousal in anger reactions, this dimension should not be ignored. Measures of cardiovascular activation, especially blood pressure and heart rate, are easily obtained. There should occur a lowering of arousal in conjunction with stressor exposure and in baseline arousal.

Cognitive changes centrally involve attaining greater flexibility in how potentially provoking events are appraised, more realistic expectations of self and others, and the ability to adjust expectations according to the situation. Efficacy expectations for dealing with problem situations should increase, associated with increases in positive self-statements and decreases in negative self-statements. The tendency to remain pre-occupied with provoking events, dwelling on aversive experiences, should also be attenuated. The capacity to generate alternative solutions to problem situations should be augmented.

The treatment method entails the development and application of behavioral skills for use in interpersonal exchanges and promoting personal well-being. Verbal and non-verbal aspects of interactional behavior can be assessed with regard to the client's handling of provocation encounters and dealing with persistent problem situations. Reductions in antagonistic style and improvements in task-oriented, problem-solving responses should be in evidence.

Generally, there should occur a lowering of the frequency, intensity, and duration of anger, as well as a reduction in antagonistic modes of expression.

CONTRAINDICATIONS

As a self-control therapy, the effectiveness depends upon the active participation of the client. Consequently, the treatment approach is not suited for those who cannot become collaborators in the treatment process. Because the intervention is cognitively-based, the treatment requires adequate cognitive functioning and would not have value for psychotic or mentally retarded populations.

BIBLIOGRAPHY

Meichenbaum, D., & Jaremko, M. (Eds.). (1983). *Stress reduction and prevention.* New York: Plenum Press.

Novaco, R. W. (1975). *Anger control: The development and evaluation of an experimental treatment.* Lexington, MA: D. C. Heath.

Novaco, R. W. (1977). Stress inoculation: A cognitive therapy for anger and its application to a case of depression. *Journal of Consulting and Clinical Psychology, 45,* 600–608.

Novaco, R. W. (1980). Training of probation counselors for anger problems. *Journal of Counseling Psychology, 27,* 385–390.

Novaco, R. W. (1981). Anger and its therapeutic regulation. In M. Chesney, S. Goldston, & R. Rosenman (Eds.), *Anger and hostility in behavioral and cardiovascular disorders.* New York: McGraw-Hill.

See: Cognitive Restructuring
     Cognitive Therapy
     Deep Muscle Relaxation
     Stress Inoculation

ANXIETY MANAGEMENT TRAINING
Richard M. Suinn

Anxiety Management Training (AMT) is a treatment technique involving coping with anxiety arousal and onset through relaxation. AMT is designed to maximize self-control training, to aid clients in early identification of cognitive or physiological cues of anxiety onset, to directly experience progress in anxiety regulation during sessions, and to enhance transfer of skills to life conditions. To achieve these objectives, AMT sessions rely upon relaxation training, imagery rehearsal, anxiety activation, graduated training, and homework assignments.

AMT uses a 6–8 session foundation, with treatment being continued or terminated depending upon client evidence of progress. Each session gradually expands the client's training and gradually fades out therapist control to increase client control. Sessions run as follows:

session 1 • relaxation training under therapist control.

session 2 • relaxation with briefer method under therapist control, anxiety arousal/coping under therapist guidance.

session 3 • client-controlled relaxation, training in anxiety cue awareness under therapist control.

session 4 • client-controlled relaxation, partial client control over anxiety arousal/coping.

sessions 5–8 • client completely in control

of relaxation, and of anxiety arousal and coping.

The specific method for anxiety activation is the use of guided imagery, whereby the client visualizes and re-experiences a real-life anxiety event. During this guided imagery, the anxiety is aroused in all of the components characteristic for the individual client, such as catastrophic thoughts, increased physiological reactivity, and/or speech or motor disruptions. Once activated, the client is then guided to reinstate emotional control through use of relaxation.

Progress is determined through use of logs and homework assignments. Logs assess level of skills on relaxation, awareness of anxiety-onset cues, and transfer of coping to in vivo settings. Homework assignments require the client to transfer the various types of skills to life conditions that are increasingly demanding as levels of skills increase.

Unlike flooding or implosive therapy, AMT sessions end with relaxation and coping and the client emotionally comfortable. Unlike the various types of desensitization, AMT was initially designed for 'free-floating' anxiety or generalized anxiety disorder, where specific anxiety hierarchies cannot be constructed. In addition, AMT differs in adding systematic, session-by-session instructions for each stage of training, fading, and homework assignments.

CLINICAL APPLICATIONS

Anxiety Management Training has proven valuable for a number of applications. Research studies have demonstrated AMT's effectiveness with specific (i.e., phobias) and generalized (i.e., general) anxiety, such as test anxiety, public speaking anxiety, music performance anxiety, mathematics anxiety, state, and trait anxiety. Published research also demonstrated AMT's efficacy

with medical and health disorders where anxiety acts in a central role, such as hypertension, dysmenorrhea, duodenal ulcers, and diabetes mellitus. AMT has also been applied to clinical populations where anxiety reduction was assumed to be important for behavioral change, such as in anxious schizophrenics, adjudicated delinquents, Type A persons, and female medical outpatients reporting depression. Preliminary study is underway on the use of AMT with impulse control and anger control. Populations receiving AMT treatment have included: community mental health center generalized anxiety disorder patients, hospitalized schizophrenics, ethnic minority high school students preparing for college, university counseling center students with multiple specific anxieties, musicians, and outpatients with medical complaints such as diabetes mellitus, dysmenorrhea, or gynecological or family stresses.

EXPECTED OUTCOMES AND TIME FRAME

The basic AMT treatment model covers 6–8 sessions, either individually or in groups. Specific determination of the length of treatment for any client will depend upon observations of client progress through data from interviews, logs, and homework assignments. Assessment of progress emphasizes behavioral information, such as the client's success in vivo.

Since the AMT sessions are structured, expectations of skills to be achieved at each session can be specified. Homework assignments following each session also help to delineate the desired skills. At the end of session 1, the client is expected to achieve relaxation within about 30–45 minutes, using the tensing-relaxing procedure, under quiet conditions. Homework is assigned along these lines. After session 2, the client is expected to be able to achieve relaxation through simple muscle review and without tensing, within about 20–30 minutes. The client is also expected to show some ability to regain relaxation following anxiety activation, but under therapist guidance. Homework expands relaxation practice outside of the home, but in non-demanding settings such as while riding quietly in a car.

By session 3, the client is expected to initiate relaxation through rapid muscle review or under cue-control. The client is also expected to show some gains in identifying the cognitive or physiological cues of anxiety onset. Finally, some early stages of self-control in preventing stress in vivo is expected as part of homework activities. After session 4, the client is expected to show early the ability to cope with anxiety arousal through withdrawal from anxiety imagery, and retrieval of relaxation. Homework continues the use of relaxation activity to prevent anxiety onset, based upon awareness of anxiety cues.

From session 5 onward, the client is expected to experience anxiety arousal via imagery, and to eliminate such arousal with relaxation, but while remaining in the anxiety situation being visualized. Homework follows the progress of the client not only in prevention, but also in coping with anxiety arousal.

The general pattern of AMT sessions separates sessions 1 and 2 by one week at the minimum. After that, sessions may be a week apart or as close as three days apart, pending client's evidence of progress in achieving the goals of each session.

POTENTIAL SIDE-EFFECTS OR CONTRAINDICATIONS

One positive side-effect can be the freeing up of patients to either utilize other therapies, or to identify core problems needing additional attention. Regarding the former,

some hospitalized schizophrenics were rated as more able to make productive use of traditional psychotherapy following AMT. Regarding the latter, some community mental health patients diagnosed as generalized anxiety disorder were able to specify other target problems (such as social skills deficits) once their major anxiety state was brought under control. In research with clients showing multiple anxieties or phobias, AMT resulted in reductions of these additional anxieties even though not addressed specifically by AMT. Further, in contrast to systematic desensitization, AMT led to reductions in both targeted and nontargeted anxieties after treatment terminated and during follow-up evaluation. Since AMT involves self-control, self-efficacy improvement appears to be a beneficial side effect reported by some patients.

The major caution for any behavioral therapy program involving anxiety activation is the possibility of the anxiety being out of control. In the rare circumstances where this occurs, the establishment of relaxation control by the therapist is a simple solution. Additionally, therapists should evaluate progress of each client before proceeding on to the next steps in training, to assure client readiness. To date, evidence is that chronic hospitalized schizophrenic patients as well as persons diagnosed as generalized anxiety disorder appear to tolerate and benefit from AMT, in spite of the presence of other psychotic manifestations or intensity of the anxiety. AMT has been applied with some elderly clients, but the training seems to occur at a slower pace. Studies have involved adolescents, although work with children is just beginning.

BIBLIOGRAPHY

Suinn, R. (1977). *Manual: Anxiety management training (AMT)*. Colorado: Rocky Mountain Behavioral Sciences Institute.
Suinn, R. (1977). Treatment of phobias. In G. Harris

(Ed.), *The group treatment of human problems: A social learning approach*. NY: Grune & Stratton.

Suinn, R. (1980). Behavioral intervention methods for stress and anxiety. In I. Kutash & L. Schlesinger (Eds.), *Handbook on stress and anxiety*. California: Jossey Bass.

Suinn, R., & Deffenbacher, J. (1982). The self-control of anxiety. In P. Karoly & F. Kanfer (Eds.), *The psychology of self-management: From theory to practice*. New York: Pergamon Press.

See: Systematic Desensitization

ASSERTIVENESS TRAINING
Eileen Gambrill

Assertiveness training is an intervention method which is designed to enhance interpersonal skills. The definition of this term is complicated by differing definitions of the construct of "assertiveness"; there is no one generally accepted definition of this term. On the most general level, it refers to the expression of preferences and opinions, both positive and negative. Some writers use the term to refer more narrowly to the expression of negative preferences: for example, refusing unwanted requests. In addition to encompassing particular kinds of response classes in particular situations, such as refusing unwanted requests and expressing opinions, the term assertion implies a value stance of "standing up for your rights." The assumption is made that people have certain rights (for example, to refuse unwanted requests) and that they should exert these rights. It is further assumed that people will feel better, have more enjoyable, equitable interpersonal exchanges, and will be more socially effective if they are assertive.

The term assertiveness is further defined by distinguishing assertive behavior from passive and aggressive behavior. Aggressive behavior refers to the hostile expression of preferences in such a way that other people's rights are violated. Passive or submissive behavior is defined as the failure to express oneself such that one's own rights are violated.

There is increasing recognition that the tripartite division of all social behavior into three categories (assertive, passive, and aggressive) is simplistic and that social behavior is far more complex than this division will allow. Also, there is considerable evidence that social behavior is situationally specific: that is, what will be effective in one situation will not necessarily be effective in another situation. Many writers advocate replacing the term assertion with the more neutral and general term "social skill." Some advocate keeping the term assertion to refer to a small subset of behaviors-in-situations.

CLINICAL APPLICATION

Assertion training has been used with a broad range of presenting concerns and associated interpersonal problems, including marital discord, depression, sexual dysfunction, antisocial aggressive behavior, substance abuse, and dependency. It has been used with psychiatric patients and mentally retarded individuals who have profound interpersonal deficits as well as with college students who have more extensive social repertoires. A careful assessment is carried out to identify the following: (1) situations of concern to the client; (2) what the client currently does in these situations; (3) current relevant repertoires that are available; (4) specific changes in verbal and nonverbal behaviors that would help clients to be more effective; (5) personal obstacles that will have to be addressed, such as interpersonal anxiety and negative thoughts; (6) environmental obstacles that will have to be addressed, such as difficult significant others or limited social contexts; (7) personal resources that can be drawn upon, such as self-reinforcement skills; (8) environmental resources, such as "buddies" who could take part in intervention programs and promising social contexts; (9) baseline information that will permit determination of progress; and (10) a hierarchy of situations of concern tailored to individual differences in skill and comfort. Assessment is complicated by a lack of information about what behaviors will be most effective in what siutations. This question is further complicated by different opinions about what criteria should be used to judge effectiveness. In addition, sources of information used to gather assessment data, such as role plays, may not necessarily represent what occurs in real-life settings.

The relationship of assertive behavior to the presenting problem is usually carefully reviewed and examples offered. Misconceptions and expectations that interfere with a willingness to become more assertive are identified and discussed; for example, the belief that requests should never be refused because this would hurt other people's feelings. Risks of becoming more assertive are carefully weighed including the risk of lost opportunities as well as the risk of negative effects. Unless misconceptions and interfering expectations are addressed, it is unlikely that clients will initiate or continue new social reactions. The comparable effectiveness found in some instances for assertion training programs that focus on altering cognitions compared to those that focus exclusively on acquisition of social skills, supports the important role of thoughts in assertion training.

A lack of assertive behavior may be related to deficits in social skills or interfering emotional reactions and thoughts. Selection of procedural mix depends on the nature of each client's unique cognitive, emotional, and behavioral deficits, surfeits, and assets in relation to situations of concern. If appropriate behaviors are available but not performed because of anxiety, the focus

may be on enhancing anxiety management skills. Discrimination training is required when skills are available but are not performed at appropriate times. If skills are absent, response acquisition procedures are used as described below.

Model presentation. Models of effective behavior in specific situations are provided using one or more of the following methods: live performances by the counselor, written scripts, videotapes, audiotapes, or films.

Behavior rehearsal. Opportunities to practice social behaviors of concern are provided.

Feedback. Positive feedback is offered following each rehearsal. Effective verbal and nonverbal reactions are noted and specific changes that could be made to enhance performance are identified.

Prompting. Instructions or signals may be offered during practice to encourage effective reactions.

Programming of change. Situations are matched to each client's individual skill and comfort levels and training progresses in accord with individual progress.

Homework assignments. Tasks are agreed on that the client carries out in real-life contexts.

Common differences in the conduct of assertion training include the following: (1) group versus individual format, (2) use of written material such as self-help manuals, (3) extent of counselor-client contact, (4) criteria used to select interpersonal situations of concern (e.g., client or counselor), (5) individualized or standardized program offered to all group members, (6) sources of assessment information used (self-report, self-monitoring, role play, reports from significant others and peers, physiological indicators), (7) involvement of significant others, (8) kinds of models used, (9) number of practice opportunities provided, (10) attention given to thoughts related to situations of concern, (11) domains tapped in evaluation of progress (physiological, overt, cognitive), and (12) attention devoted to generalization and maintenance.

EXPECTED OUTCOMES AND TIME FRAMES

Expected outcomes of assertion training include increased social effectiveness, comfort, and self-efficacy in situations of concern. If a lack of assertive behavior was thought to be associated with the client's presenting problem, then an improvement in this is also expected. The expectation that people will respond positively to assertive reactions has not always been borne out; some reports found that people do not like assertive people as much as they like passive people.

Evaluation of outcomes is complicated by lack of agreement on criteria used to determine success. Some writers use a component approach to social behavior; if predetermined verbal and nonverbal criterion behaviors occur, intervention is considered a success; for example, was an unwanted request refused? Other writers consider this focus on component behaviors far too narrow and advocate a process model of social behavior that includes attention to feelings, values, and thoughts as well as to overt behavior. They emphasize that reactions developed should match client values and goals and that comfort with new behaviors is also an important criterion.

The length of assertion training depends on the domain of social behaviors that must be developed and upon the severity of countervailing personal and environmental obstacles. If the response repertoire is narrow,

such as refusing requests, and the obstacles minor, only a few sessions may be required. If the behavior deficits are extensive, as with some psychiatric patients, many more sessions may be required even though only one or two kinds of social situations are focused on during intervention. Single-case as well as group designs have been used to evaluate the effectiveness of assertion training.

POTENTIAL SIDE EFFECTS AND CONTRAINDICATIONS

Potential adverse effects include negative reactions from other people in response to new behaviors and the possibility that clients will temporarily elicit aggressive reactions. The most worrisome potential adverse effect is related to a prime counterindication for use of assertion training: when presenting concerns are related to environmental constraints rather than personal characteristics. In such cases, a focus on the latter may result in limited effects, will deflect attention from key intervention foci, will be unnecessarily discouraging to clients, and will tend to "blame the victim" rather than address realistic environmental obstacles that limit response options and influence social consequences. Literature on gender differences in relation to social behavior offers one illustrative area. Given the lack of information about the components of effective behavior in many social situations and the ubiquitousness of stereotypes and bias concerning social behavior, a special burden is placed upon counselors to be aware of their biases and to attend to environmental constraints. Identification of specific social and personal goals of importance to clients will offer some help in protecting clients from therapist's imposed goals.

Potential positive side effects include generalization of new social skills to other situations and increased self-efficacy.

BIBLIOGRAPHY

Alberti, R. E. (1977). *Assertiveness: Innovations, applications and issues.* San Luis Obispo, CA: Impact Publications.

Bellack, A. S. & Hersen, M. (Eds.). (1979). *Research and practice in social skills training.* New York: Plenum Press.

Curran, J. P. & Monti, P. M. (Eds.). (1982). *Social skills training: A practical handbook for assessment and treatment.* New York: Guilford Press.

Jakubowski, P. & Lange, A. J. (1978). *The assertive option: Your rights and responsibilities.* Champaign, IL: Research Press.

Wolpe, J. (1973). *The practice of behavior therapy* (2nd ed.). New York: Pergamon Press.

See: Communication Skills Training
Conversational Skills Training
Social Skills Training

ASSISTED COVERT SENSITIZATION
Barry M. Maletzky

Assisted covert sensitization (ACS) is a form of aversive therapy in which noxious stimuli are combined with descriptions and fantasies of unwanted behaviors. The technique was conceived as an extension of covert sensitization when that procedure proved ineffective for some clients. However, only the presenting or unconditioned stimuli are covert; the aversive or conditioned stimuli are real and can consist of electric shock, foul odors, or noxious images (e.g., slides, movies).

ACS has been employed against a variety of target behaviors including overeating, nicotine addiction, and drug abuse. However, it has enjoyed its greatest use and success in deconditioning deviant sexual arousal. There are three basic steps in applying ACS regardless of target behavior: (1) relaxation training, (2) generation of scenes depicting the target behavior, and (3) pairing of scenes with aversive stimuli.

For example, a heterosexual pedophile might undergo relaxation training using a variety of techniques, while simultaneously working with the therapist to develop a list of scenes (7–15 usually suffice) describing typical examples of child molesting. Under relaxation, a client would then be asked to imagine such a scene and, at the appropriate moment as sexual arousal is building, an aversive stimulus, such as a putrid odor, would be presented. With suggestions of escaping the scene, the odor would be removed. The following presents a typical scene for a heterosexual pedophile:

> You and your young stepdaughter are out hiking in the woods near your home. You come to an old field and tell her to lie down. You begin to take off her clothes and when she resists you scold her and then she begins to mind you better. You can see yourself taking off her blouse and now her pants. You pull her panties down and start to feel between her legs. You can feel her young, soft skin. You start to caress her bare nipples and you can see them and feel them harden. Your hand goes down to her crotch and you start to put your finger inside of her when suddenly there is a foul, putrid odor. You look around and you see that you and she have laid down in some dog crap. You've gotten it on your body and she has it on hers, right between her legs. It is a foul, putrid odor and the brown streaking of the crap is disgusting to you. Your food catches in your throat and you start to gag. That foul odor is terrible. You can see your stepdaughter lying naked but the odor and the sight is disgusting to you. Chunks of food catch in your throat and you begin to vomit. Chunks of vomit dribble down your chin and onto her naked body. It's disgusting to be there with her that way and that foul odor is putrid. You run away quickly and clean yourself off in the creek. You begin to feel better now that you are away from sex with her. You can breathe the fresh, clean air outside and your stomach starts to settle down. You feel better away from sexual relations with her. You can breathe the fresh, clean air again.

As can be seen, there are three components to such a scene: (1) building sexual arousal, (2) introducing the aversive stimulus as sexual arousal mounts, and (3) escaping from the aversive stimulus with suggestions of ending deviant sexual behavior.

Some therapists would construct a hierarchy of scenes and begin with those lowest in sexual arousal, gradually increasing arousal as treatment progresses. Others might question the need for relaxation and begin without it, while still others would train the patient in hypnosis instead of relaxation. Regardless, the three elements within each scene are crucial for the technique's success.

Most of the work reported on this technique has employed an aversive odor (a placental culture has been typically employed) in combination with descriptions of the target behaviors. ACS has enjoyed an excellent treatment record with sexual offenders, as confirmed by penile plethysmographic measurement of pre- and post-treatment responses and has proven helpful in overeating as well; both are consumatory behaviors that may be especially sensitive to stimuli-evoking nausea. In addition, a foul odor can be presented over a broader time span than electric shock, making it especially applicable in deconditioning such behaviors in association with imagery.

In practice, ACS is generally part of a treatment package that may include standard aversive conditioning; indeed, ACS may be combined in the same treatment session with other aversive techniques. It is thus not uncommon for the aversive stimulus to be at times merely a noxious scene introduced to the client's imagination, ("covert sensitization"), a foul odor presented with a scene ("ACS"), or a foul odor or electric shock presented with a slide or movie ("aversive conditioning"). These techniques are often used randomly within a treatment session to lessen the chances of stimulus accommodation.

In order to strengthen this aversive conditioning in treatment, homework is routinely assigned. Scenes are taped, generally by the therapist, though occasionally by the patient, his wife, girlfriend, etc., and the patient is coached in using a vial of foul odor at the appropriate points within each scene. Three such scenes are usually recorded per tape and new scenes can be recorded for each session according to the level of progress being made. The client is asked to listen to the tape and use the odor at home four to five times per week.

Although control data are lacking, it would appear that ACS could be employed in a variety of unwanted behaviors, such as obsessive-compulsive illness and alcoholism. Recommendations for its use in those conditions, however, must await further study.

BIBLIOGRAPHY

Foreyt, J. P. & Kennedy, W. (1971). Treatment of overweight by aversion therapy. *Behaviour Research and Therapy, 9,* 29–34.

Janda, L. H. & Rimm, D. C. (1972). Covert sensitization in the treatment of obesity. *Journal of Abnormal Psychology, 80,* 37–42.

Liechtenstein, E. & Kreutzer, C. S. (1969). Investigation of diverse techniques to modify smoking: A follow-up report. *Behaviour Research and Therapy, 7,* 139–140.

Maletzky, B. M. (1974). "Assisted covert sensitization" for drug abuse. *International Journal of the Addictions, 9,* 411–429.

Maletzky, B. M. (1983). *The treatment of the sexual offender.* New York: Wiley.

See: Aversive Conditioning
     Contingent Aromatic Ammonia
     Covert Sensitization

ATTENTIONAL TRAINING PROCEDURES

Frances Moosbrugger Hunt

Attentional training procedures are instructional strategies used most frequently with severely developmentally delayed clients (e.g., autistic, severely retarded) to establish basic attending responses such as eye contact with the trainer or sustained focusing on an object or task. These procedures utilize "errorless learning" techniques to gradually shape, strengthen, and elaborate the target attending response. The trainer shapes the target attending response by reinforcing successive approximations. Initially, the target response may be prompted and reinforced on a continuous schedule. Once this behavior occurs consistently, the prompts are gradually faded and intermittent reinforcement is systematically introduced.

Most attentional training programs suggest that the following responses be established consistently prior to training: client sits, corrects inappropriate positioning (e.g., slumping in chair), and ceases inappropriate body movements when asked.

Attentional training procedures generally involve the following:

1. The client sits in a chair facing the trainer.
2. The trainer presents a discriminative stimulus, cue, or command every 5 to 10 seconds.
3. The trainer reinforces the client for successively closer approximations of the target response.
4. The trainer withholds all reinforcement for a brief period (usually 5 to 10 seconds) when the client fails to respond correctly within a few seconds of the presentation of the discriminative stimulus, cue, or command.
5. The trainer may initially prompt the correct response if the client consistently fails to respond correctly to the discriminative stimulus, cue, or command.
6. All prompts are systematically faded.
7. The criteria for reinforcement are gradually changed to develop a more complex response.

Attentional training procedures are commonly used to teach the client to establish eye contact with the trainer when the discriminative stimulus "Look at me" is presented. Initially, the trainer may prompt an approximation of the response (e.g., looking at the trainer's face) by holding a reinforcer near her face. When the client consistently responds under these conditions, the trainer fades the prompt and changes the criteria for reinforcement. The trainer might, for example, conceal the reinforcer in her hand and make its delivery contingent on looking at her face *plus* fleeting eye contact. The trainer continuously reinforces successive approximations of sustained eye contact until that response occurs consistently, then systematically moves to a schedule of intermittent, delayed reinforcement.

See: Positive Reinforcement
     Shaping

AUTOGENIC TRAINING

Michael Lowe

Autogenic training is a therapeutic procedure which utilizes a series of imagery-based exercises to produce mental and physical relaxation. The intended psychophysiological effects of autogenic training are opposite those elicited by stress.

There are six components of the most basic form of autogenic training, known as the "standard autogenic exercises." These steps involve the production of feelings of heaviness and warmth in the extremities, the regulation of cardiac and respiratory activity, and the production of abdominal warmth and cooling of the forehead. A number of more highly specialized exercises have been developed to complement the standard autogenic exercises. For instance, specific meditative techniques have been developed to reduce psychological distress and organ-specific exercises have been developed to help remediate particular psychophysiological disorders.

Autogenic training is applied to a variety of stress-related disorders and may be particularly appropriate with stress-related physiological problems. The technique is also used to directly modify physiological conditions which may be unrelated to stress (e.g., Raynaud's disease).

Clients are typically taught the autogenic method while reclining in an easy chair in a quiet, nondistracting environment. The client is encouraged to adopt an attitude of passive concentration during training, that is, to just let the therapist's suggestions take hold without actively trying to make this happen. In the standard version of autogenic training, the client closes his/her eyes and is then led through each of the six training components (heaviness in the extremities, bodily warmth, etc.). Each component is practiced individually, and new components are added as the client becomes proficient at earlier ones. Clients are instructed to practice the exercises at home at least several times weekly. Adaptations of this intensive training method often involve fewer training components and require less time to complete the training.

Autogenic training and biofeedback are alternative means of achieving reduction in autonomic arousal, and the two are often used together. Thus, autosuggestions of increased warmth or of a calm, regular heartbeat might be used in conjunction with biofeedback to help the client learn how successfully he or she is reducing arousal. Autogenic training, combined with thermal biofeedback is currently the most effective treatment for migraine headaches. Since the aim of autogenic training is very similar to that of the more widely used technique of progressive relaxation, the potential applications of the two techniques are similar as well. If the autogenic technique is regularly practiced between therapy sessions, then most clients are capable of self-generating a state of deep relaxation after several weeks of training.

Research suggests that the therapeutic effects of autogenic training are similar to those of progressive relaxation and that both procedures are superior to no treatment or control conditions. Researchers have found both autogenic training and progressive relaxation to be more effective than hypnosis and a control condition in producing relaxation. Others have found equal improvements in anxiety and depression and equal changes in heart rate and skin conductance with autogenic training and relaxation.

Although both autogenic training and progressive relaxation are designed to reduce stress and anxiety, autogenic training accomplishes this by reducing autonomic nervous system arousal, whereas progressive relaxation reduces muscular tension directly. There are no data on this point, but it is reasonable to expect that progressive relaxation may be the treatment of choice when muscle tension is the most prominent sign of stress, and autogenic training may be more suitable either when there is generalized physiological arousal accompanying stress or when physiological symptoms are themselves of primary concern (e.g., in tachycardia).

There are few known side effects of, or contraindications to, the use of autogenic training. As with progressive relaxation, some individuals may be more frightened than calmed by the feelings of warmth, heaviness, floating, etc., that are produced during training. The use of the technique would be contraindicated with clients who had difficulty maintaining concentration or clear mental images.

BIBLIOGRAPHY

Schultz, J. H., & Luthe, W. (1969). *Autogenic Methods* (Vol. I). New York: Grune & Stratton.

Shapiro, S., & Lehrer, P. M. (1980). Psychophysiological effects of autogenic training and progressive relaxation. *Biofeedback and Self-Regulation, 5,* 249-255.

Surwit, R. S. (1981). Behavioral approaches to Raynaud's disease. *Psychotherapy and Psychosomatics, 36,* 224-245.

Surwit, R. S., Allen, L. M., Gilgor, R. S., & Duvic, M. (1982). The combined effect of Autogenic Training on cold reactivity in Raynaud's phenomenon. *Biofeedback and Self-Regulation, 7,* 537-544.

Surwit, R., Pilon, R., & Fenton, C. (1978). Behavioral treatment of Raynaud's disease. *Journal of Behavioral Medicine, 1,* 323-335.

See: Deep Muscle Relaxation

AVERSION RELIEF
Alan S. Bellack

Aversion relief is a punishment procedure in which an aversive stimulus is presented concurrently with a negative stimulus or response, and both are simultaneously terminated contingent upon presentation of a positive stimulus or response. The negative stimulus gradually acquires conditioned aversive qualities, while the positive stimulus gradually acquires conditioned positive qualities. Aversion relief has been most commonly used in the treatment of sexual deviation and unwanted homosexuality. In a typical protocol, the client imagines or views slides of the deviant stimulus (e.g., fetish, child). He (she) is simultaneously presented with electric shock. When he (she) is sufficiently uncomfortable, he (she) can switch off the shock. The deviant stimulus is then replaced by an appropriate heterosexual stimulus. It has been presumed that this procedure would increase heterosexual arousal by pairing previously neutral heterosexual stimuli with a positive consequence (i.e., shock termination). However, there are no data to support this contention. Aversion relief has also been employed in the treatment of alcoholism, drug addiction, obsessive compulsive disorder, and cigarette smoking. Respiratory relief is a variation in which the aversive stimulus is breath holding. Used with cigarette addiction, the client takes a puff, holds his breath for as long as possible, and then stamps out the cigarette contingent on exhaling.

See: Aversive Conditioning
    Covert Aversion
    Covert Negative Reinforcement
    Covert Sensitization
    Escape Training

AVERSIVE BEHAVIOR REHEARSAL
Alan S. Bellack

Aversive Behavior Rehearsal, also referred to as Shame Aversion, is a procedure for treating exhibitionism. The central feature of treatment involves the patient exposing himself and performing his deviant ritual to staff in the clinic. Staff members are enlisted to be targets of exposure and are instructed to respond in a neutral, nonemotional manner. The procedure is not intended to humiliate the patient, so much as to teach him to develop an analytic, objective view of his behavior. Several uncontrolled clinical trials have reported positive results. The method by which the procedure works, its generality, and durability, are unclear.

See: Orgasmic Reconditioning

AVERSIVE CONDITIONING
W. L. Marshall

This term describes a variety of techniques involving systematic presentation of noxious stimuli in cases marked by an inability of the patient to either control or resist enacting certain behaviors. It is assumed that these various techniques all induce a common process which results in a change in behavior. This common process is usually thought to be conditioning of one kind or another, hence the name, but the evidence does not support this interpretation of the mechanisms of change. At the moment we are at a loss to say just why these procedures work, but we can say with some confidence that they usually do.

Whatever the theoretical basis for these effects turns out to be, it is clear that at a procedural level various applications of aversive conditioning share certain features in common. The stimulus conditions which elicit the unacceptable behavior, and perhaps the unacceptable behavior itself, are recreated or allowed to occur, and they are associated with an unpleasant experience. Typically, the unpleasant experience follows the onset of the aberrant stimulus or behavior. This, along with other features of the temporal relationship, is thought to be important by those who take a conditioning perspective of the process. However, as we have noted, the evidence does not support this perspective nor does it support the demand for precise temporal contiguities. However, at the moment, it seems best to follow the procedures outlined above. That is, the attractive but unacceptable stimuli or behavior, should precede the onset of the unpleasant event which may be continued concurrently until the deviant stimulus or response is terminated.

Note that we have not yet mentioned the nature of the unpleasant event nor whether it is best to present the eliciting stimuli or have the patient enact the aberrant behavior. Naturally the decisions concerning the nature of the aversive event, as well as the choice between stimuli or responses, are very important decisions affecting the power of aversive conditioning. Fortunately there are some guides to help us here. There is evidence suggesting that mammals are prepared by their evolutionary history to readily make associations between certain stimuli or behaviors and particular consequences. Without going into this literature in detail, it is clear that stimuli or responses are more readily affected by consquences which occur within the bodily systems that functionally relate to one another. For example, it is very easy to acquire taste aversions to foods that have made us sick, even though the sickness may not occur for some time after the ingestion of the food. Similarly, we might expect predominantly tactile experiences such as sexual behaviors to be more readily controlled by unpleasant tactile experiences. Indeed, the evidence strongly suggests that whereas unpleasant electrical stimuli have little value in aversive conditioning procedures for reducing excessive alcohol use, these electrical (tactile) events are very effective in reducing deviant sexual interests. On the other hand, insofar as aversive conditioning affects alcoholics, this seems to be most true when the aversive event is a nausea-inducing drug. Unfortunately, the use of nausea-inducing drugs is beset with many practical and ethical problems. This is particularly true concerning the distress it causes both patient and staff. Although all forms of aversive conditioning have generated considerable ethical debates, most of these objections should not apply if the procedures (other than the use of nausea-inducing drugs) are carefully and properly administered.

Whether one should present eliciting

stimuli, or have the patient engage in the deviant response, is often again based on unfounded theoretical biases, but common sense dictates that a combination of the two should be most effective. After all, in the everyday world, where the problems arise, the eliciting stimuli produce the aberrant behavior and we should attempt to replicate natural experiences as far as possible if we hope to change behavior. However, when only eliciting stimuli are used the procedures are said to match those of classical (Pavlovian) conditioning, while pairing an aversive event with the deviant behavior is said to be punishment.

Of course, it is often very difficult to recreate natural events, particularly if the therapist is determined to remain in his/her office. For this reason some clinicians prefer what is called "covert sensitization." Since this procedure is described elsewhere in this book, we will only briefly mention it here. Essentially, this procedure has the patient imagine the whole process, including the stimuli or responses as well as the aversive event. This procedure is easy to apply and appears to be effective. However, the same considerations in selecting the events apply here as they do for the overt forms of aversive therapy.

Two other procedural issues concerning covert sensitization are worth mentioning. One of the advantages of having patients imagine the chain of behaviors involved in the unacceptable response sequence is that the aversive event can be delivered at points throughout the sequence. When therapy is conducted by a therapist in an office, rather than by the patient in the natural setting, the problem is to recreate as closely as possible the natural sequence of events. Simply associating the target stimuli with an unpleasant event leaves to chance what it is that the patient is thinking and feeling. Better control is secured when the therapist instructs the patient what to think or feel. This also allows the therapist to deliver the aversive event at earlier points in the response sequence as well as at later points, and the evidence indicates that greater and more enduring suppression of a response is obtained if earlier components are punished. Such a strategy also permits the therapist to randomize the temporal occurrence of the aversive event, thereby making the delivery more uncertain from the patient's perspective. Again, the evidence indicates that uncertainty increases the aversive nature of the stimulus and thereby improves effectiveness. Finally, such a strategy more readily encourages the use of constantly changing variations on the theme to be punished which, in turn, increases generalization to the natural environment. All too often aversive therapy is highly specific in its effects so that the problem of generalization to the whole class of aberrant behaviors must be addressed in treatment.

CLINICAL APPLICATIONS

As we noted earlier, these procedures have been applied to a broad range of behaviors which are, generally speaking, not satisfactorily under the patient's control despite their best efforts. Some of the behaviors treated by aversive conditioning have been: alcoholism, eating disorders, sexual deviations, bed-wetting, self-injurious behaviors, narcotic addictions, compulsive gambling, smoking, writer's cramp, and bizarre behaviors in psychotic patients, to name the most common uses. Whether or not it is the most effective technique for all of these behaviors is doubtful, and ethical, as well as empirical, considerations are relevant to its use.

The problem then is to reduce or eliminate these behaviors, although it is very important to note that there are usually a complex of factors maintaining such problem behaviors. It is unrealistic to expect aversive conditioning alone to bring the behavior under control. This is not an unusual feature associated only with aversive therapy. Indeed, it is increasingly apparent that almost all problems are complexly maintained and consequently require the application of various procedures to enable the patient to manage independently. The clinical examples given here will illustrate this need, as well as the need to consider the issues outlined in the definition of the techniques.

A young male complained that he had an overpowering fetish for blue jeans, particularly those that had been worn by teenage boys. During masturbatory activities he would pick up the jeans, rub them against his body, and then wrap them around his penis while masturbating. The feel of the jeans was very important, so electrical (tactile) aversion was employed. The young man brought his collection of jeans to the office and, while seated in a private room, he was asked to engage in his usual ritual including the commencement of masturbation. At various points throughout his sequence of behaviors the young man was shocked by an electrical current delivered to his calf muscle. The section on *Electrical Aversion* describes this procedure in greater detail, but it is important to note that not only were the eliciting stimuli (i.e., jeans) provided, so also was the subject required to produce his typical responses. It is also of relevance to note that the intensity of the electric shock is set by the patient before therapy commences. He is instructed to increase the intensity until it is unpleasant but tolerable. The evidence suggests that aversive events do not have to be extremely unpleasant or painful to be effective, and it is certainly easier to maintain the cooperative participation of the patient if the noxious stimulus is only moderately aversive. This

tactic also reduces the relevance of at least some of the ethical objections which have been raised against aversive conditioning.

While this procedure reduced deviant activities during masturbation, it did not eliminate them and it had no impact on deviant fantasies elicited by the sight of boys wearing jeans. Other procedures were adopted to further change masturbatory fantasies by increasing the attractiveness of appropriate sexual acts, but the additional procedure of relevance here was the use of a self-managed aversive conditioning or punishment procedure. The young man was given smelling salts disguised as a nasal inhalant for colds so that his friends would not be made aware of his problem. He was told to deeply inhale the smelling salts whenever a deviant fantasy was elicited. This procedure led to a rapid reduction, and final elimination, of this aspect of his problem. Ordinarily, social skills training is required to enable men with this and other sexual deviations to act on their new-found sexual orientation; this, however, was not required with this patient who was quite competent in social interactions.

In a quite different case, illustrating other aspects of the problem of selecting appropriate procedures, we were referred a woman in her early thirties who had a significant health problem due to her inability to resist eating specific cakes. Not all people with eating problems are quite so specific in their loss of control, but for this woman there were only three types of cakes she would eat given the opportunity which, of course, she would frequently seek out. The main problem seemed to be eating chocolate cake, which was such an overwhelming compulsion that if she were to accidentally smell one she would either buy it or steal it if necessary and possible. For her, odors were extremely salient, not only in her desires for chocolate cake but also in many other areas of functioning. Accordingly, we associated foul odors with the presentation of chocolate cake. It is a little difficult, not to say unpleasant for the therapist, to present foul odors over a number of trials, owing to their tendency to linger, but lingering odors can be masked by mentholated air fanned onto the patient's face. In any case, within two sessions of 10 trials each, this woman expressed a strong repulsion to chocolate cake, which endured. However, there were other features to her problem, including a poor self-image and a host of inappropriate thoughts about herself and the value of cakes, as well as a lack of assertiveness and a need for attention; all of which impeded progress and appeared to cause her to shift her desires to yet another type of cake. It is important to note, however, that even after we had dealt with these other problems her passion for cakes remained until another program of foul-odor aversive conditioning eliminated these desires and restored her to healthful eating habits.

Another woman (aged 23 years) was referred because she could not stop herself from picking at pimples on her face. Actually she would pick at spots on her face which she took to be early signs of developing pimples. No amount of medical advice to the contrary prevented her from picking her face despite the fact that she was an intelligent person who was aware that her habit was scarring her face probably more than actual pimples would have. In discussing the behavior with her, we noticed that she shuddered whenever we asked her about the bleeding she sometimes caused and particularly when we asked if pus ever discharged when she picked at her face. This observation suggested that she might be responsive to imaginal techniques, and this was supported by her reports of frequent and complex daydreams. These daydreams, by the way, concerned having a romantic relationship with a man, which, unfortunately, she had never had despite the fact that she was quite attractive. We proposed to her a program to develop her self-confidence and social skills which required her to interact with males. She refused to participate until her face-picking was eliminated. Consequently, we explained covert sensitization to her, and described the specific procedure we would follow in treatment. This procedure required her to commence face-picking under conditions where all possible feedback was eliminated (she usually used a mirror). As she picked at her face the therapist gave graphic, although not accurate, descriptions of the possible consequences of what she was doing. He told her to imagine that blood was running down her face, over her hands and dripping onto her dress. He also urged her to imagine as vividly as possible that pus was oozing from the pimple she was squeezing and that it was running over her fingers and dropping onto her lap. The therapist suggested that the pus had a disgusting appearance and a foul odor. All of this repulsed the patient so much so that she gagged in the last of three half-hour sessions and refused to pick at her face again. Subsequent social skills training gave her the confidence to meet both males and females and develop friendships with them. Her face-picking did not return, nor did any sign of pimples emerge with its cessation.

EXPECTED OUTCOMES

There is substantial evidence testifying to the value of various forms of aversive therapy, although a good deal of this evidence takes the form of either clinical trials or controlled single case studies. There are few satisfactorily controlled group studies, although those that do exist suggest that aversive conditioning is a powerful procedure when used in an appropriate form which matches both client characteristics and features of the stimulus-response matrix. We have already seen that choosing an aversive event which affects the system involved in the aberrant behavior (e.g., electric shock for sexual aberrations; nausea-inducing drugs for alcoholics) will maximize effectiveness, while choosing an aversive event affecting an independent system will likely render the procedure inert. Alternatively, selecting an aversive event that is particularly relevant to the client (e.g., imagined noxious experiences for patients with vivid fantasies) enhances effectiveness. Where possible a combination of these choices should be optimal.

In conducting aversive therapy it is essential that careful evaluations be done before treatment commences in order that progress can be monitored. Aversive conditioning seems to progress best if treatment is given frequently (we typically have at least one session each day for office-based treatment or continuous treatment when it is self-managed by the patient). In each office-based treatment session with sex offenders, we typically present 30 pairings of the inappropriate stimuli or responses with electric shock. With foul odors it is usually only possible to present four or five pairings per session, while only one pairing is possible using nausea-inducing drugs. The great advantage of both self-administered punishment (using smelling salts, for example) and covert sensitization is that a high frequency of pairings are possible. Progress should be appraised at the end of the second week (or at the end of 10 sessions) for electrical aversion and certainly earlier (after approximately four to five sessions) when the aversive event used is either foul odors or nausea-inducing drugs. The latter events are usually rapidly effective.

When assessment or observation by the therapist or patient indicates that treatment

has been effective, it is wise to encourage overlearning by adding additional sessions. We typically have the client complete additional sessions equivalent to one-third of those completed at the time effective changes occur.

DIFFERENTIAL DIAGNOSTIC FEATURES

We have already alluded to the need to match client/behavioral characteristics with the elements in treatment, and these are probably the most important features to look for in deciding what form treatment must take. Having already elaborated on this we will do no more than mention one patient who caused us problems. This man was a child molester who failed to respond to electrical aversive therapy. After 10 sessions he told us that as an electrician he had enjoyed self-administering mild shocks in order to make himself sexually aroused. We switched to an alternative aversive event. Similarly, it has been argued that sado-masochists may not respond to aversive therapy but the evidence here suggests that this is far from always the case. However, caution should be exercised.

We have also already noted that clients seldom present with an unwanted behavior which will respond to aversive conditioning alone. Usually there are numerous other excesses or deficits in the client's repertoire which need attention in order to bring the target behavior within the client's control.

Perhaps the main diagnostic feature, which is generally taken to contraindicate the use of aversive conditioning is where treatment might constitute a health hazard to a vulnerable patient. This has been taken to be particularly true for patients with cardiovascular problems. However even here the danger may be all but eliminated by the choice of the aversive event and the site of its application. Even with electrical aversion we have markedly reduced this problem by applying the current to the calf muscle of the leg, thereby making it remote from the source of danger although the psychological stress of the anticipation of shock may be more hazardous than the actual shock itself. In any case, caution is advised and some alternative less stressful, if less powerful, technique may be more appropriate for these patients.

Other than these reservations, a well-designed aversive conditioning program may be effectively applied to a broad range of uncontrollable, but undesirable, behaviors. Of course the willing cooperation of the patient is essential for both ethical and practical reasons. Ethical concerns aside for the moment, there is no point in applying aversive conditioning to a patient who does not want to give up the behavior in question. It is doubtful that suppression of the behavior would occur in these circumstances, and even if it did, the patient could easily retrain the behavior if he/she wished. These observations introduce another note of caution having to do with ethical issues. Aversive conditioning probably does not present a great deal more in the way of ethical problems than any other behavior change program. It is wrong to apply treatment to anyone who does not consent, while for those who are either not in a position to give informed consent (e.g., children or severely retarded individuals) or for whom freedom to consent is constrained (e.g., prisoners), the therapist must take considerable care in eliminating less objectionable alternatives before turning to the use of aversive procedures.

POTENTIAL SIDE EFFECTS

It has been suggested, and indeed it was strongly believed for a long time, that the use of any aversive procedure would be ineffective and even downright counter-thera-

peutic. It was thought that these procedures at best induced only temporary suppression of behavior, while at the same time having a generally suppressive effect on *all* behavior. It is now clear that the latter effect rarely occurs and when it does it is usually the result of the careless administration of the procedure by the use of excessively painful aversive events, or by a failure to make it clear to the patient just what it is that is being punished. Also, patients will adopt strategies to avoid or escape an aversive event, and, if left to their own devices, patients may, by these strategies, develop behaviors that are equally as undesirable as the targeted aberrant response. Care should, therefore, be taken to provide appropriate avoidant or escape behaviors that will entrench patterns of responding to the stimuli which will be both beneficial to the patient and, hopefully, incompatible with the deviant act. An example of this would be to allow an obese patient to escape or avoid the aversive stimulus if, and only if, he or she ate more appropriate food, ate at a slower rate, or ate only a limited amount of food. The provision of alternative behaviors can also be facilitated by simply instructing the patient very carefully, and in precise detail, as to the changes in his behavior that the therapist aims to achieve. This is a particularly crucial aspect of treatment, not only in avoiding unwanted effects but also in shaping appropriate behaviors that will produce their own powerful rewards and thereby endure.

As far as producing only a temporary suppression is concerned, the evidence suggests that with some procedures, for some behaviors, and with some individuals, the effects are permanent. However, with most patients aversive therapy probably does induce only temporary effects, but that is not a serious disadvantage; indeed, it is rare for any one procedure, whatever its form, to produce more than temporary control. The point we have repeatedly made is that aversive therapy should be only one component in a treatment package. For example, with child molesters a reduction in their desire for the aberrant behavior induced by aversive therapy, will not guarantee the development of a sexual interest in adults nor the skills necessary to act on such changed preferences. In fact, given these observations, we would not expect aversive therapy alone to produce any more than temporary control; however, this temporary control is an essential step in the total therapeutic program.

BIBLIOGRAPHY

Grimaldi, K. E., & Lichenstein, E. (1969). Hot, smoky air as an aversive stimulus in the treatment of smoking. *Behaviour Research and Therapy, 7*, 275–282.

Lemere, F., & Voegtlin, W. (1950). An evaluation of the aversion treatment of alcoholism. *Quarterly Journal of Studies on Alcohol, 11*, 199–204.

Marshall, W. L. (1973). The modification of sexual fantasies: A combined treatment approach to the reduction of deviant sexual behavior. *Behaviour Research and Therapy, 11*, 557–564.

Rimm, D. C., & Masters, J. C. (1979). *Behavior therapy: Techniques and empirical findings* (2nd ed). New York: Academic Press.

Walker, C. E., Hedberg, A., Clement, P. W., & Wright, L. (1981). *Clinical procedures for behavior therapy*, Englewood Cliffs, NJ: Prentice-Hall.

Weitzel, W. B., Horan, J. J., & Addis, J. W. (1977). A new olfactory aversion apparatus. *Behavior Therapy, 8*, 83–88.

See: Avoidance Training
  Covert Sensitization
  Escape Training

AVOIDANCE TRAINING
Kathleen Dyer

This is a training procedure in which an individual learns to keep away from a designated stimulus in order to prevent punishment. Training first involves pairing the designated stimulus with a punisher. The individual is then negatively reinforced by performing a response that terminates the punishing stimulus. The individual subsequently learns to prevent punishment from occurring by either responding with an alternative behavior (active avoidance) or not responding at all (passive avoidance) prior to coming in contact with the designated stimulus. For example, a toilet training program might involve first outfitting an individual with a pair of shorts that would sound an alarm (a punisher) when the individual urinated in his pants (the designated stimulus). The individual would subsequently learn to prevent the alarm from sounding by either refraining from urinating (passive avoidance) or urinating in the toilet (active avoidance).

See: Aversive Conditioning
  Escape Training

AWARENESS TRAINING
Edward J. Barton

This is a discrimination training procedure in which an individual is taught to discriminate the presence or absence of an antecedent stimulus or behavior. It is an excellent educative approach to use with individuals who emit undesirable high-frequency behavior but who are unaware of when they emit such behavior. This training, which has been used mainly with the mentally retarded, involves teaching the person to discriminate such occurrences through the use of prompts and positive reinforcement (e.g., praise and hugs). If the individual fails to make the desired response, graduated guidance may be necessary in the initial training phase. Once the person begins to respond appropriately, the prompts are gradually faded and the desired behavior is reinforced on an intermittent basis. Typically, as soon as the individual begins to make the discrimination, training proceeds quickly. When used correctly, there have not been any reported side effects.

BIBLIOGRAPHY

Azrin, N. H., Gottlieb, L., Hughart, L., Wesolowski, M. D., & Rahn, T. (1975). Eliminating self-injurious behavior by educative procedures. *Behaviour Research and Therapy, 13,* 101–111.

Barton, E. J., & Madsen, J. J. (1980). The use of awareness and omission training to control excessive drooling in a severely retarded youth. *Child Behavior Therapy, 2,* 55–63.

See: Discrimination Training
      Positive Reinforcement

BACKWARD CHAINING
Laura Schreibman

This procedure involves breaking down a complex behavior into smaller component behaviors and teaching the components one at a time, so that when they are performed in sequence (i.e., the chain) the target complex behavior is achieved. It is called backward chaining because the terminal response in the chain is taught first, then the response which precedes that, and so on until the first response in the sequence is taught. For example, to teach a retarded boy to pull up his pants (complex behavior) the clinician might say "Pants up" and reinforce the child for holding the waistband on his pants. Once this step is mastered, the child would be required to pull the pants up from a few inches below the waist. Then the child would pull the pants up from knee level and so forth until the first step in the chain (e.g., foot in leghole) is taught. At the end of training, the child should perform the entire chain when told "Pants up."

See: Forward Chaining

BEHAVIOR REHEARSAL
Arnold A. Lazarus

Behavior rehearsal is the term used to describe "a specific procedure which aims to replace deficient or inadequate social or interpersonal responses by efficient and effective behavior patterns. The patient achieves this by practicing the desired forms of behavior under the direction of the therapist." Unlike other forms of role-playing such as "psychodrama," behavior rehearsal aims primarily to modify current maladaptive patterns of behavior rather than "working through" early symbolic conflicts. In applying behavior rehearsal, the therapist assumes the role of significant people in the patient's life, and in a progressive stepwise fashion, more difficult encounters are enacted.

Role-reversal is an important component wherein the therapist acts the part of the patient and models the desired verbal and nonverbal behaviors, while the patient assumes the role of the person(s) with whom he/she has (or anticipates having) a problem. The use of videotapes is helpful in monitoring the patient's tone of voice, inflection, hesitations, querulous undertones, posture, gait, and eye contact.

See: Role Playing
      Social Skills Training

BEHAVIORAL CONSULTATION
Thomas R. Kratochwill

Behavioral consultation involves indirect services to a client (e.g., a child) who is served through a consultee (e.g., parent, teacher), by a consultant (e.g., psychologist, special education teacher, social worker). Consultation has varied meanings in the mental health literature, but there are a number of characteristics that identify behavioral consultation (Bergan, 1977; Bergan & Kratochwill, in press). First of all, consultation is a problem-solving relationship between a consultant and consultee. Consultation involves an attempt to alter an existing set of problematic circumstances in the direction of a desired set of circumstances. In other words, the primary focus is to eliminate some academic or social problem. Second, consultation is an indirect service delivery approach. Typically, the consultant does not work directly with the client during consultation. Rather, the consultant works through a consultee who in turn implements a program with the client. Providing indirect services to clients is regarded as one of the attractive features of the approach in that psychological services can be established through a broader range of clients with involvement of consultees in the process.

There are three main roles associated with consultation: consultant, consultee, and client. The consultant's responsibility is to establish the stages in the consultation process and to guide the consultee through these stages. The consultant accomplishes this largely by what is discussed during consultation. Another function of the consultant is making knowledge available to the consultee through the verbal exchanges and other materials provided during the consultation process.

The consultee is expected to engage in four kinds of activities during consultation. The first involves specification and description. The consultee typically describes a specific problem to the consultant in this stage. Second, evaluation or decision-making is required. Decisions such as those related to whether or not a particular intervention plan should be put into effect or whether or not a satisfactory solution of a problem has been established would be examples. Third, the consultee must work

directly with the client. The final type of activity that the consultee must engage in is supervision. Supervision of the client's actions or those of assistants who work with the consultee is an integral part of consultation. The client can also participate in consultation. The client may establish goals of consultation and also participate in the design and implementation of plans to reach some therapeutic goal.

A major goal of consultation is to produce change in a client's behavior. Consultation for children and youths has included a broad range of behaviors in psychological and educational areas. Another goal of consultation is to change the behavior of the consultee. Based on the behavioral approach, modification in the consultee's ways of behaving toward the client is an integral part of the treatment focus in consultation. The rationale for this is that changing consultee behavior will have a direct impact on the client and the difficulties that he or she experiences. Moreover, change in the consultee may be beneficial for other clients who are not directly involved as a focus of consultation.

The consultant problem-solving model involves establishing goals of consultation in behavioral terms. Generally, consultation is aimed at producing clearly specified changes in behavior. Thus, specific operational definitions are used to describe behaviors of concern during the consultation process. Such problems as aggressiveness must be operationally broken down into specific components (e.g., threatening bodily damage on others or inflicting physical pain on another person).

The most prominent model of consultation involves four stages of a problem-solving process (Bergan, 1977). These include problem identification, problem analysis, plan implementation, and plan evaluation. Problem identification involves the specification of the problem to be solved during the consultation process. Problem identification is established through a problem-identification interview (PII). During the PII the consultant assists the consultee to describe the problem of concern. Following the exploration of the problem, the focus of the PII shifts to a discussion of procedures that can be used to measure client performance of target responses. Problem identification is completed when the consultant and consultee establish target behaviors and a goal for the desired level of performance of behaviors following treatment.

Problem analysis involves identifying variables that might facilitate solution to a problem. In other words, the consultant and consultee work together to develop a plan to solve the problem during the problem analysis phase. Again, the problem analysis is accomplished through a problem analysis interview (PAI). During the PAI the consultant and consultee discuss the client's skills and/or environmental conditions that influence the client's behavior. It is important for the behavioral consultant to utilize his or her knowledge of behavioral principles during this phase in order to develop a functional analysis of the problem.

Plan implementation is the next phase. In this phase the consultee implements or supervises the implementation of the treatment plan designed during the previous problem analysis phase. It is important for the consultee to be involved in data collection. Data collection continues so that the consultant has some idea as to whether or not the plan is effective.

Following plan implementation, problem evaluation is implemented to determine if the treatment plan is effective. The problem evaluation takes place during a problem evaluation interview (PEI). During this PEI the consultant and consultee determine whether or not the treatment has been suc-cessful. This is done by examining the data gathered over the phases of the consultation process. If the goals of the consultation program have been established and met by the client, treatment success is probable.

Consultation is usually of two broad types. *Problem-centered consultation* involves implementation of consultation services for a rather limited time or on a small number of specific behaviors of immediate concern to the consultee (e.g., eliminating disruptive behavior in the classroom, improving certain academic skills). Problem-centered consultation typically focuses on target behaviors that are relatively mild, occur over a period of several weeks or months or involve a more transient problem.

In contrast, *developmental consultation* might be implemented in order to effect changes in behaviors that require a relatively long time to treat. For example, a child may be deficient in a number of academic and social skills. An intervention plan for an entire year, or longer, might be necessary. Thus, the focus of developmental consultation is on the attainment of long-term objectives. The long-term objectives might be related to a set of subordinate objectives that can be related to the long-term goals. Nevertheless, the major feature of developmental consultation is repeated applications of the consultation problem-solving approaches, as outlined above, over a long period of time to numerous target behaviors.

BIBLIOGRAPHY

Bergan, J. R. (1977). *Behavioral consultation*. Columbus: Charles E. Merrill.
Bergan, J. R., & Kratochwill, T. R. (in press). *Behavioral consultation in applied settings*. New York: Plenum Press.

See: Behavioral Family Therapy
     Parent Management Training

BEHAVIORAL ENGINEERING
Michael Milan

The term "behavioral engineering" was first defined by Lloyd Homme and his colleagues as the application of the laws of behavior to practical problems. It represents the blending of two major technologies: (1) the technology of contingency management, which involves the arrangement of response-consequence relationships in order to increase or decrease the frequency or probability of specified behaviors, and (2) the technology of stimulus control, which involves the establishment of antecedent-behavior relationships in order to ensure that behavior occurs at appropriate times or places and not at inappropriate times or places. When analyzing and treating a practical problem, the behavioral engineer first determines exactly what behaviors are and are not to occur, what stimuli are to control them, and what reinforcers are available to influence their frequency or probability. The technologies of contingency management and stimulus control are then deployed to develop a program to deal with the problem situation. Finally, the program is implemented, monitored, and revised as necessary until the problem is resolved.

See: Contingency Management
  Stimulus Control

BEHAVIORAL FAMILY THERAPY
Karen C. Wells

Behavioral family therapy has evolved only recently as a treatment approach which is clearly distinct in conception, assessment, and implementation from other behavioral assessment and treatment strategies. As it has been most clearly articulated, behavioral family therapy is an outgrowth of the parent-consultation model for treating child behavior problems, notably aggressive disorders. Like parent-training, behavioral family therapy initially is child-focused; that is, the child (or children) in a family is (are) the identified target(s) of treatment. Unlike parent training, the behavioral family therapy conceptual model recognizes that many other variables besides, simply, skills deficits, may disrupt adults' abilities to parent their children effectively, thereby contributing to aggressive child behavior. These additional variables, identified in the empirical literature as potentially relating directly or indirectly to child behavior problems, include:

1. parent perceptions (i.e., cognitions, attitudes, labels, attributions),
2. parent psychological variables (e.g., parent depression or anxiety, parent propensities for autonomic arousal, parent antisocial behavior),
3. marital (or couples) relationship problems, and
4. social variables (e.g., family insularity, poverty, social crises).

Undoubtedly, other variables will be added to this list and formally incorporated into the behavioral family therapy conceptual model as research efforts continue.

There are several ways in which the four variables identified above can relate to behavioral family therapy for aggressive children. Negative parent perceptions (i.e., negative verbal reports or labels of the child) can result in a child being referred inappropriately to a clinic for treatment, can disrupt effective parenting, and if not modified during the therapy process, can result in failure of treatment effects to generalize across time after treatment is terminated. Parent psychological variables such as anxiety, depression, and emotional reactivity also can disrupt effective parenting skills and can bias them to perceive their children more negatively with all the attendant problems of negative labeling. Parent marital hostility and dissatisfaction also can influence parents to perceive their children more negatively than may be objectively warranted. In addition, recent research indicates that overt bickering, fighting, and hostility between the marital couple in the home can *directly* cause increases in child aggression. Finally, social variables such as poverty, poor social adjustment, and parent insularity (few extra-familial contacts and supports) can also disrupt parent perceptions and behavior. Each of these relationships has been confirmed in empirical research on variables relating to child aggressive behavior. Because one, several, or all of these variables may be operating in a family, the behavioral family therapy conceptual model includes assessment and, potentially, treatment for each of these variables.

As alluded to above, behavioral family therapy is a conceptual orientation, rooted in the empirical literature, rather than a specific technique. It is an approach which views family members as occupying several roles inside and outside the family. These roles involve their individual cognitive and psychological functioning as well as their functioning in relation to other members of the family. Furthermore, these family relationships may be dyadic, triadic, or may involve more than three family members. For example, an adult woman may occupy the roles of individual adult functioning in society, marriage partner (dyadic relationship), and may share parenting responsibilities with her husband for one child (triadic relationship). When functioning within one or more of these roles or relationships breaks down and when this dysfunction affects the child, then behavioral family therapy is likely to be the treatment of choice. Thus, while the child may be the target of change, the clinical focus may sometimes shift to other individuals or relationships (e.g., marital relationship) within the family if these are affecting the child. In this sense behavioral family therapy is often a multimodal therapy in which behavior therapy techniques are implemented to facilitate the functioning of individuals, dyads, triads, or other subgroups within a family, with the ultimate goal of improving the child's behavior. These techniques might include parent training, marital therapy, cognitive therapy with the family as a whole (e.g., relabeling) or with individuals in the family, individual anxiety management, assertiveness training, and so on. When techniques are implemented, however, it is always done with an awareness on the part of the therapist of how changes in the individual, dyad, triad, etc., will affect other members (or subgroups) of the family.

CLINICAL APPLICATION

Clinical implementation of behavioral family therapy is dependent upon and influenced by the results of the behavioral assessment. Because each of the four areas identified above (i.e., parent cognitive and psychological variables, marital variables, social variables) can relate *directly* to problematic child behavior, or *indirectly* by disrupting the adults' parenting skills, formal or informal assessment of each of these areas must occur. Formal assessment may include the use of rating scales and self-report inventories to assess for parents' perceptions of the child, parent psychological variables such as depression, anxiety, or antisocial behavior, and parent marital conflict and dissatisfaction. In addition, behavioral assessment using role-play tests and direct observation methods can help pinpoint specific aspects of parent-child interactions, or of marital communication or problem solving skills which ultimately may be targeted in therapy.

Informal assessment in family interviews also can alert the therapist to individual or relationship variables which may be contributing to the child's presenting problem. For example, it may be noticed during a family interview that one of the parents seems depressed and withdrawn, and rarely participates in the discussion. The therapist may hypothesize from this sample of behavior that the parent is similarly withdrawn at home, leaving parenting and family management responsibilities to his/her spouse. This state of affairs may lead to ineffective parenting resulting in child behavior problems, and/or may cause marital conflict which can further exacerbate the child's problematic behavior. As another example, family members may consistently use negative labels to describe other family members in the interview or may ascribe malicious intentions to the target child. Such cognitive variables can significantly interfere with family members learning or performing more adaptive patterns of behavior. In addition, negative parental labeling or summary reports of child behavior can interfere with generalization of treatment effects across time. These are just two examples of the importance of identifying early in the assessment process variables that may contribute to the child's presenting problem or interfere with the therapy process. Targeting these variables will be important for successful treatment.

Once the initial assessment process has taken place, the therapist will have an idea of the treatment modalities which will be incorporated into therapy for the particular family. Thus, formal and informal assessment may reveal a considerable degree of marital hostility and conflict. For example, a father who is only peripherally involved in parenting the target child and who blames

his wife for the child's problems, and a mother who, left with the full responsibilities of family management, is displaying poor parenting skills and, in addition, is depressed and labels herself as inadequate. It would be a clinical error to begin parenting training with the mother in this family, as this would further reinforce her own sense of inadequacy as well as her husband's labeling her as the one who is to "blame" for the child's problems. Instead, behavioral family therapy might begin with the mother, father, and child together in sessions in which the therapist skillfully relabels roles that individuals have been playing within the family, being careful to choose more neutral, uncritical labels than those currently being used by family members. The therapist may then help the couple understand that they must separate their husband/wife conflict from their mother/father parenting problems. Subsequently, a contract might be negotiated in which the couple agrees to embark on marital therapy, as well as to initiate parent training as a parental unit. This can be done in several ways. Parent training might be initiated first with the clear understanding that marital problems will subsequently be treated. Alternatively, the therapist might see the family twice a week, with one session devoted to marital therapy and the second session devoted to parent training. In this case it must be made *very clear* what goals are being dealt with each session. Finally, if the mother continues to have difficulties with depression after the first two treatment modalities have been initiated or completed, then individual therapy might be initiated utilizing behavior therapy techniques which are indicated by the assessment (e.g., individual cognitive therapy, anxiety management, assertiveness training).

The above discussion describes treatment modalities which might be applied for a typical family initially presenting to a clinic complaining of child behavior problems. The focus on treatment modalities may give the false impression that treatment is a disjointed process of disconnected interventions being applied to various individuals or subgroups in a family. However, it is worth repeating that what characterizes this approach as family therapy is the therapist's conceptual orientation which must be operating at all times. That is, while individuals or subgroups in a family may be targeted for change, treatment modalities are instituted with a clear consideration of how treatment will affect others within the family, particularly the child. In this model, family members or subgroups are involved in therapeutic modalities, whose ultimate goals are to enhance family functioning, improve the child's behavior problems, and facilitate continued adaptive functioning after therapy is terminated. In addition, considerable clinical skill is necessary in which the therapist provides structure and control in therapy sessions while maintaining a nonblaming, constructive focus.

EXPECTED OUTCOMES AND TIME FRAMES

The primary goal and outcome of behavioral family therapy is improvement in child behavior problems at post treatment and continued improved functioning after therapy is terminated (i.e., temporal generalization of treatment effects). However, several secondary outcomes can be expected when this treatment modality is used. For example, marital therapy may be undertaken primarily because of the relationship of marital conflict to child behavior problems. However, a secondary benefit of this intervention is improvement in the couple's relationship independently of any effects on the child. Likewise, individual therapy for a member or members of a family may improve individual adaptive functioning out-

side their family roles. Finally, positive generalization effects may occur for individuals within a family after behavioral family therapy even though individual therapy is not initiated. For example, many adults will experience relief from the depression and demoralization accompanying "learned helplessness" when they see themselves functioning more adequately as parents and spouses. It should be kept in mind, however, that these are secondary outcomes of behavioral family therapy. Therapeutic goal-setting must always have as its primary reference improvement in the child's presenting problems.

Because behavioral family therapy is often a complex, multimodal treatment approach, the expected time-frame may be slightly longer than for other behavior therapy strategies. The exact duration of treatment will depend to a large extent on the range of treatment modalities necessary for any given family, the process by which the family was referred for treatment, and the rate at which the family can accept and make changes. If the family was self-referred, recognizes that there are problems, is motivated to participate in the therapy process, and requires a limited number of treatment modalities, 12 to 16 sessions may be sufficient to address variables contributing to the child's presenting problem. If the family initially attends therapy only because outside agencies (i.e., the school, the welfare system) have coerced them to do so, or requires a wide range of treatment modalities to address effectively all variables contributing to the initial problem, more sessions may be necessary.

DIFFERENTIAL DIAGNOSTIC CHARACTERISTICS

Behavioral family therapy has been most clearly conceptualized in relation to treatment of aggressive disorders of childhood (DSM-III, oppositional disorder, and conduct disorder). It is not the treatment of choice for all aggressive children. Many oppositional and some conduct disordered children are treatable with parent training alone. However, for other aggressive children, parent training is not sufficient, and more comprehensive behavioral family therapy will be required. These cases include families in which (1) parental perceptions of the child are out of proportion to the child's actual behavior, (2) parental perceptions or parenting behavior is influenced by the parents' individual maladjustment or by the couple's marital conflict, and (3) parental perceptions or parenting behavior are influenced by social variables (e.g., parent social insularity, social stresses or crises). Future research will undoubtedly identify other indicators for behavioral family therapy.

It is possible that behavioral family therapy also may be useful for some cases of child anxiety or psychosomatic disorders, especially when the disorder seems to be associated with dysfunction in or among other individuals or subgroups of the child's family. However, a conceptual model relating behavioral family therapy to these disorders is lacking at the present time.

SIDE EFFECTS AND CONTRAINDICATIONS

The primary negative side effect of behavioral family therapy to which therapists constantly should be alert is the possibility that changes in an individual or subgroup in a family will have a negative impact on other individuals or subgroups in the family. For example, as a mother becomes more confident and competent in managing her children and other aspects of her life, she may generalize her new-found assertiveness to her marital relationship. If the marital relationship has historically been one in which the husband has been dominant and the wife submissive, a shift in this relationship may cause a sudden increase in marital hos-

tility, a temporary negative side effect. However, the competent behavioral family therapist will have anticipated this side effect and incorporated plans for addressing it into the therapy process (e.g., helping the husband label his wife's behavior in a neutral rather than critical manner and learn new ways of communicating with her). Therefore, while temporary negative side effects may occur, the behavioral family therapy model recognizes these as part of the change process and includes plans for addressing side effects in the comprehensive therapeutic plan.

Positive side effects of behavioral family therapy also can be anticipated. As mentioned earlier, improvements in functioning of individuals within a family may generalize to their functioning outside the family as well. For example, a woman who learns more effective communication and problem solving skills with her husband may generalize these skills to the work setting, thereby improving her professional functioning. As with negative side effects, the therapist also should be alert to such positive side effects and help family members interpret these changes in functioning outside the family in an appropriate manner.

In summary, behavioral family therapy is most clearly indicated for use with families of aggressive children in which cognitive, psychological, marital, or social variables are disrupting the parents' family management abilities and/or directly relating to child behavior problems. It is not indicated for use with families in which parenting skills deficits seem to be the only variable related to child behavior problems.

BIBLIOGRAPHY

Alexander, J., & Parsons, B. V. (1982). *Functional family therapy*. Monterey, CA: Brooks/Cole.

Griest, D. L., & Wells, K. C. (1983). Behavioral family therapy for conduct disorders in children. *Behavior Therapy, 14,* 37–53.

Patterson, G. R. (1982). *Coercive family process*. Eugene, OR: Castalia.

Stuart, R. B. (1980). *Helping couples change*. New
York: Guilford.

Wells, K. C., & Forehand, R. (in press). Conduct
and oppositional disorders. In P. H. Bornstein &
A. E. Kazdin (eds.). *Handbook of clinical behavior
therapy with children*. Homewood, IL: Dorsey.

See: Contingency Management
Parent Management Training

BEHAVIORAL GROUP THERAPY

Sheldon D. Rose

Behavioral group therapy can be defined as
the application of principles of behavior,
cognitive-behavior, and problem-solving
therapy to the treatment of children and
adults within, and by means of, the small
group. The focus of such treatment is learning and maintaining improved social problem-solving and cognitive skills which facilitate effective coping with problematic or
stressful and problematic social situations.
The small group (5–12 persons) provides
both the context of, and one set of, intervention for treatment. Behavioral group
therapy can be looked at as a continuum
from short-term training to intensive long-
term therapy. At the training end of the
continuum, groups focus solely on teaching
a narrow range of highly specific behaviors
— for example, assertion, parenting skills,
and marital communication. The groups
tend to be homogeneous as to specific presenting problem. There tends to be heavy
reliance on group exercises and working on
shared problems.

At the intensive therapy end of the continuum, a wide variety of interventions are
used as needed, individualization is much
greater, and group problems and processes
are dealt with as learning experiences. Structured exercises are also included where necessary to develop common therapeutic skills.
The groups tend to be made heterogeneous.
The problems dealt with are usually more
complex and more varied in long-term

therapy groups than those in short-term
training groups.

THE GROUP AS CONTEXT OF TREATMENT

The group appears to have both advantages
and limitations for therapy. Because many
problems are social-interactional in nature,
the presence of other clients provides an opportunity for practicing new social-interactional skills in a protected setting. The group
gives clients an opportunity to learn and
practice many behaviors and cognitions as
they respond to the constantly changing
group demands. The clients must learn to
offer others feedback, ideas, and advice; as
a result, many will develop important skills
for leadership. By helping others, clients
usually learn to help themselves more effectively than when they are the sole recipients
of therapy.

In group interaction, powerful norms
arise that serve to control the behavior of
individual clients who deviate from pro-
therapeutic norms. If these norms (informal
agreements among members as to preferred
modes of action and interaction in the group)
are introduced and effectively maintained
by the therapist, they serve as efficient therapeutic tools.

Each person in the group is given the
chance to learn or to improve his or her
ability to mediate rewards for others in social interactive situations (with spouse, family, friendship groups, work group). The
therapist can structure the group situation
in which each person has frequent opportunities, instructions, and even rewards for
reinforcing others in the group. The same
is true for giving and receiving criticism.

More accurate assessment can be another
major contribution of group therapy. Many
aspects of a problem which elude even the
most sensitive therapist often become clearly
spelled out during an intensive group discussion. The group provides clients with a

major source of feedback about what in their behavior is annoying and what makes them attractive to others. The group is especially helpful to clients who cannot pinpoint their own problems. Since the group supplies so many of its own therapeutic needs and gives simultaneous treatment to a number of people, this type of therapy appears to be less costly than individual treatment in terms of staff and money.

The group is not without major limits. Although a group contract and group agendas may prevent excessive wandering to irrelevant topics, they also may serve to deter exploration of the idiosyncratic needs of any one individual. Each person needs to be allotted some time at every meeting to discuss unique problems. Therefore, no one or two persons can be permitted to dominate it. Some clients may even feel severely restricted by such a concern for involvement of all other members.

Another disadvantage of the group is the absence of a guarantee of confidentiality. Although all clients contract to hold any discussion of individual problems in the group in confidence, they are not necessarily committed to the professional ethics of the therapist. The absence of this guarantee may also restrict the degree to which some clients are inclined to self-disclose.

For those few whose problems require more detailed and individualized examination or whose social anxiety is so great that they cannot function in a group, the group may not be the preferred context of therapy. Moreover, although psychotic patients can be treated in a group, one delusional patient in a group may be greatly disturbing to the others. This is also true of bi-polar depressives.

ASSESSMENT IN GROUPS

As in individual behavior therapy, assessment is used to determine the target behaviors, the situations in which they occur, and personal resources for coping with their problems. Behavioral checklists, goal attainment scaling, role play tests, self-monitoring techniques, and in-group or community observations are used to achieve these purposes. In group therapy, assessment is also used to determine whether a person should be in a group at all and what the composition of that group should be.

Furthermore, since assessment occurs in groups, data are often collected about the ongoing group process by means of observation and post-session questionnaires. The major variables examined are participation, satisfaction, perceived usefulness, self-disclosure, rate of homework assignment completion, and attendance.

INTERVENTION IN GROUPS

Intervention in group therapy in most cases is multi-modal. However, since social skill training lends itself especially well to group therapy and because social skill deficits are such common phenomena in most complex problems, social skill training is the most common feature of most group therapy intervention packages.

Research with psychiatric patients showed that the level of social competence, based on global measures of educational, vocational, and marital attainment, was related to the degree of psychiatric impairments. Lewinsohn and Hoberman have proposed a relationship between interpersonal deficits and such clinical phenomena as depression. Argyle has pointed out how social skill deficits can be antecedent to a variety of other clinical syndromes. For this reason, social skill training which includes modeling, rehearsal, coaching, and feedback provides a key set of procedures in this approach as one means of reducing social skill deficits.

Of course, some persons for whom social skills may or may not be lacking, are still unable to function without high levels of anxiety or other distress. For these, it appears that certain interpersonal and intra-personal events are accompanied by, or evoke, distorted cognitions which in turn elicit anxiety and other strong emotions. Under intense anxiety, the performance of adaptive or coping behavior is limited or even inhibited. For these persons, cognitive procedures such as stress inoculation can be combined with social skill training procedures to enhance social functioning and reduce anxiety. Stress management, pain management, and anger control groups draw heavily on the stress inoculation model for many of its interventions.

Research carried out by Hand and his associates with phobic and obsessive-compulsives in groups made extensive and successful use of group exposure methods.

In children's therapy groups, operant procedures are largely used. Token reinforcement which is exchanged periodically for back-up reinforcers is distributed for the completion of home behavioral assignments and appropriate in-group behavior. In the treatment of depressed adults in groups, Lewinsohn and his colleagues also use a great deal of reinforcement and reinforcement building along with cognitive and social skill training.

PROBLEM-SOLVING

Several studies have shown that emotionally distressed individuals are not very efficient problem-solvers. In the problem-solving component of training, the client learns systematically to work through a set of steps for analyzing a problem, discovering and evaluating new approaches, and developing strategies for implementing these approaches in the real world. In groups, problem-solving is first taught through problem-solving exercises in which each person brings a problem to the group and the group goes explicitly through the various steps mentioned above. Problem-solving is integrated

with social skill training and cognitive restructuring through the systematic analysis of all problem situations, through establishing the client's goals for those situations, and through the group generating specific kinds of interactive behavior and/or cognitive change for the client to evaluate. Social skill training and cognitive restructuring are usually the preparation for implementation.

GROUP PROCEDURES

Group procedures can be distinguished from individual intervention in that instructions are for interactive or cooperative activities which usually modify the group structure. Member-to-member discussion would be the most ubiquitous group intervention involved. Other, more specific, procedures include recapitulation, subgrouping, fishbowl, leadership training, group exercises, and the buddy system.

MODIFYING GROUP ATTRIBUTES

Group and individual procedures are often used together to modify group attributes which include the level of group cohesion, the distribution of group participation, the agreement to certain group norms, the status of various members in the group, and the domination of a given member over others in the group. It is this concern for influencing group phenomena to mediate the modification of individual behavior that distinguishes group from individual therapy. Most often when group data reveal a group problem (e.g., low satisfaction, a low rate of homework completion), group problem-solving is used. It should be noted that researchers have found significant differences in leader behavior and group processes among various groups of depressed patients, but that these differences had no effect on outcome. Rose, in assertive training groups, found that several processes, rate of homework completion, and degree of participation significantly correlated with outcome.

One particular group process of concern to group therapists because it differentially guides the activity of the therapist is the phases of group therapy.

PHASES OF GROUP THERAPY

One can identify at least four major, albeit overlapping, phases of group therapy: pregroup, orientation, intervention, and termination.

Pregroup phase. In the pregroup phase, the group therapist contacts potential members, tells about the activities of the group, its general purposes, and mechanics. He or she obtains preliminary agreements from the clients about their participation in the group. Assessment is initiated in the pregroup interview as well as through behavioral inventories, role play tests, sociometric tests, and self-monitoring.

Orientation phase. In the orientation phase, the therapist introduces members to each other, often dramatically, through introductory group exercises. He or she attempts to build group cohesion through other group exercises (for example, examining a case study) and roleplaying. For purposes of orientation a treatment contract is one in which the conditions of treatment are explicated, and which is presented and discussed by the members. Individual assessment is continued through direct observation of group behavior and through the introduction of a brief post-session questionnaire. In this phase, too, clients are taught basic therapeutic skills such as how to analyze situations, give feedback, roleplay, and examine and evaluate one's thinking.

Homework in this phase is usually self-observation of situations in which the client has successfully or unsuccessfully coped with a stressful or problematic social situation. Assessment in the group is continued with a detailed analysis of these situations by the group members. In this phase most of the leadership functions are held by the group therapist. The group session is usually highly structured. Should the group data reveal group problems these are presented to the group and dealt with in this as well as the following phase.

Intervention phase. In the intervention phase, in addition to problem situations being analyzed, solutions are generated and evaluated, modeled, and repeatedly practiced. At first, common problem situations are worked on. Drawing upon the data collected in assessment, the therapist designs the initial situations. Later, individual problem situations, which clients have recorded in their diaries, are the focus of treatment. Problem solving, cognitive restructuring, and social skill training are heavily used in this phase. Homework to try out solutions to problem situations in the real world is designed, carried out between sessions, and subsequently monitored. In this phase, preparation is beginning to be initiated for transfer and maintenance of change. Responsibility for decision-making is gradually shifted to the group and to individuals throughout this phase. The degree of structure is beginning to diminish. Reinforcement schedules are being thinned.

Termination phase. In preparing for termination, the attraction of other groups is increased relative to the therapy groups. Clients are encouraged to join nontherapeutic groups in order to practice their newly learned skills under less-controlled conditions. Others may be referred for further therapy. Greater reliance is placed on the decisions of the clients as they increasingly perform the major leadership tasks in the group. The role of the therapist shifts from direct therapist to consultant. These activities not only serve to make termination easier on the clients, they permit them to function independently of the therapist. This independence is necessary not only for the maintenance of changes beyond the end of the group but in making the client more comfortable in dealing with new problems should and when they happen. Clients are made ready for potential setbacks, unsympathetic relatives and friends, and unpredicted pressure through role play of situations simulating the above conditions but for which the clients are not permitted to prepare in advance.

PRELIMINARY OUTCOMES

A crucial issue of concern is whether behavioral group therapy is an effective form of treatment. Because of the methodological problems of doing research with small groups as a unit of analysis, the number of control group outcome experiments in this area is limited. A number of experiments have been carried out in the context of small groups usually without reference to the group attributes and group procedures. The results of these studies at least have suggested that social skill groups are indeed more effective in developing skills than wait-list, or placebo control groups.

In reviewing research in the treatment of anxiety-related problems in groups such as phobias, obsessions and depression, and stress, we can conclude that group therapy is in almost all cases more effective than wait-list controls. In those few studies in which group and individual treatment were compared, group therapy was equally or more effective and less costly than individual therapy. In most of the projects the specific components of group phenomena had been ignored so we do not know their peculiar contribution.

BIBLIOGRAPHY

Argyle, M. (1969). *Social interaction*. Chicago: Aldine.

Lewinsohn, P. & Hoberman, H. (1982). Depression. In A. S. Bellack, M. Hersen, & A. E. Kazdin (Eds.), *International handbook of behavior modification*. New York: Plenum Press.

Rose, S. D. (1977). *Group therapy: a behavioral approach*. Englewood Cliffs, NJ: Prentice-Hall.

Rose, S. D. (1981). How group attributes relate to outcome in behavior group therapy. *Social Work Research and Abstracts, 17*, 25–29.

Rose, S. D., Tolman, R., & Tallant, S. (1983, December). Review of group therapy research: Group process and outcome. Paper presented at Annual Convention of the Association for the Advancement of Behavior Therapy, Washington, DC.

Upper, D., & Ross, S. M. (Eds.). (1981). *Behavioral group therapy, 1981 — An annual review*. Champaign, IL: Research Press Company.

See: Modeling

BEHAVIORAL MARITAL THERAPY
Sharon L. Foster and Jean M. Griffin

Behavioral Marital Therapy (BMT) is a generic name for an approach to treating couples in unhappy relationships. The general goals of BMT are to increase mutual positive interaction, to decrease negative exchanges, and to provide couples with generalized strategies for resolving future relationship problems. A number of therapeutic tactics are used alone or (more often) in combination to achieve these goals. These include contracting, problem-solving training, communication training, increasing positive exchanges, and restructuring problem cognitions.

At the heart of BMT approaches lie contracting and problem-solving training, both sharing the goal of teaching couples to reach mutually agreeable solutions to issues that have been sources of repeated conflict. Problem-solving training generally includes teaching couples to define the problem targeted for discussion in a brief, nonaccusatory, specific fashion; to generate potential solutions to the problem; to select the best solution(s) based on evaluations of their potential effectiveness and compromise; and to implement the agreed-upon solutions at home. Problem-solving training is augmented by communication training, ordinarily necessary to reduce the accusations, defensiveness, mindreading, overgeneralizations, and quibbling about past and present wrongdoings that impede effective problem-solving. Although communication targets vary across couples, the most common skills taught are empathic and reflective listening, staying on the topic, accepting and understanding the other's point of view even if disagreeing with it, making direct requests referring to specific behaviors, expressing positive and negative feelings with "I-statements" and an indication of the behavioral antecedent of the feeling ("I feel angry when you make social commitments for us without checking with me first"), and checking out inferences and attributions about one partner's behavior with the other. Strategies used to teach couples problem-solving and communication skills include instruction, modeling, rehearsal, and therapist and/or partner feedback. Homework assignments structured to maximize compliance and success are given to enhance skill use at home.

Contracting approaches attack specific relationship problems by teaching couples to negotiate specific changes each wants from the other, along with contingencies for compliance or noncompliance with the changes. Contracts are formally written and signed by both parties. With quid pro quo contracts, the reinforcers for a change in one partner's target behavior rest on alterations in the other's target behavior (e.g., If Dorothy is home on time, Joe will put the kids to bed that night). With good faith or parallel contracts, changes in target behaviors are not used to reinforce behavior

change; instead, reinforcers involve delivery of positives that are not issues of conflict in the marriage (e.g., every time Dorothy is home on time, she and Joe will have a drink together before dinner; every time Joe puts the kids to bed, Dorothy will provide a back rub). Some complain that quid pro quo contracts, although efficient, break down more easily than parallel contracts when one partner fails to comply, due to the interdependence of spouses' behavior change. Nonetheless, research suggests that the two types of contracting used in conjunction with communication training are equally effective. Further, contracting and problem-solving communication training appear to be equally effective approaches. Use of both appears not to enhance the results of either used singly. Recently, however, the use of contracting has been downplayed in BMT, based on evidence that distressed spouses overemphasize immediate and contingent exchange of positive behaviors. This overemphasis is believed by some to be both counterproductive to relationships and encouraged by traditional contracting procedures.

Another tactic sometimes used early in therapy involves working to increase positive interactions. The goal of this tactic is to promote commitment to the marriage and to treatment via providing initial success in therapy by increasing nonconflicting relationship-enhancing behaviors. Behaviors to increase should not involve central relationship issues. Selecting and increasing positive behaviors can be accomplished by setting daily frequency goals of positive behaviors for each spouse to give, asking spouses to experiment to see which of their positive behaviors leads to the greatest increases in their partner's daily records of marital satisfaction, and/or designating special "love" or "caring days" when one spouse provides large numbers of behaviors valued by the other. Spouses can determine which behaviors are pleasing by exchanging verbal requests or inspecting self- or spouse-monitoring data collected at home during treatment. Alternatively, activities that the couple enjoys but does rarely can be scheduled more frequently.

Cognitive strategies are also used in conjunction with other BMT components when couples express unrealistic or irrational expectations, misattributions of the other's intentions and over-emphasis on the spouse as the cause of one's own unhappiness. Cognitive interventions include reframing (relabeling) negative attributions to create more benign causal explanations ("It's not that he doesn't love you, he just doesn't have the skills to express affection."), presenting factual material and contradictory evidence to correct irrational expectations, and replacing vague, partner-blame attributions of the causes of marital problems with attributions emphasizing mutual causality and changeable specific factors. Preliminary evidence tentatively suggests that addition of cognitive components to problem-solving communication training and contracting enhances BMT's effectiveness.

CLINICAL APPLICATION

BMT generally begins with a comprehensive assessment, which usually takes two or three sessions. Explaining the assessment process and its rationale to the couple and securing their agreement at the outset of treatment can enhance compliance with home data collection and help avoid disappointment when assessment sessions fail to produce behavior change. Numerous assessment methods are available to gather information about a couple's relationship. Clinical interviews may be used both to impart information to the couple and to acquire information regarding development of, and perceptions about, the relationship, relationship strengths and weaknesses, and current concerns. Audiotaping communication samples during which the couple is instructed to try to resolve a current problem, and noting the couple's interaction styles during the interview, are excellent methods for directly observing the couple's communication and problem-solving skills. Self-report questionnaires have been developed by behavioral marital therapists to elicit information about areas such as current concerns in the relationship (Areas of Change Questionnaire), the nature of daily relationship events (Spouse Observation Checklist), general relationship beliefs (Relationship Beliefs Inventory), feelings toward the spouse (Positive Feelings Questionnaire), and steps taken toward divorce (Marital Status Inventory), among others. Self- and spouse-monitoring systems designed specifically for the couple can also promote functional analyses of treatment targets not sufficiently captured by standard questionnaires.

Both partners are frequently not equally committed to working on the relationship upon entering therapy. Therefore, it is important to ascertain each partner's goals for the relationship and for treatment during the initial session(s). However, even if both spouses wish to improve the relationship rather than separating or divorcing, one or both may express reluctance to participate in treatment. One strategy for engaging a reluctant spouse in treatment involves acknowledging the reluctance, and indicating that early sessions will focus on assessing whether treatment would benefit the couple. Judicious reflection of information given by both partners that emphasizes the interdependence of both partners' thoughts, feelings, and behavior and indicates what each could gain from treatment can help the reluctant spouse to understand his or her role in the problems, as well as what benefit s/he could derive from participation. Establishing good rapport with both spouses by communicating an understanding for each partner's perspective can enhance the spouses' trust in the therapist as a change agent.

By the end of the assessment period, the therapist and couple should have reached consensual goals for therapy. The therapist can work toward this by reflecting and summarizing data and providing information about case conceptualization either at selected intervals throughout assessment, or during a specific interpretation session in which the therapist draws upon all of the assessment material gathered and discusses the treatment plan and its rationale. Positive treatment expectancies should be established, while making clear that relationship changes will be the couple's responsibility rather than the product of therapeutic magic.

Once the couple has made a verbal or written commitment to therapy, treatment proper can begin. Promoting some immediate payoffs for the couple (e.g., by working initially on increasing exchanges of pleasing behaviors) is sometimes selected as an initial step in treatment. This is based on the belief that the more arduous process of communication and problem-solving skills training will be more favorably received after couples have experienced some improvement in their daily exchanges.

Throughout treatment, the therapist should monitor the couple's perceptions regarding the nature of problems and changes. Couples tend to endorse linear, causal interpretations, which place the causes of problems and the burden of change on one of the partners. The therapist must consistently expand these one-sided interpretations to illustrate the reciprocal characteristics of relationship interactions, promoting spouses' awareness of their own contributions to a given problem and of their partner's thoughts and feelings. This process also involves encouraging couples to take a collaborative stance in problem resolution by compromising and making changes for the benefit of the relationship.

Attributions regarding the causes of partner behaviors should also be checked during treatment. In addition to reframing negative inferences regarding the meaning of displeasing partner behaviors, perceptions of positive spouse actions should also be assessed. Relationship strengths and therapy-promoted improvements are often underestimated or misattributed to factors external to the partner and relationship. The structure and presentation of therapy tasks should be designed to give spouses credit for the changes they have made to please their partners and improve the relationship.

Consistent with an emphasis on mutual contributions to problems and improvements are the therapist's equivalent distribution of attention and concern for the well-being of both spouses. Continually allying with one spouse in favor of the other can be a serious impediment to therapy. Couples cannot be expected to adopt a collaborative stance if the therapist fails to recognize the reciprocal, interactional composition of relationship problems. Alliances with one spouse should alert the therapist to the possibility that this spouse has superior expressive skills or expresses beliefs consonant with the therapist's own values, or that promoting the relationship is in fact not in the best interests of the individual spouses.

While changes will be implemented in specific problem areas, the thrust of therapy involves a focus on interactional or process issues. Problems will be encountered in all long-term committed relationships; it is the manner in which they are handled that is critical. Thus, improving the couple's communication and problem-resolution patterns will equip them to manage current and future problems effectively, irrespective of the particular content of the complaints.

EXPECTED OUTCOME AND TIME FRAMES

Numerous case studies and group outcome studies attest to the effectiveness of BMT approaches. Couples in these studies on average have been aged between 20 and 45, married under 10 years, and have been at least high school graduates. Both couples recruited through advertisement and those applying for services at outpatient mental health facilities have been shown to benefit from BMT. In general, moderately distressed couples' satisfaction with their relationship (as assessed by self-report questionnaires) improves, often into the normal range, following 8–10 weeks of weekly or biweekly treatment (assessment sessions are not included in this estimate). On average, gains are maintained at 3-month–1-year follow-ups. Severely distressed couples may require lengthier treatment. Many couples show increases in positive problem-solving communication skills and decreases in negative problem-solving behaviors in analogue discussions in the clinic, although some studies have not found these to occur. Whether couples use these skills at home has not been evaluated to date. Nor are data presently available on the percentage of couples who stay together following BMT at follow-up.

An estimated 75% of couples treated with BMT improve in marital satisfaction and/or communication, although some of these couples may voice concern that in some areas the relationship still does not meet their expectations. At present, information on characteristics of couples who do and do not improve following BMT is not available.

CONTRAINDICATIONS

In general, marital therapy, as outlined above, is contraindicated when one spouse is engaged in an ongoing extramarital relationship, when there is current or imminent spouse abuse, when divorce is the issue, when one spouse has severe individual problems extraneous to the relationship, or when one spouse will not participate in therapy.

Ongoing extramarital relationships threaten the likelihood of positive treatment gains, and terminating the extramarital relationship may be required before attempting marital therapy. This statement is predicated on the assumptions that the extramarital relationship is a source of distress in the marriage, imposes or maintains an imbalance of power in the relationship, and, if maintained despite therapeutic proscription, represents a lack of commitment to the hard work required to significantly improve the marriage. (In rare cases none of these assumptions will hold true and therapists should be alert to the possibility of imposing unwarranted assumptions regarding the significance of the affair to the couple.)

In contrast, an extramarital relationship in the couple's history, particularly recent history, is an important area to explore within the context of BMT. Discussion of the circumstances surrounding the development and termination of the extramarital relationship, its meaning to both spouses, and whether, when, and how it should be disclosed if secret may greatly facilitate case conceptualization and treatment planning.

The danger of physical harm resulting from spouse abuse immediately shifts the focus of therapy from promoting the relationship to protecting the vulnerable spouse. When the danger is imminent, effective protection may require physical separation through violence shelters or legal action. When physical harm is possible but not imminent, or when spouses choose not to seek protective services, the focus of therapy becomes one of achieving immediate control over abusive patterns, and anger control procedures may take precedence over BMT strategies outlined here.

Marital therapy is also contraindicated when one or both spouses is committed to pursuing divorce. However, when spouses are unsure about the suitability of divorce, assessment and therapy can help the couple appraise their relationship, their goals, and the efforts required to obtain them. Therapists should be aware of their personal biases regarding divorce and, as much as possible, safeguard against imposing them on the couple. When couples decide to opt for divorce, conjoint sessions are often discontinued, although in some cases couples continue to meet with the therapist to negotiate property settlement and custody agreements. Individual therapy may also be helpful to facilitate adjustment to the marital status transition and all that it entails.

When relationship problems co-exist with severe individual problems presented by one spouse, it may be necessary to postpone marital therapy until the individual problem is reduced. This will be the case when therapeutic attention to the individual problem represents a clinical priority for maintaining the well-being of the spouse, when the individual problem would interfere with effective marital therapy, and/or when eliciting or maintaining factors of the individual problem are largely outside the marriage. In the latter case, concurrent individual and marital therapy may be useful.

The dyadic focus of BMT techniques requires input and participation from both spouses. BMT is precluded when one member of an unsatisfying relationship refuses to participate in therapy. As mentioned earlier, steps taken early in BMT sometimes can elicit cooperation from a reluctant spouse. In other cases, the therapy-reluctant spouse will opt for alternatives other than therapy, such as divorce or maintaining the status quo. Therapy with the initiating spouse is then restricted to an individual, rather than relationship, focus and

the therapy process will necessarily depart from BMT. The therapeutic contract should explicitly redefine the thrust of therapy accordingly.

BIBLIOGRAPHY

Hahlweg, K., & Jacobson, N. S. (Eds.). (in press). *Marital interaction: Analysis and modification.* New York: Guilford.

Jacobson, N. S., & Margolin, G. (1979). *Marital therapy: Strategies based on social learning and behavior exchange principles.* New York: Brunner/Mazel.

Margolin, G. (1982). Ethical and legal considerations in family and marital therapy. *The American Psychologist, 37,* 788–801.

Stuart, R. B. (1980). *Helping couples change.* New York: Guilford.

See: Communication Skills Training
Contingency Contracting
Problem-Solving Training

BEHAVIORAL TREATMENT FOR CHRONIC PAIN
Paul M. Cinciripini

The treatment of chronic pain resulting from trauma, injury, or unknown etiology is a significant health care problem in the United States. Many patients stop working permanently, eliminate potentially pleasurable physical activities from their routine, and withdraw from family and friends. Recent applications of an operant model to the treatment of chronic pain have attempted to provide a basis for treatment by focusing on the behaviors a person exhibits to communicate his/her experience of pain, e.g., pill-taking, sighs, moans, limping, uptime, downtime, physical performance, and so on. Operant pain behaviors need not correspond with underlying organic disease or nociception, and hence the frequency and intensity with which they are reported may be influenced by direct reinforcement, avoidance or time out from unpleasant tasks (e.g., anxiety reduction), discouragement of well behavior, and the presence of discriminative cues which signal an increased likelihood of social reinforcement.

The results of behaviorally oriented pain programs are very promising, given the rather poor success rate of traditional medical interventions. Studies have reported favorable changes in a mixed pain population for medication intake, reclining time, daily walking distance, and hours of physical activity uninterrupted by pain or rest. Other studies have reported significant gains for low back patients in medication reduction, measures of physical functioning, such as significant increases in walking velocity and cadence, and metabolic efficiency (O_2 ml/kg-m) following multidisciplinary/behavioral treatment. Mixed chronic pain patients have shown significant reductions in medication use, verbal/non-verbal pain behavior, and improvements in physical functioning, employment status and pro-health behavior.

Likely candidates for behavioral treatment of chronic pain have included a wide array of patients with musculoskeletal, structural, and degenerative disorders. For example, much research has been conducted with migraine and tension headache sufferers, low back and lower extremity pain, upper extremity and abdominal pain, facial pain, however little work has been done with cancer pain. Other types of patients, such as those with severe burns and cancer pain, have been treated on an individual basis.

Typical patients in operant pain programs have a long history of chronic pain, and have gone through a variety of medical treatments, including surgery, physical therapy, etc., with little or no success. Often the patient presents with a past history of injury or illness, of which current pain reports are insufficiently substantiated by the status of the injury. Patients may also report pain in the absence of physical findings, or physical findings may be hypothesized, but clear evidence is lacking.

INTERVENTION

Treatment may involve both inpatient and outpatient programs, but due to the typical nature of the problem and its chronicity, inpatient treatment is preferred. If outpatient treatment is used, then it is recommended that the patient be seen frequently (e.g., twice per week) and the family be involved. Successful treatment is typically multidisciplinary and may involve general behavior therapy and biofeedback, as well as behaviorally oriented occupation and physical therapy programs.

TREATMENT GOALS

1. Reduce or eliminate dependence on psychologically and/or physically addicting medications.
2. Reduce functional impairment and approach pre-pain levels of physical activity.
3. Alter crucial elements of the patient's lifestyle to cultivate pro-health behaviors in the following areas:
   a. Exercise: physical activity and recreation
   b. Interpersonal relationships: emphasizing social skills training, assertive training, conflict negotiation.
   c. Family relationships: emphasizing reciprocity and discovering the role of pain behavior in the family life.
   d. Employability: emphasizing the behaviors necessary for job search and interviewing commensurate wtih skills.
   e. Education: improvement of life quality by encouraging participation in higher education.
   f. Stress management: emphasizing relaxation, biofeedback, cognitive stress innoculation, anger management, time management, realistic goal setting, and monitoring of progress.
   g. Improvement in personal satisfaction and self esteem: enhancement of well

being through a rational thinking style geared towards realistic goal setting and problem solving

4. Reduce inappropriate utilization of health care services.

TARGET BEHAVIORS

Some of the typical target outcome behaviors have included:

1. Subjective pain level, measured on 1–10 scale and on an hourly basis.
2. Physical activity measures, such as daily pedometer readings, stairs climbed, miles cycled, weights lifted, total up-time, total downtime, etc.
3. Medication dosage, measured by multiplying the daily frequency by the amount per occasion. Sometimes a factor for potency is also included.
4. Employment/occupation status, measured by return to the job market or previous job, pursuance of higher education or vocational retraining.
5. Compensation and disability payments.
6. Pain talk: This category consists of direct or indirect statements related to pain, for example, "My back hurts," "I feel stiff all over," or "I can't do that since the accident," "I want to see the doctor today."
7. Nonverbal pain behavior. This category refers to the subtle or covert signals used to express pain or discomfort and includes: Gesturing, defined as limping, staggering, restrained body movements, or abnormal postural adjustment (e.g., using hands to support body while sitting or other body movements used to express discomfort); Touching, defined as touching a body part associated with pain; and Grimacing, which includes frowning, gritting one's teeth, biting one's lip, and other facial expressions used to express pain or discomfort.

8. Nonpain complaints: This category consists of any verbal complaint that describes or alludes to a problem other than pain, e.g., complaints about hospital administration, dietary services, doctor's receptionist, or nonpain-related physical problems, such as colds, nausea, etc. This category may be used to determine if patients shift from pain complaints to nonpain complaints when reinforcement for pain behavior is withdrawn.
9. Pro-health talk: This behavior includes direct or indirect statements reflecting improvement in one's health or well being and contrasting with verbal and nonverbal pain measures, for example, "I feel better today," "I can do this now," "I will start this new project today," "I feel good about my exercise," or "I walked a mile today."
10. Assertive behavior: This category involves assertive verbal behavior expressed in a socially appropriate way. Attempts to compromise in disputes, requests for help or clarification, and verbalizing displeasure at being taken advantage of or unjustly criticized may be included.

PROCEDURES

Operant treatment programs have involved some or all of the following procedures:

Medication reduction. Medication reduction is usually conducted for all pain-related medications, including analgesics, tranquilizers, sedatives, and hypnotics. The procedure usually involves baseline assessment of all medications, available on a prn basis. Next, phased medication reduction techniques are implemented, consisting of a medication cocktail delivered on a fixed interval schedule. A declining percent of active medications is available in the cocktail, approaching zero within 14 days.

Physical therapy. Baseline assessment of physical functioning may entail measures of posture, gait, muscle strength, range of motion, and functional mobility. During treatment, patients are exposed to exercise routines (a.m. and p.m.), which include stretching and flexibility exercises, jogging and/or brisk walking, stair climbing, stationary cycling, and weight lifting. During the baseline, the minimum number of exercise repetitions and weight amount that can be accomplished with complete comfort is established. Patients then increase their participation in each exercise at a rate established by both the patient and the therapist. The emphasis is on gradually increased functioning in the absence of pain cues. Social reinforcement is applied for achieving incremental changes. Pain behavior is ignored or patients are asked to readjust their goals to a level where no pain is experienced and gradually work up to the new level once again.

Biofeedback/relaxation training. Biofeedback training may also be provided. Mastery of relaxation techniques, rather than pain reduction, is emphasized. Frontal EMG feedback would be typically provided and digital skin temperature also monitored. Patients may now listen to progressive relaxation tapes on a daily basis.

Behavioral group or individual therapy. Group or individual therapy may be conducted based on a social learning model. Sessions can be video taped and later reviewed with the patients, often with dramatic changes. Sessions should emphasize the fundamental role of pain behavior as a social and cognitive cue which elicits changes in the behavior of others and sets the occasion for discouragement of wellness. Patients may be asked to note the antecedents and consequences of their pain behavior, especially in relation to changes in activity level, re-

sponsibilities, marital communication, and social interaction. Alternative behaviors may be suggested which recognize the presence of discomfort, but stress the importance of positive coping skills. Patients may also learn appropriate assertive skills which preclude the use of pain behavior to manipulate family members, express anger, and so on. Additional well behaviors, including visiting friends, joining clubs, acquiring new hobbies or domestic skills, and seeking out other pleasant activities, will be encouraged. Cognitive behavioral skills may also be provided to deal directly with clinical depression and anxiety.

Contracting. Each person may also negotiate a contract with the therapist which outlines long- and short-term goals, and specifies relative intermediate steps. Expectations for change should be kept realistic and success-oriented by emphasizing gradual accomplishments. Typical goals may include analgesic medication reduction, increasing jogging time, decreasing downtime (reclining), increasing stationary bicycle activity, walking without a cane or support, initiating nonpain-related conversations, and so on. Goal reviews may be conducted once a week and contingent social reinforcement should be provided. In the care of inpatient treatment, some privileges (e.g., outdoor passes, extended free-time and access to recreational events) may also be contractually tied to changes in the individual's pain behavior and physical functioning.

Self-monitoring. Patients should self-monitor and graph daily pain levels, pedometer readings, jogging time, stairs climbed, and progress on other individual goals. Graphs should be prominently displayed in the patient's room, or at home, and serve as the basis for social- and self-reinforcement.

Family training. Spouses, family, and significant others are also asked to participate in the training sessions. Family and others can be taught to reinforce wellness, reduce and eliminate reinforcement for illness behavior, and allow the patient to assume full responsibility for the management of his/her medical concerns. The training may include lectures, discussion, and participation in the patient's daily hospital routine (in the case of inpatient treatment).

Patient education. In addition to the behavioral psychotherapy experience, patients may be exposed to lectures, discussions, and meetings in the following areas: anatomy/physiology, vocational counseling, job finding/interviewing skills, recreational planning, opportunities for higher education, completion of GED, and others.

Follow-up. Patients should be asked to attend follow-up group sessions following discharge or termination. The general focus of follow-up may be maintenance of wellness using the skills learned in treatment.

EXPECTED EFFECTS

The results of behaviorally oriented pain programs are very promising, given the rather poor success rate of traditional medical interventions. For example, favorable changes have been reported in mixed pain populations for medication intake, reclining time, daily walking distance, and hours of physical activity uninterrupted by pain or rest. Significant gains have been found for low back pain patients in medication reduction, measures of physical functioning, such as walking velocity, cadence and metabolic efficiency, and improved work status and tolerance for physical activity. Cinciripini & Floreen (1982) treated 121 chronic pain patients in a 4 week inpatient program using the package described in this chapter and noted significant reductions in analgesic medication use and verbal/nonverbal pain behavior, as well as improvements in physical functioning, employment status, and prohealth behaviors which were maintained at 12-month follow-up.

CONTRAINDICATIONS

Patients successfully treated in chronic pain programs vary widely, but the most efficacious use of the behavioral approach appears to be with patients who have pain with musculoskeletal involvement, with or without concomitant degenerative disease. The effectiveness of these procedures with terminal cancer pain and acute injury due to burn or trauma has *not* been evaluated in a programmatic way, although single case studies using relaxation and imagery techniques have been used.

BIBLIOGRAPHY

Cinciripini, P. M. (1983). Stimulus control and chronic pain behavior in low back and head/neck/face pain patients. *Behavior Modification, 7*, 243–254.

Cinciripini, P. M., & Floreen, A. (1983). Assessment of chronic pain behavior in a structured interview. *Journal of Psychosomatic Research, 27*, 117–123.

Cinciripini, P. M., Williamson, D., & Epstein, L. H. (1981). The behavioral treatment of migraine headaches. In C. B. Taylor & J. Ferguson (Eds.), *The comprehensive handbook of behavioral medicine.* New York: S. P. Medical and Scientific Books.

Fordyce, W. E. (1976). *Behavioral methods for chronic pain and illness.* St. Louis: C. V. Mosby.

Fordyce, W. E., Fowler, R. S., Lehmann, J. F., DeLateur, B. J., Sand, P. L., & Trieschman, R. B. (1973). Operant conditioning in the treatment of chronic pain. *Archives of Physiology and Medical Rehabilitation, 54*, 399–406.

Newman, R., Seres, J., Yospe, L., & Garlington, B. (1978). Multidisciplinary treatment of chronic pain: Long term follow-up of low back pain patients. *Pain, 4*, 283–292.

Thomas, L. K., Hislop, H. J., & Waters, R. L. (1980). Physiological work performance in chronic low back disability. *Journal of American Physiological and Therapeutic Association, 60*, 407–411.

See: Biofeedback
 Deep Muscle Relaxation
 Social Skills Training
 Stress Management Training

BEHAVIORAL TREATMENT OF SEIZURE DISORDERS

Paul M. Cinciripini

Behavior technology for treatment of seizures is emergent but its applications have not been widespread. Both biofeedback and operant approaches have been used with a variety of seizure disturbances.

BIOFEEDBACK APPROACHES

The use of biofeedback in the treatment of seizure disorders is a fairly recent addition to the available treatment modalities. Significant reductions in psychomotor seizures have been associated with EEG biofeedback/reward in the 12–15 cps, 18–23 cps, or 9–14 cps bandwidths. Seizure reductions have also been observed for patients exposed to an audio feedback signal which varied proportionately to the amplitude of the EEG spike/wave discharge normally associated with seizure activity.

EXPECTED EFFECTS

It appears that training in a broad band of activity (e.g., 12–23 cps) may be associated with seizure reduction, presumably by normalizing the power spectrum of the EEG and lowering slow wave activity (1–11 cps). Both extended (>10 hours) laboratory sessions and continuous home practice may be required to observe these effects. A decrease in slow wave activity during training or sleep evaluation (8–11 Hz) seems to be the common pathway associated with seizure reduction, although the clinical EEG may not always reflect decreased paroxysmal discharges. It is suggested that biofeedback training provides an opportunity for the subject to over-stimulate motor inhibitory pathways leading to neural reorganization and increased seizure threshold.

OPERANT APPROACHES

Unlike biofeedback approaches, which operate on the presumed neurological basis for seizures, operant treatment approaches attempt to alter the reinforcement contingencies associated with overt seizure behavior. The history of epileptic treatment has included several anecdotal and research quality reports of the use of strong environmental stimuli to interrupt or abort a seizure. Seizure interruption techniques include strong odors, loud verbal commands, and physically shaking the subject. The interruption techniques are applied prior to seizure climax or during the pre-seizure aura, which is present in conjunction with certain types of seizures and typically consists of stereotyped movements or unusual sensory sensations, e.g., smells or visual disturbances. In this fashion, seizures are conceptualized as a terminal link in a complex behavioral chain in which preseizure behaviors are consequated in an effort to abort or interrupt the onset of the overt seizure act. For example, preseizure limb movements have been interrupted by holding the patient's arms to his sides while shouting "No" and applying a vigorous shake to the subject at the shoulders. Differential reinforcement techniques have also been used following interruption of preseizure limb movements by gently placing the subject's arms to his sides and delivering social reinforcement for the "arms down" condition. Overcorrection and mild restraint have also been applied to preseizure limb movements, along with reinforcement for appropriate use of the hands in an academic task. Frequently, nonseizure behavior, such as on-task behavior, must be shaped in the same way as any operant, and differential reinforcement techniques and manipulation of tangible rewards provide efficacious methods for doing so. For example, token procedures have been used in which tangible rewards and social praise are delivered following seizure-free intervals. Accessible charts and graphs, and reinforcement dispensers have been used for subject feedback and implementation of reward procedures. In addition, contingent rest and time out following a seizure episode have also been used in combination with reinforcement for seizure-free intervals.

EXPECTED EFFECTS

The results of behavioral techniques for seizure reduction appear promising. The judicious and consistent application of already existing operant technology can usually be expected to result in reductions in behaviors associated with seizures. However, in the absence of painstaking assessment procedures, it is not always clear if the purported seizure behavior is associated with any neurological anomaly or whether it is adjunct behavior which is controlled by environmental contingencies. In most cases, some seizure activity is likely to be triggered by environmental or emotional cues, which may or may not have a concomitant neurological origin. This is largely irrelevant from the behavioral perspective, since the reduction in the overt behavior is of primary interest. However, one must be careful in the claims made for seizure reduction in the absence of simultaneous physiological assessment. Treatment requires a great deal of therapist vigilance and time, and procedures must be applied in both the home and clinical setting for generalization to take place.

CONTRAINDICATIONS

Most studies have been done on an experimental basis with chronic patients who are concurrently receiving anticonvulsant medication. Typically, seizures are not stabilized and further increases in medication are ruled out due to dangers of toxicity. No systematic

controlled or treatment tandem studies have been conducted using biofeedback, operant, or chemotherapeutic approaches. Psychomotor, grand mal, and petit mal seizures have all been treated with biofeedback and operant procedures but differential treatment efficacy has not been evaluated. At this time, biofeedback and operant treatment are not considered as competitive treatments with anticonvulsant therapy, but may be adjunctive in nature and, when successful, medications have been reduced. No apparent side effects have been noted.

BIBLIOGRAPHY

Cataldo, M. F., Russo, D. C., & Freeman, J. M. (1979). A behavior analysis approach to high rate myoclonic seizures. *Journal of Autism and Developmental Disorders, 9,* 413–427.

Cinciripini, P. M., Epstein, L. H., & Kotanchik, N. L. (1980). Behavioral intervention for self-stimulatory attending and seizure behavior in a cerebral palsy child. *Journal of Behavior Therapy and Experimental Psychiatry, 11,* 313–316.

Kuhlman, W. N. (1978). EEG feedback training of epileptic patients: Clinical and electroencephalographic analysis. *Electroencephalography and Clinical Neurophysiology, 45,* 699–710.

Sterman, M. B., & Shouse, M. N. (1980). Quantitative analysis of training, sleep EEG and clinical response to EEG operant conditioning in epileptics. *Electroencephalography and Clinical Neurophysiology, 49,* 558–576.

Zlutnick, S., Mayville, W. J., & Moffat, S. (1975). Behavioral control of seizure disorders: The interruption of chained behavior. *Journal of Applied Behavior Analysis, 8,* 1–12.

See: Biofeedback
 Operant Conditioning
 Overcorrection

BEHAVIORAL WEIGHT CONTROL THERAPY
Donald A. Williamson

Behavioral weight control therapy refers to a package of behavioral techniques which have been found to be effective in the treatment of obesity. Behavioral weight control therapy is based upon the assumption that obesity results from poor eating and exercise habits which lead to excessive calorie intake and inadequate calorie expenditure. Behavioral weight control therapy is designed to assist persons to lose weight by modifying eating and exercise habits. Common techniques which are used to modify eating habits are: self-monitoring of eating behavior, calorie intake, and weight; procedures to enhance stimulus control over eating; procedures to reduce the rate of eating; procedures to reduce calorie intake; and behavioral contracting to improve motivation. Procedures which are commonly used to increase caloric expenditure are: aerobic exercise, walking, and leisure sports. Behavioral weight control therapy usually produces gradual weight loss (about 1 lb. per week) and has been shown to be superior to no-treatment as well as a variety of other control conditions in numerous controlled group outcome studies.

A major deficiency of behavioral weight control therapy has been the failure to produce long-term maintenance of weight loss. Recent research has shown that weight maintenance strategies can be used to prevent regaining of weight after treatment. Strategies which have been demonstrated to be effective for weight maintenance are relapse prevention training and involvement of spouses in the initial behavioral weight control therapy program.

BIBLIOGRAPHY

Bellack, A. S., & Williamson, D. A. (1982). Obesity and anorexia nervosa. In D. M. Doleys, R. L. Meredith, & A. R. Ciminero (Eds.), *Behavioral medicine: Assessment and treatment strategies*. New York: Plenum Press.

Brownell, K. D. (1982). Obesity: Understanding and treating a serious, prevalent, and refractory disorder. *Journal of Consulting and Clinical Psychology, 50,* 820–840.

Coates, T. J., & Thoreson, C. E. (1978). Treating obesity in children and adolescents: A review. *American Journal of Public Health, 68,* 143–151.

Stuart, R. B. (1967). Behavioral control over eating. *Behaviour Research and Therapy, 5,* 357–365.

Stunkard, A. J., & Penick, S. B. (1979). Behavior modification in the treatment of obesity. *Archives of General Psychiatry, 36,* 801–806.

See: Contingency Contracting

BELL AND PAD CONDITIONING
Daniel M. Doleys

The Bell and Pad conditioning procedure is defined as the application of a urine-sensing device in the treatment of urinary incontinence. The procedure gets its name from the apparatus used which generally consists of some type of urine-sensitive "pad" which, when activated, triggers an alarm or "bell." The apparatus itself has also frequently been referred to as the urine-alarm and the Mowrer Device, after its originator, Dr. O. H. Mowrer.

The Bell and Pad procedure has most frequently been used with functional nocturnal enuresis. The fundamental aspects of the procedure require the enuretic to sleep on the urine-sensitive pad. The pad is connected to some type of battery operated buzzer or alarm system. The device is so constructed that the smallest amount of urine completes an electric circuit, activating the alarm and awakening the enuretic. Theoretically, it is postulated that, over time, bladder distention acquires discriminative stimulus properties, resulting in the child awakening to bladder distention prior to the onset of voiding. It is also postulated that, through conditioning, voiding is inhibited in such a fashion so as to not occur until the enuretic awakens from sleep.

The Bell and Pad procedure has most frequently been used with nocturnally enuretic children. It has also, however, found application with adolescents and elderly patients experiencing problems with incontinence. Smaller versions of the pad have been constructed such that they easily attach to the inside of undergarments, and therefore can be used to detect daytime wetting episodes. With this smaller apparatus, the alarm is customarily attached to the wrist or to the pants, being approximately 3–4 inches square. Treatment of nocturnal enuresis using the Bell and Pad have been effective with a variety of populations, including the mentally retarded, emotionally disturbed, and physically handicapped.

The average treatment duration varies as a function of the dryness criterion. The most common dryness criterion has been 14 consecutive dry nights. This criterion is generally achieved in 14–16 weeks with a compliant and motivated parent and child working cooperatively. Available statistics from controlled studies indicate success in 75% of cases. This percentage varies and is as high as 95% in some studies. Relapse can be anticipated in 40% of nocturnal enuretics treated by the Bell and Pad procedure. In this case, relapse is defined as wetting one or more times a week for three consecutive weeks. However, 60–70% of patients who relapse can be successfully treated by reapplication of the Bell and Pad procedure. Causes of relapse are not clear. The author, however, has found a lower rate of relapse for those children who learn to stay dry by awakening during the night and voiding, as compared to those children who remain dry by retaining through the night. There may also be a trade-off between the rapidity of treatment effect and probability of relapse. The author's approach is to require 21 consecutive dry nights with the urine alarm on the bed and then another 21 consecutive dry nights with the urine alarm in the child's room but not on the bed. This criterion results in a longer treatment duration but appears to reduce the relapse rate. Children are known to relapse up to 24 months following initial treatment and should be monitored in follow-up for this period of time.

Two modifications to the standard Bell and Pad procedure have been explored in attempts to reduce the rate of relapse. The first is intermittent scheduling of the alarm. In this instance, the alarm is programmed to operate in a specific percent of wets (usually 50% or 70%). Researchers have postulated that this intermittent operating of the alarm parallels an intermittent schedule of reinforcement known to produce behavior more resistant to extinction. Although the theoretical explanation remains questionable, Finley and his associates have reported initial success in nearly 94% of children treated, with a modest relapse rate of 25%.

Overlearning is the second researched modification. Once the enuretic has successfully reached the initial dryness criterion, the nighttime intake of fluids is increased. Early reports noted children to drink up to 32 ounces at night. A gradual increase over several nights seems more prudent. It was proposed that relapses were a result of the lack of generalization of conditioned awakening, or retention, to various degrees of bladder fullness and distention. Increased liquid intake increases bladder fullness during the night, tests the degree of control established during conditioning, and provides an opportunity for this control to cover a broad range of bladder fullness and detrusor muscle distention. The data are mixed as to the efficacy of overlearning. A negative side effect has been the loss of nighttime continence acquired with the Bell and Pad procedure if nighttime liquids are introduced too quickly or increased too rapidly.

There are a number of factors to examine when considering a particular urine alarm device. It is preferable to have one which emits a sound of approximately 100 decibels. The device should be sensitive enough to trigger the alarm in response to the smallest amount of urine. Alarms utilizing two separate pads with an absorbent sheet in between (the sandwich-type pad) are more prone to false alarms. The device must be powered and electrically constructed in such a fashion so as to avoid "buzzer ulcers," which can occur with the continual passage of current through a damp area in contact with the child's skin. The alarm should be activated immediately upon the onset of wetting. Treatment efficacy is severely compromised by even a 5-second delay.

The Bell and Pad procedure is rarely utilized with children under the age of 5. A thorough evaluation is required to rule out reinforcement factors which may be responsible for maintenance of the bed wetting, therefore rendering this technique ineffective. Children who are known to be noncompliant and disruptive may not be good candidates, depending upon their motivation and relationship with their parents and/or caregiver. The Bell and Pad procedure appears to be equally effective with primary (never been dry) and secondary (children who have experienced at least 6 months of dryness at some time in their life) enuretics. The presence of allergies, bladder infection, dysfunctional bladder, and central nervous system impairment should be ruled out in the general case. A complete urological examination, including urodynamics and intravenous pyelography, is unnecessary unless clinical findings other than the enuresis implicate a need for such. One should inquire regarding nighttime fears or night terrors which may prevent the child from awakening or utilizing the toilet facilities, thus creating the problem of enuresis.

To date, no significant negative side effects have been identified to the Bell and Pad procedure. In previous literature, there have been problems with "buzzer ulcers." These ulcers were not a function of the procedure but rather could be attributed to inadequately built equipment. Concern by psychoanalytically-oriented therapists over

the problem of symptom substitution has not been borne out. Where it has been examined, the enuretic child has generally appeared happy and more content when the enuresis has been resolved.

The technique appears appropriate and promising in the treatment of functional enuresis. Acquisition of detailed baseline data, proper introduction and explanation of the procedure and technique to parent and child, regular monitoring of progress, utilization of proper equipment, the presence of a cooperative child and parent, and a minimum 2-year follow-up appear to be the factors characterizing efficient and effective therapy.

BIBLIOGRAPHY

Ballard, J., & Nettelbeck, T. (1981). A comparison of dry-bed training and standard urine-alarm conditioning treatment of childhood bed wetting. *Behaviour Research and Therapy, 19,* 215–226.
Doleys, D. M. (1977). Behavioral treatments for nocturnal neurosis in children: a review of the recent literature. *Psychological Bulletin, 84,* 30–54.
Doleys, D. M., Schwartz, M. S., & Ciminero, A. R. (1981). Elimination problems: Enuresis and encopresis. In E. J. Mash & L. G. Terdal (Eds.), *Behavioral assessment of childhood disorders.* New York: Guilford Press.
Fielding, D. (1980). The response of day and night wetting children and children who wet only at night to retention control training and the urine alarm. *Behaviour Research and Therapy, 18,* 305–317.
Finley, W. W., Wansley, R. A., & Blenkran, M. M. (1977). Conditioning treatment of enuresis using a 70% intermittent reinforcement schedule. *Behaviour Research and Therapy, 15,* 419–427.

See: Dry Bed Training
     Dry Pants Training
     Retention Control Training

BIBLIOTHERAPY
Eileen Gambrill

This term refers to the use of written material (self-help manuals) to help clients alter their behavior, thoughts, or feelings. Use of written material for this purpose has a long history outside of behavior therapy as evidenced by the hundreds of self-help books available to the public.

CLINICAL APPLICATION

Self-help manuals have been written to help people enhance their parenting skills, decrease substance abuse and depression, enhance sexual pleasure, increase social and studying skills, and decrease smoking and excess weight. Characteristics common to the use of bibliotherapy in clinical practice include a request to read written material, application of procedures described in real-life contexts, and self-monitoring to evaluate progress. Principles on which methods are based are usually described, and examples of application of procedures are offered. The clinical use of bibliotherapy differs along the following dimensions: (1) extent of counselor-contact ranging from none to extensive; (2) individual or group format; (3) attention devoted to thoughts; (4) attention devoted to generalization and maintenance of positive effects, including development of general versus specific skills; (5) the extent to which readers are requested to "interact" with the written material in terms of completing exercises to test their understanding of content described; (6) whether bibliotherapy is used together with other methods; and (7) whether access to additional written material is made contingent on reading and understanding more elementary portions.

Requisites for successful use of bibliotherapy include reading skills that match the required reading level of the manual and a cluster of self-management skills which include the following:

1. self-diagnosis (skills in using written material to clearly define desired outcomes and plan how to achieve them; this will require skills in collecting helpful information,
2. self-monitoring skills to gather assessment information and evaluate progress,
3. skills in arranging incentives so that new reactions will occur,
4. skills in choosing next steps when positive gains are made,
5. skills in problem-solving to overcome obstacles when intervention is not working, and
6. skills in generalizing and maintaining changes.

This list illustrates the complexity of the tasks assumed in bibliotherapy; the assumption is made that people can be their own agents of change with minimal counselor contact.

The development of self-help manuals has been so great and the evaluation of these so skimpy in terms of whether they really help people do what they promise, that increasing concern has been raised in the literature and guidelines have been suggested for screening do-it-yourself-treatment books. These include:

1. What claims are made in the book? What does it promise readers?
2. Is accurate information offered concerning empirical support for procedures described?
3. Can readers check out whether they develop appropriate expectations as to what they can (and cannot) gain from reading the material?
4. Does the book describe procedures readers can use for self-diagnosis to determine (a) whether this book will be of benefit to them, and if so, in what way, and (b) how to gather required assessment information? Have these procedures been tested out?
5. Are the intervention methods described empirically supported?

6. Has the book been evaluated in terms of clinical efficacy? If so, under what conditions and with what populations? That is, does it really help people to achieve what it claims to do? Many books describe procedures which have empirical support, but often these procedures have not been evaluated within a bibliotherapy format.

7. Does evaluative data gathered support claims made?

8. How does the effectiveness of the self-help manual compare to that of other manuals or procedures?

9. Is there any evidence that positive changes last?

10. Has the possibility of negative side effects been explored?

EXPECTED OUTCOMES AND TIME FRAMES

The expectation in bibliotherapy is that the reader will be able to apply successfully instructions given in the written material in real-life situations. For example, it is expected that parents who read material about how to toilet train their child will be able to use this to achieve this outcome, or that the reader of a self-help manual designed to decrease alcohol consumption will be able to decrease drinking. Most programs using bibliotherapy are brief, 8 to 12 weeks, for example.

POTENTIAL SIDE EFFECTS AND CONTRAINDICATIONS

Potential negative side effects of bibliotherapy have not been empirically explored. The most troublesome one is encouraging the belief on the part of clients that change is impossible because bibliotherapy did not work, when, in fact, change would occur within another treatment format. Another possible negative side effect is unnecessary discomfort in the process of change due to lack of expert guidance.

A positive concurrent effect in some programs is that readers will be able to learn general coping skills that they can apply to other areas. For example, it may be hoped that if a parent learns to use positive reinforcement with one child, she/he will use this method with her/his other children as well. A basic premise, unstated in some cases, is that readers will acquire greater control over some aspect of their lives; there is a built-in self-efficacy message in many, if not all, of the books: People learn to rely on themselves rather than on someone else, such as a therapist. Written material can be readily consulted at home. Inclusion of relapse prevention guidelines will offer readers information that they can draw upon on an as-needed basis if slippage occurs.

Contraindications to use of bibliotherapy include the following: (1) limited reading ability, (2) small probability that the client will follow instructions to read and use material, and (3) small probability that the client will be able to follow-through on his own because of countervailing personal or environmental constraints. For example, perhaps drinking *is* maintained by peer support; countervailing personal characteristics might include intense emotional reactions such as anxiety. Many clients do not have the self-management skills to make effective use of written material to change their behavior. In such instances, counselor-client contact will be necessary. This support could be provided by other sources such as group members or "buddies" who are involved in similar programs.

There is a natural fascination for bibliotherapy: allowing people to achieve desired changes on their own. Some writers point out that use of self-help manuals still ties consumers to therapists since therapy experts are often the authors.

BIBLIOGRAPHY

Rosen, G. M. (1981). Guidelines for the review of do-it-yourself treatment books. *Contemporary Psychology, 26*, 189–191.

Watson, D. L., & Tharp, R. G. (1981). *Self-directed behavior: Self-modification for personal adjustment* (3rd ed.). Monterey, CA: Brooks/Cole.

See: Self-Control Desensitization

BIOFEEDBACK
Donald A. Williamson

Biofeedback refers to a number of clinical techniques which provide feedback concerning changes in a particular physiological response to the patient, so that the patient can learn to modify the physiological response. For example, if finger skin temperature biofeedback is provided, the patient may be instructed to "warm his/her hands." Feedback is usually provided using either visual or auditory modes of presentation. In some cases both sensory modes are used simultaneously. Two methods of providing information feedback have been developed by biofeedback researchers. They are called binary and analogue (sometimes referred to as proportional) feedback. Binary feedback provides yes/no information—whether the physiological response changed sufficiently to meet a pre-established criterion. For example, if EMG (electromyogram activity) is reduced by 2 micro-volts, a 500 Hz tone might be presented if binary feedback is used. Analogue feedback provides continuous information about changes in the physiological response. Changes of the feedback signal are made directly proportional to changes of the physiological response. For example, changes in EMG from 0 to 10 micro-volts could be reflected by an analogue feedback signal which varied from 300 to 1300 Hz. Using this type of feedback system, a 2 micro-volt reduction of EMG would produce a change of 200 Hz in the auditory feedback signal. From the patient's perspective, the feedback signal would change in pitch as EMG was reduced. The direction of change in pitch (i.e., either increasing or decreasing) can often be determined by the preference of the therapist or the patient depending upon the type of biofeedback equipment that is used. Basic research findings suggest that for best results, the biofeedback system should provide continuous analogue feedback which is neither too sensitive nor too insensitive to changes in the physiological response.

A variety of physiological responses have been shown to be modifiable using biofeedback. The most common physiological responses to be used clinically are: skin temperature, EMG, blood pressure, EEG (electro-encephalogram), vasomotor, and heart rate.

Skin temperature biofeedback is usually provided from a peripheral site (usually a finger). The most common instructions to the patient are to "warm the hands" or increase temperature. Analogue feedback through either auditory or visual modes is usually provided. Skin temperature biofeedback has been found to be effective for the treatment of migraine headaches, Raynaud's Disease, and a variety of stress-related illnesses. Successful treatment typically requires 8 to 20 sessions.

EMG biofeedback is usually provided from the site of muscular dysfunction (e.g., frontal area for tension headaches and masseter muscles for temperomandibular joint [TMJ] dysfunction). Analogue feedback through either auditory or visual modes is a common means of presenting EMG biofeedback. It is usually recommended that auditory feedback be used for facial muscles since the patient is expected to keep his/her eyes closed during the session. EMG biofeedback has been shown to be an effective treatment for tension headaches, TMJ dysfunction, muscle pain, and a variety of neuromuscular dysfunctions. Effective treatment generally requires 8 to 20 sessions.

Blood pressure biofeedback has been provided using a variety of methods, including binary and analogue feedback. The most widely used procedure involves provision of blood pressure biofeedback on a beat-by-beat basis using binary feedback. Recent technological advances have led to an indirect method of providing blood pressure biofeedback. This procedure is usually referred to as pulse wave velocity or pulse transit time biofeedback. The major advantage of this alternative procedure is that it does not require the use of a blood pressure cuff. Blood pressure biofeedback has been found to be useful for lowering the blood pressure of essential hypertensives. When blood pressure biofeedback has been combined with regular home practice of relaxation, clinically significant reductions of blood pressure have been reported. Most authorities have concluded that blood pressure biofeedback and related procedures are best used as adjunctive therapies to traditional medical care of essential hypertension. Treatment usually requires from 8 to 20 sessions.

EEG biofeedback has used a variety of EEG rhythms. The most widely researched EEG frequencies are alpha (8–13Hz) and sensorimotor rhythm (10–15Hz). EEG feedback is usually expressed in terms of the percentage of EEG that is within the selected frequency range. Both visual and auditory modes of presentation have been used primarily for achieving relaxation and very few studies of the clinical utility of alpha biofeedback have been reported. Sensorimotor rhythm biofeedback has been used primarily as a treatment of epilepsy. Recent research has shown that a more effective biofeedback treatment of epilepsy is to identify EEG abnormalities in a particular patient and then use a variety of EEG frequencies in biofeedback in order to "normalize" the EEG of the epileptic. Typical treatment length for this procedure is 15 to 40 sessions. Booster sessions at least once every 2 to 3 months are usually suggested following the initial treatment period.

Vasomotor biofeedback has been used as a treatment of migraine headache. Initially, vasomotor biofeedback systems utilized binary feedback for constricting the temporal artery, while recent technological advances have allowed for the provision of analogue feedback. Vasomotor biofeedback treatment of migraine headache generally involves learning to constrict the extracranial arteries for the abortion of a migraine attack. Controlled research has shown this procedure to be very effective as a treatment of migraine and mixed-tension headache. Successful treatment usually requires 10 to 20 sessions.

Heart rate biofeedback has not been used extensively for clinical purposes. When it has been used clinically, it has been applied primarily for the problems of tachycardia and cardiac arrhythmias. Heart rate biofeedback is commonly presented using analogue feedback via visual or auditory modes. Most clinical research in this area has been conducted on single subjects. Typical length of treatment is 5 to 20 sessions.

In summary, biofeedback has been used for a variety of clinical problems. Controlled group outcome studies have found biofeedback to be more effective than no-treatment for most of these disorders.

The most important considerations in conducting biofeedback treatment is proper diagnosis and utilization of a variety of therapeutic methods when indicated. No significant negative side effects of biofeedback treatment have been reported.

BIBLIOGRAPHY

Andrasik, F., Coleman, D., & Epstein, L. H. (1982). Biofeedback: Clinical and research considerations. In D. M. Doleys, R. L. Meredith, & A. R. Ciminero (Eds.), *Behavioral medicine: Assessment and treatment strategies.* New York: Plenum Press.

Blanchard, E. B., & Epstein, L. H. (1978). *A biofeedback primer.* Reading, MA: Adison-Wesley.

Blanchard, E. B., Theobald, D. E., Williamson, D. A., Silver, B. V., & Brown, D. A. (1978). Temperature biofeedback in the treatment of migraine headaches. *Archives of General Psychiatry, 35,* 581–588.

Williamson, D. A. (1979). Heart rate and blood pressure biofeedback; I. A review of the recent experimental literature. *Biofeedback and Self-Regulation, 4,* 1–34.

Williamson, D. A., & Blanchard, E. B. (1979). Heart rate and blood pressure biofeedback; II. A review and integration of recent theoretical models. *Biofeedback and Self-Regulation, 4,* 35–50.

See: Controlled Smoking

CHAINING
Diane E. D. Deitz

Chaining is a procedure in which simple behaviors already in the repertoire of an individual are reinforced in a particular sequence to form a more complex behavior. The chain of simple behaviors must occur in a definite order as one response produces the conditions for the next response, etc., until reinforcement is procured at the end of the sequence. A chaining procedure may be taught in a forward manner or a backward manner.

See: Backward Chaining
Forward Chaining

CHEMICAL AVERSION
Donald M. Prue

The major objective of aversion therapy is to reduce the frequency of clients' maladaptive behaviors. Chemical aversion procedures, one type of aversion therapy, employ chemical agents such as prescription medications (e.g., emetine, lithium, apomorphine) or commercial products (e.g., ammonia, lemon juice) within a classical or operant conditioning paradigm to decrease future occurrences of the maladaptive behavior. The selection of chemical agent and type of behavioral intervention (i.e., classical or operant) is dictated largely by the target problem and client characteristics. The administration of an aversive stimulus, such as lemon juice, follows the emission of the target behavior (e.g., rumination and vomiting, apnea) within a straightforward punishment paradigm. The punishment contingency has typically been used with children or developmentally disabled individuals. On the other hand, prescription medication is used to produce a conditioned physiological response by pairing the effects of the medication with the target behavior. The development of a conditioned response via a classical conditioning or taste aversion paradigm is the treatment of choice with adults. Again, the objective of both sets of treatment procedures is to decrease the likelihood of specific target behaviors.

CLINICAL PROCEDURES

The use of prescription medication in a classical conditioning paradigm is the most frequently employed chemical aversion procedure, and as such, will be discussed in detail. The procedures described below closely follow those proposed by Voegtlin and his colleagues over 30 years ago for the treatment of alcoholism. These procedures, with

minor variations, have been the most frequently employed and studied form of aversion therapy.

Voegtlin's conditioned aversion therapy,
more recently labeled taste aversion therapy
or chemical aversion, calls for placing the
patient in an area designed to enhance the
visibility of alcohol beverage and drinking
cues and to minimize distractions that may
interfere with the conditioning process. A
mixture of emetine-pilocarpine-ephedrine
is then administered intravenously to the
patient. Approximately 8 to 10 minutes later
the client begins to feel nauseous due to the
effects of emetine. When the first signs of
nausea become apparent the individual is
urged to pick up, smell, and swirl the drink
around. Immediately prior to emesis the individual is told to drink the liquor. Exposure
to alcohol stimuli continues during the entire session, approximately 30 to 45 minutes,
with two or three injections of emetine provided in a session. Alcohol intake is not
allowed after the nausea symptoms peak
within a trial. At times, oral emetine and
alcohol are provided at the end of a session
to induce nausea and emesis for up to an
hour after the formal session. A treatment
regimen typically calls for 4 to 7 sessions
over a 10 to 14-day period. In addition to
an inpatient phase of massed trials, booster
conditioning sessions are scheduled in an
aftercare treatment arrangement to enhance
maintenance of treatment gains. The first
booster session is typically scheduled for 2
weeks following the end of intensive treatment. Five additional sessions are distributed throughout the year after treatment.

The taste aversion procedure involves a
number of medical risks (discussed below)
and thus is employed only on an inpatient,
medically supervised basis. There are also
a number of other issues that must be considered in the design of the treatment environment and conditioning sessions. First,

it is important to consider initially limiting the number and range of stimuli in the
treatment setting. For instance, first sessions
should focus on the individual's favorite beverage, with subsequent trials adding other
alcohol stimuli in order to increase the likelihood of generalization of the conditioned
response. In fact, research has shown that
when trials are limited to clients' favorite
beverages, conditioned responses to other
beverages are not made and clients then
switch to these other beverages. Similarly,
programmed generalization of conditioned
aversions to other drinking environments,
while not yet investigated, also seems likely
to improve treatment success rates. Second,
care should be taken to avoid alcohol intake
in amounts that might interfere with the
conditioning process. Third, emetine is a
central nervous system depressant that decreases the ease with which UCS-CS rela-
tions develop. Thus, the procedure described
above, using a mixture of emetine-pilocarpine-ephedrine, should be followed to facilitate conditioning. This mixture counteracts
the depressant properties of emetine and
the hypotensive properties of emetine and
pilocarpine. A more recent procedure (Cannon, Baker, & Wehl, 1981) is to administer
a mixture of ipecac syrup and low doses of
emetine in order to avoid the toxic affects
associated with high doses of emetine.

In addition to emetine, a number of other
drugs have been used within the classical
conditioning paradigm. One drug, apomorphine, has received considerable attention
and appears to have advantages and disadvantages similar to emetine. Another drug,
succinylcholine chloride dehydrate, has very
severe effects including respiratory arrest
and has proven to be of questionable treatment efficacy. It is extremely dangerous
and should be avoided in clinical trials. Finally, there has been one report of positive
treatment outcomes with the use of lithium

as the aversive agent. The authors argued that lithium has far less potential for side effects than emetine or apomorphine and thus is the drug of choice. More evidence is needed to fully evaluate this conclusion.

Classical conditioning-based aversion procedures have also been employed in the treatment of other maladaptive behaviors. The latter include other appetitive behaviors (e.g., narcotic addiction) as well as arousal to client-designated inappropriate sexual stimuli (e.g., sadomasochistic or fetishistic stimuli). The procedures employed with these behaviors essentially parallel those employed in developing the UCS-CS associations for alcohol treatment. While some authors consider chemical aversion procedures to be restricted to those based on a classical conditioning model, others include operant procedures that use aversive chemical agents in a punishment paradigm. The latter procedures employ contingent application of the aversive stimulus on a continuous schedule following emission of the target behavior and reapplication of the aversive consequence whenever the frequency of the target behavior increases.

EXPECTED OUTCOME AND TIME FRAMES

Chemical aversion procedures rank among the most frequently evaluated alcoholism treatment paradigms. Over 6,000 clinical cases have been reported in the literature, with the results of treatment quite variable across studies. While some authors have reported treatment outcome rates in the range of 70%, others have been less optimistic. In addition, within those studies reporting high success rates, selected subsamples of individuals often differ markedly in outcome. The differences in outcome appear to be related to patient demographic variables as well as differences in other treatment procedures (e.g., individual therapy)

that have been combined with chemical aversion. Variations in the use and timing of booster sessions have also contributed to differences in outcomes.

Generally, financially secure, middle-aged, educated, married, and employed individuals have a 50% to 80% chance of maintaining abstinence for up to one year following chemical aversion treatment. Less fortunate individuals have a much less positive prognosis. In addition, individuals who attend intermittent booster sessions have the best overall prognosis. Post-treatment affiliation with abstinence-oriented organizations also improves success rates. The high abstinence rates at one year follow-up decrease to approximately 50% after 2 years and 40% at 5 years. These success rates also decrease as the number of positive demographic and treatment program characteristics listed above decrease. Thus, positive outcomes are tempered by the very low success rates (i.e., 20% or less) for individuals who are unemployed, unmarried or having marital problems, and subsisting on financial assistance.

In addition to problems associated with determining the effects of chemical aversion across various patient characteristics, studies have not examined chemical aversion treatment independent of multimodal or broad-spectrum therapies. Thus, it is difficult to specify the independent contribution of chemical aversion to the success rates reported above. Despite this fact, it appears that success improves when a comprehensive program is supplemented by chemical aversion therapy regardless of patient characteristics.

The outcome of chemical aversion procedures applied to other classes of behaviors (e.g., maladaptive sexual arousal) has not been as well researched. Extant research has consisted solely of single subject investigations or clinical case studies; comparisons with other treatment procedures and no-treatment controls have not been made. Similarly, research on the contingent application of aversive stimuli within a punishment paradigm has also been largely limited to small, uncontrolled evaluations. Although this research has shown very promising outcomes, including life-saving suppression of rumination, more definitive conclusions on their success rates await further investigation.

POTENTIAL SIDE EFFECTS/ CONTRAINDICATIONS

The administration of an emetic agent, besides being a physically intrusive procedure involving a prescription drug, carries specific medical risks. Thus, the procedure must be carried out under the supervision of a physician. A complete medical history must be obtained to insure that the individual does not have any of the following contraindicative conditions: psychosis, organic brain syndrome, history of cardiovascular or renal disease, hepatic cirrhosis, esophageal varices, hernias, gastrointestinal bleeding, cervical fusion, or hypertension. The presence of any of these medical conditions may result in side effects that range from exacerbation of the medical conditions to death. Thus, extreme care must be taken in screening individuals prior to treatment via chemical aversion. When more common, non-prescription products are used as the aversive stimulus there are less severe side effects; however, care should still be taken in the administration of the procedures. Finally, one important note that has yet to be addressed is the role of client motivation. The possibility of greater risks in the use of chemical aversion procedures than for other behavior therapy procedures makes it imperative to insure the cooperation of those being treated. Careful steps should be taken to maintain the highest eth-

ical standards and to avoid the use of coercion. The therapeutic as well as legal risks of inattention to high professional standards could prove disastrous to the widespread application of these promising procedures as well as to behavior therapy.

BIBLIOGRAPHY

Baker, T. B., & Cannon, D. S. (1979). Taste aversion therapy with alcoholics: Techniques and evidence of a conditioned response. *Behaviour Research and Therapy, 17*, 229–242.

Cannon, D. S., Baker, T. B., & Wehl, C. K. (1981). Emetic and electric shock alcohol aversion therapy: Six- and twelve-month follow-up. *Journal of Consulting and Clinical Psychology, 49*, 360–368.

Davidson, W. S. (1974). Studies of aversive conditioning for alcoholics: A critical review of theory and research methodology. *Psychological Bulletin, 81*, 571–581.

Lemere, F., & Voegtlin, W. (1950). An evaluation of the aversion treatment of alcoholism. *Quarterly Journal of Studies on Alcohol, 11*, 199–204.

Voegtlin, W., & Broz, W. B. (1979). The conditioned reflex treatment of chronic alcoholism. X. An analysis of 3125 admissions over a period of ten-and-a-half years. *Annals of Internal Medicine, 30*, 580–597.

Weins, A. N., & Menustik, C. E. (1983). Treatment outcome and patient characteristics in an aversion therapy program for alcoholism. *American Psychologist, 38*, 1089–1096.

See: Aversive Conditioning
     Classical Conditioning

CLASSICAL CONDITIONING
Thomas R. Kratochwill

Classical conditioning, discovered almost simultaneously by Edwin Twitmyer, is a theory of learning first reported by Ivan Pavlov in 1902 and more fully described in 1927. Pavlov noted that reflexive reactions (unconditioned responses) may be activated by a previously neutral stimulus (conditioned stimulus) after repeated pairings with a stimulus (unconditioned stimulus) which unavoidably produces the response. The strength of this new response (conditioned response) is dependent upon the relationship in time between the unconditioned and conditioned stimulus, with the conditioned stimulus immediately following the unconditioned stimulus producing the strongest response. If a stimulus similar to the conditioned stimulus also produces a conditioned response, generalization is said to occur. If only the particular conditioned stimulus produces the conditioned response, differentiation is said to occur. If the conditioned stimulus is continuously presented without the unconditioned stimulus, the conditioned response will weaken and eventually extinguish altogether. Classical conditioning is generally represented by the following schema, in which UCS = unconditioned stimulus, UCR = unconditioned response, CS = conditioned stimulus, and CR = conditioned response:

$$UCS \rightarrow UCR$$
$$CS \rightarrow UCS \rightarrow UCR$$
$$\rightarrow CR$$

CLASSROOM MANAGEMENT
Johnny Matson

Classroom management is a general term used to describe a multi-faceted group of learning-based strategies as they are applied to children in the classroom. These approaches are typically implemented by teachers and have, by and large, been operantly oriented learning strategies as opposed to cognitive-behavioral methods or classical conditioning. To date, little has been done in the way of measuring the effects of enhanced academic performance on classroom disruptions and lack of attention, although the relationship between these variables is well-known. Rather, most efforts at management or enhancing compliant behavior have been directed specifically at suppressing the inappropriate act, and or increasing alternative appropriate behaviors. Some controversy about the type of behaviors selected for treatment, and acceptable classroom values have been questioned. Several authors have argued that there is excessive emphasis on rigid order and control as the norm for classroom management, and that the goals of being still, quiet, and docile should be questioned. Conversely, it has been argued that these complaints are an overgeneralization, and that goals of classroom management may vary widely depending on the type of child treated. For example, less impaired children might benefit from a less regimented system but unmotivated, hyperactive, withdrawn, blind, and deaf children may benefit more from a more structured program.

Despite these concerns, behaviors which have traditionally been targeted for treatment include several broad categories of behavior. These include social skills, emotional problems, academic behavior, and self-help skills. A list of specific behaviors which exemplify those behaviors treated in each of these four categories are listed below.

Social Skills
  Speaks too often or too loud
  Initiates interactions
  Disruptive to class
  Bossy
  Has friends
  Makes pleasant comments

Emotional Problems
  Phobias
    School
    Animals
  Depression
  Autism
  Childhood schizophrenia
  Hyperactivity

Academic Behavior
  Spelling
  Reading
  Writing
  Attending to task

Self-Help Skills
  Dressing
  Pedestrian skills
  Gross motor skills
  Fine motor skills
  Toileting skills

The range and severity of the disorders noted above can vary considerably from child to child. Also, the age, number of children per class, and type of handicaps the children in the class have may dictate whether or not the behavior would be viewed as problematic. Thus, for example, some mild stereotypic behaviors such as rocking, hand-gazing (staring at one's hand or hands for 15–30 minutes at a time), and the accompanying deficiencies in attention, might be viewed as highly problematic in a typical classroom of nonhandicapped children. Conversely, such behaviors may be considered mildly, if at all, problematic with severe and profoundly mentally retarded children.

The types of problems identified as classroom disruptions are typically those behaviors which are most problematic to the teacher. Therefore, problems such as depression or social withdrawal are rarely identified, whereas problems such as hitting other children or yelling and screaming in class would almost always immediately be targeted for treatment.

TREATMENT TECHNIQUES

The most frequently used treatment techniques for classroom management are the various forms of reinforcement, time-out, token economies, and, to a lesser degree,

response cost, self-reinforcement and other self-control procedures, systematic desensitization, group contingencies, and overcorrection. There are also other procedures that have been used on a very limited basis, but the methods noted here tend to have the best empirical support. The type of classroom management procedures used varies to some degree based on the population that is treated. Obviously, children in special education classrooms for mentally retarded, learning disabled, and behaviorally disordered/emotionally disturbed children, on average, have a much higher rate of disruptive and related classroom management problems than is found in nonhandicapped classrooms. Also, there are more children with serious acting-out or self-help problems (e.g., toileting accidents). Because of this, those children who receive treatment in special education are more likely to receive time-out, overcorrection, and related punishment procedures. Also, since many of these children, particularly those in classrooms for the mentally retarded or behaviorally disordered, have poorer cognitive abilities, they are unlikely to receive self-reinforcement or self-control training as opposed to tangible reinforcement.

There are also particular problems which are more likely to receive treatment with specific strategies. Token reinforcement programs, for example, have been used to enhance the attentive behavior of severely mentally retarded children: for being quiet in class, hanging up coats, paying attention while sitting at their desks; for enhancing academic achievement such as reading, writing and arithmetic, and enhancing various social behaviors. Time-out or the removal of a child from a reinforcing situation has been used for aggression, disobedience, resisting directions and other forms of noncompliance, and temper tantrums. Reinforcement procedures have been used for almost all forms of behavior that fall under the general category of classroom management, either alone or in combination with various punishment procedures.

As noted, several methods, while used frequently, are less commonly employed than the methods noted in the preceding paragraph. Systematic desensitization, for example, is the most frequently used of the behavioral approaches with phobic behaviors. Self-reinforcement is used generally for skills such as attending to task, and refraining from acting out in class.

Classroom management then, constitutes a rather broad range of problem behaviors, child populations, and treatment procedures deemed appropriate as a means of curbing inappropriate behavior. The primary impetus of treatment is to insure an acceptable learning atmosphere. What is acceptable may vary depending on the population treated and the views of each particular teacher.

BIBLIOGRAPHY

Bijou, S. W., & Ruiz, R. (1981). *Behavior modification: Contributions to education.* Hillsdale, NJ: Lawrence Erlbaum Associates.

Matson, J. L., & McCartney, J. R. (1981). *Handbook of behavior modification with the mentally retarded.* New York: Plenum Press.

Sternberg, L., & Adams, G. L. (1982). *Educating severely and profoundly handicapped students.* Rockville, MD: Aspen.

Wehman, P. (1979). *Curriculum design for the severely and profoundly handicapped.* New York: Human Sciences Press.

Winett, R. A., & Winkler, R. C. (1972). Current behavior modification in the classroom: Be still, be quiet, be docile. *Journal of Applied Behavior Analysis, 5,* 499–504.

See: Group Contingency
   Overcorrection
   Positive Reinforcement
   Response Cost
   Self-Reinforcement
   Systematic Desensitization
   Time Out
   Token Economy

COGNITIVE RESTRUCTURING
Cynthia G. Last

Cognitive restructuring is a term used to denote techniques that are aimed at directly modifying specific thoughts and/or beliefs believed to mediate maladaptive behavioral and physio-emotional responses. Since "cognitive restructuring" subsumes a variety of treatment procedures, several of the more popular approaches will be outlined below.

Ellis's *rational-emotive therapy* primarily attempts to alter certain "core" irrational beliefs that are conceptualized as maintaining most psychological disorders. The clinical approach to using the treatment generally would include: (1) presentation of the therapeutic rationale (i.e., that irrational thoughts play an important role in subjective distress), (2) monitoring of thought patterns, so that clients can become aware of their irrational self-verbalizations and the situations in which they are likely to be elicited, and (3) development of more adaptive thought patterns. In addition, clients usually are assigned in vivo homework in order to "test out" newly acquired beliefs.

Beck's *cognitive therapy* is somewhat similar to rational-emotive therapy in that treatment is aimed at clients': (1) discovering maladaptive cognitions, (2) recognizing the consequences of these thought patterns, and (3) substituting more adaptive thoughts for the maladaptive ones already in use. However, while rational-emotive therapy endorses direct confrontation of the client by the therapist, the cognitive therapist's role is less confrontative, essentially leading the client to discover for him or herself that thoughts are inaccurate and maladaptive, through non-directive reflection. As in rational-emotive therapy, cognitive therapy also includes in vivo homework assignments, since behavioral experience is considered to be an important means for changing irrational and maladaptive cognitions.

Meichenbaum's *self-instructional training*, or cognitive-behavior therapy, is similar to rational-emotive therapy and cognitive therapy in that the technique focuses on modifying self-verbalizations or "self-talk," which are viewed as the precipitant for a wide range of emotional and behavioral disorders. Clients are taught to become more aware of their negative or irrational thoughts and to change them by substituting more adaptive, coping self-statements. Clients also are encouraged to develop their own idiosyncratic coping statements, through a skills development approach. Like rational-emotive therapy and cognitive therapy, behavioral experience often is incorporated into the treatment package. It should be noted, however, that while rational-emotive therapy places emphasis on the rationality of a thought, self-instructional training places greater emphasis on its adaptiveness and constructive alternatives.

The length of treatment with cognitive restructuring techniques varies among clients and according to the technique utilized; however, 12–20 sessions may be anticipated for optimal outcome. Empirical findings indicate that cognitive restructuring procedures may be effective in treating a variety of clinical problems including: mild-moderate depression; chronic or explosive anger; impulsivity, hyperactivity, and aggression in children; test anxiety in students; stuttering; tension headaches; social anxiety; chronic pain; and mild fears and phobias. Although clinically the technique often is incorporated into exposure-based treatment packages for clients with severe anxiety disorders, research to date does not support its inclusion.

There are no known side effects or contraindications for using cognitive restructuring procedures.

BIBLIOGRAPHY

Beck, A. T. (1976). *Cognitive therapy and the emotional disorders.* New York: International University Press.

Ellis, A. (1962). *Reason and emotion in psychotherapy.* New York: Stuart.

Last, C. G. (in press). Cognitive treatment of phobia. In M. Hersen, R. M. Eisler, & P. M. Miller (Eds.), *Progress in behavior modification* (Volume 16). New York: Academic Press.

Mahoney, M. J., & Arnkoff, D. (1978). Cognitive and self-control therapies. In S. Garfield & A. Bergin (Eds.), *Handbook of psychotherapy and behavior change.* New York: Wiley.

Meichenbaum, D. H. (1977). *Cognitive behavior modification.* New York: Plenum Press.

See: Anger Control Therapy

COGNITIVE THERAPY
Michael E. Thase

The term cognitive therapy in the strictest sense describes a comprehensive treatment approach developed by Aaron T. Beck and associates. In a broader perspective, cognitive therapies encompass a wide range of approaches, conceptually grouped by explicit hypotheses that: (1) cognitive factors (thoughts, images, memories, etc.) are intimately related to dysfunctional behavior, and (2) modification of such factors is an important mechanism for producing behavior change. To avoid semantic confusion, the term *cognitive behavior modification* should be used to classify the overall field, with *cognitive therapy* being reserved to describe Beck's specific form of treatment. In either case, cognitively-based assessment and treatment are generally conducted, at least to some extent, simultaneously with more traditional behavioral methods. While cognitively-oriented approaches are a relatively new development within behavior therapy, they are rapidly gaining acceptance and empirical support as useful treatments for a variety of problems experienced by adults and children.

The basic tenets of Beck's cognitive theory of dysfunctional behavior are as follows: (1) certain psychopathological states are either caused and/or maintained by rather automatic distorted and dysfunctional patterns of thinking, (2) cognitive distortions reflect unrealistic and frequently negative views of self, world, and future (the cognitive triad), (3) dysfunctional cognitions may appear illogical to others but are consistent with the patient's personal views of reality, (4) clinically troublesome cognitive distortions are often triggered by adverse life events, yet are maintained by fixed perceptual rules or schemata, (5) schemata provide the basis for organizing, categorizing, evaluating, and judging new experiences and recollections of past events, and (6) schemata often develop early in life and are shaped by relevant experiences.

Examples of dysfunctional cognitive distortions seen in patients with depression include: "Why bother, I can't do anything right," "I am weak and fail at anything I try," and "I am not worthy of the love of others." Although such automatic self-statements are not specific to depression, patients with other broadly defined conditions are likely to evidence other themes or patterns of dysfunctional thoughts. For example, patients with anxiety-based disorders frequently express cognitions regarding impending doom or increased expectations of harm. Nevertheless, such distortions generally reflect a diminished sense of self-efficacy and some degree of helplessness to solve problems competently. Frequency of cognitive distortions often covary with the severity of the behavioral disorder.

Dysfunctional thoughts are further intertwined with a variety of logical errors in information processing and decision making. Such errors are felt to be the result of faulty underlying schemata or basic assumptions. Logical errors follow the pattern of excessive

personalization (inferring personal meaning from a neutral event), arbitrary inference and selective attention (drawing a conclusion from insufficient data and ignoring positive aspects of the situation), and magnification of the importance of an event.

Schemata are more basic and durable beliefs about one's self. They are considered to be unspoken premises rather than conscious thoughts. For example, a patient with marked anxiety and rejection sensitivity might be inferred to have the following silent assumption: "If I am left alone, I will die."

The process of cognitive therapy relies on an active interchange between therapist and patient. This has been described as "collaborative empiricism." The therapist introduces the basic tenets and goals of treatment to the patient in order to provide a rational and coherent context, as well as given explanatory meaning to the subsequent use of assignments and homework. While traditional therapeutic qualities (empathy, warmth, support, etc.) are of obvious value, the therapist's principal role is to serve as a teacher or guide. The therapist assumes an objective and non-judgemental stance, and must convey the notion that problems are understandable within the context of cognitive theory. Similarly, the utility of cognitive therapy must be demonstrated directly through data collected in the various tasks and assignments, rather than simply instilled through persuasion or enculturation.

Effective cognitive therapy should accomplish the following goals: (1) patients learn to objectively identify, evaluate, and examine their thoughts and images in relation to specific distressing behaviors or events, (2) patients are taught to weigh such cognitions against objective evidence and correct distortions, (3) patients learn to identify more pervasive and unspoken silent assumptions or schemata, (4) patients practice various cognitive and behavioral strategies such that they may be applied in vivo, i.e., during novel situations or during unexpected stresses, and (5) patients develop new, more adaptive cognitions about self, world, and future, as well as less dysfunctional schemata.

Actual therapeutic strategies involve a tailored combination of behavioral and cognitive techniques. The direction for such interventions is based on an assessment of the nature of the presenting problem and the type of cognitive distortions. Self-monitoring and detailed recording of automatic thoughts and dysfunctional cognitions serves a dual purpose by providing ongoing assessment and empirical data for work within therapy sessions. Homework is an integral part of treatment. Patients should be given explicit instructions, a clear rationale, and relatively simple tasks early in the course of treatment. Initial strategies include use of graded task assignments and activity scheduling. As in most behavioral interventions, an early goal in the treatment of depression is to increase activity level. Similarly, in patients with anxiety-based disorders, it is important to increase exposure to feared settings. Mastery and pleasure ratings recorded during completion of assigned tasks are useful to establish self-efficacy and test negative distortions of incompetence. Reattributional techniques are used to redefine behaviors initially perceived to represent personal inadequacies, with step-by-step analysis of particular behavioral sequences employed to demonstrate partial successes which were first viewed as complete failures. Both cognitive and behavioral rehearsal are employed to enhance coping abilities in anticipated difficult situations, as well as to learn from previously stressful events. Once dysfunctional thoughts and images readily are identified, patients are taught to carry on a pro-con dialogue to test

the objective evidence supporting a particular cognitive distortion. Finally, as treatment progresses and some successes have been achieved, specific attention is given to identification and testing of the validity of underlying maladaptive schemata. Efforts also are directed towards development of new and more adaptive basic assumptions.

Cognitive therapy is generally a relatively short-term approach (12–30 sessions). In severely symptomatic patients, beginning a course of treatment with twice-weekly (or even three times a week) sessions facilitates therapy. A successful course of acute treatment is often followed by a number of less frequent "maintenance" sessions. Conversely, periodic "booster" sessions are sometimes employed with recovered patients who are experiencing a new stressor or who report reemergence of minor symptoms.

Although cognitive therapy generally is conducted as an individual approach, group and couples applications have been described. Preliminary evidence indicates that the group format may be equally useful in patients with milder problems, while individual therapy is preferred in more severely impaired clinical samples.

Efficacy of cognitive therapy is best established in treatment of mild-to-moderately severe nonbipolar major depression. Results from a number of trials conducted with subclinical samples indicate superiority to both waiting-list and nonspecific treatment controls. Moreover, results from at least four controlled investigations conducted with clinical samples demonstrate that cognitive therapy either matches or exceeds the effects of tricyclic antidepressants. In such studies, a favorable outcome generally is seen within 12 weeks in 60%–90% of nonbipolar major depressives.

There is little evidence to suggest that cognitive therapy is effective as a primary treatment for patients with more severe or "biological" depressions, such as melancholia, bipolar affective disorder, delusional depression, or in hospitalized patients. Cognitive therapy may prove to be useful as an adjunctive treatment in such patients. However, routine combination of cognitive therapy and pharmacological treatment in patients with nonbipolar major depression has not been shown to be convincingly superior to either treatment modality administered alone.

Efficacy of cognitive behavior modification also is well established in patients or subclinical samples with mild to moderately severe anxiety or phobic disorders. There is some indication that use of cognitive strategies may enhance treatment programs for panic disorder and agoraphobia. However, definitive studies contrasting effects with exposure-alone and/or pharmacological interventions have not yet been completed. Similarly, the utility of cognitive therapy or cognitive behavior modification with more of the pervasive and complex conditions currently classified as personality disorders is not established. A longer course of therapy may ultimately be needed here. There is little evidence that cognitively-oriented therapies will play a major role in treatment of schizophrenia or the dementias.

Cognitive behavior modification has shown promise in applications with children with problems of impulse control or conduct disorders. Again, further study is needed. Several investigators have applied cognitive treatments to patients with alcoholism or substance abuse. However, results from one recent, major comparative trial with alcoholic patients indicate that Beck's cognitive therapy was no more effective than a traditional form of psychotherapy emphasizing emotional expression and development of insight.

Cognitive therapies would seem most indicated for outpatients with mild-to-moderately-severe anxiety or depression. In practice, such strategies may be preferred for patients who evidence a number of distorted or dysfunctional cognitions. Unfortunately, empirical support for this intuitive choice of modalities is not yet available. At this time, relative contraindications for use of a short-term course of cognitive therapy or cognitive behavior modification as a singular modality would include the presence of delusions, existence of impaired cognitive abilities and memory deficits, severe melancholic depression, and borderline personality disorder. However, in each case cognitive strategies might prove helpful in combination with other interventions and/or in a hospital setting. Cognitive therapy does not have specific side effects or adverse reactions, although it must be noted that between 10%–40% of apparently appropriate patients may not respond to this treatment. Attrition rates are relatively low in most studies, especially when compared to pharmacotherapy-alone conditions. It is recommended that patients who do not appear to benefit from 3 months of regular therapy (i.e., 12–20 sessions) should be reassessed for treatment with an alternative modality.

BIBLIOGRAPHY

Beck, A. T. (1976). *Cognitive therapy and the emotional disorders*. New York: International Universities Press.
Beck, A. T., & Rush, A. J. (1978). Cognitive approaches to depression and suicide. In G. Serban (Ed.), *Cognitive defects in development of mental illness*. New York: Brunner/Mazel.
Beck, A. T., Rush, A. J., Shaw, B. F., & Emery, G. (1979). *Cognitive therapy of depression*. New York: Guilford Press.
Miller, R. C., & Berman, J. S. (1983). The efficacy of cognitive behavior therapies: A quantitative review of the research evidence. *Psychological Bulletin, 94*, 39–53.
Rush, A. J. (1983). Cognitive therapy of depression: Rationale, techniques, and efficacy. *Psychiatric Clinics of North America, 6*, 105–127.

See: Covert Conditioning
Self-Control Therapy
Self-Statement Modification
Self-Verbalization

COMMUNICATION SKILLS TRAINING
Donald A. Williamson

Communication skills training is a behavioral technique which is commonly used in marital and family therapy. The purpose of communication skills training is improvement of communication between two (or more) persons. Common problems of communication which are targeted for treatment by communication skills training are: appropriate expression of emotions, resolution of conflict, assertion, provision of positive feedback to others, compromising, and planning of activities. The components of communication skills training are: role-playing, modeling, feedback (often using videorecording techniques), and homework assignments for practicing communication skills which have been learned in the clinic.

See: Behavioral Family Therapy
     Conversational Skills Training
     Social Skills Training

COMMUNITY REINFORCEMENT APPROACH
William R. Miller

The Community Reinforcement Approach (CRA) is a multidimensional, broad spectrum approach to treatment introduced by Nathan Azrin and his colleagues. Although it could easily be applied to other problems, CRA research to date has focused on alcoholic populations.

The purpose of CRA is "to rearrange the vocational, family, and social reinforcers of the alcoholic such that time-out from these reinforcers would occur if he began to drink" (Hunt & Azrin, 1973, p. 93). Noting that most alcoholism treatment programs have focused on the individual but ignored the social environment, Azrin reasoned that

behavior change would be more likely to be maintained if the treatment program brought about changes in the social contingencies that encourage or discourage drinking. Family, employment, and social relationships were chosen as significant sources of positive reinforcement to be modified.

The content of CRA has evolved since its introduction in 1973. The original program included job-finding counseling for unemployed clients, problem-solving training, behavioral family therapy, social counseling (scheduling activities, encouraging hobbies and recreation, seeking company of friends who do not tolerate drinking), and "reinforcer access counseling." The latter provided encouragement and assistance to the client in having access to common information and sources of reinforcement: a radio or television in the home, newspaper and magazine subscriptions, a driving license, and a telephone. A special social club was initiated that provided an alcohol-free environment in which there was access to many social and recreational activities, and clients were given a one month free membership. For the first month post-discharge, clients were visited once or twice weekly, then twice monthly, and eventually once monthly, for problem-solving sessions with a counselor. This comprehensive program required an average of 50 hours of individual counseling per client.

Improvements in this initial program were suggested by Azrin (1976). These included: (1) prescription for disulfiram, a drug that punishes any alcohol consumption by causing an adverse physical reaction; (2) a program to encourage compliance with disulfirm dosage, involving supervision of self-administration, dosage at a regular time and place, and rehearsal of situations likely to encourage discontinuation; (3) a "buddy" system whereby each client was paired with a recovering alcoholic peer-advisor; and (4) an "early warning" system of daily mood ratings, so that counseling could be reinstituted at the first sign of impending relapse. In addition, the format for CRA was changed from individual to group counseling, reducing the required time from 50 to 30 hours per client.

The outcome studies on CRA are among the best controlled and most encouraging evaluations in the alcoholism field. The initial research put CRA to an exceedingly stringent test by applying it to an inpatient chronic alcoholic population with a history of physical addiction, and evaluating whether it would produce treatment gains beyond those from a standard hospital alcoholism treatment program. Random assignment was used to assign inpatients to receive or not receive CRA in addition to the hospital program (didactic lectures and Alcoholics Anonymous). The CRA program produced such large effects that there was little overlap between the experimental and control groups by the time of the 6-month follow-up. CRA-treated patients were drinking on 14% of days (accounted for mostly by one client), compared with 79% drinking days in the hospital-treated control. Unemployed days were 12 times higher in the control group, and institutionalized days were 15 times higher in controls relative to those in CRA. All marriages in the CRA group remained intact, whereas 25% separated in the control group. Self-reports were corroborated by collateral interviews, and group differences were highly significant statistically as well as clinically.

Azrin's (1976) "improved" CRA program produced equally encouraging results. At 6-month follow-up, CRA clients (again addicted inpatient alcoholics) showed only 2% drinking days (compared with 55% in the controls), 20% unemployed days (vs. 56%), 7% of days away from home (vs. 67%) and no days of institutionalization (vs. 45%).

Further, it is noteworthy that the *same* counselors administered the traditional hospital program (their usual modality) and the additional CRA module. A 2-year follow-up was included and showed excellent maintenance of gains, with over 90% abstinent days at 12, 18, and 24 months, based on data from 100% of cases.

Two subsequent studies have begun "dismantling" the CRA program to evaluate the contribution of its components. Azrin, Sisson, Meyers, and Godley (1982) evaluated a traditional outpatient alcoholism treatment program with or without the addition of: (1) the disulfiram-compliance component alone, or (2) the full CRA program. At 6-month follow-up, traditionally-treated outpatients reported over 50% drinking days, and about one-third of days intoxicated and unemployed. The disulfiram-compliance program reduced these rates by about half, but the full CRA program yielded almost total suppression of drinking (0.9 days/month), intoxication (0.4 days), and unemployment (2.2 days). Consistent with Azrin's prior findings, the traditionally treated group showed almost total relapse within 3 months (the modal pattern following alcoholism treatment), whereas little relapse was evident in the CRA group.

Mallams, Godley, Hall, and Meyers (1982) tested the "social club" component of the CRA program by encouraging vs. not encouraging attendance among outpatient alcoholics (random assignment). Those given the encouragement program attended the alcohol-free social club more often, and showed significantly more reduction in drinking, behavioral impairment, and time spent in heavy drinking contexts relative to the control group. Although it is difficult to compare across studies, the gains appear to be less than those resulting from the full CRA program.

Thus, CRA has been shown to be very

effective with both inpatient and outpatient alcoholic populations, including chronically addicted individuals. Azrin (1976) has suggested that CRA techniques are equally applicable to abstinent or controlled drinking goals, although no program to date has evaluated CRA with a moderation goal. Azrin et al. (1982) found that the full CRA program was differentially beneficial to unmarried clients, whereas married alcoholics derived equal benefit from the disulfiram-compliance program alone, a much simpler approach. It is reasonable to assume that the reinforcement-rebuilding value of CRA will be differentially greater for clients who have less-stable social support systems, are unemployed, and/or lack supportive immediate or extended family. This is noteworthy in that the greater the chronicity of alcoholism, the more likely CRA is to be beneficial. Other differential predictors of favorable response are unknown at present.

Contraindications to CRA would seem few. The primary consideration would be one of cost-effectiveness, in that it is apparently more than is needed for some clients, especially married and socially stable individuals. Even the streamlined CRA program requires 30 hours of counselor time per client, although more minimal versions may be quite beneficial. For chronic alcoholics, who have a notoriously high relapse rate, the investment of this additional staff time is obviously justifiable, based on the sizable effects evidenced in controlled research to date. Certain components of the program (e.g., job-finding) are unnecessary for some individuals (e.g., those already employed). When CRA includes the disulfiram-compliance component, clients must be screened for medical risks associated with the use of this drug. Research reports to date, however, have included very few unfavorable responses, particularly when CRA results are compared with the outcome of traditional alcoholism treatment.

In summary, CRA is a very promising method for treating chronically addicted alcoholics. The experimental support of effectiveness of CRA is quite strong, and compares very favorably with traditional approaches to treatment. It is applicable in either inpatient or outpatient settings, with either abstinence or moderation goals, in either individual or group counseling formats. Similar broad-spectrum methods have been applied with good results in Norway, and CRA appears to be a valuable contribution to the effective treatment of alcohol problems.

BIBLIOGRAPHY

Azrin, N. H. (1976). Improvements in the community-reinforcement approach to alcoholism. *Behaviour Research and Therapy, 14*, 339–348.

Azrin, N. H., Sisson, R. W., Meyers, R., & Godley, M. (1982). Alcoholism treatment by disulfiram and community reinforcement therapy. *Journal of Behavior Therapy and Experimental Psychiatry, 13*, 105–112.

Duckert, F., & Aasland, O. G. (1980). Rehabilitation of alcoholics and drug addicts: An experimental approach. *Journal of Studies on Alcohol, 41*, 368–372.

Hunt, G. M., & Azrin, N. H. (1973). A community-reinforcement approach to alcoholism. *Behaviour Research and Therapy, 11*, 91–104.

Mallams, J. H., Godley, M. D., Hall, G. M., & Meyers, R. A. (1982). A social-systems approach to resocializing alcoholics in the community. *Journal of Studies on Alcohol, 43*, 1115–1123.

See: Controlled Drinking
     Job Club Method

CONDITIONED PUNISHMENT

See: Conditioned Reinforcement

CONDITIONED REINFORCEMENT
Sandra Twardosz

Conditioned positive reinforcement refers to the presentation of a stimulus contingent on a behavior that results in an increase in the frequency or strength of that behavior. The stimuli, called *conditioned reinforcers*, were previously neutral events. They acquired their reinforcing value through repeated association with primary or unlearned reinforcers, which are generally those that satisfy biological needs, or with other conditioned reinforcers. For example, praise may acquire reinforcing value if it is repeatedly presented immediately before food following a behavior. Tokens, money, attention, smiles, and physical affection are also considered to be conditioned reinforcers. However, the reinforcing value of some social behaviors may be unlearned.

Conditioned negative reinforcement refers to the removal of a stimulus contingent on a behavior that results in an increase in the frequency or strength of that behavior. The stimuli, called *conditioned negative reinforcers*, were previously neutral events that acquired their aversive value through pairing with primary aversive events such as pain or discomfort, or with other conditioned aversive events. Examples include disapproving facial expressions and reprimands.

Conditioned punishment refers to the presentation of a conditioned aversive stimulus, such as a frown, or the removal of a conditioned reinforcer, such as attention, contingent on a behavior that results in a decrease in the frequency or strength of that behavior.

Conditioned reinforcers and aversive stimuli must be paired periodically with primary or other conditioned stimuli in order to retain their power to increase or decrease behavior. Generalized conditioned reinforcers and aversive stimuli have been associated with a variety of events and are generally more effective than those that have been paired with only one event.

See: Conditioned Punishment

CONTACT DESENSITIZATION
Thomas R. Kratochwill

Contact desensitization is a form of behavior therapy treatment combining graduated modeling and guided participation. The procedure has been employed with both children and adults. In the usual application, a model demonstrates a desired behavior under relatively secure conditions. Subsequently, the client is guided through further modeled demonstrations and performance of progressively more difficult responses. After modeling each step in a hierarchy, the therapist helps the client perform that step by guiding the client, encouraging the client with various motivating statements, and praising the client for progress. The therapist then gradually withdraws prompts until the client can perform each step alone. In summary, the treatment procedure consists of three major components: modeling desired behavior, use of physical and verbal prompts, and gradual withdrawal of therapist's assistance and contact. A fourth component, which has sometimes been recommended is a highly positive therapist relationship with the client.

CLINICAL APPLICATION

Contact desensitization has a fair amount of research support. For example, in one study 44 snake-avoidant children were assigned to three treatment groups: contact desensitization, live modeling, and a no-treatment control condition. Children in the two treatment groups received 35-minute small group sessions. Results of this study indicated that both treatment conditions were superior to a no-treatment control group on a behavioral avoidance test, and children in a contact desensitization group showed more improvement than children in the modeling group. In a subsequent study with snake-avoidant children, it was found that contact desensitization was superior to a contact desensitization treatment without a touch condition. More recently the contribution of various components of contact desensitization was evaluated with snake-avoidant 4- and 5-year-old children. Children were assigned to one of five experimental conditions: contact desensitization, contact desensitization without therapist touch, verbal input (information about the snake) plus therapist modeling, verbal input alone, and a no-treatment control condition. Results of this investigation suggested that all groups improved significantly from pretest to posttest on a behavioral avoidance test. Moreover, contact desensitization was found to be as effective in reducing children's avoidance behavior as the contact desensitization without the therapist touch. Both groups were found to be significantly more effective than a no-treatment control condition but no other differences were found.

An example of a clinical application follows:

In the application of this method to the elimination of snake phobia, at each step the experimenter, himself, performed fearless behavior and gradually led subjects into touching, stroking, and then holding the snake's body first with the glove and then bare hands while he held the snake securely by the head and tail. If the subject was unable to touch the snake after ample demonstration, she was asked to place her hand on the experimenter's and to move her hand gradually until it touched the snake's body. After subjects no longer felt any apprehension about touching the snake under these secure conditions, anxieties about contact with

the snake's head and entwining tail were extinguished. The experimenter again performed the task fearlessly, and then he and the subject performed the responses jointly; as subjects became less fearful the experimenter gradually reduced participation and control over the snake until the subjects were able to hold the snake in their laps without assistance, to let the snake loose in the room and to retrieve it, and let it crawl freely over their bodies. Progress through the graded approach task was paced according to subject's apprehensiveness. When they reported being able to perform one activity with little or no fear, they were eased into a more difficult interaction. (Bandura, 1969, p. 185)

EXPECTED OUTCOMES AND TIMEFRAME

The expected outcomes of contact desensitization are systematic progression through a hierarchy such as that described in the table. The time needed for this therapy will depend on the nature of the hierarchy and the subject's characteristics, as well as the specific fear that is the focus.

POTENTIAL SIDE EFFECTS OR CONTRAINDICATIONS

No negative side effects of contact desensitization have been reported in the literature. However, subjects may experience anxiety during initial phases of the hierarchy depending upon the type and nature of experiences with the feared object.

BIBLIOGRAPHY

Bandura, A. (1969). *Principles of behavior modification.* New York: Holt, Rinehart, & Winston.
Ritter, B. (1968). The group desensitization of children's snakes phobias using vicarious and contact desensitization procedures. *Behaviour Research and Therapy, 6,* 1–6.
Ritter, B. (1969a). Treatment of acrophobia with contact desensitization. *Behaviour Research and Therapy, 7,* 41–45.
Ritter, B. (1969b). The use of contact desensitization, demonstration plus participation and dem-

Table 1. Hierarchy for Children Afraid to Enter a Swimming Pool

1. Let's begin by walking into the pool room to the white marker (one-quarter of the way to the pool).
2. Walk to the yellow marker on the floor (half of the way).
3. Walk to the red marker on the floor (three-quarters of the way).
4. Walk to the green marker by the edge of the pool.
5. Sit down right there (by the edge of the pool).
6. Let's see you put your feet in the water, while I slowly count to 9. 1 . . . 2 . . . 3
7. . . . 4 . . . 5 . . . 6
8. . . . 7 . . . 8 . . . 9
9. Get up and walk into the water to the red marker and stay there until I count to 6. 1 . . . 2 . . . 3
10. . . . 4 . . . 5 . . . 6
11. Walk to the green marker (halfway down ramp) and stay there until I count to 6. 1 . . . 2 . . . 3
12. . . . 4 . . . 5 . . . 6
13. Walk to the yellow marker (bottom of ramp: 2'6" deep) and stay there until I count to 9. You can hold onto the edge. 1 . . . 2 . . . 3
14. . . . 4 . . . 5 . . . 6
15. . . . 7 . . . 8 . . . 9
16. Let's see if you can stand there without holding on (only if person held on in previous step).
17. Walk out to the red marker (3' from edge) and then come back to me.
18. Splash some water on yourself: hold on to edge if you like.
19. Do that without holding on (only if person held on in previous step).
20. Splash some water on your face: you may hold on to the edge if you like.
21. Do that without holding on (only if person held on in previous step).
22. Squat down and blow some bubbles in the water. You can hold on if you like.
23. Blow bubbles without holding on (only if person held on in previous step).
24. Put your whole face in the water. You may hold on if you like.
25. Do that again without holding on (only if person held on in previous step).
26. Put your whole body under water. You can hold on if you like.
27. Do that again without holding on (only if person held on in previous step).
28. Walk out in the water up to your chin (if pool depth permits).
29. Hold onto the kickboard and put your face in the water.
30. Hold onto the kickboard and take one foot off the ground.
31. Hold onto the kickboard and take both feet off the ground.
32. Put your face in the water again and take your feet off the bottom.
33. Let's go down to the deep end of the pool. Sit on the edge and put your feet in the water.
34. O.K. Now climb down the ladder.
35. Now hold onto the edge right here by the green marker.
36. While still holding on, put your whole body under water.
37. Hold onto the kickboard.
38. While still holding on put your face in the water.
39. Do that again, but now put your whole head under water.
40. O.K. Now climb out of the pool and come over to the blue marker. Jump in the water right here (at pool depth of 3'6" or 5' depending on person's height).

Source: Morris, R. J. (1976). *Behavior modification with children: A systematic guide.* Cambridge, MA: Winthrop. Reprinted with permission.

onstration-only in the treatment of acrophobia. *Behaviour Research and Therapy, 7,* 157–164.

Morris, R. J., & Dolker, M. (1983). A constituent analysis of contact desensitization with snake fearful children. *Education and Treatment of Children,* in press.

See: In vivo Desensitization
     Modeling

CONTINGENCY CONTRACTING

E. Thomas Dowd and Douglas H. Olson

Contingency contracting is a behavioral change procedure in which an agreement is made between the persons who desire behavior to change (i.e., parents, teachers, counselors, etc.) and those whose behavior needs to be changed (i.e., child, student, client, etc.), or in which a bilateral contract is made between two (or more) people each of whom desires mutual changes in the other(s). Contingency contracts, usually in the form of written agreements, specify the relationships between behaviors and consequences. The contract clarifies the positive and negative consequences that can be expected to follow specific behaviors. Contracts often imply an "if–then" relation between behaviors and consequences (e.g., "if you make the meal, then I'll do the dishes"). The contingency arrangements are actively negotiated by those involved. The contents of the written contract are then mutually agreed upon and signed by both parties.

CLINICAL APPLICATION

The clinical application of contingency contracts can take many varying shapes and forms. It is possible for an individual to engage in a self-contract, where another person provides only minimal supervision and monitoring (i.e., student and an aca-demic advisor). Contracts are also possible between an individual and a group (i.e., child and family members or student and class, etc.). Contracts can be unilateral, where one party engages in the change program without expecting specific contributions from the second party. More commonly, bilateral contracts are utilized (i.e., husband and wife or student and teacher, etc.) which specify the obligations and mutual reinforcements for each of the parties.

The persons in bilateral contingency contracts (e.g., husband and wife) openly negotiate each feature and include only contents which have been mutually agreed-upon. This process can help those participating learn to bargain and compromise without force or coercion. Allowing each of the parties involved to engage in the design and implementation of the contract may enhance such things as personal commitment to the program, behavioral performance, and the perceived fairness of the contingencies included.

Most contracts are in written form and are signed by the parties involved, following mutual agreement on its contents. The written format provides the parties involved with an excellent record of the agreement, as well as an opportunity to evaluate progress. The explicit, written record reduces the chances of confusion and disagreements about expectations, responsibilities, or consequences for behavior.

The process of designing and negotiating contingency contracts provides the parties with practice in the process of clearly defining desired behaviors and establishing realistic steps to attain them. Clinical application of contracts often includes a series of contracts designed to gradually improve behavior successively over a period of time. In utilizing a graduated series of contracts, an individual would not be faced with unrealistic expectations of performing beyond capabilities or the overwhelming task of eliminating the undesirable behavior all at once.

The explicit nature of contingency contracts clarifies expectations and is useful in providing some structure to the relationships of the parties involved. By clarifying and following through on reinforcement given for desirable behaviors, the relationship between the parties may be enhanced. Some basic ideas upon which contingency contracting rests are as follows: (a) reinforcement is a privilege which must be earned, not a right; (b) good relationships are based on even exchanges of reinforcement; (c) the value of a relationship is influenced by the reinforcements received; and (d) a contract increases freedom within a relationship for the parties to earn the reinforcement they desire.

The focus in the designing and negotiating of a contract revolves around four major content dimensions: (a) the desired behavior, (b) positive consequences, (c) negative consequences, and (d) bonuses. The parties involved must come to consensus on the specific desired behaviors which will be goals of the program. The behavioral criterion expected should be consistent with the realistic capabilities of the person at that point in time. The positive reinforcements or privileges contingent upon fulfillment of each behavioral criterion should be clearly specified. The privileges to be gained should be in proportion to the amount of performance required. In addition, penalties for violating specific aspects of the agreement should be negotiated. Finally, a bonus clause is generally used which provides additional positive consequences for going above and beyond the behavioral criterion established or for performing the desired behavior consistently over time.

It is important to follow explicit guidelines in designing effective contingency contracts. The 14 guidelines presented here have been gleaned from the literature and are organized according to the major content dimensions of contracts discussed earlier.

CENTRAL FEATURES AND GUIDELINES OF AN EFFECTIVE CONTINGENCY CONTRACT

General Principles.

(1) Each feature of the contract should be openly negotiated and its contents should be mutually agreed upon by the parties involved.

(2) The contract should usually be in written form, with the parties involved signing it following mutual agreement on its contents. The signing procedure is understood to be a personal and public commitment to follow through on the agreement.

(3) Recognition should be given for accomplishments and not payment for obedience.

(4) An effective contract is often one in a larger series of contracts which are used to gradually shape behaviors.

(5) The content of any one contract is not legally binding and is open to re-negotiation by any party at any point in time.

Specifying Desired Behavior.

(6) A clear and detailed description of the desired behavior should be provided. The behaviors should be short-range approximations of the eventual goal(s).

(7) Some specific criterion should be set for the time or frequency limitations (i.e., when, where, how often, etc.) which constitute the behavior required on the contract.

(8) The contract should require reason-

able behavior that the parties are capable of performing.

(9) The specific behavior required must be observable and measurable, so that each party can monitor when the required behavior is met and privileges can be granted. Ability to monitor the contract will provide the parties with immediate and constant feedback on progress made.

Positive Consequences.

(10) The positive reinforcements or privileges contingent upon fulfillment of each behavioral criterion should be specified.

(11) The reinforcer should be perceived by the parties as worth the behavior required to earn it.

(12) The timing for delivery of reinforcement contingencies should be arranged to follow the desired behavior as quickly as possible.

Negative Consequences.

(13) The contract should specify, in advance, the penalties for each person's failure to carry out the parts of the contract pertaining to them. By having small penalties for various specified offenses, it will reduce the likelihood that one single violation can result in termination of the contract.

Bonuses.

(14) The contract should provide a bonus clause for additional privileges to be earned if the person exceeds minimal demands of the contract and/or performs the desired behavior(s) consistently over a prolonged period of time.

EXPECTED OUTCOMES

Generalizations concerning the efficacy of contingency contracting with specific disorders should be made cautiously due to the relatively small number of studies conduct-

ed. However, successful contingency contracting has been investigated in studies which examine the effects of contracting on specific problem areas. Contracts which have been investigated can be narrowed down into five major categories of problem behavior: (a) academic or school related behaviors; (b) independent living and social skills; (c) habit control, such as alcohol and drugs; (d) marital problems; and (e) delinquent behavior.

In dealing with academic or school-related behaviors, successful contracts have been used in the reduction of fighting behavior at school in a young child, reduction of absenteeism in high school students, and increasing the study rate of undergraduate students of a wide range of abilities.

Contingency contracts have also significantly reduced problem behaviors (i.e., refusing meals and medication, making delusional statements, physical assaults, etc.) in former psychiatric patients attempting to develop independent living skills in a foster home setting.

A number of studies have successfully utilized contingency contracts in dealing with drug and alcohol usage. Contingency management has been shown through research to be effective in reducing alcohol abuse, although it has not been shown that the treatment effects persist once the contingencies are removed. However, these techniques have been shown to have only modest success with drug abusers, especially regarding their contribution to successful treatment outcome.

Excessive smoking has also been the target of contracting research. Participants in one study significantly reduced their excessive smoking behavior through contingency contract interventions, although significant effects were not maintained between treatment conditions at a 1-year follow-up period. Contingency management has been used successfully for obesity treatment, but it has not been demonstrated that weight loss can be maintained for any length of time once the contingencies are removed.

Successful contracts have also been utilized in dealing with marital discord and have been recommended to improve communication patterns among family members of delinquents. Contingency contracting has also been shown to be helpful in increasing the rates of particular targeted marital behaviors.

POSSIBLE SIDE EFFECTS OR CONTRAINDICATIONS

General conclusions about side effects or contraindications of contingency contracts cannot be made due to the lack of consensus among various studies that such effects occur. However, tentative conclusions regarding side effects and contraindications might be derived from the limited data available.

The A-B-A-B reversal design that has been utilized in studies on contingency contracting makes it clear that caution must be used in the methods used to withdraw contracts and maintain treatment gains. Haphazard withdrawal of contracts, or a series of contracts, may result in a return of the problem behaviors to previous baseline levels. Since most contingencies must be managed externally, this is an important limitation. Inconsistency and unpredictability of treatment strategies by an external agent is a serious limitation on effectiveness.

Adherence to the features and guidelines of effective contracts outlined above may become even more important when working with young children or persons of any age with less cognitive and verbal skill than normal adults. For example, required behaviors must be easy to identify, tasks broken down into components, a series of contracts should be used, and recognition should be given for accomplishments rather than payment for obedience.

A clinician, parent, or teacher who might feel a need to dominate the arrangement of contingency requirements on a contract, may meet with little success. In fact, it has been shown that higher rates of academic-related behavior occurs when the pupil arranges the contingency requirements, as opposed to when the teacher specifies them. The ultimate aim of contingency contracting is, in fact, self-contracting.

Caution should be exercised in using contingency contracts with delinquents or those with other severe disorders. The use of contracting with delinquents may have potential difficulties. It may not be the contents of the contracts themselves which cause change, but the process of changing communication patterns between the persons developing the contract.

BIBLIOGRAPHY

Bristol, M. M., & Sloane, H. N. (1974). Effects of contingency contracting on study rate and test performance. *Journal of Applied Behavior Analysis, 7*, 271–285.

DeRisi, W. J., & Butz, G. (1975). *Writing behavioral contracts: A case simulation practice manual.* Champaign, IL: Research Press.

Homme, L. E., Csangi, A., Gonzales, M., & Rechs, J. (1969). *How to use contingency contracting in the classroom.* Champaign, IL: Research Press.

Kanfer, F. H. (1980). Self-management methods. In F. H. Kanfer & A. P. Goldstein (Eds.), *Helping people change.* New York: Pergamon Press.

Kazdin, A. E. (1980). *Behavior modification in applied settings.* Homewood, IL: Dorsey Press.

See: Behavioral Family Therapy
Behavioral Marital Therapy
Contingency Management
Operant Conditioning

CONTINGENCY MANAGEMENT

Trevor F. Stokes

Contingency management involves the analysis and change of the functional contingencies in the environment that determine a person's behavior. As a result, the behavior changes from its initial rate to a different rate of occurrence. In clinical practice, this typically involves the development of new or alternative forms of adaptive behavior. These changes are made with attention to the discrimination and generalization of behavior changes.

Within a certain environmental setting or context, a contingency describes a functional relationship among stimuli antecedent to a particular behavior, the behavior which is the clinical target, and the consequences which follow the occurrence of the behavior. An antecedent stimulus or a consequence is functional if it maintains or has an effect on the behavior of a person. The functional environment for one person is often different from the functional environment for another person. Many stimuli or events occur in a person's environment, yet have no effect on his/her behavior. Therefore, that part of the environment is not functional. It is simply present.

An antecedent discriminative stimulus controls the occurrence of a behavior by its presentation prior to the performance of the behavior. Functional consequences are defined by their effects. Reinforcing consequences increase the frequency of behaviors. In the operation of positive reinforcement, a stimulus presented following a behavior functions to increase its frequency. In the operation of negative reinforcement a stimulus removed following a behavior functions to increase its frequency. Punishing consequences decrease the frequency of behaviors. In the operation of positive punishment (or

punishment by addition), a stimulus presented following a behavior functions to decrease its frequency. In the operation of negative punishment (or punishment by removal or cost), a stimulus removed following a behavior functions to decrease its frequency. In the operation of extinction, a stimulus that has been a reinforcer for a particular behavior is removed or prevented from being presented following that behavior. Subsequently, the frequency of that behavior decreases. Contingency management, therefore, involves the analysis and modification of contingencies involving discriminative stimuli, reinforcement, punishment, and extinction.

Contingency management frequently focuses on public and observable behaviors and controlling environments. The environment of interest is primarily that part which is observable and measurable and which functions to increase, decrease, or control the occurrence of certain behaviors. The behaviors of focus are primarily those which are observable and measurable by other people, e.g., conversation skills. Of equal validity is contingency management that focuses on behaviors or environments less well-observed or measured by others, i.e., behaviors and environments that are covert, "within the skin" (e.g., thoughts). Most contingency management efforts concentrate on overt behaviors and functional environmental contingencies because of the less reliable analysis of covert behaviors and environments. Because the functional analysis and modification of overt behaviors and environments accounts for a large proportion of effective interventions, extensive analysis of covert behavior and environments is often unnecessary.

Contingency management within clinical practice typically is concerned with appropriate discrimination and generalization of adaptive behavior changes. An effective behavior change program needs to incorporate procedures both to restrict the occurrence of behaviors to the presence of certain environmental events (i.e., discriminative stimuli), and also to accomplish the generalization or transfer of behavior changes across relevant persons, settings, behaviors, and time. The particular procedures incorporated into an intervention program to accomplish initial discriminated behavior change may be different than the manipulations required in order to program for the generalization of behavior changes. Procedures to accomplish both the initial behavior changes and generalized changes should be incorporated into the contingency management program from the outset of therapy.

A therapeutic intervention involves both the analysis and the modification of the functional contingencies of certain behaviors. Completing a functional analysis is not a straightforward, foolproof endeavor. It involves some retrospective review of the history of a behavior's interactions with the functional environment and a thorough analysis of current maintaining contingencies. The analysis of the current environmental function is best conducted through repeated sessions of direct observation of the behavior(s) in the relevant natural setting. These analyses will reveal the nature and extent of the clinical problems over time, as well as focusing attention on relevant discriminative stimuli, reinforcers, and punishers for certain behaviors. Unfortunately, the analysis of a functional history may be difficult — information may be lost, inaccessible, or inaccurate for a variety of reasons. Therefore, whether or not this information is beneficial to the therapist, it is often unobtainable. Probably the more important assessment is the analysis of current controlling contingencies. This is especially important if the contingencies that maintain current behavior are different than the contingencies origin-

ally responsible for development of the behavior.

Prior to a thorough functional analysis, a therapist needs to assess the precise nature of the behavior(s) which will become the target for intervention. With the involvement of the client and relevant other persons (e.g., parents), the therapist should develop a precise and objective description of the behavior and the circumstances under which it occurs (or should occur). Relevant to this assessment is an analysis of factors such as discriminative control, frequency, duration, and quality of the targeted behavior(s). The more precise the description and definition of the target behavior, the more readily and reliably the client, relevant other persons, and/or the therapist will be able to monitor the occurrence of behavior. The therapist should also consider the client's behavior repertoire beyond the initial presenting behaviors. An appropriately broad assessment should consider the client's behavioral excesses, deficits, and assets.

Part of an assessment will also be a survey of a client's functional environment for a range of behaviors. This analysis will provide information regarding the relative frequency of certain behaviors and events in the person's environment. It will also allow an overview of current functional consequences which may provide clues as to which consequences may function as reinforcers or punishers for the behaviors that will be targeted in the intervention.

Three final points regarding the conduct of functional analyses can be made. First, every person has a different history of interaction with the functional environment. Few targeted behavior problems are likely to have closely related histories and current topographies. Similar behaviors may come effectively under the control of similar procedures, but to neglect each person's circumstances entirely is both an insult to the dignity of the individual and not good practice. Second, there is no guarantee that a functional analysis of a client's behavior is correct, adequate, or sufficiently comprehensive. The only test is to develop an intervention based upon as thorough an analysis as can be conducted, and then determine if the modifications of the functional environmental contingencies change the rate of the target behavior(s). Third, contingency management does not just deal with simple and uncomplicated behavior and intervention procedures. The complexity of the behaviors targeted is limited only by the limited focus and/or skill employed in the functional analysis and intervention programming. A broad focus with clinical problems, especially in initial contacts, as well as creativity and flexibility on the therapist's part in attempts to identify functional consequences, will enhance the likelihood of correct analysis and modification of functional contingencies for a diversity of target behaviors.

After a comprehensive functional analysis of environmental contingencies, the therapist plans a program of intervention to modify contingencies to change the rate of the target behavior(s). The information gathered through interview and direct observation is used to focus plans on certain techniques, antecedent stimuli, and consequences manipulations. For example, the current rate of a behavior and the presence of that behavior in the client's repertoire (history), will determine whether prompting and fading or shaping may be the procedure of choice. Some experimentation by a therapist in the use of different procedures is also likely, e.g., will the client's behavior be positively reinforced by certain consequences? How reliably will certain consequences function as punishers? Flexibility and problem solving by the therapist is essential here.

Another important aspect of contingency management is the assessment of outcome. Depending upon the nature of the target behavior(s) and the environment(s) in which it occurs, the therapist may assess the circumstances under which the behavior occurs, and/or take frequency, duration, or time-sampling measures. These program data are collected by the client, by relevant other persons, and/or by the therapist. Typically, these data are graphed to reveal progress towards program success and are compared with a pre-intervention baseline assessment of the same target behavior(s). These data are useful in documenting progress, in promoting a client's participation, and in providing services in an accountable fashion.

Monitoring of progress is also important because an ineffective program needs to be changed. Without assessment of outcome, it is unclear when changes should be made. In an extinction program, for example, there may be an initial increase in the rate of a behavior following the implementation of the program. The therapist, therefore, needs to recognize this and maintain the program long enough to establish the effectiveness of the extinction procedure. Changing too quickly (e.g., within a week or two), when a program is not going smoothly is often inappropriate. Frequently, persistence and careful implementation of procedures will prove successful, especially when a client has a history of outlasting new contingency manipulations by pressuring contingency managers back to the use of previously ineffective management strategies. Nevertheless, as important as it is to persist and give a program a reasonable time to be effective, it is also important that a therapist be flexible and ready to change a program which clearly is not being effective. A broad focus in assessment of outcome also will allow documentation of positive generalized behavior changes or negative side effects of the procedures.

Most of the documented research regarding contingency management concerns interventions with children. They are a frequent target of such procedures because parents, teachers, and other program mediators are able to gain control over controlling contingencies. The control of reinforcers and punishers provides both the opportunity for effective contingency management and the responsibility for maintaining ethical and reasonable practice. The therapist usually will maximize a child's participation in the development and implementation of the intervention. For example, the incorporation of self-management procedures often facilitates client involvement and promotes effective and generalized changes. Work with mediators who manage contingencies for children broadens the focus of the therapist's role. The involvement and contingency management skills of the program mediators (e.g., parents, institution staff members) must also be developed and maintained by the therapist. This, in itself, is an additional management program. Of these types of programs, probably the most effective occur when the mediator has some relatively prompt initial successes and/or has much to gain if the program is successful, e.g., a child's behavior is particularly aversive for the parent.

Applications of contingency management procedures with adults are similar to those with children. However, they often involve more participation by the client (i.e., more extensive self-management of antecedent stimuli and consequences), as well as program assessment. The advantages of self-management and self-control procedures often are seen in client participation, efficiency of program completion, and generalization of behavior changes. A disadvantage though, is that naturally occurring environmental contingencies frequently maintain behavior(s) that are counter to the therapeutic

goals. For example, a client may avoid implementing an aversive procedure (an intended punishment operation) and is negatively reinforced for not implementing such a contingency. Another example of a short-circuited contingency would be when a client sets a contingency that certain chores must be completed before watching a football game on television, yet when the game time arrives, the client watches despite the fact the chores have not been completed. In this case, the natural consequence, watching TV, reinforces the behavior of avoiding the set contingency and going straight to the positive consequence. Such natural contingencies and potential pitfalls need to be assessed and some control over them exerted whenever possible, e.g., occasional therapist monitoring of program compliance.

Specific procedures of contingency management and their application will be detailed elsewhere in this dictionary. What is being emphasized here is that effective contingency management is not just an unsophisticated approach that recommends, for example, to reinforce a behavior to increase its frequency. If done appropriately, it involves a thorough functional analysis of controlling contingencies, a flexible and creative approach to rearranging the functional environment, and a careful monitoring of outcome to document the effectiveness of procedural changes.

BIBLIOGRAPHY

Bijou, S. W., & Baer, D. M. (1978). *Behavior analysis of child development*. Englewood Cliffs, NJ: Prentice-Hall.

Craighead, W. E., Kazdin, A. E., & Mahoney, M. J. (1981). *Behavior modification: Principles, issues, and applications*. (2nd ed.). Boston: Houghton Mifflin.

Martin, G., & Pear, J. (1983). *Behavior modification: What it is and how to do it*. Englewood Cliffs, NJ: Prentice-Hall.

Stokes, T. F., & Osnes, P. G. (in press). Programming the generalization of children's social behavior. In P. S. Strain, M. J. Guralnick, & H. Walker

(Eds.), *Children's social behavior: Development, assessment and modification.* New York: Wiley.

Sulzer-Azaroff, B., & Mayer, R. G. (1977). *Applying behavior analysis procedures with children and youth.* New York: Holt, Rinehart, & Winston.

See: Behavioral Family Therapy
Contingency Contracting
Group Contingency
Positive Reinforcement
Punishment

CONTINGENT AROMATIC AMMONIA
Frances Moosbrugger Hunt

Contingent aromatic ammonia is a punishment procedure which involves the presentation of an unconditioned aversive stimulus contingent on some inappropriate target response. The strategy involves crushing an aromatic ammonia capsule ("smelling salts") near the client's nose each time the target behavior occurs. A negative reinforcement contingency can supplement the punishment procedure when removal of the aversive stimulus is contingent on cessation of the target response.

Advantages of using contingent aromatic ammonia include: rapid suppression of the target behavior, easy handling and concealing of ammonia capsules, and the stimulus is less controversial than other unconditioned aversives such as electric shock. As with all punishment procedures, contingent aromatic ammonia should be used only when less restrictive procedures have been ineffective or when the nature of the problem calls for rapid suppression of the response. Because prolonged exposure to the ammonia capsule may damage the skin and nasal mucosa, staff should be well-trained and monitored closely when using this procedure. Negative side effects of punishment (e.g., emotional outbursts) have been reported, and generalization training may be required for response suppression in all settings.

Contingent aromatic ammonia is typically used to suppress severe behavior problems such as self-injurious behavior (SIB). For example, after assessing baseline levels of self injury, the therapist would crush the ammonia capsule near the client's nose each time the client initiated the SIB response. If the negative reinforcement contingency was part of the treatment, removal of the capsule would be contingent on cessation of the SIB. If data indicated procedure effectiveness, contingent aromatic ammonia would be used in all settings and situations until SIB rates were near zero. Maintenance and generalization strategies would then be implemented.

See: Aversive Conditioning
Chemical Aversion

CONTROLLED DRINKING
William R. Miller

Controlled drinking is not a technique, but rather a goal of treatment for problem drinkers. It is a term usually applied to a particular type of outcome: moderate alcohol consumption that does not result in negative consequences or symptoms of dependence, occurring in an individual whose prior drinking has been associated with such problems. The term "controlled" may be an unfortunate one, in that it connotes a certain tenuousness or a temporary respite between relapses. One of the earliest uses of the term, in fact, is found in the 1935 "big book" of Alcoholics Anonymous (A.A.), where it describes an outcome that the A.A. philosophy purports to be impossible for any alcoholic to attain. Nevertheless, "controlled drinking" has become a definitive descriptor for the treatment goal of moderate and nonproblem drinking.

Early reports of controlled drinking outcomes were observations of moderate, nonproblem drinking among individuals who had been treated for alcoholism, typically with a goal of total and lifelong abstinence. Indeed, follow-up studies of abstinence-oriented treatment programs have commonly reported this type of "improvement" in a certain percentage of treated individuals, usually ranging between 5% and 20%. Such "accidental" or "incidental" moderation outcomes have been reported since the earliest alcoholism treatment outcome studies. The widely publicized "Rand report" (Polich, Armor, & Braiker, 1981) described abstinent as well as successful nonabstinent outcomes from programs where the goal was abstention and where no training was provided to help clients achieve a goal of moderation.

In 1970, however, there appeared the first of a long series of studies evaluating the effectiveness of intervention procedures specifically designed to teach problem drinkers how to drink in a controlled fashion. The ultimate goal of such treatment is the same as that of abstinence programs: to eliminate, or at least reduce, the problems and suffering attendent to overdrinking. The difference lies in the means chosen to pursue that end. Whereas abstinence programs emphasize total avoidance of alcohol, controlled drinking programs offer an individual the option of reducing alcohol consumption to a level where it no longer endangers health or evokes life problems.

Techniques used to teach controlled drinking have varied widely. A variety of aversive conditioning procedures have been employed, as has biofeedback of blood alcohol concentration (BAC). Direct training in moderate drinking has also been provided in simulated bar settings, and video-feedback self-confrontation has been used as a motivational strategy. In the 1980s, however, practice has moved away from these techniques toward a simpler, equally effective, less aversive, and less controversial set of procedures drawing on basic principles of behavioral self-control training. Typical components of such programs include: (1) specific goal-setting, (2) self-monitoring, (3) modification of the topography of drinking to reduce consumption rate, (4) self-reinforcement, (5) functional analysis, and (6) training in alternative coping skills.

Clinical application of behavioral self-control training (BSCT) is possible in a number of different formats. Research has supported the effectiveness of BSCT offered as either individual or group therapy. Several investigators have applied BSCT principles in secondary prevention programs, and have found reductions in drinking and alcohol-related problems with populations including drunk driving offenders, incipient problem drinkers, and Native American adolescents. A surprising finding, now replicated in at least four studies, is the equivalent effectiveness of a counselor-administered "bibliotherapy" intervention using only minimal therapist contact, self-monitoring, and a self-help manual. Research suggests that when BSCT is therapist-administered, an average course of treatment consists of 6–10 weekly outpatient sessions. Marked reduction in consumption and BAC level is often observed in the first few weeks of intervention (even with bibliotherapy), and failure to show improvement within 6–10 weeks of treatment has been found to be predictive of a poor prognosis for successful controlled drinking in the long run. Some clinicians have recommended that clients be encouraged or required to sustain a period of abstinence (ranging from 2 weeks to 2 years) as a prerequisite for controlled drinking training, although no empirical findings exist at present to support this requirement.

As of 1984 there have been more than two dozen controlled or comparative treatment outcome studies evaluating intervention techniques with a goal of controlled drinking.

To date, there is no other treatment approach for problem drinkers that has been so thoroughly evaluated and scrutinized. The results of these evaluations have been encouragingly consistent, and as a consequence, we know more about the effectiveness and limitations of controlled drinking therapies than about any other approach for treating alcoholism. Across a wide variety of populations and geographic settings, research has documented favorable outcomes ranging from 60% to 80% (including abstainers, who constitute 0% to 50%) at 12-month follow-up. Most evaluations of controlled drinking training have included random assignment to comparison groups, follow-up of 12 months with high interview rates, and confirmation of self-report by interviews with collaterals, breath testing, blood tests, or other procedures. A typical array of 1-year outcomes is about 40% fully controlled drinkers, 10% abstaining, and 20–30% showing reduced consumption and problems but not full remission. A 2-year evaluation of BSCT reported a 67% success rate, with very little change from prior 1-year findings, and again, equivalent maintenance of gains in bibliotherapy and therapist-directed conditions.

At least four studies however, have reported less-favorable outcomes following treatment aimed at controlled drinking, including the recent widely publicized 10-year follow-up and reevaluation of the work of Mark and Linda Sobell. The methodologies of these studies have been criticized, but it is noteworthy that all negative studies to date have had one thing in common: the population being treated consisted of "gamma" alcoholics with a documented history of pharmacologic addiction (dependence) to alcohol. By contrast, in the 20 studies evaluating controlled drinking with less-dependent problem drinkers there is not a single negative study; all have yielded positive outcomes, averaging between 60% and 80%. This is in agreement with two other consistent findings. In studies of abstinence-oriented treatment it has been found that clients who become controlled drinkers are those who, at intake, showed less problem severity and fewer symptoms of alcohol dependence. Secondly, when evaluations of moderation-oriented treatment have included predictive analyses, clients who succeed at moderation have been found to be the less-severe problem drinkers, whereas those attaining abstinence have tended more to resemble the classic syndrome of gamma alcoholism. To be sure, the separation is not complete. There are a number of well-documented cases of controlled drinking outcomes maintained over many years in individuals clearly diagnosable as gamma alcoholics. Likewise, nonaddicted problem drinkers can and do choose total abstinence. Yet the trend is clear: The more severe the alcoholism (dependence), the lower the chances of achieving and maintaining controlled drinking and the greater the probability of success with abstinence. Conversely, the *less* severe the problems and dependence, the greater the chances of successful moderation and the lower the probability that the individual will accept, pursue, and sustain total abstinence. The 4-year Rand follow-up found that among severely dependent drinkers, relapse was about three times more likely from controlled drinking than from abstinence. By contrast, among young, less-dependent single men, relapse was 10 times more likely from abstinence than from controlled drinking. Thus, the success and advisability of a controlled drinking approach depends, in part, on the individual or population to be treated.

In helping clients to select an optimal treatment goal there are a number of important differential diagnostic considerations. One pragmatic consideration is the client's own preference. Those who choose abstinence need not be persuaded otherwise; those who refuse to consider abstinence are likely to reject treatment if that is the sole goal available. Common sense criteria also apply, with the general rule that any condition in which the individual's health and safety would be endangered by even moderate drinking constitutes a contraindication to a moderation goal. Such conditions include liver disease, alcoholic cardiomyopathy, alcohol idiosyncratic intoxication (DSM-III 291.40), and current or planned pregnancy. Concurrent abuse of drugs having synergistic or otherwise dangerous interaction with alcohol represents a contraindication to moderation. Other conditions, such as diabetes, epilepsy, or psychosis, require careful consideration and evaluation of potential negative consequences of moderate consumption. Furthermore, the above-mentioned findings point to severe pharmacologic dependence as a contraindication to controlled drinking. On the other hand, younger, less-dependent, less-severe problem drinkers appear to be more likely to accept and respond favorably to a moderation-oriented approach than to a lifelong-abstinence orientation. Neuropsychological impairment, which is evident in about half of a typical sample treated for alcoholism, represents still another consideration in selecting a goal. It is clear that neuropsychological deficits are at least partially reversible in most cases if abstinence is sustained. Less information is available regarding recovery of adaptive abilities with moderate drinking. Although it seems likely that cognitive functions, like liver enzymes, will improve with moderation, until further data become available it is prudent to regard severe neuropsychological deficits as a contraindication to a moderation goal. An argument against this can be made in the case where chronic impairment exists (whether of brain, liver, heart, etc.), and the individual is unable or unwilling to sustain abstinence. In such cases, a mod-

eration-oriented treatment may succeed where all else has failed, reducing risk and enabling greater improvement than would occur with contined excessive drinking.

If the above contraindications are observed, the risks attendant to BSCT with a moderation goal appear to be minimal. Some clinicians express concern that a controlled drinking goal "plays into the alcoholic's denial system" and delays "acceptance of the necessity of abstinence." On the other hand, a competent trial at controlled drinking may be the best differential diagnostic procedure available, and can serve as a very effective confrontation. Rather than taking an oppositional stance to the client who refuses abstinence, the therapist poses a challenge: show me that you can do it. Such an "acid test" was recommended more than three decades ago by Marty Mann and continues to be used within A.A., although the terms usually have been excessively simplistic (no more than three drinks per day for 3 months; one violation represents proof of inability to control), the instruction has usually been given with the clear expectation that the client will fail, and no guidelines have been provided to help the client achieve this goal. By contrast, the challenge of a competent BSCT program includes encouragement and the teaching of concrete skills for self-control, giving the client his or her best reasonable chance (based on what we know at present) for achieving moderate, non-problem drinking. If it is successful, both client and therapist should be satisfied. If not, the client can and should be encouraged to consider abstention as an alternative to continued harmful drinking.

It should be noted that greater risks and side effects are attached to some of the older procedures for teaching controlled drinking. The use of overt aversive agents, such as electric shock and nausea-inducing drugs, must be governed by strict health considerations. Serving alcohol to clients during treatment sessions is subject to public law restrictions, and requires health safeguards as well as protection of the client until BAC returns to zero. Videotape-feedback self-confrontation has been shown to induce distress and depression, lower self-concept, and perhaps yield an increased probability of drop-out and proximal relapse. Current data indicate that such procedures add little or nothing to the effectiveness of a basic BSCT program, so that the risks and difficulties posed by the clinical applications of these methods do not seem to be offset by increased benefit from treatment.

In sum, behavioral self-control training strategies have proved quite successful in teaching problem drinkers to moderate their alcohol consumption to a nonproblematic level. The overall success rates from moderation programs have been at least as high as those resulting from typical abstinence programs, and favorable outcomes seem to endure over at least 2 years of follow-up, with relapse rates comparable to those observed in programs emphasizing total abstention. Although controlled drinking therapies can rightly be termed "experimental" in the sense that further research is needed, it must likewise be recognized that no other approach for treating problem drinkers has received such consistent support from so many controlled and comparative outcome studies.

BIBLIOGRAPHY

Heather, N., & Robertson, I. (1983). *Controlled Drinking* (rev. ed.) London: Methuen.
Miller, W. R. (1983). Controlled drinking: A history and critical review. *Journal of Studies on Alcohol, 44*, 68–83.
Miller, W. R., & Hester, R. K. (1980). Treating the problem drinker: Modern approaches. In W. R. Miller (Ed.), *The addictive behaviors: Treatment of alcoholism, drug abuse, smoking, and obesity*. Oxford: Pergamon Press.
Miller, W. R., & Muñoz, R. F. (1982). *How to control your drinking* (rev. ed.). Albuquerque, NM: University of New Mexico Press.
Polich, J. M., Armor, D. J., & Braiker, H. B. (1981). *The course of alcoholism: Four years after treatment*. New York: Wiley.

See: Aversive Conditioning
       Community Reinforcement Approach
       Self-monitoring
       Self-reinforcement

CONTROLLED SMOKING
Russell E. Glasgow

Controlled smoking is an individualized multicomponent treatment approach to the modification of cigarette smoking behavior which focuses on making substantial reductions in several dimensions of smoking behavior, without requiring complete abstinence. Controlled smoking (CS) has been utilized to make sequential reductions in three aspects of participants' smoking behavior: substance (e.g., brand smoked), rate (e.g., number of cigarettes smoked), and topography (e.g., how the cigarette is smoked — inter-puff interval, depth or duration of inhalation, how much of each cigarette is smoked) in a sequential fashion.

CS should be distinguished from: (a) the goal of controlled or reduced smoking, which may be achieved via a number of approaches, and from (b) several related smoking reduction approaches. CS consists of the component techniques of self-monitoring, goal setting, instructions to sequentially modify different smoking behaviors, suggested strategies for achieving these reductions, and frequent feedback on one's progress. CS is distinguished from several other dosage reduction approaches such as nicotine fading and brand fading because it is more comprehensive (focusing on changes in multiple dimensions rather than a single target behavior.

CLINICAL APPLICATION

CS was developed in an effort to overcome several problems encountered with traditional approaches to smoking modification. For example, CS may appeal to many smokers who feel they are either unable or unwilling to quit completely, but are concerned about the health consequences of smoking. In addition, many recent quitters use the consumption of even a few cigarettes as justification for returning to baseline levels of smoking. Initial CS programs were characterized by daily meetings with subjects in a laboratory setting in which their smoking behavior was observed. Treatment included comprehensive assessment of smoking behavior, individualized goals based upon baseline smoking patterns, an emphasis on the regulation of smoking behavior as opposed to abstinence, and the development of both general skills for coping with stressful situations and specific skills for modifying different smoking behaviors. Feedback on carbon monoxide (CO) levels, including the CO "boost" resulting from smoking a single cigarette in a specified manner, was also an important feature of early CS programs. Evaluations of this CS package consisted of intra-subject multiple-baseline across behaviors designs that focused mainly on the modification of topographical variables such as puff frequency, puff duration, and cigarette duration. Number of cigarettes smoked was stabilized through the use of behavioral contracting.

More recently, this early work has been replicated and extended. This research has typically employed larger sample sizes, used weekly small group meeting formats for 5–7 treatment sessions, and combined intra-subject, multiple baseline across behaviors designs with between-subjects comparative treatment outcome designs. The work has focused on achieving 50% reductions in each of three target behaviors: nicotine con-tent of cigarette brand smoked, number of cigarettes smoked per day, and amount (percentage) of each cigarette smoked. Intervention consists of sequentially (a) providing subjects with lists containing the tar and nicotine content of different cigarette brands and having subjects choose 2–3 brands to try which contain approximately half the nicotine content of their current brand, (b) having subjects select one or more of the following strategies for reducing smoking rate — controlling accessibility (e.g., keeping cigarettes in a locked drawer), temporal control (e.g., limiting smoking to one cigarette per hour), and/or situational control (e.g., not smoking while watching TV); and (c) cueing adherence to the goal of smoking less of each cigarette by having subjects mark their cigarettes at the desired length.

This approach has been extended to smokers who want to quit, as well as to those who want to reduce but not quit completely, and to programs in worksite settings (rather than in clinics or laboratories). Additional research has also determined that such factors as weekly CO feedback, graphical feedback on daily nicotine consumption, and abrupt versus more gradual reduction goals do not improve the success of the basic CS program.

EXPECTED OUTCOMES AND TIME FRAME

The results of CS studies consistently show that subjects are successful in modifying their smoking patterns. Inspection of multiple-baseline figures reveals that subjects promptly achieve reductions in targeted behaviors following the introduction of treatment, and that these changes are fairly well-maintained. There is some relapse evident at 6-month to 2-year follow-ups, but follow-up smoking levels are still below baseline levels. The data suggest that the programs are more effective in reducing nicotine content (M reductions = 49–56% across four studies) than number of cigaretts smoked per day (M reductions = 28–30%) or percentage of the cigarette smoked (M reductions = 19–34%). All CS investigators assessing carbon monoxide levels have reported reductions in CO levels as a result of treatment. Some researchers have also reported that the smoking topography changes observed in the laboratory generalize to more naturalistic settings.

The long-term effects of CS on both smoking status and health risks are not known at this time. A small number of subjects (roughly 15–25%) quit smoking while undergoing CS treatment. Preliminary, but encouraging data suggest that subjects who become abstinent during CS are quite likely to maintain their abstinence.

DIFFERENTIAL DIAGNOSTIC CHARACTERISTICS

Although CS has been applied with a wide variety of smokers, there is no evidence that subject characteristics are associated with treatment outcome. CS has been successfully used with chronic, addicted smokers as well as with younger smokers having less firmly established habits. Unlike controlled drinking, variables such as chronicity, severity, and strength of addiction do not seem to be consistently associated with the success (or failure) of CS. Additional work is needed in this area.

POTENTIAL SIDE EFFECTS AND CONTRAINDICATIONS

Like controlled drinking, CS is a controversial treatment. Critics have variously claimed that subjects will not be able to make or maintain reductions in their smoking patterns; that if subjects are successful in making these changes, they will compensate by increasing their nicotine intake in other ways; and that CS approaches may deter subjects from participating in abstinence-based programs. The data on CS, however, do not support any of these claims. Controlled investigations of CS suggest that: (a) subjects are able to make and maintain reductions in targeted behaviors for at least 6 months (the longest time that a sizable number of CS subjects have been followed); (b) participants do not compensate for these behavior changes by increasing their smoking on nontargeted dimensions that have been assessed, and CO reductions are consistently observed following CS programs; and (c) some subjects are able to achieve abstinence using the CS approach.

What remain unanswered are questions concerning the long-term health significance of changes of the magnitude observed with CS and the relative effectiveness of CS versus abstinence based treatments. As Lichtenstein (1982) concluded in his review of behavioral approaches to smoking modification, "Abstinence remains the preferred goal, but the extension of CS to larger and more diverse populations seems warranted" (pg. 811).

BIBLIOGRAPHY

Frederiksen, L. W. (1979). Controlled smoking. In N. A. Krasnegor (Ed.), *Behavioral analysis and treatment of substance abuse* (NIDA Research Monograph 25, DHEW Publication No. ADM 79–839). Washington, DC: U.S. Government Printing Office.

Frederiksen, L. W., Peterson, G. L., & Murphy, W. D. (1976). Controlled smoking: Development and maintenance. *Addictive Behaviors, 1,* 193–196.

Frederiksen, L. W., & Simon, S. J. (1978). Modification of smoking topography: A preliminary analysis. *Behavior Therapy, 9,* 946–949.

Glasgow, R. E., Klesges, R. C., Godding, P. R., & Gegelman, R. (1983). Controlled smoking, with or without carbon monoxide feedback, as an alternative for chronic smokers. *Behavior Therapy, 14,* 386–397.

Glasgow, R. E., Klesges, R. C., Godding, P. R., Vasey, M. W., & O'Neill, H. K. (1984). Evaluation of a worksite controlled smoking program.

Journal of Consulting and Clinical Psychology, 52, 137–138.

Lichtenstein, E. (1982). The smoking problem: A behavioral perspective. *Journal of Consulting and Clinical Psychology, 50,* 804–819.

See: Biofeedback
Self-monitoring
Nicotine Fading
Rapid Smoking

CONVERSATIONAL SKILLS TRAINING
Steven Paul Schinke

Conversational skills include appropriate eye contact, smiles, gestures, voice volume, fluency, statements, questions, and compliments. Conversational skills training is primary or adjunctive therapy for depression, anxiety, shyness, social isolation, and relationship problems. In group and individual settings, conversational skills may be taught via instruction, modeling, reinforcement, rehearsal, and feedback. Improved conversational skills are generally seen in 1 to 5 training sessions. Training may heighten clients' self-reported anxiety. Training should not be implemented without supportive assessment data. Because conversational skills vary with race and ethnicity, caution is warranted in cross-cultural training.

See: Heterosocial Skills Training
Social Skills Training

COVERANT CONTROL
E. Thomas Dowd

Coverants, or covert operants, are private cognitive events, such as thoughts or mental images. Coverant control refers to the management of those cognitive phenomena through operant conditioning procedures. The basic strategy entails first rehearsing a negative coverant, then rehearsing a positive one, and finally engaging in a behavior of higher operant probability (i.e., the Premack Principle). The same principles and techniques used for the management of covert behavior are used in the management of coverants, and thus coverant control represents a direct transfer of behavioral technology to the control of cognitive events. Coverant control can be seen as a naive form of cognitive control in that it assumes that reinforcing events automatically strengthen cognitive phenomena. Subsequent research has shown this assumption to be untenable, and clinical outcome data have shown that this technique does not consistently produce positive results.

See: Cognitive Therapy
Covert Conditioning

COVERT AVERSION
Donald M. Prue

Covert aversion is one type of aversion therapy procedure which employs therapist- or client-generated images as the aversive stimuli. Covert aversion procedures parallel aversion and chemical aversion procedures and are related to assisted covert sensitization and covert sensitization.

Covert aversion procedures rely on imagined consequences and thus avoid the use of electrical shock or chemicals as aversive stimuli. This makes the procedures extremely safe relative to other aversion techniques. Covert aversion is employed in either a classical or operant conditioning framework, although most applications conceptualize procedures within the latter paradigm. A typical application of covert aversion would be to ask the client to imagine a target behavior such as a drinking scene, and then imagine an aversive consequence, such as vomiting. The objective of the procedure is to reduce future occurrences of the target behavior.

This covert aversion procedure has been employed to decrease a wide variety of maladaptive behaviors, but most research has investigated substance abuse (e.g., cigarette smoking, food intake) or inappropriate sexual arousal. Generally, the covert aversion procedures have been successful with sexual disorders, but less so with the appetite behaviors.

See: Assisted Covert Sensitization
Aversive Conditioning
Chemical Aversion
Covert Sensitization

COVERT CONDITIONING
Joseph R. Cautela

Covert conditioning is a theoretical model which, in addition to involving a set of assumptions, refers to a set of imagery-based procedures which alter response frequency by manipulation of consequences. The term *covert* is employed because the client is asked to *imagine* both the target behavior and the consequences. The term *conditioning* designates that the behavioral change is a conditioning process. While covert conditioning focuses on imagery, thoughts and feelings are also included as covert processes that can be manipulated by covert conditioning procedures (e.g., instructing a subject to say to him/herself, "I am not going crazy," and then instructing him/her to imagine a pleasant scene, or "You walk into the exam room and you feel relaxed and confident" [reinforcement]).

The covert conditioning procedures are: covert sensitization, covert reinforcement, covert extinction, covert negative reinforcement, covert response cost, covert modeling, and the self-control triad.

A BRIEF DESCRIPTION OF COVERT CONDITIONING PROCEDURES

Covert sensitization, covert extinction, covert response cost and the self-control triad are employed to decrease the frequency of undesirable behaviors. These procedures are administered as follows:

Covert Sensitization. The client is instructed to imagine performing the target behavior (e.g., injecting heroin, and then imagine an aversive consequence).

Covert Extinction. The client is instructed to imagine the target behavior (bragging), and then imagine that the reinforcer maintaining the behavior is not presented (no one pays attention to him/her).

Covert Response Cost. The client is instructed to imagine the target behavior and then imagine that he/she is deprived of a reinforcer (not the reinforcer that is maintaining the behavior).

The Self-control Triad. The client is instructed to yell "stop" (to himself), take a deep breath and exhale, and imagine a pleasant scene whenever the target behavior occurs.

Covert reinforcement and covert negative reinforcement are used to increase the frequency of desirable behavior.

Covert Reinforcement. The client is asked to imagine the target behavior (feeling comfortable and relaxed walking onto a plane), and then is asked to imagine a pleasant scene (listening to his/her favorite music).

Covert Negative Reinforcement. The client is asked to imagine an aversive stimulus (being screamed at by his boss), and then terminate the aversive scene and switch immediately to the response to be increased (making an assertive response).

Covert Modeling. Covert modeling can be used both to increase or decrease the target response. The client is instructed to imagine observing a model performing the target behavior, and then imagine either a reinforcing or aversive consequence, depending on whether the response is to be increased or decreased.

ASSUMPTIONS

Behavioral processes can be classified into three categories:

1. Overt behavior, (observable behavior).
2. Covert psychological responses, which include: (a) thinking, or talking to oneself; (b) imaging, or making responses similar to those that are made to particular external stimuli when these stimuli are not present; and (c) feeling, or reproducing sensations (bodily cues) which one learns (via the verbal community) to apply to certain inferred responses (e.g., pain).
3. Covert physiological responses of body systems, organs, cells of which one is unaware, or responses of which one is aware, but which are not observable to others.

The covert conditioning procedures are based on three main assumptions:

1. *Homogeneity.* There is a continuity or homogeneity between overt and covert behaviors. This assumption has variously been labeled the continuity assumption, or the assumption of functional equivalence. Since "continuity" implies different substantive categories of response, and "equivalence" implies a separateness or distinction between overt and covert behaviors, the term "homogeneity" is preferred so that empirically derived con-

clusions about overt phenomena can be transferred to covert phenomena.

Covert and overt processes share similar importance and similar properties in explaining, maintaining, and modifying behavior. However, covert conditioning does not make the assumption that covert responses correspond to the real world any more than do overt responses; that is, covert conditioning does not assume that our sense modalities register photocopies of the real world.

2. *Interaction.* There is an interaction between overt and covert events. That is, when an individual makes covert responses, whether at the prompting of another individual (e.g., a therapist) or other stimulus events, these responses can influence overt and covert behavior in a manner similar to overt behaviors. Similarly, overt events can influence covert behavior. This assumption does not, of course, deny that sometimes covert events occur concomitantly with overt events and that sometimes covert events involve more labeling of current overt events. Furthermore, when we conceptualize overt and covert behaviors or physiological and psychological behaviors as different levels of activity, it is only for convenience of analysis, since the terms "covert" or "psychological" actually refer to a particular set of physiological events. Therefore, when we speak of covert or psychological events influencing overt or physiological events, we are not referring to purely covert events influencing physiological events. Rather, we are talking about a particular class of physiological events influencing another class of physiological events. In other words, the covert conditioning assumptions are not positing the same laws as governing qualitatively different classes of events.

3. *Learning.* Covert and overt behaviors are

similarly governed by laws of learning, more specifically, operant conditioning. Moreover, overt and covert behaviors interact according to these same laws.

RATIONALE

Before the covert conditioning procedures are applied, the clients are given the following rationale:

> Your undesirable behaviors occur primarily because they are being maintained by the environment. The environment has many ways of influencing you. People in the environment may be rewarding, punishing, or ignoring you, and thereby maintaining a particular behavior. Your observation of what other people do and what happens to them also affects your behavior. These are just a few examples. By changing how the environment influences you, we can change your behavior. If you are rewarded for a desirable behavior, the desirable behavior will increase. If you are punished for an undesirable behavior, it will decrease. Studies indicate that if you imagine a reward after you imagine yourself performing the desirable behavior, then you will also experience an increase in the actual desirable behavior. I shall teach you techniques in which you imagine yourself or another person performing a particular behavior, and then you imagine the appropriate consequences. When you imagine your scene, it is important that you involve all your senses. If you are walking through the woods, imagine that you can feel the wind on your face, hear branches rubbing against one another, see the rays of sun filtering through the leaves, and smell the earth. Experience the movements in your body. The most critical part of your imagining is that you feel that you are actually experiencing the event rather than just seeing yourself.

GENERAL DESCRIPTION OF PROCEDURES

The client is then asked to imagine a scene in order to demonstrate his imagery ability. He is asked to raise his right index finger when the scene is clear. Inquiry is made concerning the scene's clarity and emotive capacities. If the client's imagery is deemed adequate, he is asked to imagine the scene by him/herself. If a client experiences difficulty in imagining in general, or in any sense modality in particular, appropriate imagery training is given.

The therapist then adds the behavior to be changed to the imagery sequence. If the client wishes to become more assertive, for example, the therapist describes a scene in which the client is asserting him/herself properly. He requests the client to signal when this experience is clear. He then instructs the client to reinforce him/herself with the previously practiced scene. At the end of the sequence and every forthcoming sequence, the therapist inquires as to the clarity and other characteristics of the sequence. The therapist then instructs the client to complete the entire sequence on his/her own. There are many possible themes and variations of the therapist-client imagining. The most commonly used sequence is a series of 20 alternating trials where the therapist describes a scene, and the client then imagines 10 scenes by him/herself. The covert conditioning scenes are usually audio taped and the client is asked to play them at least once (preferably twice) every day until the next session.

APPLICATIONS

When originally conceived, the covert conditioning procedures were applied mostly to an adult clientele in private practice or in outpatient settings. Currently the procedures are being extended to other populations, such as children, adolescents, and the elderly in a variety of situations, including residential institutions, schools, and hospitals.

The therapeutic intervention of various covert conditioning procedures, both individually and as a composite package, has been applied to cases of dental fear in children and sibling aggression. It has also been used to increase social interaction in the autistic, and to curb maladaptive behaviors, such as hand flapping and inappropriate hitting, in the retarded. Covert conditioning has been reported to reduce the urge to set fires in an adjudicated delinquent and has been applied to the modification of organic dysfunction, for example, epilepsy.

Adolescent problem behaviors such as poor study habits, test anxiety, obsessive sexually deviant thoughts, and inadequate social skills have all been treated.

Recently, the procedures were presented in an attempt to enhance physical rehabilitation in special needs children.

Covert conditioning procedures now are being applied in the field of behavioral medicine. Besides treatment of persistent cough, epilepsy, and asthma, covert conditioning has been employed in reducing pain associated with rheumatoid arthritis. It is assumed that if an individual can follow directions, is cooperative, has imagery ability, or can be trained in imagery, then covert conditioning can effect behavioral change.

IMAGERY PROBLEMS IN THE APPLICATION OF COVERT CONDITIONING

The problem that occasionally arises with the covert conditioning procedures, and also arises with other imagery-based procedures, concerns the client's ability to develop appropriate imagery. Appropriate imagery refers to sufficient clarity to perform the scenes and adequate controllability over imagery while practicing the scenes. In addition, the attitude of the client while he or she is engaging in the covert procedure is important.

When any of the imagery procedures are to be employed, an inquiry is made as to the extent of clarity and pleasantness or aversiveness of the scene. If covert positive

reinforcement is used, the client is asked to rate the scene on a 1-to-5 basis in terms of clarity, 1 representing "not at all clear" and 5 representing "very clear." When an aversive stimulus is presented, the client is asked to rate stimuli in terms of clarity and aversiveness. Reinforcing or aversive stimuli are only employed if the client reports either a 4 or 5 on clarity and pleasantness or unpleasantness.

It is important to emphasize that imagery should not be equated with visual imagery. Usually the client is able to obtain adequate imagery with the use of one or more sense modalities.

If a client has difficulty employing visual imagery, the therapist has a number of options. First, he may teach the client to use visual imagery more efficiently. The therapist may have the client practice looking at particular objects or scenes, closing his eyes, and attempting to reproduce the object or scene as accurately as possible in imagination. The client needs to continue this practice until he/she is able to reproduce the scene with clarity. For example, if a particular stimulus is involved, such as boats, the client may go to a marina for practice or pictures of ships may be employed in the same manner. A second method for increasing visual imagery ability is to have the client practice looking at various objects in the office, and then have him describe them to the therapist with his eyes shut. As homework, he may be asked to carefully note the visual details of any new situation encountered, such as visiting another person's home for the first time or seeing a beautiful sunset.

COVERT CONDITIONING AS A SELF-CONTROL PROCEDURE

One of the goals of treatment for any client is to teach procedures that can be used after therapy has been terminated, even though treatment has been successful. Before clients leave treatment, the rationale of covert conditioning should be explained to them, and they should be taught how to use covert conditioning as a self-control procedure.

Clients should be instructed to scan their behaviors as they occur in different situations throughout the day. If they find that they have made inappropriate responses, then at some time before going to sleep at night they are to imagine that they are making the desirable, correct responses, using one or more covert conditioning procedures. For example, if a patient determines that he/she should have been more assertive to his/her roommate, then he/she can imagine that the situation is occurring again, but this time he/she makes the appropriate assertive response, feels comfortable, and then imagines a pleasant scene (covert reinforcement).

If clients deliberately did not take their medicine during the day, they are to imagine observing someone else not taking prescribed medicine and then immediately becoming ill (covert modeling). Also, they can imagine that when significant others discover that they are not taking prescribed medication, the others ignore the matter completely (covert extinction). Again, in dealing with the same response, clients can imagine that they are about to throw medications down the drain, but decide not to, feel very good about this, and then imagine pleasant scenes (covert reinforcement). Covert sensitization can also be used by having clients imagine that medication has been omitted for some time and that this has been followed by serious illness. Another covert conditioning procedure that can be used to decrease maladaptive behaviors is covert response cost. The client is instructed to imagine the response to be reduced, (e.g., refusing medication) and then imagine that a reinforcer is removed (finding one's wallet is missing). On an a priori basis, one would expect that clients such as the elderly, who experience many losses, would find that this procedure would only reinforce their feelings of loss or abandonment. However, empirically it appears that they not only feel less alone and less helpless, but also recognize that they have a procedure that they can use to control their behaviors.

Clients can use one or more covert conditioning procedures to modify almost any inappropriate response that occurs during the day. They should repeat each procedure until the desired effect is achieved. The use of covert conditioning in this manner on a day-to-day basis can gradually result in elimination of inappropriate behavior or can prevent behavior from occurring at such a high rate that it becomes inappropriate.

Clients can be told that they now have procedures that can be used to modify any response if they apply them diligently and appropriately. If they empirically demonstrate this for themselves, they develop strong feelings of coping ability and competence. Clients should practice daily use of covert conditioning as a means of self-control before therapy is terminated. Also, they should be told that if they ever need re-education concerning any procedures at any time in their lives, they should feel free to contact the therapist for an appointment.

COVERT CONDITIONING VARIABLES THAT INFLUENCE APPLICABILITY

There are some populations for which covert conditioning is difficult or possibly not applicable because of inability to follow directions. These populations include special needs individuals, very young children, and individuals with severe behavior disorders. While covert conditioning is difficult with the above populations, it is not impossible to apply it successfully with *some* members of these populations. Covert conditioning has been attempted with some success with some members of the above groups. Special training is needed in following directions, teaching parts of the procedures, and then chaining responses. It is probably wise not to exclude any population on an a priori basis from the possible benefits of covert conditioning.

Another important factor concerning the applicability of covert conditioning is to achieve cooperation. Presentation of the rationale and examples of treatment are particularly important in this regard. Cooperation is necessary not only in the therapeutic session but also in practicing the procedures at home and using scenes in vivo.

Covert conditioning can be difficult to apply if the tension level is high or there are interfering images. Relaxation training has been useful in both situations.

BIBLIOGRAPHY

Cautela, J. R., (1973). Covert processes and behavior modification. *Journal of Nervous and Mental Disease, 157,* 27–36.

Cautela, J. R. (1977). Covert conditioning: Assumptions and procedures. *Journal of Mental Imagery, 1,* 53–64.

Cautela, J. R., & Baron, M. G. (1977). Covert conditioning: A theoretical analysis. *Behavior Modification, 1,* 351–368.

Cautela, J. R., & Bennett, A. K. (1981). Covert conditioning. In R. Corsini (Ed.), *Handbook of innovative psychotherapies.* New York: Wiley.

Cautela, J. R., & McCullough, L. (1978). Covert conditioning: A learning theory perspective on imagery. In J. L. Singer & K. S. Pope (Eds.), *The power of human imagination.* New York: Plenum Press.

Kazdin, A. E. (1977). Research issues in covert conditioning. *Cognitive Therapy and Research, 1,* 45–58.

Upper, D., & Cautela, J. R. (1977). *Covert conditioning.* New York: Pergamon Press.

See: Covert Sensitization

COVERT EXTINCTION
Joseph R. Cautela

Covert extinction is a covert conditioning procedure employed to decrease the probability of target behaviors. In covert extinction the client imagines the behavior to be reduced in frequency and then imagines that the reinforcement that usually overtly follows this behavior *does not* occur (e.g., if the target behavior is complaining to his/her spouse, then there is no response by the spouse: either attention or sympathy).

The therapist should be aware that during the extinction procedure two possible side effects can occur:

1. There can be a temporary increase in the target behavior when the extinction procedure is first employed (extinction burst).
2. Aggression toward the therapist or agent perceived as not delivering the reinforcement sometimes occurs (extinction-produced aggression).

See: Covert Reinforcement
      Covert Sensitization

COVERT MODELING
Joseph R. Cautela

Covert modeling is a covert conditioning procedure that is analogous to overt modeling. Modeling, or observational learning, refers to the learning that occurs from the observation of others. In modeling, the individual whose behavior is observed and is the center of focus is designated as the model. Live modeling involves direct observation of a live model. Symbolic modeling refers to the observation of a model who is presented indirectly through film, audio tape, or through the printed word. Covert modeling is a logical extension of symbolic modeling. Covert modeling has the creative advantage of tailoring a scene for each individual client. Also, there is more economy of time and money in employing covert modeling. Covert modeling can also be taught as a self-control procedure. In employing covert modeling, the client is asked to imagine observing a model and particular consequences.

ASSUMPTIONS

Covert modeling assumptions include:

1. Overt modeling is operant behavior taught to children (when they imitate and are reinforced) and this modeling behavior is maintained throughout life by intermittent reinforcement.
2. The parameters that influence overt modeling also influence covert modeling in a similar manner.

RATIONALE PRESENTED TO THE CLIENT

"The procedure we are going to use is based on a number of experiments in which people learn new habits by observing other people in various situations. The way this is usually done is that people actually observe others doing things. What I am going to do is vary this procedure somewhat, by having you observe certain scenes in imagination rather than having you directly observe a movie or actual interaction among people. I am going to use scenes that I think will help you change the behavior we agreed needs changing. In a minute, I'll ask you to close your eyes, and try to imagine, as clearly as possible, that you are observing a certain situation. Try to use all the senses needed for the particular situation (e.g., try to actually hear a voice or see a person very clearly). After I describe the scene, I will ask you some questions concerning your feelings about the scene and how clearly you imagined it."

DESCRIPTION OF PROCEDURE

After the presentation of the rationale the client is told: "Now sit back and relax. Close your eyes. I am going to describe a scene or situation to you. I want you to pay attention to my voice and try to imagine exactly what I tell you. Try not to think of anything else except what I tell you. Do you understand?" After the covert modeling scene is presented to the client, he/she is asked to describe the nature of his/her imagery. The nature of the imagery includes clarity of imagery, the type and degree of affect, and the extent to which the client imagines the scene as presented by the therapist. The following are some examples of scenes:

EXAMPLES OF COVERT MODELING

Covert modeling has been found to be useful in modifying both approach and avoidance behavior, especially with children. This technique can be used with all age groups and can be modified according to intellectual and verbal development.

Below is an example of three covert modeling scenes employed to decrease the very frequent and aversive whining-voice behavior of a 6-year-old girl who will be referred to as Linda. After several shaping sessions, Linda was able to close her eyes, relax, and imagine the scenes as directed by the therapist. The following is an example:

Linda, I would like you to imagine you are sitting in a movie theater watching the big screen in front of you. On that screen you see a young girl about 6-years-old. She has blond hair and blue eyes and a very pretty smile. Her name is Minda. (This description closely resembles the client. The particular ficticious name avoids any possible association between the client and someone with a valid, similar name, such as Belinda.) Minda is walking into her livingroom, and she sees that her mother and sister are talking. In her hand, Minda is carrying one of her dolls. As she approaches her Mom, Minda says in a very whiney voice, "Mom, my doll is broken, and I don't know how to fix her." But her mother and sister ignore her completely. They act as though Minda never even spoke, and they continue talking, so the little girl says again in a squeaky voice, "My doll is broken, Mom. Help me fix her!" Again Minda is ignored. So, she decides to try to fix the doll by herself, and she leaves the room. But as she leaves, she hears her mother and sister say something. Her Mom says, "You know, I wish Minda wouldn't whine that way. It sounds so awful! She has such a pretty voice when she isn't whining. I wish she would stop that terrible whining." Minda's sister agrees with the mother, "I know what you mean, Mom," the sister says, "She does have a nice voice when she doesn't whine. I wish she'd stop, too." Minda hears this conversation and gets very sad. She doesn't like to be ignored, and she doesn't like to hear her mother and sister talk as though they are disappointed in her (first scene). She decides to try again at getting some help to fix her broken doll, but this time she is going to ask them without whining. Minda walks back into the livingroom and up to her mother who is now reading the newspaper. Minda thinks to herself, "I'm not going to whine; I'm going to speak in a regular voice." Now out loud, she says, "Excuse me, Mom, are you busy?" Her mother says, "Not really Minda, what is it?" Minda says, "My doll is broken, see?" and she shows her mother the doll. "Do you think you can fix her?" Minda asks, without whining. Minda's mother says to her sister, "Hmmm, Minda asked so nicely! She didn't whine or cry at all!" Then her mom says, "Well, let me try." Before long, Minda's mother has fixed the broken doll and returned it to the little girl. "Oh thank you so much!" says the girl as she hugs her mother. "She's all better now." says Minda. Her sister smiles (second scene). Minda takes the doll and leaves the livingroom to play with the doll in her bedroom. But as she leaves, she hears her mother say, "Wow! Did you hear how nicely Minda spoke? She didn't whine at all that time!" The sister says, "Isn't that great. I'm so glad she's trying not to whine anymore." The mother and sister are very proud of Minda. Minda is proud of herself and she feels very very happy. She decides to try not to whine but instead to talk in her very nice regular voice (third scene).

A male cross-dresser was given the following scene:

You are standing behind a one-way mirror. You see a bare room except for two single beds with clothes on them. One bed has male clothes on it and the other has female clothes on it. Straight ahead at the other end of the room, you see a door open and a naked man about your age walks into the room. He walks toward the beds which are next to each other about four feet apart. He starts to go toward the bed with the female clothes on it. He looks at the clothes; suddenly you can see a painful expression on his face. He sits down on the bed. Now he starts to sweat and looks sick. He reaches for a bra and he starts to gag. As he puts the bra on he starts to vomit all over the clothes and on himself. He groans in agony as he doubles over and falls down to the ground. He is lying with the bra on and wallowing in vomit.

A covert modeling scene can then be given in which he puts on the male clothes and looks happy.

DESCRIPTION OF PROCEDURE

The time between scenes may vary from 1 minute to 5 minutes. In some cases (with special populations) only one scene per session is given.

After the scene is presented the client is asked to describe the scene and comment on the clarity and the type and degree of affect achieved. When it appears that the client knows the scene well, he/she is asked to imagine the scenes without description by the therapist. Sometimes the client is asked to verbalize the scene while he/she is imagining it. The scenes used during each session are usually taped and the client is asked to play the scenes two times a day until the next therapeutic session.

CLIENT CHARACTERISTICS

Originally, covert modeling was designed for clients who could not imagine themselves in a particular situation and therefore desensitization or covert positive reinforcement was not applicable. Now it is used with clients even if they can readily experience themselves in a particular situation. Covert modeling is particularly suited for some clients who have so much anxiety when they imagine themselves in particular situations that they are not able to cooperate. If covert positive reinforcement or desensitization is appropriate with these clients, they can be shaped into experiencing themselves in a particular situation by covert modeling. First they can imagine observing a model like themselves. When they can observe the modeling situation with a minimum of anxiety, they are asked to imagine themselves as the model. After this sequence, they are more apt to imagine themselves in covert positive reinforcement or desensitization scenes since the anxiety has been reduced somewhat.

RELATIVE PARAMETERS

As stated above, it is assumed that similar variable characteristics influence covert modeling and overt modeling. As in overt modeling, covert modeling is apt to be more effective if the model is the same age and sex as the observer. Multiple models are more apt to increase generalization effects. Cop-

ing models produce more behavior change than mastery models.

COVERT MODELING WITH CHILDREN

Covert modeling appears particularly suited for children. Children constantly require new learning for adaptation, and the covert modeling scenes can help provide information (e.g., how to be tactfully assertive to peers). Children have a great familiarity with symbolic modeling through TV and movies. Also, children are more apt to cooperate if they don't see themselves as the wrong-doers. Covert modeling appears to be the covert conditioning procedure of choice in modifying children's behavior.

COVERT MODELING AS SELF-CONTROL

As with any other covert conditioning procedure, covert modeling can be taught as a self-control technique. Before discharge, the client is taught how to construct the scenes to produce the desired behavior change. The client practices the construction of covert modeling scenes concerning possible maladaptive behaviors that can occur in the future.

Covert modeling is more flexible to use than other covert conditioning procedures. Both maladaptive approach and avoidance behaviors can be treated by covert modeling. If the target behavior is to be increased in frequency, then the client imagines positive consequences occurring when a model performs the behavior. If the behavior is to be decreased in frequency, then the client imagines aversive consequences occurring when a model performs the behavior.

BIBLIOGRAPHY

Cautela, J. R., Flannery, R., & Hanley, E. (1974). Covert modeling: An experimental test. *Behavior Therapy, 5*, 494–502.

Kazdin, A. E. (1975). Covert modeling, imagery assessment, and assertive behavior. *Journal of Consulting and Clinical Psychology, 43*, 716–724.

Kazdin, A. E. (1976). Effects of covert modeling, multiple models, and model reinforcement on assertive behavior. *Behavior Therapy, 7*, 211–222.

Kazdin, A. E. (1978). Covert modeling: The therapeutic application of imagined rehearsal. In J. L. Singer & K. S. Pope (Eds.), *The power of the human imagination.* New York: Plenum Press.

Rosenthal, T. L., & Reese, S. L. (1976). The effects of covert and overt modeling on assertive behavior. *Behaviour Research and Therapy, 14*, 463–469.

See: Covert Rehearsal

COVERT POSITIVE REINFORCEMENT
Joseph R. Cautela

Covert positive reinforcement is a covert conditioning procedure which is used to increase the probability of covert or overt behavior. The client is asked to imagine the target behavior, then asked to imagine a pleasant or reinforcing scene, e.g., if the target behavior is initiating conversation, then he/she is asked to perform the target behavior while feeling comfortable and confident, and then asked to imagine a pleasant (reinforcing) scene. Often a sequence of scenes is presented involving the target behavior, e.g., walking into a room full of people and feeling comfortable (reinforcement), walking over to a group of people to talk to them and feeling comfortable (reinforcement), or introducing oneself and feeling confident (reinforcement).

See: Covert Conditioning

COVERT REHEARSAL
Alan S. Bellack

Covert rehearsal is a treatment procedure in which new behaviors are "practiced" in imagination before being carried out in vivo. The therapist directs the client to first imagine a situation in which the target response might occur. The client then visualizes himself/herself performing the target response effectively and receiving reinforcement. Covert rehearsal has been used most frequently in social skills training. For example, a shy male might imagine himself approaching an attractive female, initiating a conversation, and asking for a date. An unassertive woman might imagine herself asserting her desires to her husband. These imaginary trials would be repeated several times, and followed by trials of different imaginary events, in a manner analogous to live role playing in standard social skills training. Ordinarily, the client receives instructions and modeling of appropriate behavior before covert trials begin, but this is not necessary with mild problems (e.g., the client already knows how to perform the response). Covert rehearsal can be used as an intermediary step whenever in-session training must be translated to in vivo performance.

See: Assertiveness Training
    Heterosocial Skills Training
    Rehearsal
    Social Skills Training

COVERT REINFORCER SAMPLING
Patricia Wisocki

Covert reinforcer sampling is an extension of the reinforcer sampling technique originally utilized by Ayllon and Azrin in 1968 to increase the use of various facilities, services, and products among chronic institutionalized patients by directly exposing the patients to the activity or product concerned. Reinforcer sampling via instructions to imagine participation in an event or consumption of an item has shown promise as a clinical procedure with limited empirical support. It may also be regarded as one of the components of other imagery-based techniques.

The procedure is especially useful with clients whose treatment programs call for increasing the range and/or intensity of pleasurable activities in daily living. Typically, clients who are depressed, socially withdrawn, grieving, apathetic, or simply inactive physically might find CRS helpful therapeutically. The procedure involves the following steps: (1) the selection of activities which are of at least moderate interest to the client; (2) instructions to the client to engage in detailed imagery about the target activity without any contingencies (For example, to increase the activity of playing tennis, a client would be asked to imagine him/herself on the tennis court, in a white outfit, in an appropriate stance, lifting the racket, seeing one's opponent serve the ball, hearing the ball hit the racket, feeling the strain of returning the serve, and so forth); (3) instructions to practice the selected scenes about 20–30 times per day, while the client is relaxed, generating as much vivid imagery and positive feelings as possible; and (4) encouragement to actually engage in the activity. No stimulus events or consequents are suggested.

See: Covert Conditioning
     Covert Positive Reinforcement

COVERT SENSITIZATION
Joseph R. Cautela

Covert sensitization is a covert conditioning procedure that is analogous to the operant procedure of punishment. If a response is followed by a stimulus and the possibility of the response's occurrence is decreased, then punishment is said to have occurred. The term covert is used because both the behavior to be reduced in frequency and the consequence are imagined by the individual. Sensitization designates that the individual is to be sensitized or taught to avoid a maladaptive approach response such as drinking alcohol, rape, overeating, or stealing.

DESCRIPTION OF PROCEDURE

When employing the covert sensitization procedure, the client is asked to close his/her eyes and imagine that he/she is about to perform or is performing the target responses to be weakened, and then he/she is told to imagine an aversive stimulus (e.g., getting nauseous, vomiting, or seeing insects). Some typical scenes are:

Alcoholism. "You are walking into a bar. You decide to have a glass of beer. You are now walking toward the bar. As you are approaching the bar, you have a funny feeling in the pit of your stomach. Your stomach feels all queasy and nauseous. Some liquid comes up into your throat and it is very sour. You try to swallow it back down, but as you do this, food particles start coming up your throat into your mouth. You are now reaching the bar and you order a beer. As the bartender is pouring the beer, puke comes up into your mouth. You try to keep your mouth closed and swallow it back down. As soon as your hand touches the glass, you can't hold it down any longer.

You have to open your mouth and you puke. It goes all over your hand, all over the glass and the beer. You can see it floating around in the beer. Snot and mucous come out of your nose. Your shirt and pants are all full of vomit. The bartender has some on his shirt. You notice people looking at you. You get sick again and you vomit some more. You turn away from the beer and immediately you start to feel better. As you run out of the bar room, you start to feel better and better. When you get out into the clean, fresh air, you feel wonderful. You go home and clean yourself up."

Stealing. "You are walking down a street. You notice a really sharp sports car. You walk toward it with the idea of stealing it. As you're walking toward it, you start to get a funny feeling in your stomach. You feel sick to your stomach and you have a slight pain in your gut. As you keep walking, you really start to feel sick, and food starts coming up into your mouth. You're just about to reach for the handle of the door and you can't hold it any longer. You vomit all over your hand, the car door, the upholstery inside, all over your clothes. The smell starts to get to you and you keep puking from it. It's all over the place. It's dripping from your mouth. You turn around and run away and then you start to feel better."

Exhibitionism. "You feel kind of tense and bored at home. You decide that you want to get in your pickup truck and cruise around. You want to find some young girls walking with no one else around. As soon as you make the decision to expose yourself to them you start to feel faint and very weak. You start to sweat and you feel awful. As you go out to your truck you start to feel sick to your stomach. You are starting to feel cramps and you feel very sick but you are determined to get in the truck. As soon as you get into the truck vomit comes into your mouth, but you are determined to expose yourself no matter how lousy you feel. As you drive along you see two young teenagers under a street light. You drive your truck over to them. Now you are so sick you think you are going to faint. You stop your truck and pull down your pants and open the door. As soon as you open the door, you get violently ill. You start to vomit all over yourself, including your pants and penis. Snot is coming out of your nose. Your vomit stinks and looks awful; it is green and yellow. You feel sticky and slimy all over your body. You slump over the seat. The next thing you know the police have you handcuffed."

As can be observed from the above example, the aversion starts at the beginning of the response chain and continues until the response is about to be performed or is performed. This procedure has the advantage of making all the maladaptive approach responses aversive conditioned stimuli.

A Case of Compulsive Folding. "You're in the laundry room. There's a pile of clothes in front of you. You take one thing . . . it's a towel and you fold it and put it aside. You think it's not quite wrinkle-free and you decide to re-fold it. As soon as you have that thought, you get a queasy feeling in the pit of your stomach. Vomit comes up into your mouth. It tastes bitter and you swallow it back down. Your throat burns, but you take the towel and start to refold it anyway. Just as you do that, your stomach churns and vomit comes out of your mouth, all over the clean clothes, your hands, the table, over everything. You keep vomiting and vomiting. Your eyes are watering. Your nose has snot and mucous coming out of it. You see vomit over everything. You think that you should never have tried to fold that towel a second time. A few wrinkles make no difference, and you run from the room. Immediately you feel better. You go and clean yourself up and smell fresh and clean and feel wonderful."

After the scene is described, the client is asked to indicate the clarity of imagery and the degree of aversiveness of the noxious stimulus imagined. The procedure is practiced or modified until the client reports high clarity of imagery and rates the consequences as highly aversive. The client is then asked to imagine the covert sensitization scene by himself (i.e., without the description being given by the therapist). Typically, there are 20 scenes in each therapy session, 10 scenes described by the therapist and 10 scenes imagined without description. The 10 covert sensitization scenes are different ones involving possible situations in which the maladaptive approach behavior is likely to occur. The covert sensitization scenes are usually taped and the client is instructed to listen to the tapes twice a day. The client is also instructed to practice covert sensitization in vivo. He/she is told to imagine that if a stimulus (such as a glass of bourbon) produces an urge, he/she is to immediately imagine that the stimulus (bourbon) is covered by vomit, or another noxious stimulus such as bugs or fecal matter. Finally, the client is asked to perform covert sensitization in the evenings concerning situations during the day where he/she had a strong urge, or performed the maladaptive responses. If the client smoked after a cup of coffee in the morning, then he/she is to do three covert sensitization scenes involving being about to smoke after drinking a cup of coffee in the morning, and then getting sick or vomiting as the cigarette is being put into his/her mouth.

It is important to establish face validity for the procedure by describing the rationale to the client (which includes why the procedure is likely to work). The client is told: "Of course, the reason you smoke (drink, overeat, exhibit yourself, etc.) is because you enjoy it or it is somehow rewarding. It is a bad habit that has been rewarded over a long period of time. What we have to do is to make smoking disgusting or not pleasurable. One way to do this is to try to imagine oneself being punished for smoking so that smoking will lose its rewarding qualities. We have found that by just imagining you are about to smoke or have started smoking and then imagining some disgusting or fearful stimulus, you will gradually lose the urge to smoke and therefore stop smoking. It is important to remember that the more you are imagining that you are smoking and enjoying it, the stronger the habit will become." It is important to emphasize that covert sensitization should be employed until all strong urges are eliminated, even beyond the time when the behavior is reduced to "0" frequency (overlearning), otherwise the smoking behavior is apt to reoccur at its original strength.

Covert sensitization is usually combined with covert reinforcement for more effective treatment. Covert reinforcement, in this case, involves having the client imagine that he/she has refused to make the maladaptive response and then imagine a pleasant scene (i.e., punishment combined with reinforcement of an incompatible response is more effective than just punishment alone).

CAUTIONS

It is important to employ covert sensitization on the *urge* to perform the maladaptive response and not just the consummation of the undesirable stimulus or the undesirable stimulus itself. This prevents the likelihood of inappropriate generalization, e.g., feeling sick when someone else is smoking, or seeing a young child (as for pedophiliacs).

As with any aversive procedure, other covert conditioning techniques such as covert modeling and covert reinforcement should be employed as the treatment of choice, if possible. Covert sensitization is especially indicated if the behavior is very strong and further performance of the response can be quite dangerous (e.g., self-injurious behavior, rape, or alcoholic drinking that can result in job loss or family breakdown).

It is usually not effective to employ covert sensitization with children, since the aversive nature could lead to the avoidance of therapy sessions and lack of cooperation. Also, it is more difficult to control the aversive characteristics of the scene with children. Some children have a tendency to incorrectly report the clarity and intensity of the scenes. Other covert conditioning procedures, such as covert modeling, can produce cooperation and more effective results with children.

POSSIBLE SIDE EFFECTS

Since covert sensitization is an aversive procedure, one of the possible side effects is resentment or aggression. Even though clients voluntarily come for treatment, and understand the covert sensitization procedure, they sometimes indicate resentment, since they perceive the therapist as someone who is taking something away from them (extinction-produced aggression). Also, receiving aversive stimulation sometimes results in aggressive behavior. The hostility can be attenuated somewhat by the learning theory explanation of the resentment.

There is more apt to be a lack of cooperation when the client is being treated for maladaptive approach behaviors as compared to the treatment of maladaptive avoidance behaviors. Therefore, it is often a necessary therapeutic strategy to try to increase the client's reinforcing activities before starting covert sensitization procedures that will result in a loss of reinforcement.

VARIANTS OF COVERT SENSITIZATION

Some therapists have employed assisted covert sensitization. When employing this procedure, the client imagines the target behavior and then an overt aversive stimulus is presented (e.g., electric shock to the forearm or a strong odorous substance). Assisted covert sensitization appears particularly helpful in treating exhibitionism.

Another variant is to instruct the client to imagine an aversive scene immediately upon being confronted with an external stimulus that usually starts the chain of imagining performing the undesirable behavior and overtly fulfilling it.

ADVANTAGES OF COVERT SENSITIZATION

1. It has now become axiomatic, in behavior therapy, to use the least-aversive procedure necessary to modify behavior. Covert sensitization is a less-aversive procedure than many externally applied aversive stimuli, such as painful electric shock and chemical aversion.
2. While it can be argued that, trial for trial, covert sensitization may not be as effective as external aversive stimuli, more covert sensitization trials can usually be applied.
3. Covert sensitization can be more readily used as a self-control procedure than external punishment. During treatment the clients learn to make their own scenes. They are also taught how to do a behavioral analysis and tailor the scenes for their particular problem. They then can apply covert sensitization to themselves if they need a booster after discharge or if other maladaptive approach behavior occurs.

4. No equipment is necessary.
5. This therapeutic technique can be effective to insure generalization. The covert sensitization scenes can be tailored to many different situations.
6. The procedure can make aversive the chain of responses leading to the undesirable behavior.

BIBLIOGRAPHY

Barlow, D. H., Leitenberg, H., & Agras, W. S. (1969). Experimental control of sexual deviation through manipulation of the noxious scene in covert sensitization. *Journal of Abnormal Psychology, 74*, 597–601.
Brownell, K. D., Hayes, S. C., & Barlow, D. H. (1977). Patterns of appropriate and deviant sexual deviation. *Journal of Consulting and Clinical Psychology, 45*, 1114–1115.
Cautela, J. R. (1967). Covert sensitization. *Psychological Record, 20*, 459–468.
Hughs, R. C. (1977). Covert sensitization treatment of exhibitionism. *Journal of Behavior Therapy and Experimental Psychiatry, 8*, 177–179.
Little, L. M., & Curran, J. P. (1978). Covert sensitization: clinical procedure in need of some explanations. *Psychological Bulletin, 85*, 513–531.

See: Assisted Covert Sensitization
Aversive Conditioning
Covert Conditioning

CUE-CONTROLLED RELAXATION
F. Dudley McGlynn

Cue-controlled relaxation is an anxiety management skill training package in which the goal is that of teaching patients to control mild anxiousness by relaxing in response to a privately self-produced signal.

Typically, cue-controlled relaxation training occurs in six or so two-part sessions, each of which is basically the same. During the initial phase of each session, 20–30 minutes are devoted to relaxation training per se. This is usually done with a 16 muscle-group "progressive" relaxation sequence but other relaxation methods have been used.

During the second phase of each session, cue-association training is carried out. Without any break in the procedure, the now relaxed patient is instructed to pair repeatedly his/her relaxed muscular state with a self-produced private cue word such as "calm" or "control." Cue-association training is begun by instructing the patient to focus his/her attention on the slow regular breathing that comes with relaxation. Soon, the patient is instructed to privately rehearse the word "calm" (or a similar word) with each upcoming exhalation. The therapist then audibly utters the word "calm" for five or so exhalations, says "continue," and sits quietly as the patient exhales 15 more times. After the first series of 20 cue-relaxation pairings the patient is instructed to "discontinue" and to focus attention on being relaxed. A one-minute pause ensues, then a second series of 20 pairings is undertaken. During the second series also, the therapist vocalizes the cue word in synchrony with the patient's first five or so exhalations. After the first session, the patient is instructed to practice relaxation and cue association for 30 minutes or so each evening. After the third or fourth session, the patient is encouraged to rehearse self-cued relaxation in response to mild anxiousness. On subsequent sessions the patient is interviewed supportively about success and/or failure during these rehearsals. After the final treatment session, the patient is instructed to use self-cued relaxation at the first sign of tension or anxiousness.

More than a dozen case study reports have described globally successful applications of cue-controlled relaxation. Numerous reports of single and multiple group experiments have done so as well. Ordinarily, treatments have taken 5 to 7 weeks and treatment effects have been observed toward the end of the planned sessions.

Case studies have reported successful application of cue-controlled relaxation to problems such as peripherally cued anxiety, nonspecific anxiety, migraine headache, nervous habits, and seizures. Systematic therapy outcome research with cue-controlled relaxation has shown successful application to college student problems such as test anxiety and heterosocial shyness. Generalization of treatment effects has not been documented satisfactorily. Further, there are reasons to believe that only mild anxiousness has been represented in the more systematic therapy outcome studies, and that much of the observed clinical and experimental success of cue-controlled relaxation derives from demand/placebo factors.

Clinicians are justified in using cue-controlled relaxation with mild anxiety problems and with fears involving negative social evaluation. Particular clinical circumstances might also provide justification for using the technique with conditions such as migraine headache and "nervous habits" where good case study reports exist. As a sole or primary approach, cue-controlled relaxation is not recommended for agoraphobia, for strong simple phobias, or for extreme social phobia.

Cue-controlled relaxation is a very conservative skill training approach that presents no side effects and has no contraindications except for those few associated with muscular relaxation per se. Among factors that occasionally are problematic in relaxation are specific physical disabilities, muscle cramps, spasms, tics, intrusive cognitions, unusual bodily sensations, and feeling of impending loss of control. Adequate orientation to relaxation training will forestall most of these potential problems. Care can be taken also to tailor relaxation around existing physical disabilities.

BIBLIOGRAPHY

Cautela, J. (1966). A behavior therapy approach to pervasive anxiety. *Behaviour Research and Therapy, 4*, 99–111.

Grimm, L. G. (1980). The evidence for cue-controlled relaxation. *Behavior Therapy, 11*, 282–293.

Marchetti, A., McGlynn, F. D., & Patterson, A. S. (1977). Effects of cue-controlled relaxation, a placebo treatment, and no treatment on self-reported and psychophysiological indices of test anxiety among college students. *Behavior Modification, 1*, 47–72.

McGlynn, F. D., Bichajian, C., Giesen, J. M., & Rose, R. L. (1981). Effects of cue-controlled relaxation, a credible placebo treatment, and no treatment on shyness among college males. *Journal of Behavior Therapy and Experimental Psychiatry, 12*, 299–306.

Wells, K. D., Turner, S. M., Bellack, A. S., & Hersen, M. (1978). Effects of cue-controlled relaxation on psychomotor seizures: An experimental analysis. *Behaviour Research and Therapy, 16*, 51–53

See: Deep Muscle Relaxation

CUEING
Joel Hundert

Cueing is the presentation of a stimulus to signal the occurrence of a particular behavior. Through pairing the cue with contingent reinforcement, the individual learns to associate the presentation of the stimulus with the target behavior. Cueing can be used to signal when a particular behavior should occur (e.g., verbal instruction to a parent to use time-out with a child) or when a particular behavior should cease (e.g., raising an open hand to signal a child to stop interrupting). The cue given may take different forms (e.g., verbal comments, a buzzer, visual stimuli) according to the needs of the situation.

See: Stimulus Control

DEEP MUSCLE RELAXATION
Joseph Wolpe

Deep muscle relaxation is the activity of undoing the tonic contraction of muscle fibers. Successful relaxation has autonomic consequences: parasympathetic responses are enhanced and sympathetic responses attenuated, heart rate slows, blood pressure falls, breathing becomes slower and more regular, palmar resistance (GSR) rises. In step with these changes, an anxious person feels less anxious.

MODES OF RELAXATION TRAINING

Progressive Relaxation. This is the procedure originally introduced by Jacobson (1938). Instruction begins by drawing the attention of the subject to the sensations produced by minimal contraction of small groups of muscles. He is then directed to release the contraction progressively — "to go further and further in the negative direction." Each muscle group receives individual attention. Training by Jacobson characteristically took 50 to 200 sessions, with daily homework practice of an hour or more. He (1964, p. 29) later described an abridged regime called "self-operations control" that compressed instruction into 20 1-hour sessions.

Jacobson was well aware that it was insufficient to confine relaxation to practice periods, and that to be of therapeutic value the reduction of emotional tension had to be extended into the subject's daily life. He made this possible by teaching subjects to develop the habit of constantly relaxing muscles not in use, which he called *differential relaxation*. A marked degree of emotional calmness can, with practice, be achieved if a person relaxes muscles that he is not actively using. For example, he may relax the muscles of his arms and legs while talking, or some of his facial muscles while driving a car.

Very substantial benefit frequently results from Jacobson's method. Out of 23 cases with anxiety problems (1938, pp. 417–419), 21 were "markedly" or "very markedly" improved. Jacobson did not, however, ob-

serve that two different kinds of changes were achieved in his cases. In some, lasting change developed: the target anxieties and related complaints were gradually diminished, so that active relaxation was less and less required, and finally not needed at all. Apparently, repeated counteraction of the anxiety responses sometimes led to their progressive extinction. Other subjects needed to continue, apparently indefinitely, to use their relaxation skills to counteract anxiety. Eight cases that Jacobson (1964) described in detail provide a sampling of the two kinds of outcome. Only one case became independent of relaxation after a modest amount of treatment — 20 hours over 7 months. The other seven were much improved, displaying fundamental recovery in some directions after treatment periods ranging between 8 months and 3 years. But 6 of the 7 continued to use progressive relaxation to deal with significant discomfort.

Abbreviated Relaxation Training. Although the most profound relaxation is doubtless achieved by Jacobson's prolonged and exacting regime, it is more often preferable to aim for a relatively modest degree of calming in a short time — notably for the purposes of systematic desensitization.

An abbreviated relaxation training schedule for use in systematic desensitization was initiated by Wolpe (1954). Awareness is directed to individual muscle groups through strong, rather than minimal contraction, and then the subject is instructed to let go progressively in the manner of Jacobson. The usual order of training is: arms, face, jaws, tongue, neck, shoulders, trunk, and lower limbs. In some cases, relaxation of the extrinsic eye muscles is emphasized because of its exceptional emotional potency.

Many modifications of this schedule have been described. Some have advocated the use of tape recordings, but these are not very helpful unless the subject has previously had personal training. Cue-controlled relaxation and biofeedback-based relaxation are valuable when it is desirable to make relaxation reponses automatic. The same autonomic effects as are induced by deep muscle relaxation are also obtained by transcendental meditation and by autogenic training.

APPLICATIONS OF DEEP MUSCLE RELAXATION

Relaxation for Breaking Fear Habits. Systematic desensitization is the most common vehicle for this use of relaxation. In the standard technique, the subject has received abbreviated relaxation training. Then, while he is in a calm state, progressively more disturbing scenes within the problem area are presented to his imagination. He is eventually able without distress to imagine even the "strongest" scenes in that area; and there is transfer of the change to real life. However, it is imperative for the preliminary training in relaxation to be adequate. Otherwise, poor results are to be expected.

To decondition anxiety by competing relaxation, one may also elicit the anxiety by real instead of imaginery stimuli (in vivo desensitization). There is no alternative to this in patients who are unable to imagine realistically. This method is widely applicable, even to some cases of agoraphobia who, after thorough relaxation training, are instructed in differential relaxation, which they then employ on journeys of increasing length both on foot and by car. In the course of a few weeks, some patients are able to go any distance without anxiety, and thereafter gradually dispense with relaxation on journeys.

Relaxation as Sole Treatment. A great many unadaptive anxiety response habits have been ameliorated by relaxation alone, no matter by what method the skill has been taught — but, as noted above, few patients attain the kind of change that ultimately enables them to do without relaxation. The beneficial effects of relaxation as sole treatment are attributable to differential relaxation, which lowers the level of ongoing anxiety and diminishes the impact of stressful experiences. Administered in groups, differential relaxation is an economical way of diminishing anxiety in substantial numbers of people.

Relaxation training alone is particularly recommendable in some syndromes that have traditionally been called "psychosomatic" — notably migraine, tension headache, insomnia and essential hypertension. Recent studies have shown that about 65% of patients with tension headache and 50% of those with migraine obtain marked benefit from muscle relaxation. Follow-ups suggest that most of the nonresponders are those who fail to practice. In insomnia not due to medical or psychiatric conditions, relaxation training appears, in general, to be the most effective treatment available.

The ability of relaxation to lower blood pressure, first noted by Jacobson (1938), has in recent years been widely confirmed. In an extensive series of studies, Agras (1983) found that weekly half-hour sessions for 8 weeks resulted in a mean decrease of 12 mm. in diastolic pressure compared with 2 mm. in a control group. The improvement transferred to the work situation and persisted at 15-month follow-up.

Another role for relaxation is to control the emotional overreactions of the coronary-disease-prone Type A personality, the core of which appears to be excessive arousability to anger, manifested in part by a liability to be irritated by trivial things. It is interesting that although this form of hyperemotionality and neurotic anxiety are markedly different, differential relaxation training affects both.

There has recently been great interest in relaxation for the purpose of "stress-control," i.e., diminishing the effects of daily stresses. The involvement in this of large corporations has encouraged the emergence of poorly trained self-proclaimed "stress control experts." This is unfortunate, but mass education in relaxation would be a major prophylactic advance if it were provided by competent practitioners.

BIBLIOGRAPHY

Agras, W. S. (1983). Relaxation therapy and hypertension. *Hospital Practice,* May, 129–137.
Borkovec, T. D., & Sides, J. K. (1979). Critical procedural variables related to the physiological effects of progressive relaxation: A review. *Behaviour Research and Therapy, 17,* 119.
Jacobson, E. (1938). *Progressive Relaxation.* Chicago: University of Chicago Press.
Jacobson, E. (1964). *Anxiety and tension control.* Philadelphia: Lippincott.
Wolpe, J. (1954). Reciprocal inhibition as the main basis of psychotherapeutic effects. *Archives of Neurology & Psychiatry, 72,* 205–266.

See: Anxiety Management Training
     Autogenic Training
     Cue-controlled Relaxation
     Self-control Desensitization
     Stress Management Training
     Systematic Desensitization

DELAYED AUDITORY FEEDBACK
Louise Kent-Udolf

Delayed auditory feedback (DAF) refers to the experience of hearing ones own voice played back into ones own ears while speaking, at a time delay interval greater than normal. The experience is considered to be aversive, because speakers subjected to DAF learn to reduce their speaking rate and prolong vowels and continuant speech sounds as they speak in order to reduce the "echo" effect produced by the delayed feedback. DAF also refers to clinical procedures used to reduce speaking rate, to induce flu-

ency, or to calibrate speaking rate. DAF procedures have been used clinically with persons who stutter (more typically with adults than with children), and with persons diagnosed with apraxia of speech, a neurogenic speech disorder.

Descriptive information on equipment used to accomplish the delay may be obtained from Phonic Ear Inc. (DAF also refers to the machinery being used.)

From a perceptual point of view, under conditions of DAF speakers do not hear themselves as they usually do. Instead of an almost simultaneous feedback of hearing oneself talk, there is a slight delay in hearing what has just been said. This "echo" effect initially tends to disrupt normal patterns of articulation, resulting in disfluences, variable in all respects. The subjective experience is generally reported as aversive.

A clinically popular DAF unit marketed by Phonic Ear Inc. offers continuously variable delay rates from 25 milliseconds to 220 milliseconds, and a continuous volume control for gains of 11 dB to 33 decibals. The unit is small enough to be worn in a pocket or attached to a belt and operates on two 9 volt transistor radio type batteries.

The use of DAF as a clinical procedure has not been described as fully for the management of apraxia of speech as for stuttering. Indeed, numerous clinicians have developed rate control therapies for stuttering using DAF. What follows here is a procedural example of the use of DAF in the Shames and Florance stutter-free speech program. Training begins by instructing the client to speak very slowly, stretching each word into the next to produce continuous phonation throughout the phrase (from one punctuation mark to the next), and to eliminate pauses or interruptions that disrupt the flow of speech. To effectively train a consistent slow rate of speech, a delayed auditory feedback signal of 250 milliseconds is used. The client is instructed to slow down his speech until he is no longer aware of any delay through the earphones. If the client needs further explanation, the clinician explains that the DAF is simply a tape recorder that plays the client's speech back at a specific rate of delay. The major objective for the client is to slow his speech down until the speech on the "tape loop" and his on-line speaking are at the same rate and he is no longer aware of any delay through the earphones.

When stuttering therapy begins, the client is required to complete 30 minutes of stutter-free speech under 250 millisecond delay. A correct response is one that is slow enough so that the speaker does not hear the delayed feedback and one in which continuous phonation is produced between words within the phrase. The clinician may ask the client to evaluate continuous phonation and rate of his or her own speaking behavior during the clinical session. Once the client is able to report accurately regarding these two aspects of the speaking response, the clinician directs the client to monitor (in his or her own speech) continuous phonation and rate, and to continue talking until he/she achieves 30 minutes of stutter-free speech, in which appropriate rate, prosody and continuous phonation have been maintained. The client is successively required to complete 30 minutes of stutter-free speech at each of five delay intervals on the DAF machine (250, 200, 150, 100 and 50 milliseconds). Dependency on DAF for rate calibration is faded systematically, client responsibility for self-monitoring outside the therapy situation is increased systematically, and amount of time in therapy is gradually reduced. In the later phases of therapy self-monitoring is faded.

CLINICAL GUIDELINES

Clinical use of DAF to modify rate should be part of a comprehensive behavioral therapy plan; that is, DAF alone does not con-

stitute a therapeutic procedure. Numerous references in the literature suggest that for young children, clinical approaches that involve DAF procedures are not as effective as those that make use of other rate modifying methods. Regarding the use of DAF in the management of apraxia of speech, DAF appears to influence articulatory accuracy by slowing the patient's speech. If slowing the patient's speaking rate improves articulatory performance and intelligibility, then DAF may contribute to a palliative effect. The patient will need to be instructed in the use of DAF and be allowed to adjust to it. Optimum delay intervals, loudness, and stimuli are unknown. It is suggested in the literature that the use of DAF is apt to be facilitating only for patients with mild-to-moderate apraxia who are capable of phrase and sentence-length utterances.

BIBLIOGRAPHY

Costello, J. M. (1983). Current behavioral treatments for children. In D. Prins, & R. J. Ingham (Eds.), *Treatment of stuttering in early childhood: Methods and issues.* pp. 69–112. California: College Hill Press.
Curlee, R. F., & Perkins, W. H. (1969). Conversational rate control therapy for stuttering. *Journal of Speech and Hearing Disorders, 34*, 245–250.
Flanagan, B., Goldiamond, I., & Azrin, N. H. (1958). Operant stuttering: The control of stuttering behavior through response contingent consequences. *Journal of Experimental Analysis of Behavior, 1*, 173–177.
Rosenbek, J. C. (1978). Treating apraxia of speech. In D. J. Johns (Ed.), *Clinical management of neurogenic communicative disorders* . pp. 191–241. Boston: Little, Brown.
Ryan, C., & Van Kirk, B. (1974). The establishment, transfer and maintenance of fluent speech in 50 stutterers, using delayed auditory feedback and operant procedures. *Journal of Speech and Hearing Disorders, 39*, 3–10.
Shames, G., & Florance, C. (1980). *Stutter-free speech: A goal for therapy.* Columbus, OH: Charles E. Merrill.

See: Fading
    Self-Monitoring

DIFFERENTIAL ATTENTION
Edward Konarski

Differential attention is the contingent application of human attention to designated target behaviors in conjunction with the contingent witholding of human attention (ignoring) for other designated target behaviors. It is a variation of differential reinforcement, with the secondary reinforcer of attention serving as the consequent stimulus event to be manipulated. The application of attention contingent upon certain behaviors is designed to increase those behaviors by means of the behavioral principle of positive reinforcement. The withholding of attention for other behaviors is designed to decrease those behaviors by means of the behavioral principle of extinction. Therefore, the use of this technique can simultaneously increase the performance of desired behaviors while decreasing the performance of undesirable behaviors. Differential attention has also been conceptualized as a way of forming a discrimination for a person between which behaviors to perform and not to perform.

CLINICAL APPLICATION AND PROCEDURES

Differential attention has been successfully applied to a wide range of behaviors, across a variety of clinical and non-clinical populations, and in many different settings. However, a review of the research literature indicates that it has been most frequently used in classrooms, pre-schools, and home settings to modify the deportment, academic, compliance, and mild tantrum behaviors of children. Usually, teachers and parents have served as administrators of the technique. The widespread use of differential attention is due mainly to the powerful effect attention has in controlling many human behaviors. Therefore, the use of this technique is indicated in almost any situation where attention is indicated as the reinforcer currently maintaining the undesirable behaviors of the client, the behavior to be ignored is not dangerous to the client or others, and a relatively slow rate of change in the target behavior can be tolerated. It is most appropriate in situations where an increase of specific-appropriate and a decrease of specific-inappropriate behaviors are both desired. However, it may also be used in situations where the primary focus is to singularly increase or decrease a particular behavior. However, when dual effects are intended, it is suggested that differential attention will be most effective where the targeted appropriate and inappropriate behaviors are mutually exclusive.

Differential attention is often effective in controlling behavior when used by itself. However, it also is often used as part of a package treatment; that is, other behavioral techniques are used in combination with differential attention to change behavior. This treatment approach is taken when any of the previously described criteria regarding appropriateness of the technique are in question. The techniques most often used in combination with differential attention include the addition of more potent reinforcers to enhance the effects of attention as a reinforcer, instructions to prompt the occurrence (what to do) or nonoccurrence (what not to do) of the target behaviors, and/or the use of another technique designed to decrease undesirable behavior (e.g., time-out from positive reinforcement).

The first step in the application of this technique is to determine that attention is currently acting to reinforce the undesirable behavior of the client. This indicates that attention is clearly a potent reinforcer for that client. Next, a list of the behaviors that will be given attention is constructed, along with a list of those that will be ignored. A baseline assessment is then taken on these behaviors. If paraprofessionals are being used as the behavior change agent, the therapist must then instruct them how to apply the principles of positive reinforcement and extinction. It must be kept in mind by whoever applies the treatment that attention takes several forms: verbal (e.g., praise, acknowledgement), physical (e.g., hug, pat on the back), and gestural (e.g., smile, nod). Each or any combination of these may be delivered contingently for desirable behavior and all forms must be witheld for undesirable behavior. Finally, the program is implemented and the target behaviors are systematically monitored to assess the effects of the treatment. The rate of behavior change will likely be increased if instructions are added to the program which inform the clients of what they are expected to do and what they are not expected to do. If the target behaviors show little or no change, a more potent reinforcer may be added to the program or an additional technique for decreasing behavior may be initiated for the undesirable behavior.

EXPECTED OUTCOMES

If attention is the reinforcer currently maintaining the undesirable behavior of the client it is clearly a potent reinforcer for that person. It is therefore expected that the systematic application of differential attention will result in the desired changes in behavior. The rate of behavior change will be directly related to the potency of attention as a reinforcer; that is, the more potent attention is, the more rapidly the behaviors will change. The rate of change is also related to the consistency of application of differential attention. Inadvertent deliveries of attention for the undesirable behavior or repeated failure to reinforce the desirable behaviors with attention will retard behavior change. It can be generally stated, however, that the rate of behavior change using differential attention will likely be less than programs which employ more powerful primary reinforcers (e.g., food) or more powerful generalized secondary reinforcers (e.g., tokens), or employ more powerful methods than extinction for decreasing behavior (e.g., overcorrection, time-out from positive reinforcement, or response cost). If rapid behavior change is required, other techniques will have to be used in addition to differential attention.

SIDE EFFECTS AND CONTRAINDICATIONS

The most obvious negative side effects of the application of differential attention are those associated with the use of extinction. They include extinction burst and spontaneous recovery. Extinction burst refers to the increase in behavior which typically occurs when the reinforcer for a behavior is first withdrawn. This means that a temporary increase of undesirable behavior may occur before a decrease is seen. In a related vein, a behavior may also increase in intensity when extinction is first implemented, and sometimes even mild aggression may be induced. All of the above effects related to the extinction burst will likely be temporary if extinction is systematically applied; that is, no reinforcement is delivered for the undesirable behavior, and adequate reinforcement is given for desirable behavior. The problem of spontaneous recovery refers to the reappearance of the undesirable behavior after a time once it has been extinguished. If this occurs, the behavior should again be systematically ignored and it will extinguish quickly once again.

Differential attention should not be used if the behavior to be ignored cannot be allowed to occur, such as the case in self-injurious and aggressive behavior. It should also not be employed alone in the absence of convincing evidence, via observation or direct manipulation, that attention is the reinforcer maintaining the undesirable behavior. Particular clinical populations for which the use of differential attention alone may be inappropriate due to the likelihood of the ineffectiveness of attention as a reinforcer might include autistic children and extremely withdrawn schizophrenics. However, differential attention might still be employed as part of a package treatment which contains powerful primary reinforcers so that through association, attention might become a potent secondary reinforcer for these individuals.

BIBLIOGRAPHY

Budd, K. S., Green, D. R., & Baer, D. M. (1976). An analysis of multiple misplaced parental social contingencies. *Journal of Applied Behavior Analysis, 9*, 459–470.

Hall, R. V., Lund, D., & Jackson, D. (1968). Effects of teacher attention on study behavior. *Journal of Applied Behavior Analysis, 1*, 1–12.

Herbert, E. W., Pinkston, E. M., Hayden, M. L., Sajwaj, T. E., Pinkston, S., Cordua, G., & Jackson, C. (1973). Adverse effects of differential parental attention. *Journal of Applied Behavior Analysis, 6*, 15–30.

Madsen, C. H., Jr., Becker, W. C., & Thomas, D. R. (1968). Rules, praise, and ignoring: Elements of elementary classroom control. *Journal of Applied Behavior Analysis, 1*, 139–150.

Roberts, M. W., Hatzenbuehler, L. C., & Bean, A. W. (1981). The effects of differential attention and time-out on child noncompliance. *Behavior Therapy, 12*, 93–99.

See: Differential Reinforcement of Low Rate
        Behavior
     Differential Reinforcement of Other
        Behavior
     Extinction

DIFFERENTIAL REINFORCEMENT OF LOW RATE BEHAVIOR
Samuel M. Deitz

The differential reinforcement of low rate behavior (DRL) is a schedule of reinforcement which results in the reduction but rarely the elimination of behavior. There are three ways to program DRL schedules. In *Spaced Responding DRL*, a behavior is reinforced if it has been separated from a previous instance of that behavior by a minimum amount of time (the interresponse time, or irt). In *Interval DRL*, reinforcement is delivered at the end of an interval of time if fewer than two instances of a behavior occur during the interval; if a second behavior occurs, the interval is reset, thus delaying the availability of reinforcement. In *Full Session DRL*, reinforcement is delivered at the end of the whole observation session if fewer than a prescribed number of behaviors have occurred (the DRL Limit).

In each case, the initial requirement is determined by examining baseline levels of behavior. For example, if behavior is occurring about once every 5 minutes in baseline, the initial irt requirement (Spaced Responding DRL) would be set at 5 minutes as would the initial interval size (Interval DRL). If sessions were 60 minutes, the initial Full Session DRL Limit would be set at 12. As soon as reinforcement is regularly earned, irt and interval lengths would be gradually increased, or the DRL Limit would be gradually decreased, until an acceptable low level of behavior was achieved.

Spaced Responding DRL is most suited to behaviors which are only inappropriate because of their high rate. If, for example, one student was "hogging" class discussion, the problem is the extent of the behavior rather than its topography. After all, making a comment during discussion is appropriate;

making too many comments, however, limits the opportunities for other students and is therefore inappropriate. In this case it would help to put some "space" between the student's comments. To do that with Spaced Responding DRL would require setting an acceptable irt, possibly 5 minutes between comments. Then, if the student has waited at least 5 minutes between comments, his answer would be reinforced, perhaps by commenting favorably on the quality of the statements. If the 5 minute irt requirement had not passed, the comment could be ignored or the student could be told that enough time had not passed since his last comment and the irt timer would be reset to 5 minutes.

Interval DRL is useful when young children, for example, need more direct feedback to control minor behavior problems. If students are interrupting others during "show and tell," the teacher could set an interval of 2 minutes, for example. If during the interval no more than one interruption was noticed, the teacher would immediately deliver reinforcement, possibly a gold star or piece of fruit. If a second interruption was noticed before the 2 minutes were concluded, no reinforcement would be delivered and the timer would be reset.

Full Session DRL is useful in any case where the overall number of behaviors need to be reduced, but it would be acceptable if some of the behaviors occasionally occurred close together. If a client of a therapist was bothered by excessive thoughts of failure, Full Session DRL could be used to reduce the number of thoughts to a more "normal" level. A DRL Limit of 10 could be set based on baseline averages of 15 per day. If 10 or fewer such thoughts occurred, reinforcement such as self-selected and enforced access to television would be earned. If more than 10 occurred, no TV would be allowed. Later the DRL Limit could be re-

duced to five, then three, and eventually even one. If the DRL ever was set at zero, the schedule would have changed to DRO (Differential Reinforcement of Other Behavior).

Full Session DRL and its variations (see the Good Behavior Game) have been used most frequently in applied settings. This procedure has been used to decrease a number of different types of misbehavior, such as off-task talking, wasted time between activities, self-stimulatory behaviors, and noise levels. "Group" behaviors as well as individual behaviors have been reduced through Full Session DRL. Interval DRL has been used less frequently but has been successful in reducing interruptions of very young children, talk-outs, and other inappropriate behaviors. Spaced Responding DRL, the most cumbersome of the types of DRL, has been used primarily in laboratory research. Still, it has been successful in reducing inappropriate classroom questions and stereotyped behavior of normal and retarded individuals.

All three types of DRL, when properly programmed, have been shown to be effective, and changes in behavior occur quite rapidly. When requirements for reinforcement are increased, further reductions are also possible. Problems can occur at two points, however. First, in setting the initial irt, interval, or limit, effectiveness of the procedure will be limited if the requirement makes earning reinforcement too difficult. The requirement should be initially close to baseline levels of behavior. Second, in subsequently reducing the limit or increasing the irt or interval, changes should be slow. Too abrupt a change will make reinforcement unlikely, therefore decreasing chances of success.

While no adverse side effects have been noted with any of the forms of DRL, some restrictions should be placed on their use.

For serious self-injurious or aggressive behaviors, no form of DRL is suitable since behavior is usually only reduced, and these forms of behavior should be eliminated. Also, Full Session DRL and Interval DRL do not provide complete response-dependent feedback mechanisms. Since under those conditions some misbehaviors receive no consequence, these contingencies may be unsuitable (i.e., ineffective) for individuals from populations with any of a variety of learning difficulties. Finally, while Full Session DRL is an easy procedure for practitioners to use, Interval DRL and Spaced Responding DRL are more difficult to implement in some settings.

In any case, with proper planning and programming, each of the types of DRL provides three distinct advantages. First, DRL is designed to reduce, rather than eliminate, inappropriate behavior. Young children, for example, are not required to be "perfect"; they can improve and earn reinforcement. Since some behaviors are only inappropriate because of their excessive frequency, once they are reduced the problem disappears.

Second, each type of DRL can be easily combined with other response reduction procedures to increase its effectiveness. With Spaced Responding DRL, reinforcement is delivered if the irt requirement is met; if it is not met, a behavior could result in time out, for example, and when the time out was complete, irt timing would begin again. Interval DRL could be combined with punishment, for example, by reinforcing at the end of the interval if zero or one behavior occurred; in this case, punishment would be delivered to the second behavior within the interval and a new interval would then begin. With Full Session DRL, reinforcement would be delivered at the end of the session if the DRL Limit was not exceeded; if it was exceeded, overcor-

rection, among other procedures, could be required.

The final advantage of DRL is that it uses reinforcement rather than aversive events to reduce misbehavior. The pleasant nature of the applied environment is therefore as enhanced while reducing behavior as it is while increasing or establishing behavior.

BIBLIOGRAPHY

Chappel, L., & Leibowitz, J. M. (1982). Effectiveness of differential reinforcement as a function of past reinforcement and present schedule. *Psychological Reports, 51*, 647–659.

Deitz, S. M. (1977). An analysis of programming DRL schedules in educational settings. *Behaviour Research and Therapy, 15*, 103–111.

Deitz, S. M., & Repp, A. C. (1973). Decreasing classroom behavior through the use of DRL schedules of reinforcement. *Journal of Applied Behavior Analysis, 6*, 457–463.

Deitz, S. M., Slack, D. J., Schwarzmueller, E. B., Wilander, A. P., Weatherly, T. J., & Hilliard, G. (1978). Reducing inappropriate behavior in special classrooms by reinforcing average interresponse times: Interval DRL. *Behavior Therapy, 9*, 37–46.

Singh, N. N., Dawson, M. J., & Manning, P. (1981). Effects of spaced responding DRL on the stereotyped behavior of profoundly retarded persons. *Journal of Applied Behavior Analysis, 14*, 521–526.

See: Differential Attention
      Differential Reinforcement of Other
         Behaviors
      Omission Training

DIFFERENTIAL REINFORCEMENT OF OTHER BEHAVIOR
Samuel M. Deitz

The differential reinforcement of other behavior (DRO) is a schedule through which reinforcement is delivered at the end of a period of time (interval) during which no instances of the target behavior occurred. If during that period of time a behavior does occur, the interval is reset and the opportunity for reinforcement is delayed.

The name of the schedule references "other behavior" because with any active individual some "other behavior" will probably be occurring at the end of the interval and therefore temporally correlated with reinforcement. Actually, since no other behavior is required for reinforcement to be delivered, this accidental correlation should not be in the name of this schedule. A more suitable reference would be the differential reinforcement of the *omission* of behavior for that is what is required for reinforcement to be delivered.

In DRO, the initial interval size is determined from baseline levels of responding. For example, if the target behavior is occurring about once every 7 minutes during baseline, the initial interval would be set at 7 minutes, thus maximizing the opportunity for reinforcement. If after 7 minutes, no instances of the target behavior were observed, reinforcement would be immediately delivered and a new interval would begin. If a behavior occurs, the timer would be reset to 7 minutes. Once behavior is under control, the size of the interval could be gradually increased.

Since DRO works to eliminate behavior, it is useful for such serious problems as self-injurious actions. If a client was head-banging at an average baseline rate of three times per minute, the therapist would start with 15- or 20-second intervals to insure maximum access to reinforcement such as some special food. If during the interval no head-banging were noticed, the client would receive the food immediately at the end of the interval. If head-banging did begin during the interval, the client would be stopped, no food delivered, and a new interval would begin. Soon, the length of the interval could be extended to 30 seconds, then 60 seconds and higher, depending on continued success.

DRO schedules have been effective in reducing many different forms of behavior, ranging from classroom noise to self-destructive behaviors. Sibling conflict, vomiting, and spitting, seizure-like behaviors, and thumbsucking have all been effectively treated with DRO. These successes have been achieved with individuals and groups of both normal and special population.

Reduction of these behaviors is usually quite rapid and tends to be durable. If DRO is correctly implemented it is usually very successful. The major difficulty arises with either initially setting too long an interval or increasing the size of the interval too rapidly.

DRO has some minor disadvantages. First, since accurate timing and observation are required, DRO is somewhat difficult to implement in situations such as classrooms where one adult is in charge of many individuals. Second, although rare in applied situations, DRO can produce superstitious behavior. This occurs when the "other behavior" at the end of the interval is strengthened. Since it usually fades away rapidly, such an event is only a small bother.

The advantages of DRO are important. First, it is effective across a very wide range of behaviors, from those which are minor annoyances to severe social problems. Second, when properly carried out, DRO has been shown to be more effective than many other behavior reduction procedures. Third, DRO can be easily combined with other behavior reduction procedures such as punishment, response cost, or time out. If no behavior occurs during the interval, reinforcement would be delivered; if a behavior does occur, the other procedure would be immediately applied and a new interval would begin.

Finally, since DRO uses positive reinforcement to decrease misbehavior, it does not suffer from legal sanctions or the problematic side effects of aversive procedures such as punishment. Using positive reinforcement adds to the general pleasant nature of the applied setting.

BIBLIOGRAPHY

Deitz, S. M., Repp, A. C., & Deitz, D. E. D. (1976). Reducing inappropriate classroom behavior of retarded students through three procedures of differential reinforcement. *Journal of Mental Deficiency Research, 20,* 155–170.
Homer, A. L., & Peterson, L. (1980). Differential reinforcement of other behavior: A preferred response elimination procedure. *Behavior Therapy, 11,* 449–471.
Leitenberg, H., Burchard, J. D., Burchard, S. N., Fuller, E. J., & Lysaght, T. V. (1977). Using positive reinforcement to suppress behavior: Some experimental comparisons with sibling conflict. *Behavior Therapy, 8,* 168–182.
Repp, A. C., & Deitz, S. M. (1974). Reducing aggressive and self-injurious behavior of institutionalized retarded children through reinforcement of other behaviors. *Journal of Applied Behavior Analysis, 7,* 313–325.
Zeiler, M. D. (1976). Positive reinforcement and the elimination of reinforced responses. *Journal of the Experimental Analysis of Behavior, 26,* 37–44.

See: Differential Attention
Differential Reinforcement of Low Rate Behavior
Omission Training

DIRECTED MASTURBATION

See: Orgasmic Reconditioning

DISCRIMINATION TRAINING
Alan M. Gross

Discriminination training is used to teach people when to perform a given behavior. It is achieved by establishing antecedent stimuli as cues signaling which behavior will be reinforced in a particular setting. Training involves reinforcing a specific response in the presence of one stimulus and not reinforcing the response in the presence of other stimuli. When a response is con-

sistently reinforced in the presence of one stimulus and consistently not reinforced in the presence of other stimuli, each stimulus setting becomes a cue indicating whether or not certain consequences are likely to occur for the performance of the behavior. The stimulus associated with reinforcement is called a discriminative stimulus. The probability of a behavior may be altered by adding or subtracting a discriminative stimulus to (from) the environment. When an individual responds differently in the presence of different stimuli, a discrimination has been made. Teachers often use discrimination training procedures to alter the behavior of the mildly disruptive student who talks to classmates during lessons. In order to show the youngster that talking to friends is not acceptable behavior during lessons and should primarily occur during free play, the teacher will ignore (extinction) or punish the child for talking out in the classroom and provide social reinforcers to the youth when he engages in this behavior on the playground.

See: Classroom Management
Cueing
Extinction
Punishment

DRY-BED TRAINING
Johnny Matson

Dry-bed training is one particular strategy for decreasing nocturnal (nighttime) bed wetting. Enuresis was originally derived from the term, "I make water." A frequent definition of nocturnal enuresis is the nighttime, repeated, involuntary discharge of water after the age of 3 years. The age of 3 has been chosen since this is the age at which most children achieve urinary continence at night. Encopresis or defecating in the bed may also occur but is infrequent.

The number and amount of nocturnal

wetting episodes which must occur to constitute a problem varies widely. It is not uncommon for children to wet their beds occasionally, even after having learned to be continent. Wetting two or three times a week is a commonly accepted minimum figure to consider the response highly problematic.

Wetting has been found to be nocturnal only in 60% to 80% of enuretic children, diurnal (daytime) only in about 5%, and nocturnal and diurnal in 20% to 40%. When both nocturnal and diurnal wetting are present, it is typically found that nighttime wetting is treated first and that in half of the cases daytime enuresis remits spontaneously, as success occurs in the training of the nighttime problem.

Some of the distinctive aspects of dry-bed training are positive reinforcement for nighttime urination in the toilet, practice in arising to urinate in the toilet, an artificially increased need to urinate, immediate detection of correct toileting as well as bed wetting, and punishment of accidents. Training is intensive and the objective is to eliminate the problem in one day.

About half-an-hour before bedtime the resident is given two cups of a preferred drink such as flavored punch. A urine-alarm device is used which buzzes when the person voids in the bed. Every hour, a staff member is to awaken the resident by using the minimal prompt needed. Sometimes the person could be awakened by manually guiding them to a sitting position, while in other instances more involved and intense, or less involved and intense, procedures (merely touching the individual) could be employed. Next, the bedwetter is guided to the toilet to void. If urination does not occur within 5 minutes the person would be returned to bed and given two more cups of fluid to drink. This procedure is repeated hourly. Training is continued until the bedwetter has one or no accidents for an evening.

When a wetting episode is observed, the trainer immediately discontinues the buzzing night alarm. The bedwetter is awakened, if not already awake, and occupied for 45 minutes. The bedwetter is reprimanded for having an accident. The bedwetter is then required to attempt urinating in the toilet while the trainer removes the urine-alarm apparatus and the wet bedding. When the bedwetter returns to the bedroom, (s)he is required to engage in Cleanliness Training. This procedure consists of having the person remove the soiled bedding and put it in the laundry room. Next, (s)he must select clean bedding and make the bed. Then, the bedwetter is required to engage in Positive Practice which consists of lying down in the bed for 3 minutes, getting up and going to the toilet, where the person sits on the toilet bowl for up to 30 seconds and then (s)he is directed back to the bed. No reinforcement is given to the person, even if they urinated in the toilet. This procedure is repeated for 45 minutes or 8 to 10 toileting trials.

BIBLIOGRAPHY

Azrin, N. H., Sneed, T. J., & Foxx, R. M. (1973). Dry bed: A rapid method of eliminating bedwetting (enuresis) of the retarded. *Behaviour Research and Therapy, 11*, 427–434.

Azrin, N. H., Sneed, T. J., & Foxx, R. M. (1974). Dry-bed training: Rapid elimination of childhood enuresis. *Behaviour Research and Therapy, 12*, 147–156.

Barmann, B. C., Katz, R. C., O'Brien, F., & Beauchamp, K. L. (1981). Treating irregular enuresis in developmentally disabled persons: A study in the use of overcorrection. *Behavior Modification, 5*, 336–346.

See: Bell and Pad Method
     Dry Pants Training

DRY PANTS TRAINING

Johnny Matson

The Dry Pants Training program is very similar to the Dry Bed Training program. However, this procedure is aimed at diurnal toileting accidents, which may consist of enuresis (wetting), and encopresis (defecating in one's pants). Encopresis rarely occurs without enuresis but enuresis often occurs without encopresis. The occurrence of enuresis and encopresis together is much more frequent than in nocturnal problems.

The major difference between the Dry Pants and Dry Bed methods is the location of the urine-alarm. In the Dry Pants procedure a device called the *wet pants alarm* is attached directly to the person's undergarments. Two moisture-detecting snaps are fastened to the person's briefs, and two flexible wires leading from the snaps, which are located in the crotch area, lead to a circuit box located on a belt just above the person's waist. A tone sounds in the circuit box when urine or feces moistens the area between the clothing snaps.

A systematic number of steps are followed in the training procedure and are listed below:

I. *When no accidents occur*: (1) Resident seated in chair when not seated on toilet bowl, (2) Resident drinks fluids every half-hour, (3) Scheduled toileting of resident every half-hour, (4) Resident given edible and social reinforcer every 5 minutes while dry, (5) Shaping of undressing and dressing during toileting, and (6) Resident given edible and social reinforcer following elimination in toilet bowl and returned to chair.

II. *When accidents occur*: (1) Trainer disconnects pants alarm, (2) Trainer obtains resident's attention, (3) Resident walks to laundry area to obtain fresh clothing, (4) Resident undresses himself, (5) Resident walks to nearby shower, receives shower, and dresses himself, (6) Resident obtains mop or cloth and cleans soiled area on chair or floor, (7) Resident handwashes soiled pants, wrings pants out, and hangs pants up to dry, (8) Trainer removes resident's chair from use, and (9) 1-hour time-out procedures: (a) no edibles or social reinforcers every 5 min., (b) no fluids every 30 min., (c) chair not available, (d) continue 30-min. scheduled toilet periods.

BIBLIOGRAPHY

Azrin, N. H., & Foxx, R. M. (1971). A rapid method of toilet training the institutionalized retarded. *Journal of Applied Behavior Analysis, 4*, 89–99.

Azrin, N. H., & Foxx, R. M. (1974). *Toilet training in less than a day.* New York: Simon & Schuster.

Butler, J. E. (1976a). Toilet training a child with spina bifida. *Journal of Behavior Therapy and Experimental Psychiatry, 7*, 137–140.

Butler, J. E. (1976b). Toilet training success of parents after reading "Toilet training in less than a day." *Behavior Therapy, 7*, 185–191.

Matson, J. L., & Ollendick, T. H. (1977). Issues in toilet training normal children. *Behavior Therapy, 8*, 549–553.

See: Bell and Pad Method
Dry-Bed Training

ELECTRICAL AVERSION

W. L. Marshall

Electrical aversion (also sometimes called "faradic aversion") is a specific form of aversive conditioning (see major section) where the aversive event is an electrical stimulus. The goal is to reduce or eliminate an undesirable behavior by associating either the stimuli that elicit the behavior, or the execution of the behavior itself, with the electric shock. However, the particular nature of the other elements (eliciting stimuli, aberrant response, and whether the therapist or patient delivers the shock) again depends on factors similar to those relevant to aversive conditioning.

There is some debate about the intensity of the electrical stimulus, but most therapists have the patient set the shock at an intensity which is unpleasant but tolerable. While the animal literature suggests that, up to a point, more intense shocks are associated with greater and more rapid suppression of the targeted behavior, this same literature indicates that more intense shocks lead to generalized suppression of other responses, a greater tendency toward the initiation of aversive control, development of inappropriate avoidance behavior, or behavioral rigidity. The use of moderately aversive shocks seems to be the best choice at the moment.

The location of delivery of the shock is important, as is the type of electric current used. Electric shocks are response-interfering, so that if the patient is required to use his/her hands and arms as part of an approach, and particularly if part of an escape or avoidance behavior, then the stimulus should be delivered to the leg. On no account should electrical stimuli be applied to the trunk of the body or the head.

Several of the marketed devices for delivering aversive electrical stimuli use power from electrical outlets which do not permit increases in voltage and, in any case, involve high levels of amperage to generate the current. A current whose intensity is primarily a function of high amperage is quite dangerous and frequently causes tissue damage at the site of application. Such devices should definitely be avoided. The best current generator is provided by a simple inductorium which is driven by dry-cell batteries (we use #6 Ignition batteries because they have a long shelf life). This permits increases in intensity to be made by increasing voltage while holding amplitude constant at negligible levels. Currents produced in this way are quite safe, do not cause local tissue damage, and patients seem not to habituate to them whereas they do to the low voltage/high amperage current. A device of this type is marketed by Farrell Instruments (Mark III, Behavior Modifier).

CLINICAL APPLICATION

The evidence indicates that electrical aversion is most effective in reducing deviant sexual interests, possibly because these behaviors involve significant tactile experiences (i.e., electric shock is primarily a tactile aversive stimulus). Whatever the reason, electric aversion does not seem to be effective with behaviors predominately involving gustatory (taste) or olfactory (smell) systems.

It is important to note that it is rare, indeed, for the misbehavior of sexual deviants to be maintained by aberrant sexual preferences alone, so that the use of electrical aversion to reduce deviant interests should be seen as one element in a comprehensive treatment program. Given that this is understood, the actual form of the aversive procedure should be tailored to the unique features of the individual. However, certain types of sexual deviance present particular features that suggest advantages for particular forms of components in treatment. For example, the behaviors involved in most fetishisms or transvestisms can be readily produced in the therapist's office. And these behaviors, along with the eliciting stimuli (female clothing, or leather boots, etc.), should be the features which are associated with the electric shock. Indeed, wherever possible, *both* stimuli and the responses to them should be the targets for punishment. However, with some behaviors (e.g., exhibitionism, child molestation, and rape) it obviously is neither possible nor acceptable to reproduce the behaviors in the office. For many therapists this has meant restricting treatment to the presentation of the eliciting stimuli in representational forms (e.g., slides or videotapes), but fortunately, some creative therapists have devised ways of producing relevant responses.

Abel, for example, uses audiotapes based on the patient's own descriptions of his typical behavioral sequence when enacting the deviant response. The patient is required to imagine this sequence and is punished at various points throughout the response chain until the fantasy loses its provocativeness. Quinsey measures the erectile responses of sexual offenders to depictions of the deviant stimuli and punishes responses above a set criterion level. It is very important to note that the electrical shock in this procedure is delivered to the arm or leg and *not* the penis as opponents of aversive therapy often suggest. We have also provided exhibitionists with portable shock devices to self-administer electrical aversion in their natural environment when urges to expose occur. In all of these variations, there is an attempt to replicate the natural environment where the eliciting stimuli and deviant responses occur. This should serve to increase generalization to the patient's everyday life.

EXPECTED OUTCOMES

Careful evaluations (and with sexual deviants this should include physiological assessments of sexual preferences) should be conducted after no more than 10 sessions (preferably massed over 2 weeks), with each involving approximately 30 shocks. By this time, benefits should be evident or the procedure should be abandoned and an alternative sought.

While we have already pointed out that sexual deviates are the best target for electrical aversion, whether or not changes in the sexual preferences of these men is desired depends to a large extent on both the therapist's and patient's views. However, most therapists nowadays do not consider homosexuality, for example, to be a devi-

ance and are, therefore, reluctant to attempt to change orientation in these cases. Perhaps a more compassionate world would think the same of fetishists and transvestites. If these men steal, or engage in other unacceptable behaviors to procure their favored articles, then these aberrant behaviors can be dealt with independently of their sexual preferences.

The use of electrical aversion, or, indeed, any other aversive strategy with masochists may not be appropriate, although the evidence is not clear on this issue. Similarly for those persons familiar with, and unaffected by electric shocks (e.g., some electricians), use of some alternative aversive event is probably more sensible.

POTENTIAL SIDE EFFECTS

As is the case for aversive therapy generally, electrical aversion should be avoided when the patient has a significant cardiac problem, although use of low-amperage current reduces these obstacles significantly as does placing the delivery of the current at a peripheral site.

Use of moderately intense, rather than painful electric stimuli, will probably avoid any unwanted side effects, but the therapist should watch for those we have already noted (e.g., generalized suppression of behavior, etc.).

BIBLIOGRAPHY

Abel, G. G., Levis, D. J., & Clancy, J. (1970). Aversion therapy applied to taped sequences of deviant behavior in exhibitionism and other sexual deviations: A preliminary report. *Journal of Behavior Therapy and Experimental Psychiatry, 1*, 59–66.

Blakemore, C. B., Thorpe, J. G., Barker, J. C., Conway, C. G., & Lavin, N. I. (1963). The application of faradic aversion conditioning in a case of transvestism. *Behaviour Research and Therapy, 1*, 29–34.

Marks, I. M. (1976). Management of sexual disorders. In H. Leitenburg (Ed.), *Handbook of behavior modification and behavior therapy*. Englewood Cliffs, NJ: Prentice Hall.

Marks, I. M., & Gelder, M. G. (1967). Transvestism and fetishism: Clinical and psychological changes during faradic aversion. *British Journal of Psychiatry, 113*, 711–729.

Quinsey, V. L., Chaplin, T. C., & Carrigan, W. F. (1980). Biofeedback and signalled punishment in the modification of inappropriate sexual age preferences. *Behavior Therapy, 11*, 567–576.

See: Aversive Conditioning

EMOTIVE IMAGERY
Arnold A. Lazarus

The use of anxiety-inhibiting emotive images (i.e., images that arouse feelings of pride, mirth, serenity, affection, joy, self-assertion, and elation) was introduced into the literature by Lazarus and Abramovitz (1962). It is particularly useful as a pediatric technique with phobic children. The technique consists of the following steps:

1. As in desensitization, a graduated hierarchy is compiled.
2. By sympathetic inquiry, the clincian establishes the nature of the child's hero images and the fantasies that accompany them.
3. The child is told a story, close enough to his or her everyday life to be credible, within which the child's favorite hero or alter ego models fearless behavior and provides support and encouragement.
4. Step-by-step, the child is to imagine himself/herself confronting his or her feared situations, accompanied by the hero-images. Thus, a child who feared visiting the dentist soon overcame his phobic reactions when picturing Batman and Robin receiving dental attention. Next, he was to imagine himself in the dentist's chair while his heroes stood by and observed him. He practiced this image several times a day for a week. Subsequently, according to his mother, he sat through four fillings without flinching.

BIBLIOGRAPHY

Lazarus, A. A., & Abramovitz, A. (1962). The use of "emotive imagery" in the treatment of children's phobias. *Journal of Mental Science, 108*, 191–195.

See: Covert Rehearsal

ENVIRONMENTAL DESIGN
Leonard Krasner

Environmental design represents an approach to changing human behavior which derives from several streams of investigations in psychology. Environmental design represents the application of empirically derived principles of behavior influence to the modification and design of environments. Behavior influence principles and the multitude of behavioral and environmental research provide environmental design with both a data base and a philosophy for intervention.

In recent years the behavioral (environmental, social learning) model of man has broadened to the point where it now represents a comprehensive approach to human behavior with major social and political ramifications. This expanded version of the behavioral model can be labeled "environmental design," a term which is both eloquently simple and sufficiently broad to convey the complexities of the approach.

Using a term such as environmental design may be viewed as a kind of territorial growth for the behavioral model in that there are few fields indeed which do not encompass man's involvement with his environment. Heimstra and McFarling (1974) note that, "The relationship between man and his environment is of interest to individuals in many areas, including architecture, urban and regional planning, civil and sanitary engineering, forest and parks management, geography, biology, sociology, and psychology, to name only a few" (p. 3).

Colman (1975) offers a useful description of environmental design that incorporates most of the elements in this orientation:

> A more useful definition of environmental design would relate the planning of a coherent program and set of procedures to affect the total human and nonhuman environment in ways that increase the probability that certain goals or 'needs' will be achieved. The goal of environmental design would relate to social behavior, such as planning an educational or therapeutic system, as much as to aesthetics such as constructing an awe-inspiring church. Input into environmental design problems must then include knowledge related to modifying human behavior and social systems as well as structural information from engineering and perceptual psychology. The field would expand toward a new view of man, always powerfully affected by his physical and social environment, now actively developing an environmental design model and methodology that would place the effect of the total environment on his behavior more in his own control, and the responsibility for the design and control of the environment of his behavior, in himself. (p. 411)

The environmental design approach represents a conceptual and applied linking of behavior modification with environmental and ecological psychology. It involves a process of training people to conceptualize the environment in which they are working in such a way that they can apply the general principles of environmental design. Succinctly stated, these principles include:

(1) A hypothesized model of human behavior which conceptualizes the locus of influence as in the *interaction* between an individual's behavior and his environment.

(2) An individual learns by observing and doing.

(3) Behavior followed by a rewarding event is likely to be repeated.

(4) Any situation can be analyzed so that the designer can set up specific behavioral goals that are socially desirable, taking into consideration both social and individual needs and desires.

(5) Techniques should not be developed in isolation, but only in the context of learning environments with which the individual designer is dealing. The broader influences on behavior, such as social roles and the impact of institutional rituals and restraints, must be considered.

(6) The professional influencer is part of the influence process itself; in effect, a participant observer. As such, he must be aware of, and in control of, the influence on himself.

(7) There is a symbiotic relationship between therapist and patient, influencer and influencee, designer and designee—both need each other.

(8) Research and application, theory and practice are mutually interactive and inseparable.

(9) Social and personal change is a continuous process.

(10) The variables of influence lie in the environment (man-built, natural, and social), but they may differentially influence as a function of the history of the individual.

(11) Meaning or truth is not intrinsic but is imposed currently and repeatedly by the observer, investigator, or designer.

Perhaps the most fundamental issue in environmental design is design for what and by whom? This is not a new issue in that it was expressed early in the behavioral movement in terms of modification "for what" and "by whom." A major point which derives from this viewpoint is that the goal of helping individuals is to enable them to learn how to control, influence, or design their own environments. Implicit in this is a value judgment that individual freedom is a desirable goal, and the more an individual is able to affect his environment the greater is his freedom. Of course, there is no absolute freedom in this sense. In this context, "environment" is both the people and physical objects in one's life.

The goals of environmental design may be explicated by noting that:

> The best way to increase freedom is not merely to say people *may* choose, but to work so that people *can* choose. Just as humans have gone far in changing their physical environments, we hope the next decade will see humans controlling and changing their psychological environments. The how is being developed rapidly in schools, clinics, families, and formal organizations. An attempt is being made to reduce the gap between decision makers and the populations they affect, especially in the areas of education and consumer affairs and to a lesser extent in political and industrial settings. (Krasner & Ullmann, 1973, p. 502)

BIBLIOGRAPHY

Colman, A. D. (1975). Environmental design: Realities and delusions. In T. Thompson & W. J. Dochens (Eds.), *Applications of behavior modification*. New York: Academic Press.

Heimstra, N. W., & McFarling, L. H. (1974). *Environmental psychology*. Monterey, CA: Brooks/Cole.

Krasner, L. (Ed.). (1980). *Environmental design and human behavior: A psychology of the individual in society*. Elmsford, NY: Pergamon Press.

Krasner, L., & Ullmann, L. P. (1965). *Behavior influence and personality: The social matrix of human action*. New York: Holt, Rinehart & Winston.

Proshansky, H. M. (1976). *Environmental psychology: People and their physical settings* (2nd ed.). New York: Holt, Rinehart & Winston.

ENVIRONMENTAL ORGANIZATION

Sandra Twardosz

Environmental organization involves changing relevant aspects of the physical, social, and programmatic context to produce changes in behavior. Physical environmen-

tal variables include architectural features, furnishings and equipment, play materials and activities, food, and signs. Social and programmatic variables include the presence and location of people, the division of responsibilities among staff, activity schedules, and the method of presenting academic tasks. In contrast to most behavior therapy procedures, which are personally mediated, organizational variables usually do not need to be delivered through the behavior of another person each time they are used. Once established, they operate continuously on behavior as people interact with their environment.

Organizational variables may sometimes operate as reinforcers, punishers, or discriminative stimuli. In many cases, however, they cannot be conceptualized as immediate antecedents or consequences of behavior and are more usefully classified as setting events.

CLINICAL APPLICATION

This approach is used when settings are not providing individuals with sufficient opportunities for participation and learning or are maintaining dysfunctional behavior. In contrast, the purpose of most behavior therapy procedures is to change the behavior of individuals so they can function more effectively in their environment. The goals of environmental organization are to set the occasion for desired behavior, to remediate and prevent behavior problems, to prevent the deterioration of skills from lack of practice, and to support the implementation of educational and therapeutic procedures. The latter function (for which there is limited empirical demonstration) includes setting the occasion for desired behavior so it can be shaped and reinforced, providing a variety of potential reinforcers so that contingency management procedures, such as time-out, are more effective. This increases the likelihood that newly acquired behaviors will be maintained and generalize beyond the training setting.

Environmental organization has been used primarily in group care settings such as day care centers, nursing homes, institutions for the retarded, and classrooms, with a focus on both client and staff behavior. Several examples of its use in families and other community settings exist. Examples of specific applications include the provision of play materials and activities to increase participation and decrease inappropriate behavior, use of family-style dining to increase social interaction, spacing children to decrease mild disruptive behavior, scheduling activities concurrently rather than sequentially to increase participation, and use of signs to decrease shoplifting.

EXPECTED OUTCOMES AND TIME FRAMES

Changing relevant aspects of the environment produces clinically or socially significant results in many cases. In others, only minimal change occurs, and contingency management procedures must also be implemented to obtain the desired results. Whether or not environmental organization is sufficient to produce important change is determined by variables, such as individuals' behavioral repertoires and their physical condition. For example, different outcomes would be expected when providing play materials or activities to nonhandicapped preschoolers, the severely retarded, or the elderly in a nursing home.

Environmental variables produce change almost immediately after implementation if the desired behavior is in the individuals' repertoires. Behavior quickly returns to baseline levels when the procedures are discontinued. Because most studies have been conducted over a short period of time, little information regarding the long-term effects of this approach is available; however, studies from a variety of disciplines provide evidence for the long-term benefits of stimulating and responsive environments.

DIFFERENTIAL DIAGNOSTIC CHARACTERISTICS

Settings in which many clients are exhibiting the same problem behavior, such as sitting passively throughout the day, engaging in mild forms of disruptive behavior, or interacting rarely with others are prime candidates for this approach. An individually-tailored behavior therapy program, such as some type of contingency management, would be more appropriate when only a few clients exhibit the above problems. However, such programs could also include environmental modification.

Indications that environmental organization may be beneficial include: low levels of client participation, an inappropriate noise level, absence of a daily schedule or staff assignments, infrequent or inappropriate interaction between staff and clients or among staff, and long periods of waiting when clients have little or nothing to do.

Use of environmental organization alone is not recommended for decreasing dangerous or well-established aggressive or disruptive behavior and is no substitute for training in specific skills. However, it should be used as an adjunct to the contingency management or other educational or therapeutic procedures that are used to remediate those problems.

POTENTIAL SIDE EFFECTS OR CONTRAINDICATIONS

There is no information available on side effects. Contraindications are described in the preceding section.

BIBLIOGRAPHY

Center, D. B., Deitz, S. M., & Kaufman, M. E. (1982). Student ability, task difficulty, and inappropriate classroom behavior: A study of children with behavior disorders. *Behavior Modification, 6*, 355–374.

Horner, R. D. (1980). The effects of an environmental "enrichment" program on the behavior of institutionalized profoundly retarded children. *Journal of Applied Behavior Analysis, 13*, 473–491.

LeLaurin, K., & Risley, T. R. (1972). The organization of day care environments: "Zone" versus "man-to-man" staff assignments. *Journal of Applied Behavior Analysis, 5*, 225–232.

Melin, L., & Götestam, K. G. (1981). The effects of rearranging ward routines on communication and eating behavior of psychogeriatric patients. *Journal of Applied Behavior Analysis, 14*, 47–51.

Twardosz, S. (1984). Environmental organization: The physical, social, and programmatic context of behavior. In M. Hersen, R. M. Eisler, & P. M. Miller (Eds.), *Progress in behavior modification* (Vol. 18). New York: Academic Press.

ESCAPE TRAINING
Kathleen Dyer

This is a training procedure in which an individual learns to perform a response in order to terminate a punishing stimulus. For example, an escape training procedure designed to increase the frequency of seatbelt wearing might involve sounding a loud buzzer when the individual sits in a car and starts the engine. The buzzer could only be turned off by the individual fastening his or her seatbelt. Thus, the individual learns to fasten the seatbelt in order to terminate the buzzer.

See: Aversive Conditioning
   Avoidance Training

EXPOSURE
W. L. Marshall

Exposure is any procedure that confronts the person with a stimulus which typically elicits an undesirable behavior or an unwanted emotional response. Often, other procedures are also employed (e.g., repeated response evocation in the case of satiation, or an anxiety-competing response in the case of desensitization) in which case it is usual to consider exposure as simply an element within a particular treatment package. It is only when exposure on its own is expected to lead to changes in behavior that it is properly considered to be an independent treatment technique. This is best exemplified in certain forms of "flooding" therapy, aimed at reducing unpleasant emotional and motor responses.

In exposure, as defined in these terms, then, the patient is presented (either imaginally or in vivo) with examples of the stimuli that elicit the unwanted responses until these responses no longer occur. Many writers restrict the use of the term "exposure" to those procedures involving direct confrontations with the actual eliciting stimuli. While the evidence clearly indicates that these in vivo procedures are more effective than imaginal exposure, there are instances when it is not possible to have the patient confront the actual situation as part of treatment. For example, therapists cannot usually arrange to have thunderstorms happen at convenient times when treating astraphobia. In these cases, having the patient imagine the feared event is usually the only alternative, although some resourceful therapists have managed to create reasonable facsimiles of certain phobic stimuli (e.g., use of a planetarium to produce storm-like experiences).

Ordinarily, in exposure procedures the patient is required to remain in the situation until the distressful emotion has abated either as a result of exhaustion of the response system involved, or as a result of the patient recognizing that the stimulus does not cause the dreaded consequences. Often, the patient is encouraged to develop a new perspective toward the phobic event while exposure is taking place. This certainly seems to both enhance and accelerate occurrence of the benefits derived from treatment. With height-phobics, for example, we typically suggest the positive aspects of being able to view the surrounds from on high, and we urge patients to reconstruct their thoughts about being in a high place and supply them with positively worded self-statements regarding their experiences during exposure. Of course, this means we are doing more than just exposure, but the benefits are clear.

It is also clear from the evidence that exposure should be prolonged until the patient has reappraised the stimulus so that it is no longer threatening. Usually, and somewhat surprisingly, this can be achieved without too much distress on the part of the patient. However, in treating pathological grievers with this method the patient is typically very upset, and this taxes the therapist's resilience. It has been observed that conducting exposure in groups reduces the intensity of individual distress, and in other ways helps to keep patients in prolonged contact with the disturbing situation. Similarly, recruiting a close friend or relative as a co-therapist to assist in exposure to everyday occurrences of the upsetting stimuli can significantly enhance treatment benefits. However, in these cases it is essential to properly prepare the patient's companions so that they encourage appropriate behaviors and thoughts.

CLINICAL APPLICATIONS

As already noted, exposure procedures are typically applied to the reduction of unpleasant emotional responses elicited by particular, although often rather vaguely defined, events. Indeed, one of the initial tasks of the therapist is to arrive at a clear understanding of the eliciting stimuli, and with most phobics these distressing events often include anticipatory worrisome thoughts about what might happen. In its extreme form, this fearful anticipation of consequences may be seen as a "fear of fear." Whatever their form, these dysfunctional thoughts need to be included in exposure treatment. Indeed, in the application of these procedures to the treatment of compulsive individuals, the target of this component in the treatment package is the thoughts of what might happen if a ritual is not enacted. In addition, the physiological concomitants of anxiety (or any other distressing emotion) are often an important source of disturbance which the patient may learn to fear. Gradually, this fear of fear will sensitize the patient to these internal cues, making it necessary for the patient to experience physiological arousal as part of the exposure procedure.

We will give brief illustrations of the use of exposure involving the treatment of different emotional states. Anxiety of one form or another is the typical target of exposure treatments, and we will illustrate its use with one of the more complex forms, namely, agoraphobia. Exposure is conducted in the natural environment, where a group of fellow-sufferers is led by a therapist through various situations which typically make them phobic. They are urged to allow fear to develop, and to attend to the fear in all its manifestations, including their usual ways of thinking about the events which are taking place. Although group members can offer crucial support to one another for remaining in the phobic situation, they must not be allowed to encourage particularly fearful group members to avoid in any way any aspects of their fearful response. As their fears diminish, or at least come under their control, the patients are advised to offer one another new, more positive, perspectives on being in the phobic situation. It is wise practice to include as many different evocative situations as can be reasonably managed over the planned treatment program to ensure generalization. Each treatment session should last until each phobic's fear is well under control and this may take from 2 to 4 hours. While this seems like a considerable amount of therapist time, it must be remembered that several patients are being seen at once, and that generally treatment benefits occur within a few sessions.

We have applied these same procedures to the treatment of pathological grievers, where the distressing stimuli predominantly include thoughts about the deceased person (or departed lover), many of which concern guilt over assumed neglect by the patient. However, we have often used places or articles, which serve to remind the patient of the deceased, as additional elements in the exposure process. Again, the patient is urged to allow the distressful emotion to occur as the therapist describes the thoughts the patient has that upsets him/her. This is continued until the patient is no longer upset, at which time the therapist suggests new, more constructive, ways of remembering the dead person.

Such procedures have also been used to help patients deal with uncontrollable anger, particularly when this is not expressed, but rather, brooded upon to the continued distress of the patient. We present the evocative stimulus (which may be a person or a behavior and usually both), while encouraging the patients to get angry and urging them to attempt to articulate the reasons for their anger. We usually have someone role-play the provoker in order to make the situation more realisitic and manageable. Again, we not only continue until anger abates, but we also have them reconstruct their thinking, rationalize their feelings, and train them to develop alternative, more constructive, responses (e.g., become more assertive).

EXPECTED OUTCOMES AND POTENTIAL SIDE EFFECTS

Unless positive benefits are apparent after five exposure sessions (providing each session is continued to the above-noted criteria), the procedure should be stopped, and either revamped or an alternative sought out. Usually, five sessions will produce marked benefits, although we typically continue treatment until we have at least two consecutive sessions with no signs of distress.

Exposure treatment is appropriate for any unpleasant or disadvantageous emotional response, although to date it has not been applied to depression except when this is reactive to a loss as in the case of grief. It was at one time feared that exposure of this kind, invoking as it sometimes does extreme distress in the patient, might exacerbate rather than attenuate unpleasant emotions. This certainly does seem likely, although far from certain, when exposure is terminated while the patient is still upset. If, however, exposure is continued until positive changes are observed, unfortunate reactions are rare and seem to happen only in psychotic or pre-psychotic individuals. One side effect fearful patients often anticipate is that they will faint or have a heart-attack. Neither of these consequences has ever happened to our patients nor to the patients of over 20 other exposure therapists we contacted. This was true even when the patient was found later to have cardiovascular problems.

Perhaps the greatest obstacle to this form of treatment is the frequently encountered resistance of the patient to participate for fear of something dreadful happening. After all, phobics fear certain events just because they are sure something awful will follow. Properly preparing the patient for the experience is essential and it is important for the therapist to also believe that unfortunate experiences will not befall the patient as a result of treatment.

BIBLIOGRAPHY

Emmelkamp, P. M. G. (1982). Exposure in vivo treatments. In A. Goldstein & D. Chambless (Eds.), *Agoraphobia: Multiple perspectives on theory and treatment*. New York: Wiley.

Foa, E. B., & Goldstein, A. (1978). Continuous exposure and complete response prevention in the treatment of obsessive-compulsive neurosis. *Behavior Therapy, 9*, 821–829.

Gauthier, J., & Marshall, W. L. (1977). Grief: A behavioral/cognitive analysis. *Cognitive Therapy and Research, 1*, 39–44.

Marshall, W. L., Gauthier, J., & Gordon, A. (1979). The current status of flooding therapy. In M. Hersen, R. Eisler, & P. Miller (Eds.), *Progress in behavior modification* (Vol. 7). New York: Academic Press.

Mathews, A. M., Gelder, M. G., & Johnston, D. W. (1981). *Agoraphobia: Nature and treatment*. New York: Guilford Press.

See: Flooding

EXTINCTION
Alan Poling

Extinction is a response-weakening operation which can involve either: (a) consistent failure to deliver a reinforcer following an operant response which had previously produced that reinforcer, or (b) consistent failure to follow a conditional stimulus (CS) with an unconditional stimulus (US) which previously had reliably followed that CS. The former operation ([a] above) is termed operant extinction and eventually results in nearly complete elimination of the operant response, although a transient rate increase (response bursting) is frequently observed soon after operant extinction is arranged. The latter operation ([b] above) is termed respondent and eventually results in the CS no longer eliciting a conditional response (CR).

Reducing a depressed client's rate of negative self-evaluative statements by failing to verbally acknowledge them is an example of operant extinction. Respondent extinction is evident in the failure of conditioned reinforcers, such as money or tokens, to exercise control over behavior unless at least occasionally paired with other, established, reinforcers.

See: Differential Attention
Differential Reinforcement of Other Behavior
Omission Training
Operant Conditioning

FACIAL SCREENING
Vincent B. Van Hasselt

Facial screening is a mildly aversive technique that has been used to suppress a wide variety of self-stimulatory and self-injurious behaviors in developmentally disabled persons. Some of these include: face-slapping, self-biting, hand-flapping, body-rocking, inappropriate vocalizations, and trichotillomania (compulsive hair-pulling). The procedure consists of briefly covering the individual's face with a non-abrasive terrycloth bib contingent upon the occurrence of the target behavior(s). (A similar approach, *visual sensory extinction*, employs an eye screen instead of a bib.) The bib is positioned in a manner such that the person can breathe in a normal and comfortable fashion. The duration of bib placement over the face has ranged from a few seconds to several minutes. Recent evidence, however, shows that a 1-minute interval may be optimal for affecting behavior change. Release from facial screening generally is contingent upon non-disruptive behavior following expiration of the minimum time requirement for administration of the screening procedure.

There are a number of advantages in

using facial screening relative to other aversive methods. First, the technique requires minimal training and has been effectively carried out by paraprofessionals, parents, and teachers. Second, its application rapidly and significantly reduces the frequency of maladaptive behaviors. Improvement has been observed across settings (laboratory, classroom, home). Further, follow-up data ranging from 6 to 18 months have documented the durability of gains with this strategy. Also, positive collateral effects (e.g., improved social behavior, increased play) have been observed as a function of facial screening. Finally, in contrast to more severe aversive approaches, this technique involves no physical risk and produces no negative side effects.

A problem with employing facial screening is the possible resistance to treatment (e.g., pulling the therapist's hands away) mentioned earlier. Consequently, the intervention may have limited utility with strong and agile children. In addition, the technique requires special equipment (i.e, terrycloth bib, eye screen) that may prove inconvenient to implement in certain settings. As a result, the efficacy of *visual* screening, a variant of facial screening, has been examined. In visual screening the child's eyes are covered by the therapist's hand rather than a bib or eye screen. This procedure has produced significant decreases in stereotypic behaviors and compulsive rituals in mentally retarded and autistic children.

BIBLIOGRAPHY

Barmann, B. C., & Vitali, D. L. (1982). Facial screening to eliminate trichotillomania in developmentally disabled persons. *Behavior Therapy, 13,* 735–742.
McGonigle, J. J., Duncan, D., Cordisco, L., & Barrett, R. P. (1982). Visual screening: An alternative method for reducing stereotypic behaviors. *Journal of Applied Behavior Analysis, 15,* 461–467.

Singh, N. N. (1980). The effects of facial screening on infant self-injury *Journal of Behavior Therapy and Experimental Psychiatry, 11,* 131–134.
Singh, N. N., Beale, I. L., & Dawson, M. J. (1981). Duration of facial screening and suppression of self-injurious behavior: Analysis using an alternating treatments design. *Behavioral Assessment, 3,* 411–420.
Zegiob, L. E., Jenkins, J., Becker, J., & Bristow, A. (1976). Facial screening: Effects on appropriate and inappropriate behaviors. *Journal of Behavior Therapy and Experimental Psychiatry, 7,* 355–357.

See: Visual Screening

FADING
Laura Schreibman

Fading refers to the gradual change in a stimulus dimension when teaching a discrimination. Typically, fading is used when teaching a difficult discrimination, and it is deemed desirable to make the discrimination easier by adding a dimension and then gradually fading this dimension as the individual masters the discrimination. For example, in teaching a child to discriminate between a hexagon and an octagon a teacher might make this difficult discrimination by adding a color dimension and coloring the hexagon blue and the octagon red. As training progresses and the child continues to respond correctly, the color cue is *faded* by gradually having both forms change to black. At the end of training the color is completely faded and the child responds to black hexagon versus black octagon — a discrimination that was originally too difficult for the child to learn.

See: Backward Chaining

FEEDBACK
Joel Hundert

As a technique, feedback refers to the presentation of information to an individual following a target behavior so as to guide the future occurrence of that behavior. As a result of this information, the individual learns to change the behavior in more desired directions. The type of information provided and the format of its delivery may vary widely according to the situation from as general as an observer's comments or as specific as a written score representing an individual's measured performance in a skill area. Although often a component of other procedures (e.g., reinforcement, public posting, biofeedback), feedback alone is typically used to train an individual in a new skill area where motivation is not so much a problem.

See: Biofeedback
     Public Posting
     Reinforcement

FLOODING
Larry Michelson

Flooding is a generic term used to depict a varied and complex set of therapeutic procedures which are primarily utilized in the treatment of phobic and obsessive-compulsive disorders. While anecdotal description of the concept and its application dates back to at least the ancient Greeks, the vast majority of its historical development can be traced over the past three decades during which time it was the focus of much empirical study. Flooding procedures entail exposure to anxiety-arousing stimuli (i.e., objects, situations, individuals, etc.) to which clients have become phobically conditioned. While the clinical dimensions of flooding techniques may differ markedly across studies,

the underlying conceptualization of exposure facilitating habituation and extinction remains evident.

The basic theoretical and applied model of flooding derives from animal research literature, whose focus was on increasing the proximity of the phobic stimulus, not the anxiety levels of the animals, as a means of achieving habituation of the phobic response. Gradually increasing the proximity and duration of the exposure, without permitting either escape or avoidance behaviors, resulted in diminution and/or elimination of the phobic pattern of elevated physiological indexes, overt distress, and avoidance.

However, flooding strategies have been misunderstood and mistakenly associated with implosion therapy, which employs horrific, frightening, and psychodynamic cues in order to maximize anxiety arousal, which in turn was presumed to enhance rapid extinction. However, empirical studies have found that such cues are often ineffective, and in many instances may be contra-therapeutic. Thus, the deliberate use of fear-enhancing or anxiety-arousing cues needs to be re-examined, as the basic conceptual model of flooding requires only increased exposure, not phobic arousal. Hence, for purposes of clarification, use of the term "flooding" should denote the behavioral (non-horrific/non-psychodynamic) model which eschews excessive phobic arousal, while facilitating phobic exposure.

IMAGINAL VS. IN VIVO

Within the purely behavioral framework, flooding strategies differ on a number of important clinical dimensions. One of the most significant factors involved in applying flooding is whether it is performed in imagery (imaginal) or is undertaken in vivo (naturalistic settings). Presently, the literature suggests that flooding in actual phobic situations is more effective than merely presenting visual, auditory, tactile, etc., cues in imagery. This is not surprising given the fact that many clients cannot evoke imagery powerful or detailed enough for a sufficient period of time to allow habituation to occur. Another limitation is that clients may block their anxiety arousal by minimizing and neutralizing many phobic elements of their imagery experience. This blocking phenomena may be difficult to monitor and remediate as the clarity, potency, and duration of flooding in imagery is subject to all the weaknesses of self-report data. Advantages of in vivo exposure include the direct facilitation of client coping, more rapid exposure to real-life situations, and insurance that the individual does not avoid or escape his/her contact with the phobic stimuli. Flooding in vivo also does not require any imagery training or visualization ability on the part of the client. Moreover, it also possesses the inherent advantages of social validity and treatment generalization. First, the phobic targets are selected and practiced in their natural states. Should certain stimuli either prove to be more or less phobic than was originally conceptualized, other more problematic and therapeutically valid phobic targets can be readily substituted. Conversely, when evaluating the efficacy of flooding in imagery, the exact degree of association with corresponding in vivo counterparts remains unknown. However, imaginal flooding may be a viable strategy when phobic stimuli cannot be utilized due to its unavailability in vivo, or being primarily of an imaginal nature (e.g., fear of dying).

INTENSIVE VS. GRADUATED

Another dimension of flooding concerns its speed of presentation, e.g., rapid vs. gradual. The current body of clinical research supports a graduated approach to flooding. Flooding, conducted in an ascending hierarchy, not only reduces client drop-out, noncompliance, and resistance, but also facilitates enhanced self-efficacy, self-mastery, and coping strategies. Graduated flooding allows the client to participate actively in structuring the level of difficulty of the phobic tasks. This, in turn, results in decreased anticipatory and conditioned fear and diminished physiological reactivity, both prior to and during the tasks. Moreover, it accelerates inter- and intra-session habituation and generalization processes by precluding unnecessary and extreme levels of phobic response.

DURATION OF SESSIONS

A series of studies has also examined whether flooding, in vivo, is more efficacious with longer sessions. Almost without exception, the literature supports the need for, and effectiveness of, *prolonged* in vivo exposure for the treatment of anxiety and phobic disorders. Prolonged in vivo flooding treatment evinces significantly superior habituation across the tripartite domains of physiological, cognitive, and behavioral functioning. While differences in client population, diagnoses, and symptoms make specific recommendations difficult, between 90 minutes and 180 minutes of flooding per session are requisite to obtain maximal therapeutic benefit.

SPACED VS. MASS PRACTICE

A dimension of flooding procedures subjected to systematic inquiry concerns the differential efficacy of spaced vs. massed treatments. While long-term outcome does not seem to be significantly affected, the treatment literature generally favors the use of massed (frequent and temporally close applications) versus the use of less intensive interventions (e.g., once a week).

THERAPIST VS. CLIENT-DIRECTED

Another variant of flooding in vivo concerns whether it is therapist- or client-directed. Based upon the research, to date, it appears that therapist-directed flooding may be important and even necessary during the initial and middle stages of treatment. However, treatment and generalization effects may be further enhanced via increased competency attributions, on the part of the client, by their assuming gradual and progressively more responsibility for designing and subsequently undertaking their own flooding sessions.

MODELING

The effects of modeling vis à vis flooding have also been examined and depend, in some degree, upon the particular dysfunction being treated and modeling strategy employed. Briefly, the use of participant modeling aids may be quite useful, as adjunct clinical tools with flooding. However, they are generally regarded as neither essential nor sufficient for the remediation of major anxiety disorders among clinical populations.

CLINICAL DESCRIPTION

Examples of flooding include the prolonged in vivo exposure of obsessive-compulsive clients with washing rituals and dirt/germs/contamination obsessions who are encouraged to touch and handle doorknobs, bathroom walls, or garbage bins, etc., until their urge to escape and/or wash abates. Similarly, agoraphobics who typically avoid traveling unaccompanied would be invited to venture beyond their "safety radius" and remain in their phobic environments for several hours. In both cases, of course, the exposure would be hierarchically structured, with the most difficult flooding tasks being attempted only

after less-anxiety-provoking gradations have been successfully undertaken. Likewise, acrophobics who avoid elevators, bridges, and tall buildings would be instructed to engage in prolonged graduated in vivo exposure practice on a daily basis, with the more phobic situations reserved for the latter phases of treatment.

GROUP TREATMENTS

Flooding has been extensively studied in a variety of formats with diverse analogue and clinical populations. Several conclusions can be drawn from the available research. First, flooding techniques are readily adapted for use with groups of clients with similar phobic disorders such as agoraphobia. Group treatment represents an efficient, and for most patients, an equally effective modality as compared to the one-to-one therapeutic approach. Indeed, factors including increased support via group cohesion and social reinforcement can facilitate more rapid flooding, and hence improvement.

SPOUSE CO-THERAPISTS

Flooding interventions also appear to benefit from the addition of a relative or close friend who might serve as an adjunct co-therapist, encouraging the client between formal treatment visits to engage in prolonged in vivo exposure practice sessions. While short-term results may not markedly differ, those clients with trained spouses and/or relatives (providing they are both supportive and follow the therapist's instructions) appear to fare better over long-term follow-up evaluations.

TREATMENT RESPONSE

Therapeutic response to flooding procedures is generally reported in the 60% to 75% range. Generalizations regarding prediction and/or delineation of temporal patterns of improvement depend upon myriad single- and higher-order interactions including (but not limited to): diagnosis, age of client, severity of condition, duration of symptoms, presence of secondary depression, marital dysfunction, medical conditions, therapist experience and competency, social support network, and client expectations, attributions and cognitive coping skills, to name but a few of the more salient factors.

As culled from the clinical-research literature, a general rule of thumb is that most phobic and obsessive-compulsive clients who respond favorably to flooding should begin to manifest noticeable gains during the first 4 to 8 weeks consisting of two weekly, 2-hour sessions of prolonged graduated therapist-assisted in vivo exposure. The improvements, of course, are considered marked from the relative perspective of the client's dysfunction and not in an absolute sense. For example, a completely housebound agoraphobic, whose safety radius is expanded to one mile of independent and panic-free functioning, would be evidencing major strides. This initial favorable response, judging from both the research and clinical literature, is likely to continue and result in both qualitative and quantitative improvements if flooding treatment is further pursued. Hence, initial responsivity (e.g., 4–8 weeks) to flooding is associated with subsequent improvement. The converse, however, is not necessarily always true. For a variety of clinical reasons, certain clients who may not obtain benefit from flooding during the initial stages may, with therapist assistance, subsequently evince major gains. Specifically, if particularly problematic symptoms are present (e.g., panic attacks, horrific ideation, severe counterproductive and/or anxiety-enhancing cognitions, overvalued ideas, etc.), they may necessitate preliminary reduction prior to conducting flooding proper.

THERAPEUTIC RATIONALE

While many research protocols utilize flooding sessions lasting several hours, conducted over a 3–6 month period, it is not unusual for some clients to require more prolonged treatment, conducted over 6–12 months. Similarly, flooding strategies with phobic clients should always include a thorough rationale for the client (and relatives, if appropriate), instructions to practice self-directed flooding on a daily basis between formal treatment sessions, daily monitoring of target symptoms, therapeutic reassurance regarding the effectiveness and efficiency of the procedures, their non-harmful nature, and the positive benefits the client is likely to experience as a result of the intervention. Clients are also uniformly instructed that although they may have slight increases in perceived anxiety during the initial phases, these experiences are mild in degree and transient in nature. Furthermore, habituation and extinction processes are described to the client to facilitate their understanding of the impact of the strategy and the need to eliminate avoidance and/or escape behavior. Flooding modalities are highly efficacious for remediation of anxiety disorders whose primary clinical dimension is comprised of phobic avoidance and phobic anxiety, including many forms of obsessive-compulsive disorder. Flooding treatments, however, for disorders with only minimal avoidance, such as panic disorder or generalized anxiety disorder, presently lack strong theoretical or empirical support.

FOLLOW-UP

Longitudinal follow-up studies of flooding, ranging from a month to 9 years, reveal marked stability of gains and moderate generalization phenomena to other domains of functioning including affective and interpersonal dimensions for agoraphobics, simple, and mixed phobics. Obsessive-compulsive clients evince more intractable patterns and may be more vulnerable to periodic exacerbation of symptoms. Thus, the use of periodic, programmed, flooding-booster sessions should be given serious consideration as a vehicle for the secondary and/or tertiary prevention of more severe symptomatology.

POTENTIAL SIDE EFFECTS

Potential side effects of flooding include marked increases in anxiety, caused by unduly large gradations between exposure practices. Likewise, clients may escape flooding situations if they are significantly more difficult than previously successful steps. In both cases, the therapist can remedy or preferably prevent this problem by employing a graduated hierarchy, designed in close collaboration with the client.

Although the client, on ethical grounds, always has the ultimate say with regard to terminating flooding sessions, the experienced therapist will consistently posit the therapeutic benefit of both the exposure and the mild concomitant anxiety experienced by the client. Indeed, the therapist's reframing of the client's mild exposure-related discomfort may facilitate further exposure as behavioral avoidance, rather than concomitant anxiety. The therapeutic rationale also includes an emphasis on the long-term positive effects of flooding on eliminating phobic avoidance, anxiety, physiology and cognitions. However, clients need to be reassured that the major channel to which treatment is directed is behavioral. (Hence, the physiological and cognitive components of the phobia will subsequently be eliminated following reduction in behavioral avoidance.) This rationale enhances client compliance and motivation.

Potential side effects of flooding, such as medical risks and psychiatric deterioration,

are rare. However, with routine medical clearance and careful psychological/psychiatric diagnosis of the presence of an anxiety disorder (and absence of concurrent psychopathology), these remote possibilities can be even further reduced. There are no empirically-derived or universally accepted contraindications for conducting prolonged graduated in vivo exposure. However, clients who manifest alcohol and/or drug abuse are generally poor candidates for treatment prior to their detoxification and/or withdrawal. Similarly, clients taking anxiolytic medication (Valium, Librium) might be encouraged, with their physician's support, to reduce and eventually eliminate their use as they may inhibit habituation and reduce self-efficacy attributions.

WHEN FLOODING FAILS

When flooding strategies do not affect significant clinical improvement, which, unfortunately, occurs in approximately 15%–35% of the cases treated, the therapist will need to reformulate the client's treatment plan with consideration being given to alternative modalities, including cognitive (paradoxical intention, self-statement training, etc.), marital, individual, family, and adjunct pharmacological interventions. While the majority of recommendations will be applicable for most clients, there are always difficult clinical cases which require innovation in the application of flooding techniques, guided by an essential knowledge of flooding's theoretical base.

BIBLIOGRAPHY

Chambless, D. C., Goldstein, A. N. (Eds.). (1982). *Agoraphobia: Multiple perspectives on theory and treatment*, New York, Wiley.

Emmelkamp, P. M. M. G. (1982). *Phobic and obsessive-compulsive disorders: Theory, research, and practice.* New York, Plenum Press.

Mathews, A. M., Gelder, M. G., & Johnston, D. W. (1981). *Agoraphobia: Nature and treatment.* New York, Guilford Press.

Mavissakalian, M., & Michelson, L. (in press). Role of self-directed in vivo exposure in behavioral and pharmacological treatments of agoraphobia. *Behavior Therapy*.

Michelson, L., Hersen, M., & Turner, S. (Eds.). (1982). *Future perspectives in behavior therapy*. New York: Plenum Press.

Rachman, S. J., & Hodgson, R. (1980). *Obsessions and compulsions*. Englewood Cliffs, NJ: Prentice Hall.

Turner, S. M., & Michelson, L. (1984). Obsessive-compulsive disorders. In S. M. Turner (Ed.), *Behavioral theories and treatment of anxiety*. New York: Plenum Press.

See: In Vivo Desensitization

FORWARD CHAINING
Diane E. D. Deitz

Forward chaining is a teaching procedure in which a sequence of responses is developed by first reinforcing the initial step in the sequence, then reinforcing the *addition* of the second step in the sequence, etc., until the entire sequence has been acquired and is emitted as a unitary complex behavior. The different responses which compose the complex behavior are simple behaviors already in the repertoire of the individual. For example, a child can usually verbalize individual numbers before performing the complex behavior of "counting to 10." Using a forward chaining procedure to teach rote counting to 10, the trainer would first reinforce the child for saying "1"; then reinforcement would be contingent on saying "1, 2." Step three would require the response "1, 2, 3" for reinforcement, etc., until the entire sequence of 1 through 10 is acquired. While forward chaining is common, backward chaining is generally a more effective chaining procedure.

See: Backward Chaining
     Chaining

GOOD BEHAVIOR GAME
Samuel M. Deitz

The Good Behavior Game (GBG) combines several procedures into an unusually effective system designed either to eliminate inappropriate behavior or to increase appropriate behavior. The GBG includes: (1) rules specifying the exact behavior(s) to be changed, (2) posted feedback, and (3) reinforcement based on the comparative performance of two groups of students or clients. The population to be treated is divided into two (or more) groups and each group is given a name or label. Rules about the appropriate or inappropriate behaviors to be changed are explained to members of the groups and are then posted in a public place. As behaviors occur, they are publicly noted under the name of the team whose member emitted the behavior. Reinforcement for appropriate behavior is provided to both teams if a *minimum*, predetermined, and posted standard is met or exceeded by both teams. If that standard is not met, the team with the highest total "wins" and receives reinforcement. Reinforcement for appropriate behavior is provided to both teams if a *maximum*, predetermined, and posted standard is not exceeded by either team. If that standard is exceeded, the team with the lowest total "wins" and receives reinforcement. Rapid success with no harmful side effects has been achieved with the GBG in increasing proper sentence structure and work performance and in decreasing a variety of classroom misbehaviors.

For example, one could use the Good Behavior Game to increase spelling performance in a classroom. Like the traditional "spelling bee," the class would be divided into two teams. Each member would be asked to correctly spell one of the assigned words. If correct, that team member would remain on the team to later spell another word. If incorrect, the team would lose that member for the rest of the game. When all the words have been correctly spelled by one member or another, the team with the most members remaining would receive reinforcement (often just the "honor" of winning). Unlike the traditional "spelling bee," with the Good Behavior Game in effect, both teams could win if only a prespecified number of members had to sit down on either team.

For misbehavior, the teacher could divide the class into teams and specify several misbehaviors such as talkouts, interruptions, out-of-seats, hitting, pushing, throwing paper, and not following directions. Cumulative totals for each team for all of the misbehaviors would be kept. At the end of the class period, the team with the lowest total would win unless both teams stayed below the pre-set minimum. Then, both teams could win and earn reinforcement.

BIBLIOGRAPHY

Barrish, H. H., Saunders, M., & Wolf, M. M. (1969). Good behavior game: Effects of individual contingencies for group consequences on disruptive behavior in a classroom. *Journal of Applied Behavior Analysis, 2,* 119–124.

Harris, V. W., & Sherman, J. A. (1973). Use and analysis of the "good behavior game" to reduce disruptive classroom behavior. *Journal of Applied Behavior Analysis, 6,* 405–417.

Lutzker, J. R., & White-Blackburn, G. (1979). The good productivity game: Increasing work performance in a rehabilitation setting. *Journal of Applied Behavior Analysis, 12,* 488.

Maloney, K. B., & Hopkins, B. L. (1973). The modification of sentence structure and its relationship to subjective judgements of creativity in writing. *Journal of Applied Behavior Analysis, 6,* 425–433.

Medland, M. B., & Stachnik, T. J. (1972). Good behavior game: A replication and systematic analysis. *Journal of Applied Behavior Analysis, 5,* 45–51.

See: Operant Conditioning

GROUP CONTINGENCY
Carolynn C. Hamlet

A behavior-consequence paradigm in which the receipt of reinforcers or punishers by one or more group members is contingent, at least in part, upon the behavior of other group members is known as *group contingency*. It should be noted, however, that a group contingency is not an instructional procedure, but rather a social structure within which systems such as token economies and response cost can advantageously control group and member behavior. In addition to its capacity to direct the use of peer control, group contingencies also afford benefits to the implementer such as the economical and practical use of time and resources.

CLINICAL APPLICATION

The diverse and effective applications of group contingencies across varied settings, populations, and ages has established its versatility and credibility. Group contingencies have been employed in schools, homes, businesses, and other institutions to achieve social aims such as increased reading accuracy, decreased cafeteria disruption, increased pro-social interactions among geriatric as well as retarded residents, reduced frequencies of racial slurs (in settings where an instigator was unidentifiable), reductions in cash shortages in a neighborhood market, and increased creativity in elementary students' art work.

Applications of group contingencies, regardless of the populations or behaviors targeted, usually take one of two forms. In the first form, the performance of a single member or of selected members determines the consequences for the entire group. One example might be the reduction of a future homework assignment for an entire class contingent upon completion of the previous day's assignment by three targeted students. In the second type of application, every group member plays a role in determining the group outcome. Frequently this arrangement calls for the criterion for group performance to be expressed in one of two ways. One, a level of performance may be expressed for all group members as a set criterion, such as a correct rate of at least 45 and an error rate of no more than 3 on a multiplication worksheet. Two, a level may be determined in averaging either all performances, high performances, or low performances of group members' scores.

EXPECTED OUTCOMES, TIME FRAMES, AND DIFFERENTIAL DIAGNOSTIC CHARACTERISTICS

In using a group contingency, one should expect the outcomes and the immediacy of effects essentially to be determined by the procedure (e.g., positive reinforcement) which is associated with the group contingency. Lesser effects should be attributed to the group contingency context within which the procedure is applied. In addition to the primary effects, however, one might find that a group contingency arrangement may account for many desirable secondary effects as well as the enhancement of primary effects.

Peer-administered contingencies may: (1) function as a source of reinforcement for an individual who will work for the opportunity to interact with a peer, (2) enhance social interactions among group members, (3) result in increased skills for the peer group members, (4) facilitate skill maintenance and transfer, and (5) simultaneously make available individualized instruction and attention to large numbers of learners. Thus, a unique contribution which a group contingency may provide is its capacity to promote the concurrent attainment of several

desirable outcomes for both the targeted and non-targeted participants.

POTENTIAL SIDE EFFECTS AND CONTRAINDICATIONS

As with outcomes, one might expect the side effects observed in a group contingency arrangement to be more closely associated with the procedure in use than with the group contingency format. Thus, a punishment procedure which would produce emotional outbursts and attempts to escape the environment when applied in an individual contingency, could be expected to produce similar effects in a group contingency application. In addition to the procedure-related outcomes, however, one also might observe secondary side effects unique to the group contingency relationship. For example, a group contingency which employs a punishment procedure might call for class members to lose 5 minutes of free time contingent upon the failure to submit completed homework assignments. In such a situation, cries of inequitable treatment are likely to be heard from those individuals who diligently completed their assignments and, yet, lost free time. Such side effects may be controlled, however, by selecting reinforcers which are not normally available in the environment. This practice ensures that those who meet the criterion will retain the reinforcers to which they normally had access.

BIBLIOGRAPHY

Kazdin, A. E. (1980). *Behavior modification in applied settings*. Homewood IL: Dorsey Press.

Kazdin & Geesey, S. (1977). Simultaneous-treatment design comparisons of the effects of earning reinforcers for one's peers versus for oneself. *Behavior Therapy, 8,* 682–693.

Litow, L., & Pumroy, D. K. (1975). A brief review of classroom group-oriented contingencies. *Journal of Applied Behavior Analysis, 8,* 341–347.

Marholin, D., II, & Gray, D. (1976). Effects of group response cost procedures on cash shortages in a small business. *Journal of Applied Behavior Analysis, 9,* 25–30.

Neumann, J. K. (1977). The analysis of group contingencies data. *Journal of Applied Behavior Analysis, 4,* 755–758.

See: Classroom Management
　　　Contingency Management
　　　Response Cost
　　　Token Economy

HABIT REVERSAL

Steven Beck

The habit reversal method appears to be the most carefully developed and best validated treatment technique for eliminating nervous habits and tics. The rationale for this approach is that nervous habits or tics originally develop as normal reactions to physical injury or stress, or the behavior may have started as an infrequent, but normal, behavior that has increased in frequency. While most individuals inhibit these behaviors due to personal or social awareness of their peculiarity, occasionally these movements are performed at such a high rate that they become strongly established habits that become automatic. For some tics, the continued execution of the movement may even strengthen the specific muscles required for that movement, and opposing muscles become unused and may atrophy.

Habit reversal consists of two procedures. The primary procedure involves teaching the client to be aware of every occurrence of the habit and to emit a physically competing response so that it no longer will be part of the chain of normal movements. The second procedure involves a more general behavior therapy strategy that consists of identifying persons or situations that may trigger the tic behavior, relaxation training, daily self-monitoring of the tic behavior, and social support by family members for not exhibiting tic behavior.

CLINICAL APPLICATION

Several studies have reported successful control or elimination of various tic behaviors for children and adults. The following tics have been modified: thumb sucking, head jerking (spasmodic torticollis), arm jerking, shoulder jerking, fingernail biting, tongue thrusting, excessive eye blinking, and hair pulling (trichotillomania).

Habit reversal treatment is usually conducted in the following manner. The client is first taught to become aware of every execution of the habit behavior. Clients are then taught to practice an isometric exercise which is topographically incompatible with the tic response and involves the same muscles used in the tic. For example, an individual who plucks his eyelashes is taught to grasp objects with both hands for a brief time (from 1 minute to 3 minutes) at the earliest sign of hand movements towards his eyelashes. The competing response for an individual who displays head jerking is isometric contraction of the neck flexors by pulling the chin in and down. The competing response for an individual who exhibits uncontrollable eye blinking is to stare at selected objects without blinking for 3 seconds. The client is then told to make one deliberate blink after the count of three. The competing response is to be performed as inconspicuously as possible. The client is then to recall all situations, persons, and places where the habit is likely to occur and have him discuss and practice how he will implement the competing responses in these situations.

Habit reversal treatment also encompasses having the client review with the therapist inconveniences caused by the tic, identification of antecedents associated with high or low probability of tic episodes, heightening awareness of the tic by deliberately performing and viewing it in a mirror, relaxation training, daily-self monitoring of tic episodes, and social support by family members for exhibiting control over the tic behavior.

EXPECTED OUTCOME AND TIME FRAME

This method appears to produce immediate substantial results (after a few sessions) for motivated clients. On the other hand, negative practice, drugs, and shock aversion have been successful with one-third to one-fourth of clients with tics, while the habit reversal method appears to be successful with virtually every motivated client. Treatment has been reported to be successful for up to 1 year after treatment, although it is not uncommon that telephone contacts by the therapist reminding clients of the techniques may be necessary to overcome some relapses. This technique also appears to be effective with young children with the aid of parents (one study reported successful treatment with an 8-year-old boy).

POTENTIAL SIDE EFFECTS OR CONTRAINDICATIONS

There have been no reports of negative side effects or contraindications for this technique. One study did suggest that relatively mild cases of nervous habits or tics that have not yet become stereotypical behaviors (resistant to personal awareness) may benefit by merely having the client self-monitor the occurrence of each tic behavior.

BIBLIOGRAPHY

Azrin, N. H., & Nunn, R. G. (1973). Habit-reversal: A method of eliminating nervous habits and tics. *Behaviour Research and Therapy, 11,* 619–629.

Azrin, N. H., Nunn, R. G., & Frantz, S. E. (1980). Habit reversal vs. negative practice treatment of nervous tics. *Behavior Therapy, 11,* 169–178.

Beck, S., & Fedoravicius, A. S. (1977). Self-control treatment of an eye blink tic. *Behavior Therapy, 8,* 277–279.

Glasgow, R. E., Swaney, K., & Schofer, L. (1981). Self-help manuals for the control of nervous habits: A comparative investigation. *Behavior Therapy, 12,* 177–184.

Rosenbaun, M. S., & Ayllon, T. (1981). The habit-reversal technique in treating trichotillomania. *Behavior Therapy, 12,* 473–481.

See: Positive Practice

HETEROSOCIAL SKILLS TRAINING
Richard G. Heimberg

Heterosocial skills training is the label typically applied to therapeutic procedures designed to enhance one's interactions with the opposite sex. It refers to a complex and varied behavioral repertoire and includes initiating contact, making conversation, demonstrating interest in the other person, date initiation, self-disclosure, expression of praise, affection, sexual attraction, and so on. In many ways, heterosocial behavior is no different than other types of social behavior, and heterosocial skills training is no different than other forms of social skills training. However, a person's ability to make and maintain satisfying social contact with the opposite sex may affect his or her adjustment throughout the life span. Therefore, heterosocial behavior is worthy of special attention.

The label heterosocial *skills* training implies a specific theoretical position (i.e., that inadequate heterosocial performance occurs because the client's behavioral repertoire does not include the necessary adaptive behaviors). Several studies have therefore attempted to isolate the key differences between heterosocially successful and unsuccessful performers. Early studies isolated relatively few differences, although successful groups tended to talk more. It has been demonstrated, however, that unskilled and anxious persons differ from skilled-nonanxious persons in the timing and placement of some responses and not in the absolute frequency with which these responses occur. However, this "known-groups" approach to heterosocial behavior misses an important point. Specific deficits in heterosocial behavior may be highly idiosyncratic and situation-specific. A client's failure to successfully execute any of the following behaviors requires attention for that individual: eye contact; affect, including smiles, voice quality, facial expression, head nods, appropriate laughter; duration of speech; conversational questions; self-disclosing statements; complimentary comments; follow-up or acknowledgment statements; and requesting a date. Heterosocial skills training programs designed to modify deficient performance of these behaviors typically include: (a) instructions regarding appropriate heterosocial behavior, (b) modeling of the skillful performance of the behavior in roleplayed heterosocial interactions, (c) behavior rehearsal or roleplayed practice of the target behavior, (d) feedback about the positive aspects of the client's response and specific aspects that require modification, (e) social reinforcement or praise and encouragement from the therapist for successive approximations to the desired level of performance, and (f) systematic homework assignments for application of the newly-acquired skills in the client's natural environment.

Poor heterosocial performance may or may not occur because the client has a "heterosocial skill deficit," and the training procedures outlined above may or may not have their effect by remediating that deficit. Other formulations of heterosocial difficulties have been advanced and include the related notions that the client's effective heterosocial performance is interfered with by the experience of anxiety or disrupted by cognitive factors such as inappropriately negative evaluations of one's social perform-

ance, low self-esteem, or expectation of social failure. Neither of these formulations contradicts the skills-deficit notion, and clients may have heterosocial difficulties as a result of anxiety, cognitions, skill deficits, or any of the three. Relaxation training and systematic desensitization have been suggested as methods of anxiety reduction while several cognitive restructuring strategies have been attempted including self-statement substitution, systematic rational restructuring, rational emotive therapy, and modification of standards for self-evaluation and self-reinforcement.

CLINICAL APPLICATION

Heterosocial skills training packages have been applied to a number of target populations, including college students, mentally retarded persons, and psychiatric patients of mixed diagnoses. College students have served as subjects in the overwhelming number of studies. Their utilization as subjects is usually justified on the very legitimate basis that heterosocial behavior represents for them an important developmental challenge. Survey studies document college students' concern with heterosocial interaction, but other equally viable subject groups such as middle school or high school students have been thoroughly overlooked.

Clinical treatment of heterosocial difficulties is typically conducted in a group setting and includes the basic components of instructions, modeling, behavior rehearsal, feedback, social reinforcement, and homework assignments. Relaxation training, imagery procedures, or cognitive restructuring techniques are often integrated into the treatment package. Groups of 5–10 clients may meet for 8–12 weekly sessions of 1.5–2 hr. duration. Groups are typically administered by male and female co-therapists, but unisex and mixed-sex groups have both been reported. While empirical data on the latter issue are lacking, mixed-sex groups may be easier to conduct because of the increased pool of opposite-sex persons available for use during behavior rehearsals. Session time may be divided among: (a) discussion of heterosocial interactions during the past week, especially those initiated as part of homework assignments, (b) focus on the specific situations of concern to particular group members, with some attention to each client in each session whenever possible, and (c) construction of homework assignments to be implemented during the next week. In focusing on the concerns of a particular group member, the following sequence of events might be employed: (a) discussion of situations in which the concern arises, (b) isolation and detailed description of a specific instance, (c) role-play demonstration by the client of his/her likely or typical response, (d) comments, feedback, and discussion involving the client, other group members, and therapists, (e) modeling by the same-sex therapist of effective performance of a single target behavior selected for attention, (f) rehearsal of the behavior by the client, (g) praise for positive aspects of the client's response, (h) feedback regarding modification of other targeted aspects of the response, (i) self-evaluation and integration of discussion by the client, and (j) repetition of steps (f) through (i) as needed until the target behavior can be skillfully performed. Several repetitions may be necessary to assure a smooth performance. At this point, other behaviors in need of training may be targeted, other role-play partners may be included, or the partner's behavior may be altered in some way so that the client is trained to respond in a flexible manner. A homework assignment is then developed to help the client implement newly-acquired skills in the real-life situations for which they are intended.

EXPECTED OUTCOMES

Most investigations have involved treatment of college students in settings such as that just described. Overall outcomes have been very positive when assessed immediately after treatment or after a brief (less than 6 months) follow-up period. However, most assessments have consisted of self-report questionnaires or role-plays of social interactions conducted in the clinic. Client self-monitoring and unobtrusive observation of naturally-occurring social behaviors have been underutilized. Full evaluation of expected outcomes requires a more complete assessment conducted over a longer follow-up period for a more diverse selection of clients.

CONTRAINDICATIONS

No specific data are available on side effects or contraindications of heterosocial skills training. However, emphasis should be placed on careful and complete assessment of clients' behavioral, cognitive, and physiological responses to heterosocial interactions so that the most appropriate techniques may be matched to client difficulties. It is also necessary to carefully monitor treatment generalization since such generalization has not automatically occurred in many applications of skills training procedures.

BIBLIOGRAPHY

Arkowitz, H. (1977). Measurement and modification of minimal dating behavior. In M. Hersen, R. Eisler, & P. Miller (Eds.), *Progress in behavior modification* (Vol. 5). New York: Academic Press.

Curran, J. P. (1977). Skills training as an approach to the treatment of heterosexual-social anxiety: A review. *Psychological Bulletin, 84,* 140–157.

Galassi, J. P., & Galassi, M. D. (1979). Modification of heterosocial skills deficits. In A. S. Bellack & M. Hersen (Eds.), *Research and practice in social skills training.* New York: Plenum Press.

Heimberg, R. G., Madsen, C. H., Jr., Montgomery, D., & McNabb, C. E. (1980). Behavioral treatments for heterosocial problems: Effects on daily self-monitored and roleplayed interactions. *Behavior Modification, 4,* 147–172.

Kelly, J. A. (1982). *Social skills training: A practical guide for intervention.* New York: Springer.

See: Communication Skills Training
     Conversational Skills Training
     Social Skills Training

HOME BASED REINFORCEMENT

Benjamin Lahey

The term *home based reinforcement* refers to any number of methods in which reinforcement is provided at home for a socially valued behavior that occurs in a school, day care, or similar setting. Most commonly, school children bring a "daily report card" home to their parent or guardian on which the teacher has noted their behavior during that day. In this way, an adult who is not part of the school system can provide systematic reinforcement for behavior that he or she did not directly witness. When the parent or guardian is not a responsible individual or does not have custody of the child, such reinforcement can be delivered by a school counselor, principal, corrections counselor, or other similar adult. The primary advantage of home based reinforcement programs is that they make it possible to modify classroom behavior even when teachers are not willing or able to implement classroom behavior modification programs. They also appear to be efficient in terms of the time and effort required of the teacher, parent, and consultant.

Home based reinforcement programs have been used successfully to modify the general behavior and academic performance of "predelinquent" adolescents (Bailey, Wolfe, & Phillips, 1970), children with learning problems (Hawkins, Sluyter, & Smith, 1972), aggressive children (Bristol, 1976), and normal kindergarten children (Lahey, Gendrich, Schnelle, Gant, & McNees, 1977). Most of the research on home based reinforcement has been reviewed by Broughton, Barton, and Owen (1981).

Clinically, the use of home based reinforcement appears to be most successful when the following guidelines are followed:

1. The daily report card should clearly specify one, two, or three behaviors that are of primary concern. The description of these behaviors must be unambiguous to the teacher, and should neither be overly vague nor overly specific. It is always necessary to discuss the meaning of these behavior categories with the teacher, both before and after making up the card. The teacher must be included in the selection of the target behaviors, and then he or she must be in agreement with the consultant and the parent as to the specific meaning of the behavior categories.

   The most common problem in using daily report cards from the teacher's perspective involves the use of an excessively high or low criterion for getting a "yes" for a behavior category. The teacher should initially mark "yes" if the child is doing well in that category relative to his or her past performance ("He wasn't in his seat every minute, but for him, he had a pretty good day."). Later, the teacher can usually raise the criterion after the child is behaving better if further improvement is needed.

2. The responsibilities of all persons involved in the system must be clearly articulated. It is the responsibility of the *consultant* to prepare the card in consultation with parent and teacher, to duplicate sufficient copies, and to monitor (and perhaps modify) the system. It is the responsibility of the *parent* to provide the card to the child each day and to provide the ap-

propriate consequences. It is the responsibility of the *teacher* to evaluate the child's behavior and to sign the card at the end of the day. It is the *child's* responsibility to take the card to school, ask the teacher to fill it out each day, and to bring it home to the parent. If the child does not bring it home signed, the consequence is the same as if the card contained all "no" marks. This is done to prevent the child from "losing" bad cards and "remembering" them as being marked with all "yeses" when he or she gets home.

3. If the child has more than one teacher each day, the card can have categories for each teacher to rate and sign. These categories can even be different in some ways for different teachers. It is generally best, however, to limit the daily report card initially to the one or two teachers for whom the child's behavior is most inappropriate.

4. The most important aspect of the home based reinforcement system is the delivery of response consequences by the parent. It is essential to adhere to the following guidelines:

(a) The parents must be told that punishment can *never* be given as a consequence for bad report cards. Parents will want to do this as they are usually angry with the child by the time they reach the consultant, but they must agree to use positive consequences. If the consultant is not convinced that the parents will refrain from using punishment, one probably should not use the daily report card system. Otherwise, daily feedback to parents of the child's bad behavior may increase frequency of inappropriately coercive, or even abusive, control by the parents. This will often increase the child's inappropriate behavior in school, which will further escalate use

of punishment, possibly creating a maladaptive iatrogenic spiral.

(b) The parents must deliver positive consequences without "barbs." For example: "Well, its about time you had a good day." "That's good, but don't you *ever* have a bad day!" "See, we knew you could do it, dear." Positive consequences should be delivered with a brief compliment—"That's great!" "Good!" If the card is not acceptable (usually set as all "yeses," but it could be set as all "yeses" and one "no," especially if more than one teacher and more than one behavior is involved), then the positive consequence is simply not given. Again, the parents must be cautioned to not criticize or punish the child for a bad card, and to avoid spending a lot of time being "interested" or "solicitous" contingent upon bad cards as that might reinforce the child for inappropriate behavior.

(c) The positive consequences should be potent and easily delivered. Furthermore, if the child gets consistently good cards, the consequences should represent a net gain in "good" things. Examples of effective positive consequences include: after-school snacks, money, TV-viewing time, time spent alone with a parent playing games or talking, and points that can be accumulated to earn a large prize (baseball glove, trip to an amusement park, etc.). Money is a commonly used positive consequence and should be delivered in the following way. Suppose, for example, that a boy receives $1.00 a week allowance. A contract could be negotiated with him such that he will continue to get 50¢ non-contingently, but that he can earn 20¢ per day for each card brought home with all "yeses." In that way, he could earn $1.50 per week if he behaves well all week. The parent must feel comfortable with giving him this amount of money, however, because of the next point.

(d) When behavior improves to appropriate levels, the cards should be "faded" out. One effective way of doing this is to shift (after 2 or 3 weeks of acceptable behavior) to a weekly report card. In this system, the teacher rates the child for the entire week and he or she can earn the full week's consequences ($1.00 extra allowance, for example). If that is not successful and the child's behavior worsens, the daily system should be reinstituted. If the weekly system is successful (for 2 weeks or so), then the child should be told that he has earned the right to go off the system entirely. But he should still get the full consequence (e.g., 50¢ plus $1.00 in allowance) noncontingently. If his behavior deteriorates, he can be placed back on a weekly or daily system.

(e) The parents need to watch out for forgeries, especially with older children! For this reason, each report should be dated and signed with a full signature.

Not enough research has been conducted with any one clinical population to estimate the magnitude of treatment effects, or expected time until improvement, with any confidence. Clinical experience with elementary school children with mild learning and behavior problems, however, suggests that modest to considerable improvement generally occurs within 2–10 days of implementation. As mentioned above, home based reinforcement is contraindicated when the parents are unstable, and particularly when they are potentially abusive, unless suitable precautions are taken to protect the children.

BIBLIOGRAPHY

Bailey, J., Wolfe, M., & Phillips, E. (1970). Home-based reinforcement and the motivation of pre-delinquents' classroom behavior. *Journal of Applied Behavior Analysis, 3*, 223–233.

Bristol, M. (1976). Control of physical aggression through school-and-home based reinforcement. In J. Krumboltz & C. Thoresen (Eds.), *Counseling methods*. New York: Holt, Rinehart, & Winston.

Broughton, S. F., Barton, E. S., & Owen, P. R. (1981). Home-based contingency systems for school problems. *School Psychology Review, 10*, 26–36.

Hawkins, R. P., Sluyter, D. J., & Smith, C. D. (1972). Modification of achievement by a simple technique involving parents and teacher. In M. B. Harris (Ed.), *Classroom uses of behavior modification*. Columbus, OH: Charles E. Merrill.

Lahey, B. B., Gendrich, J. G., Gendrich, S. I., Schnelle, J. F., Gant, D. S., & McNees, M. P. (1977). An evaluation of daily report cards with minimal teacher and parent contacts as an efficient method of classroom intervention. *Behavior Modification, 1*, 381–394.

See: Parent Management Training

HOMEWORK
Cynthia G. Last

Homework refers to any tasks assigned to clients to be completed outside of regular treatment sessions. Such tasks may be undertaken for assessment and/or therapeutic purposes. For example, assessment homework may include self-monitoring of relevant target behaviors or completion of questionnaires and surveys. Therapeutic homework assignments most commonly include continued practice by clients of techniques acquired during formal treatment sessions (e.g., practice using cognitive restructuring procedures, relaxation exercises, thought-stopping, self-exposure to feared situations, etc.). Homework generally is thought to increase the efficacy of most behavioral and cognitive-behavioral interventions.

See: Covert Rehearsal
    Operant Conditioning
    Systematic Desensitization

IMPLOSION
Cynthia G. Last

Implosion, or implosive therapy, is a technique intended to eliminate avoidance responses. The treatment procedure was first described in 1961 by Thomas Stampfl. Essentially, the technique consists of increasing anxiety to high or intense levels through imaginal presentation of scenes depicting avoided behavior and stimuli. However, imagery used in treatment is intended to represent "conflict areas" that are thought to be the source of most avoidance behaviors. As such, implosion is based upon clearly specified assumptions concerning the psychodynamics of clients under treatment, and relevant issues at various psychosexual stages are considered to be the substance of treatment. Areas of conflict include: orality, anality, sexual concerns, aggression, rejection, loss of impulse control, and central or autonomic nervous system reactivity.

Scenes are presented in a hierarchical fashion, beginning with less anxiety-provoking items. However, even initial scenes are intended to elicit intense anxiety. Clients are prevented from engaging in any form of avoidance behavior, since such behavior is thought to reduce the effectiveness of treatment. If avoidance occurs, the therapist should stop the client at that point and begin the scene again.

The mechanism of action for implosion is thought to be the extinction of conditioned anxiety responses. In this sense, implosive therapy is similar to flooding or response-prevention techniques. However, proponents of implosion assume that conditioned anxiety responses always are acquired during childhood traumas, which usually are of a psychodynamic nature.

Although initial reports of the effectiveness of this treatment were quite positive, controlled research has not supported the efficacy of implosion. Further, it remains unclear as to whether the psychodynamic content of implosive themes and/or maximization of anxiety (through dramatization of hypothesized "repressed" material) are necessary, especially since these characteristics are two ways in which the technique differs from flooding and response prevention techniques.

Implosive therapy has been used most extensively with fearful and phobic clients. Treatment generally lasts from 10–15 sessions. Potential side effects include high degrees of subjective/physiological distress. No contraindications to the use of this technique have been reported to date.

BIBLIOGRAPHY

Hogan, R. A. (1968). The implosive technique. *Behaviour Research and Therapy, 6*, 423–432.

Hogan, R. A. (1969). Implosively oriented behavior modification: Therapy considerations. *Behaviour Research and Therapy, 7*, 177–184.

Levis, D. J. (1980). Implementing the technique of implosive therapy. In A. Goldstein & E. B. Foa (Eds.), *Handbook of behavioral interventions: A clinical guide.* New York: Wiley.

Stampfl, T. G., & Levis, D. J. (1967). Essentials of implosive therapy: A learning-theory-based psychodynamic behavioral therapy. *Journal of Abnormal Psychology, 72*, 496–503.

Stampfl, T. G., & Levis, D. J. (1968). Implosive therapy—A behavioral therapy? *Behaviour Research and Therapy, 6*, 31–36.

See: Flooding

INCREASED CALORIC PRESENTATION
Michel Hersen

Increased caloric presentations is a straight-forward strategy generally followed as part of a more comprehensive behavioral approach for the treatment of anorexia nervosa. Basically, while in the hospital, the anorexic patient will be presented with several large servings per day, totaling some 6,000 calories. Clinical research in this area indicates that with increased caloric presentation from 3,000 to 6,000 calories a day there is increased consumption from about 2,500 to 2,800 calories a day. Indeed, when combined with feedback and reinforcement this technique is powerful in making food cues salient for the anorexic patient.

BIBLIOGRAPHY

Agras, W. S., Barlow, D. H., Chapin, H. N., Abel, G. G., & Leitenberg, H. (1974). Behavior modification of anorexia nervosa. *Archives of General Psychiatry, 30*, 279–286.

Elkin, T. E., Hersen, M., Eisler, R. M., & Williams, J. G. (1973). Modification of caloric intake in anorexia nervosa: An experimental analysis. *Psychological Reports, 32*, 75–78.

See: Behavioral Weight Control Therapy
Feedback

INSTRUCTIONS
Kathleen Dyer

Instructions are stimuli provided to describe to an individual how to perform a desired response or set of responses. Instructions can be presented verbally (e.g., "Take out your pencil"), or in written form (e.g., Put your name on the top of this page). Additionally, individuals may also engage in self-instruction, where their own verbal behavior guides their response. Instructions generally are not used alone to change clinically significant or strongly maintained behavior. Rather, they serve as a component of a more extensive program (e.g., social skills training or parent management training).

See: Parent Management Training
Social Skills Training

IN VIVO DESENSITIZATION
Robert E. Becker

In vivo desensitization consists of a series of techniques which are similar to systematic desensitization, but involve exposure in real life rather than in imagination. This therapeutic approach is usually applied to anxiety disorders best conceptualized as phobias. The first procedure is specification, in as much detail as possible, of the environmental stimuli which produce the anxiety response. Next, these stimuli are graded from those which produce the most intense response, to those producing a minimal anxiety response. Then the client is instructed in the skill of progressive muscle relaxation. Once this skill is mastered desensitization proper begins, and consists of actual exposure to the environmental stimulus lowest on the graded list of situations while the patient remains relaxed. For example, a client who is afraid of heights might be asked to lean out of a window on the second floor of a building. If after an exposure of several minutes the client feels no subjective anxiety, this exposure is stopped. Some therapists may conduct a second exposure to this same situation just to be sure. Once again, if no anxiety is experienced by the patient, the next highest item on the graded list is presented to the patient (e.g., lean out of a third story window). Therapy proceeds in this manner until the highest ranked item can be presented. Upon completion of this final presentation the therapy is complete. If the patient signals subjective anxiety (usually by a hand signal) the stimulus presentation is stopped and the patient is asked to rate the intensity of the anxiety on a subjective unit of discomfort scale (SUDS). Therapy proceeds from this point by re-relaxing the patient and presenting the stimulus situation one lower than the stimulus which produced the signal of anxiety. If this stimulus is experienced without anxiety then the next highest stimulus is presented once again.

See: Control Desensitization
     Deep Muscle Relaxation
     Exposure
     Systematic Desensitization

JOB CLUB METHOD
Louise Kent-Udolf

The Job Club Method is a counseling method for teaching unemployed persons behaviors necessary to get jobs of the highest possible quality in the shortest possible time. Detailed descriptions of procedures, standard forms, scripts, and samples to be used by participants are included in the *Job Club Counselor's Manual: A behavioral approach to vocational counseling* (Azrin & Besalel, 1980).

The Job Club Method is based on a behavioral counseling model and consists of techniques for getting interviews, arranging transportation to interviews, getting family support, finding and creating unadvertised jobs, utilizing friends and relatives, and other job-seeking strategies. As the name implies, the method is a group approach. It is characterized by adherence to standardized procedures, a directive manner, emphasis on positive statements and constant encouragement, highly structured training procedures, and special focus on final outcome, namely employment. Each training session is designed to fulfill a specified series of objectives. The topics to be covered are specified in advance, and the skills to be learned are stated in task-specific terms. After minimal instruction in any particular lesson or job seeking activity, the client practices the behavior, giving the counselor the opportunity to reinforce correct actions. While in the Job Club Office or lab, the clients prepare resumes, search for job leads, telephone or write letters to potential employers or other sources of information about jobs, make transportation arrangements, write out job search schedules, or complete other pertinent assignments. Except for the actual employment interviews, clients carry out the procedures in the counseling room under the counselor's supervision and instruction. Behaviors are taught and practiced at the office, and interviews are extensively rehearsed. Everything that can be anticipated is done to minimize the efforts required of the client by providing materials and facilities needed in the job search. Clients are urged to come to the office every day until they get a job. To increase the probability of attendance at the training sessions, the Job Club provides coffee, soda, and a smoking area so that the situation is associated with reinforcement. Multiple reinforcers are used to avoid satiation or loss of effectiveness of a single reinforcer. Peer reinforcement and support from the client's family is arranged in addition to counselor praise. The opportunity for attendance is unlimited.

Job Club clients have included normal job seekers, the handicapped, professionals, welfare recipients, youth, and college students. The method is intensive and demanding for clients and counselors, but the results are promising. Highly correlated with success in job finding are consistency of attendance and the number of interviews obtained. It has been demonstrated that job finding effectiveness is greater when the techniques are taught by supervision of actual job-seeking behaviors rather than through a lecture, discussion, written, and role-playing format.

BIBLIOGRAPHY

Azrin, N. H., & Besalel, V. A. (1980). *Job Club Counselor's Manual: A behavioral approach to vocational counseling.* Baltimore: University Park Press.

Azrin, N. H., Besalel, V. A., Wisotzek, I., McMorrow, M., & Bechtel, R. (1982). Behavioral supervision versus informational counseling of job seeking in the Job Club. *Rehabilitation Counseling Bulletin, 25,* 212–218.

Azrin, N. H., Flores, T., & Kaplan, S. J. (1975). Job-finding club: A group assisted program for obtaining employment. *Behaviour Research and Therapy, 13,* 17–27.

Azrin, N. H., Philip, R. A., Thienes-Hontos, R., & Besalel, V. A. (1980). Comparative evaluation of the Job Club program with welfare recipients. *Journal of Vocational Behavior, 16,* 133–145.

Azrin, N. H., Philip, R. A., Thienes-Hontos, R., & Besalel, V. A. (1981). Follow-up on welfare benefits received by Job-Club clients. *Journal of Vocational Behavior, 18,* 253–254.

See: Behavioral Group Therapy

LEMON JUICE TREATMENT
Vincent B. Van Hasselt

Lemon juice treatment was developed by Thomas Sajwaj and his colleagues to reduce chronic and life-threatening rumination (i.e., regurgitation of food without nausea or retching, followed by its ejection or reswallowing) in infants and young children. The procedure involves injecting five to 10 cc of lemon juice from a 30 cc medical syringe into the child's mouth contingent upon rumination or one of its precursors, such as lip-smacking or vigorous tongue movements. To minimize the possibility of aspiration, the lemon juice is injected into a corner of the child's mouth. This decreases the force with which the liquid strikes the inside of the mouth. Also, the head is positioned upright or down (not back), thus allowing the lemon juice to be ejected.

While an aversion therapy technique, lemon juice treatment has several advantages over other punitive methods. First, the procedure is relatively simple to carry out. It can be implemented by paraprofessionals and parents with instruction and close supervision by the therapist. Second, the effects of treatment are immediate. Substantial decreases in ruminative responses generally are observed after just a few administrations of the juice. Further, collateral positive side effects, such as increased play, smiling, and motor development have been observed as a function of the intervention. Lemon juice treatment also causes less physical discomfort and is more socially acceptable than other aversive strategies (e.g., electric shock, aromatic ammonia). Finally, this approach is more cost-effective than massive noncontingent attention and less severe than corrective surgical procedures which previously have been employed to decrease rumination.

Drawbacks of the intervention include possible medical complications resulting from its use. The acidity of the juice may cause some irritation of the interior and immediate exterior of the mouth. However, this quickly subsides once use of lemon juice is decreased or eliminated. The second, and potentially more serious, problem concerns aspiration of lemon juice into the lungs. This risk can be minimized by taking the precautions mentioned above.

Although lemon juice treatment primarily has been applied to chronic rumination, it would appear to have value in the remediation of other behaviors commonly associated with but not necessarily part of the ruminative process. Some of these include: mouthing of fingers and objects, choking, and tongue-thrusting.

BIBLIOGRAPHY

Becker, J. V., Turner, S. M., & Sajwaj, T. E. (1978). Multiple behavioral effects of the use of lemon juice with a ruminating toddler-age child. *Behavior Modification, 2,* 267–278.

Sajwaj, T., Libet, J., & Agras, S. (1974). Lemon juice therapy: The control of life-threatening rumination in a six-month old infant. *Journal of Applied Behavior Analysis, 7,* 557–563.

Van Hasselt, V. B., Hersen, M., & Myers, B. (1983). *Lemon juice treatment of chronic rumination in a multihandicapped child.* Unpublished manuscript, Western Pennsylvania School for Blind Children.

See: Punishment

MASSED PRACTICE
Michel Hersen

Massed practice is a paradoxical treatment technique derived from Hull's learning theory that has been applied clinically in tic disorders. The theoretical basis for the treatment is that by *voluntarily* practicing the tic in many trials over a concentrated period of time, fatigue (i.e., reactive inhibition) will build up. When such fatigue reaches a critical point the patient no longer is able to perform the tic. The habit of not performing the tic presumably is associated with drive reduction and, hence, reinforced.

Clinical studies and a number of single case experimental analyses have yielded positive results ranging from a total absence of the tic to reduced frequency of its emission. In one study the patient was asked to perform the tic 400 times consecutively on four occasions per day. In another case report, massed practice was carried out for 1-minute periods alternating with 1-minute rest periods. In the absence of controlled outcome studies, however, there are no specific recommendations for rate of practice and use of rest periods. Also, there is one possible contraindication to the use of massed practice. Since patients with tic disorders such as spasmodic torticollis already tend to suffer from hypertrophy of the sternocleidomastoid muscle, massed practice, if unsuccessful, may lead to further hypertrophy.

BIBLIOGRAPHY

Hersen, M., & Eisler, R. M. (1973). Behavioral approaches to study and treatment of psychogenetic tics. *Genetic Psychology Monographs, 87,* 289–312.

Turner, S. M., Hersen, M., & Alford, H. (1974). Effects of massed practice and meprobamate for spasmodic torticollis: An experimental analysis. *Behaviour Research and Therapy, 12,* 259–260.

Yates, A. J. (1970). Tics. In A. J. Yates (Ed.), *Behavior Therapy.* New York: Wiley.

See: Extinction
    Paradoxical Intention

MATERIAL REINFORCEMENT
Thomas R. Kratochwill

Material reinforcement is also known as *tangible* reinforcement. A functional relationship between a material or tangible reinforcer and a behavior serves to strengthen, increase, or maintain that behavior. *Material reinforcers* are those objects in the environment that can be touched, smelled, tasted, looked at, eaten, worn, or manipulated. Material reinforcers are therefore distinguished from two other categories of positive reinforcers: Social reinforcers and intrinsic reinforcers. Material reinforcers may, however, be either primary or secondary reinforcers. Examples of material reinforcers include candy, toys, a new tennis racket, a bicycle, or clothes.

See: Positive Reinforcement

MEMORY RETRAINING
Roger L. Patterson

Memory retraining is a collection of techniques used to restore memory functioning in brain-damaged people who have lost part of their memory capacity. Major interventions include the teaching of the use of mnemonics, the skilled use of prompts, reinforcement, or some combination of these techniques. Assessment to determine the exact nature of the deficit is an important part of the process.

CLINICAL APPLICATION

As a behavior therapy technique, memory retraining is well explicated by Lewinsohn and his associates at the University of Oregon Neuropsychology Laboratory. This group has developed a treatment model which included: (a) pinpointing the memory deficit by means of laboratory assessment procedures, (b) designing and evaluating intervention intended to alleviate deficits as demonstrated in the laboratory, (c) generalizing improvements to real-life situations, and (d) maintaining these improvements.

The initial assessment is a critical part of the procedure, since memory complaints may be very vague or inaccurate, and the actual deficit may not be easily observed in casual interactions. Also, as noted by Lewinsohn and his colleagues, "memory" is a very loose, global term and may refer to many diverse phenomena.

The Oregon group employs standardized tests (Halstead Battery, Wechsler Adult Intelligence Scale, two short-term memory tests) initially in order to provide information about the general level of functioning and to suggest areas of impairment. These assessments are followed by an interview in which the interviewer seeks to identify specific areas of concern to the client (Examples: (1) remembering what he/she has done, (2) remembering where he/she put things, (3) remembering what he/she needs to do in the future, etc.). The third stage of assessment is to determine how these deficits are revealed on laboratory tasks. Examples of these tasks are paired-associate learning, associating faces (photographs) and names, recognizing faces, and remembering parts of a story. The reason for the third step of assessment is that it is considered necessary to demonstrate both the deficit and ways to control it in the laboratory before attempts are made to improve memory in the real-life setting.

The therapeutic interventions used by the Oregon group as well as most others have consisted largely of training the subjects in the use of one or more of a variety of mnemonics. These mnemonics are taken from experimental psychology as well as other sources. The particular mnemonic(s) used is determined by the nature of the deficit. One useful method is visual imagery, which can be applied in several ways. The basis of visual imagery is that items to be associated, such as pairs of words, or faces and names, may be remembered much better if they are imagined as being objects or animals which are involved in physical interaction. For example, "dog" and "umbrella" may be associated by imagining a dog carrying an umbrella. With faces and names, some characteristic of the name, such as the letter "I" in Ivory may be associated with Mr. Ivory's long, thin nose. Visual imagery is also involved in the place-loci method, in which things to be remembered are imagined to be located in different rooms of one's house. Another mnemonic system involving visualization is the Peg system. The Peg system is based on words which rhyme with the numbers 1 through 9. Words which rhyme with these numbers (e.g., 2 is a shoe) are then associated with items to be remembered by means of visual memory. Mnemonics which do not require visual imagery include association based upon rhyming, categorization, learning initials as cues for names, including items to be remembered as part of a story, and so on.

The mnemonics used in memory retraining of brain-damaged people are essentially the same for normals, but the techniques of teaching the use of these devices to the clinical population may be more complex.

For example, brain-damaged people may have difficulties in forming and utilizing visual imagery. Drawings may be used to provide images of object interactions, and these prompts may be faded carefully after this method is learned. Verbal cues may be similarly introduced and faded. In addition to methods relying on training people to use mnemonics, the importance of reinforcement used without mnemonics to improve memory in brain-damaged persons has been documented. In general, more explicit training using well-defined stimuli, careful fading of prompts, frequent feedback, and frequent reinforcement may be useful with the brain-damaged.

EXPECTED OUTCOME AND TIME FRAMES

In general, many studies show that many brain-damaged people can learn to improve their performance on laboratory memory tasks if the techniques are properly suited to the needs of the individual. In a few cases, such training generalized to real-life tasks. However, the potential for such techniques to improve the functional capacities of these people on a routine basis remains to be demonstrated. In a number of studies the following results have been found: (1) dramatic improvements in experimental inpatient groups trained by reinforcement to recognize ward staff and to answer questions regarding ward routine, but no changes were noted on a rating scale reflecting normal ward behavior; (2) significant improvement on a face-name task 30 minutes after training, but these effects disappeared after one week; and (3) a severely disabled victim of Korsakoff's psychosis was able to spontaneously identify, and greet by name, several staff members and to locate his locker and several items in it.

With regard to time frames, it would be expected that a few weeks would be needed to provide training on laboratory tasks. Much more time would be needed to provide for proper generalization and maintenance, depending upon the extent and nature of the deficits.

POTENTIAL SIDE EFFECTS AND CONTRAINDICATIONS

Specific guidelines have been provided for mnemonics training. First, training materials must be clearly perceivable and understandable by the subjects. Also, for written materials, subjects must be able to read. For almost all training tasks, subjects must be able to hear and comprehend spoken words. Severely retarded and severely aphasic persons may not meet these criteria. Persons with major psychiatric complications may have various problems which prevent participation. Tolerance for participating in a lengthy series of repetitive tasks may also be a limiting factor in some cases. Caretakers of Alzheimer's disease patients may become more depressed after attending sessions with the affected persons. This is so because the caretaker may recognize, for the first time, the extent of the deficits of the patient.

BIBLIOGRAPHY

Cermak, L. S. *Improving your memory.* (1975). New York: McGraw-Hill.

Dolan, M. P., & Norton, J. C. (1977). A programmed training technique that uses reinforcement to facilitate acquisition and retention in brain damaged patients. *Journal of Clinical Psychology, 33,* 496–501.

Gianutsos, R., & Gianutsos, J. (1979). Rehabilitating the verbal information processing of brain injured patients. A demonstration using single-case methodology. *Journal of Clinical Neuropsychology, 1,* 117–133.

Glasgow, R. E., Zeiss, R. A., Barrera, M., & Lewinsohn, P. M. (1977). Case studies on remediating memory deficits in brain damaged individuals. *Journal of Clinical Psychology, 33,* 1049–1054.

Lewinsohn, P. M., Danaher, B. G., & Kikel, S. (1977). Visual imagery as a mnemonic aid for brain-injured persons. *Journal of Consulting and Clinical Psychology, 45,* 717–723.

Zarit, S. H., Zarit, J. M., & Reever, K. E. (1982). Memory training for severe memory loss: Effects on senile dementia patients and their families. *Gerontologist, 22,* 373–377.

See: Shaping

METRONOME-CONDITIONED SPEECH RETRAINING
John Paul Brady

Metronome-conditioned speech retraining (MCSR) is a procedure for the treatment of stuttering in which the patient/client paces his speech with the regular clicks of an auditory metronome. The principal underlying MCSR is that most stutterers are more fluent if they pace their speech with an iterated auditory stimulus. Even very severe stutterers will be more fluent and show a marked reduction in secondary symptoms (lip tremors, exaggerated eye blinks, jerking motions of the head, and so forth) by pacing one syllable to each beat of a desk top metronome set at a slow rate (e.g., 30 to 60 beats per minute). The fluency obtained in this manner is of limited use to the patient because of the slow rate of the speech, its monotonous quality, and the fact that it is generated only in the quiet and secure confines of the therapist's office. In metronome-conditioned speech retraining, the patient's fluency is systematically extended along two dimensions; the quality of the speech is improved by successively approximating (shaping) speech of normal rate and cadence and by gradually extending the environmental context of the newly fluent speech from the therapist's office into the everyday ecology of the patient.

The rate of speech is gradually increased by increasing the rate at which the metronome is beating and by having the patient pace larger units of speech with a single beat (e.g., from syllables, to short words,

to polysyllabic words, to groups of words). This is done in a series of small steps with the patient practicing extensively (20 to 40 minutes per day) between therapy sessions. The fluency acquired at each step increases the patient's sense of mastery and self-confidence, and insures success at the next step. Speech of normal cadence is acquired by having the patient allow some beats to be planned silences (where sentences are normally junctured) and pacing several short words which are syntactically associated to a single beat. This is also done gradually and with extensive practice. At the same time that the patient is improving the quality of his speech, he is gradually and systematically extending his fluency to more complex situations in his natural environment. Thus, when he can speak fluently and confidently with the therapist or when practicing alone at home, he begins to practice MCSR with other persons with whom he anticipates minimal difficulty. Then, he may begin to pace his speech in the presence of two or more persons or while conversing with a person with whom he previously experienced substantial difficulty. Again, the increased self-confidence and sense of mastery associated with each step in the hierarchy of speaking situations facilitates success at the next most difficult step. The task of extending metronome-paced speech into the patient's natural environment (the classroom, restaurants, and other public places) is made possible by the use of a miniaturized electronic metronome, which is worn behind the ear like the hearing aid it resembles. With this device, designed with a control for both the rate and loudness of the beats, the patient can now practice MCSR in virtually any situation.

In the course of this program, many patients experience temporary relapses (i.e., episodic increases in difficulty maintaining fluent speech). On these occasions it is important that the patient return to a slower rate of speech and that he practice MCSR in less-difficult situations to insure that he regains a high degree of fluency. When his fluency and confidence are regained, he can again systematically increase the rate of the metronome (and hence the rate of speech) and again enter more difficult speaking situations.

Once the patient is able to speak with a high degree of fluency in virtually all situations, he can begin to *discontinue* use of the miniaturized metronome, beginning in the least-difficult situations first. He then proceeds to systematically discontinue use of the metronome in more and more situations until he is speaking fluently in all situations without the device. Often, patients will continue to consciously pace their speech, but without the aid of an external stimulus.

EXPECTED OUTCOMES AND INDICATIONS

Most stutterers who undertake MCSR systematically and practice faithfully between weekly treatment sessions show substantial improvement in their speech. Some stutterers experience periodic relapses (i.e., periods of increased dysfluency), often in relation to identifiable stresses in their daily lives. On these occasions, patients should return temporarily to the use of the metronome until fluency is regained and then again systematically discontinue its use. Some very severe stutterers find that they are indeed substantially more fluent with the aid of the device, but report that efforts to be adequately fluent without it are unsuccessful. Many such patients find the wearing of this prosthesis in most speaking situations is justified and do not have any plan to discontinue its use. For them, the metronome makes possible comfortable and effective communication which is otherwise unobtainable.

The time required for obtaining fluency in most situations is highly variable, ranging from a matter of several weeks to over a year. Most treatment failures occur in patients who, for whatever reasons, fail to practice their new speech patterns between treatment sessions.

Treatment results are most striking in severe stutterers, perhaps because this group is often the most motivated to work at refashioning their manner of speaking and are the most willing to wear the prosthetic device as a step in their treatment.

The results with MCSR are best if other indicated treatments are included in the total therapy program. In particular cases this may include: (1) social skills training, for the unassertive and shy young stutterer; (2) relaxation training, for the physically tense speaker; and (3) cognitive restructuring for the stutterer with persistent negative attitudes and expectations about himself and/or excessively critical attitudes about his own speech performance.

CONTRAINDICATIONS

The one kind of stutterer for whom this procedure is inappropriate is the person whose dysfluent speech pattern is being maintained by its consequences. An example is the patient who makes use of his stuttering as a means of avoiding promotion at work because the prospect of such a change is too threatening to him for some reason. However, such consequences of being a stutterer are rarely major maintaining factors in adult cases.

A more common occurrence is the patient who makes rapid and dramatic improvement in his speech over a short period of time but begins to feel uneasy, anxious, or even threatened. Other persons may begin to relate to him differently, often with increased expectations of a social or vocational nature. The patient may feel that his way of relating to others and his way of meeting life's daily challenges and demands must change as a result of his new fluency. It is the problem of giving up what is familiar, even if dysfunctional, for what is new. Some stutterers react to this situation by not practicing between therapy sessions or by discontinuing treatment completely. A solution to this situation is to discuss the problem with the patient and plan his program so that new and more fluent speaking patterns are required more gradually. This allows the patient time to change his view of himself and to "grow into his new pair of shoes." It is during this period that ancillary treatment procedures, such as social skills training, are often carried out.

BIBLIOGRAPHY

Berman, P. A., & Brady, J. P. (1973). Miniaturized metronomes in the treatment of stuttering: a survey of clinicians' experience. *Journal of Behavior Therapy and Experimental Psychiatry, 4,* 117–119.

Brady, J. P. (1971). Metronome-conditioned speech retraining for stuttering. *Behavior Therapy, 2,* 129–150.

Burns, D., & Brady, J. P. (1980). The treatment of stuttering. In A. Goldstein & E. B. Foa (Eds.), *Handbook of behavioral interventions: A clinical guide.* New York: Wiley.

Hotchkiss, J. C. (1974). Some reactions and responses of stutterers to a miniaturized metronome and metronome-conditioning therapy: A follow-up report. *Behavior Therapy, 5,* 574–575.

Hutchinson, J. M. (1976). A review of rhythmic pacing as a treatment strategy for stuttering. *Rehabilitative Literature, 37,* 297–303.

See: Social Skills Training

MODELING
Johnny Matson

Modeling is an important and powerful social learning theory method that is receiving increasing attention. There are a number of variations of the approach, but the basic procedure involves the presentation of a live demonstration, a filmed or pictoral presentation, or an imagined one. Exposure to this model also includes many details of the model's response, such as cues and situations that surround the model's behavior, so that the situations under which it occurs may also be observed. Based on the presentation, the viewer learns a method of responding and/or the contingencies under which the targeted response will fall.

There are at least three terms that are frequently used with respect to this phenomenon: modeling, imitation, and observational learning. Modeling is a more generic term encompassing the other two. Imitation is the observation and then displaying of this series of responses. Observational learning, on the other hand, refers to the learning that occurs from the observation of others, and often the behaviors learned are not precisely imitated. Thus, knowledge that this learning has occurred may be demonstrated through verbal report. Similarly, the individual may learn a particular set of responses but may choose to exhibit other behaviors which may be more or less desirable.

There are several characteristics which enhance the effectiveness of modeling, including the characteristics of the model himself/herself and the characteristics of the observer. With respect to the model, the proficiency and clarity with which the response is performed and the esteem that the observer holds for the model are important. Thus, in the latter case, professional athletes and actors are held in high esteem by many people. With respect to the observer, there are several steps that seem to be of considerable importance. These include: (1) the attentional process itself (e.g., sensory capacity, arousal level, perceptual set and post reinforcement); (2) retention processes (symbolic coding, motor rehearsal, and cognitive organization); (3) motor reproduction processes (e.g., physical capabilities, accuracy feedback, and availability of component responses); and (4) motivational processes (external reinforcement, self-reinforcement).

There are, in practice, a number of variations from the basic modeling paradigm which are used as training procedures. These include graduated modeling, where the presentation of increasingly difficult behaviors is made; guided modeling, where some physical prompting is used, usually in a gradual manner; and, guided modeling with reinforcement. These methods are primarily used to train particular responses. Participant modeling or contact desensitization involves body contact with the therapist in the guiding of the client's participation and is used primarily as a means of eliminating undesirable response patterns such as phobias.

Modeling procedures which are typically used in conjunction with reinforcement and other training strategies have been successfully employed to train many behaviors in addition to phobias. Some of these responses are social skills, pedestrian skills, cooking skills, and dressing behaviors.

BIBLIOGRAPHY

Bandura, A. (1969). *Principles of behavior modification.* New York: Holt, Rinehart & Winston, Inc.

Bellack, A. S., Hersen, M., & Kazdin, A. E. (1982). *International handbook of behavior modification and therapy.* New York: Plenum Press.

Matson, J. L., Marchetti, A., & Adkins, J. A. (1980). Comparison of operant and independence-training procedures for mentally retarded adults. *American Journal of Mental Deficiency, 84,* 487–494.

Shapiro, E. S. (1981). Self-control procedures with the mentally retarded. In M. Hersen, R. M. Eisler, & P. M. Miller (Eds.), *Progress in Behavior Modification* (Vol. 12). New York: Academic Press.

See: Contact Desensitization
 Covert Modeling
 Symbolic Modeling

MULTIMODAL BEHAVIOR THERAPY
Arnold A. Lazarus

Multimodal therapy is a systematic and comprehensive assessment-therapy approach that postulates that "personality" and psychological dysfunctions may be viewed in terms of seven modalities: behavior, affect, sensation, imagery, cognition, interpersonal relationships, and biological considerations. BASIC ID is derived from the first letters of each of these modalities, but by referring to the biological modality as "Drugs/Biology" (since one of the most common biological interventions is the use of neuroleptic medication), we have the more compelling acronym BASIC ID, or the preferred BASIC I.D. [B = Behavior, A = Affect, S = Sensation, I = Imagery, C = Cognition, I = Interpersonal relationships, D = Drugs/Biological factors.] Multimodal therapy is *behavioral* inasmuch as it adheres to the principles, procedures, and findings of psychology as an experimental science. Nevertheless, the multimodal orientation transcends the traditional behavioral approach by delving in greater depth and detail into sensory, imagery, cognitive, and interpersonal factors and their interactive effects. Multimodal therapy should not be confused with the multidimensional and multifaceted assessment and treatment procedures that many clinicians employ. The unifying feature that sets multimodal therapy apart from diverse, eclectic, multiform approaches is the thorough assessment of significant deficits and excesses across the client's BASIC I.D.

The multimodal framework allows the therapist to take into account the uniqueness of each individual and to tailor treatment accordingly. There are virtues not only in using a variety of techniques, but even a variety of therapists. The client always comes first, even if it means referring him or her to someone else. Clearly, multimodal assessment and treatment procedures are applied differently in institutional settings than with adults seen in private practice. Similarly, special adaptations are necessary when treating children.

The multimodal framework provides an integrative assessment and treatment plan that considers the whole person in his or her social network. People are troubled by a multitude of specific problems that call for a wide range of particular interventions. By constructing a Modality Profile (i.e., a list of specific problems in each area of the BASIC I.D., together with proposed treatment strategies for each identified problem), the clinician obtains a "blueprint" and is able to distinguish idiosyncratic factors, and thus guards against molding clients to preconceived treatments.

Here is the Modality Profile of a 30-year-old woman who complained of shyness:

The client's "shyness" appears to be related to several specific, identifiable problems. Seventeen such areas are matched to nine treatment recommendations. Typically, client and therapist examine the Profile and determine treatment priorities. The initial BASIC I.D. or Modality Profile provides a *macroscopic* overview of the client's "personality." Thorough assessment calls for an accurate and comprehensive examination of each modality and the interactions between and among the seven modalities.

A recursive application of the BASIC I.D. to itself (a "second-order" assessment) often helps to shed new diagnostic light and helps to overcome some seemingly recalcitrant problems. The Second-Order BASIC I.D. consists of subjecting any item on the initial Modality Profile to a more detailed inquiry in terms of behavior, affect, sensation, imagery, cognition, interpersonal factors, and drugs or biological considerations. This procedure is usually invoked when treatment impasses occur. For example, when the aforementioned "shy woman" found desensitization ineffective in overcoming her fears of rejection, the following Second-Order assessment was carried out:

Therapist: Imagine someone rejecting you. (Pause) What do you see yourself *doing*?

Modality	Problem	Proposed Treatment
BEHAVIOR	Reticent, compliant Flat tone of expression	Assertiveness training Voice projection
AFFECT	Fears criticism, rejection; anxious Tense; unable to relax	Desensitization Relaxation training
IMAGERY	Images of helplessness, loneliness, and ridicule from others	Coping imagery exercises
COGNITION	Overvalues pleasing others Perfectionistic	Cognitive disputation
INTERPERSONAL	Avoids social situations Does not initiate conversations Withdrawn	Risk-taking assignments
DRUGS/BIOLOGY	Drinks six cups of coffee per day Overeats—minimal physical activity	Cut down on coffee Institute fitness regimen

Client: (Thinks) I'm just sitting quietly, sort of withdrawn, or I'm walking away with my head down.

Therapist: And what are you *feeling* at the time?

Client: Sad, and hurt, and angry, oh, and I'm probably starting to cry as soon as I'm sure nobody can see me.

Therapist: What bodily *sensations* would you experience?

Client: (Pause) My throat would be tight, and my teeth would probably be clenched. I'd feel very tight and tense.

Therapist: What sorts of *images* come to mind?

Client: At what stage?

Therapist: You've been rejected. You have walked away. You feel hurt and angry, and you start to cry. You feel tense. What mental image goes with all that?

Client: The first thing that popped into my head was me as a child. I feel diminished. I see myself as a little baby. I look tiny in my own mind. I'm surrounded by giants.

Therapist: And what *thoughts* or ideas go along with that?

Client: I think of myself as ineffectual, almost useless. I think people have a valid reason for rejecting me.

Therapist: In your day-to-day dealings with other people, are you aware of feeling that they are all adults and that you are a child?

Client: (Thinks) I've never really thought of it just in those terms, but it hangs together. I do see the world through the eyes of a timid, frightened child.

Second-Order BASIC I.D. for Rejection

B   Withdraws; cries
A   Sad, hurt, angry
S   Throat and jaws tight. General tension.
I   A small child or a baby surrounded by giants.
C   Ineffectual. Gives too much credence to others.
I.   Approaches others timidly.
D.   —

The upshot of this Second-Order Assessment was to change the treatment focus to the use of additional coping imagery exercises (in which she deliberately and systematically pictured herself as an adult dealing with other adults) and to place more emphasis on assertiveness and social skills training.

Whereas Modality Profiles list specific problems in each dimension of the BASIC I.D., Structural Profiles provide a quantitative self-rating of the client's proclivities in each of the seven modalities. In everyday terms, some people are primarily "doers," whereas others are "feelers," or "thinkers," or people-oriented "relaters," and so forth. Clients are asked to rate the extent to which they perceive themselves as Doing, Feeling, Sensing, Imagining, Thinking, and Relating. They are also requested to rate how closely they observe and practice "health habits"—regular exercise, good nutrition, abstinence from cigarettes, etc. A high D score on the Structural Profile indicates a healthy and health-minded individual. Structural Profiles are especially useful in marriage therapy. Spouses may be asked to draw up their own profiles, their estimate of how their mate might perceive them, and a Profile of how they see their spouse. Table 1 illustrates the Structural Profile of a cou-

Table 1 . Self-Ratings of Husband and Wife

Modality	Husband	Wife
Behavior	6	4
Affect	1	6
Sensation	2	5
Imagery	2	3
Cognition	6	5
Interpersonal	1	6
Drugs/Biology	4	5

ple for whom divorce counseling proved more effective than marriage therapy.

This couple was especially incompatible in the Affective, Sensory, and Interpersonal modalities. The wife depicted herself as a particularly "feeling" and "relating" individual (the husband's two lowest self-ratings). He, in turn, regarded himself as a "doer" and a "thinker." Their domestic problems centered around issues of affection and caring (the wife felt deprived; the husband felt overwhelmed by her demands) and a constant struggle raged regarding her desire for companionship and friendship, and his wish for solitude. The Structural Profile led the husband to declare that "this marriage should never have taken place," a view with which the wife reluctantly concurred. In general, Structural Profiles provide a springboard for fruitful discussions of specific and precise measures that spouses may undertake for remedying particular discrepancies. Moreover, when therapist and client explore the meanings and relevance behind each rating, important insights are often gained.

Another assessment procedure that is unique to the multimodal approach is called Tracking. This refers to a careful scrutinizing of the "firing order" of the different modalities. For example, some clients tend to generate negative emotions by dwelling first on unpleasant mental pictures (images) followed by catastrophic ideas (cognitions), that trigger heart palpitations and tremors (sensations), culminating in avoidance or withdrawal (behavior). The foregoing ICSB pattern (images, cognitions, sensations, behavior) may call for different treatment strategies than, say, a SCIB pattern (sensations, cognitions, images, behavior), or a CISB sequence (cognitions, images, sensations, behavior). Clinically, it appears to be more productive to administer techniques in the same sequence as the client's "firing

order." Thus relaxation and biofeedback would be favored as initial treatments for a client with a SCIB order (i.e., predominantly sensory techniques to meet the client's sensory trigger), whereas a client with a CISB pattern would be expected to respond less well to sensory techniques, until some improvement was evident in cognitive and imagery areas.

Another strategy that multimodal therapists employ is called Bridging. This refers to a deliberate tuning in by the therapist to the client's preferred modality, and thereafter branching off into other dimensions that seem more productive. Thus, if a multimodal therapist is eager to obtain affective reactions, *feeling statements*, from a client who is *intellectualizing* and presenting only cognitive material, a "bridging maneuver" would be invoked. Instead of challenging the client, or even pointing out that he or she tends to eschew the expression of feelings by erecting intellectual barriers, the multimodal therapist would first enter into the client's domain and then gently lead him or her into other (potentially more productive) channels. By joining the client in his/her preferred modality, it permits the client to be "heard," whereupon it is usually simple to guide him/her into other areas of discourse.

Multimodal therapy overlaps with cognitive behavior therapy and rational-emotive therapy in certain important respects, but there are significant points of difference. For one thing, it is more comprehensive. The deliberate and systematic assessment of the BASIC I.D.; the use of Second-Order BASIC I.D. procedures; and the construction of Modality Profiles and Structural Profiles are unique to multimodal therapy. They yield clinical information often not gleaned by other assessment procedures. Moreover, methods such as Bridging and Tracking provide a structure that keeps the therapist "on target." Apart from its heuristic virtues, the multimodal structure permits an examination of its own efficacy. While all multimodal therapists are eclectic, all eclectic therapists are not multimodal in outlook or in practice.

BIBLIOGRAPHY

Brunell, L. F., & Young, W. T. (Eds.), (1982). *Multimodal handbook for a mental hospital.* New York: Springer.
Keat, D. B. (1976). Multimodal therapy with children: Two case histories. In A. A. Lazarus (Ed.), *Multimodal behavior therapy.* New York: Springer.
Lazarus, A. A. (Ed.). (1976). *Multimodal behavior therapy.* New York: Springer.
Lazarus, A. A. (1981). *The practice of multimodal therapy.* New York: McGraw-Hill.
Lazarus, A. A. (1984). Multimodal therapy. In R. J. Corsini (Ed.), *Current psychotherapies* (3rd ed.). Itasca, IL: Peacock.

See: Cognitive Therapy
Rehearsal
Systematic Desensitization

NEGATIVE PRACTICE
Kathleen Dyer

Negative practice is a procedure designed to decrease the occurrence of an inappropriate behavior by requiring the individual to repeatedly perform the behavior. For example, a negative practice procedure designed to decrease the frequency of swearing by an individual might involve several sessions where the person is required to swear repeatedly for a predetermined amount of time.

See: Massed Practice
Paradoxical Intention

NEGATIVE PUNISHMENT
Alan Poling

Negative punishment is an operant conditioning procedure in which a response is followed by the termination or reduction of a stimulus (negative punisher), and is thereby weakened. The response-weakening effects of negative punishment typically involve a decrease in the future rate or probability of occurrence of the response, although other changes in behavior (e.g., an increase in response latency, or a decrease in response magnitude) may also be indicative of negative punishment. Negative punishment, by definition, weakens the response class for which it is arranged, although it may strengthen, weaken, or have no effect on other behaviors.

Briefly reducing the intensity of music piped to her study carrel each time a student engages in off-task behavior, and thereby reducing the rate of occurrence of the response, is an example of negative punishment.

See: Negative Reinforcement
Positive Punishment
Punishment

NEGATIVE REINFORCEMENT
Alan Poling

Negative reinforcement is an operant conditioning procedure in which a response is followed by the termination or reduction of a stimulus (negative reinforcer), and is thereby strengthened. The response-strengthening effects of negative reinforcement typically involve an increase in the future rate or probability of occurrence of the response, although other changes in behavior (e.g., a decrease in response latency, or an increase in response magnitude) may also be indicative of negative reinforcement. It is important to recognize that negative reinforcement, by definition, strengthens the response class for which it is arranged, although it may strengthen, weaken, or have no effect on other behaviors. Care must be taken not to confuse negative reinforcement with punishment, which inevitably weakens responding.

An example of negative reinforcement is increasing a mildly mentally retarded individual's appropriate use of a table napkin by briefly removing his or her bib each time the response occurs. This procedure would, of course, involve negative reinforcement only if the response were strengthened. If the rate of napkin use decreased as a function of the treatment, it would then be a negative punishment procedure.

See: Negative Punishment
     Operant Conditioning
     Punishment

NICOTINE FADING
Richard M. Foxx

Nicotine fading is a procedure for treating cigarette smokers that involves requiring them to systematically change their brand of cigarettes to those brands containing proportionately less nicotine until they are smoking the lowest nicotine cigarette commercially available. At that point, the smoker either quits smoking or engages in controlled smoking by continuing to smoke the low-nicotine brand. The nicotine fading rationale is based on the assumption that the nicotine in cigarettes produces physiological dependence. As a result, gradually reducing this dependence should serve to minimize nicotine withdrawal effects while simultaneously reducing health risks since the nicotine content of cigarettes is highly correlated ($r = 0.96$) with their tar content.

See: Fading

OMISSION TRAINING
Frances Moosbrugger Hunt

Omission training is a differential reinforcement procedure used to reduce or eliminate inappropriate behaviors. It involves the delivery of reinforcement contingent on the complete absence of the target behavior throughout a prespecified time interval: The client is reinforced for omitting, rather than emitting a response. The near-elimination of the target response can be achieved by gradually increasing the length of the interval during which the behavior must be absent. Omission training is sometimes combined with punishment procedures to speed up the reduction of the target response.

When using this procedure, the therapist should continuously monitor the acceptability or appropriateness of the behaviors, if any, which are emitted by the client in place of the target response, as well as possible increases in the target response in nontreatment settings (i.e., behavioral contrast effects).

A typical application of omission training would be to reduce self-stimulatory behavior of a severely retarded student during instructional sessions. Baseline assessment might indicate that the student refrains from self-stimulation for up to 5 seconds at a time, so the initial criterion for reinforcement is no self-stimulation for 5 seconds. Throughout the instructional session, the client is reinforced for each interval of 5 or more seconds during which no self-stimulation occurs. The length of the other interval is gradually increased until the client consistently refrains from engaging in self-stimulatory behavior for the entire instructional session.

See: Differential Reinforcement of Low Rate
     Behavior
     Differential Reinforcement of Other
     Behavior

OPERANT CONDITIONING
Thomas R. Kratochwill

Operant conditioning is a theory of learning most closely associated with B. F. Skinner. There are commonly thought to be two types of conditioning: Type S, or classical conditioning, and Type R, or operant conditioning. In operant conditioning, the probability of the reoccurrence of a response is increased if the response is followed by a reinforcing stimulus. A discriminative stimulus may be presented before the response, informing the organism that the conditions of reinforcement are in effect. A previously non-occurring response may be shaped by reinforcing closer and closer approximations to the desired response. The frequency of occurrence of the response is affected by its schedule of reinforcement. If reinforcement does not follow the response, the probability of its reoccurrence will diminish, until it eventually returns to pre-reinforcement levels. Operant conditioning is generally represented by the following schema, in which S^D = discriminative stimulus, R = response, and S^R = reinforcing stimulus: $S^D \rightarrow R \rightarrow S^R$.

ORGASMIC RECONDITIONING
Barry M. Maletzky

Orgasmic reconditioning (OR) is a technique employing a client's own sexual fantasies to reduce or eliminate deviant sexual arousal. As such, its sole application has been in the treatment of the sexual offender, occasionally with dramatic results. It is generally introduced in treatment when sufficient trust has been built to discuss masturbation fantasies and is usually employed as one among a number of techniques, such as aversive conditioning, shame aversion, or assisted covert sensitization for the sexual offender. All authors on this subject, and many clients as well, stress the importance of sexual fantasy in the initiation and maintenance of deviant sexual arousal.

There exist four separate techniques which can be employed utilizing the clients' own masturbation fantasies:

1. *Directed Masturbation* — In directed masturbation the client is simply asked to masturbate to non-deviant fantasies, as often as daily, and to avoid masturbation to any deviant fantasies. Theoretically, the association with fantasy, orgasm, and an appropriate stimulus, such as a same-aged female, will eventually increase non-deviant sexual arousal. However, many sexual offenders already have a normal sexual response to non-deviant stimuli. It is unlikely that simple extinction could occur so rapidly, often within weeks, to strongly conditioned sexual stimuli. Nonetheless, reports of this technique have been quite positive and indicate larger clinical trials.

2. *Alternate Imagery* — In this technique the client is asked to masturbate for a block of time as short as one day or as long as several weeks to deviant fantasies during the first block and to non-deviant ones during the second. For example, in daily alternation, days one, three, five, seven, etc. are devoted to deviant fantasies, while days two, four, six, eight, etc. to non-deviant ones. Again, the success of this technique is difficult to explain based upon a simple conditioning model and other hypotheses have been invoked to explain the beneficial results in reducing or eliminating deviant sexual arousal.

3. *The Satiation Technique* — In this technique the client is asked to masturbate to fantasies or pictures of sexual activity with an appropriate stimulus (such as a like-aged female) until reaching climax. At that point he is directed to continue masturbating for 15 to 60 minutes to deviant fantasies (such as exposing himself or

sexual activity with a young girl or boy). This forces the deviant fantasies to be experienced during the period of time when sexual arousal is at its lowest; thus, some writers have hypothesized that this technique is helpful through the principles of aversive conditioning as well as through other mechanisms, such as cognitive self-control and changes in self-perception.

4. *Masturbatory Fantasy Change (MFC)*— In this technique the client is asked to masturbate with fantasies or materials of deviant sexual arousal just to the point of ejaculatory inevitability and then to suddenly switch to non-deviant fantasies or materials for climax. Then, with each subsequent masturbatory session the client is instructed to make this switch earlier and earlier in the course of masturbation until he finally is masturbating to non-deviant fantasies and materials alone. The optimum time course for such a change is not as yet specified but in clinical practice the client usually reports successful completion of total fantasy change, from deviant to non-deviant stimuli over a course of 1 to 2 months. Successful case studies have appeared in the recent literature.

Each of these four techniques has been successful with some sexual offenders but studies comparing them to each other and to other techniques of treatment are not yet at hand. One difficulty such studies will encounter is the private nature of the masturbatory act. Attempts to partially circumvent this obstacle have been reported: the client is often asked to masturbate in a special treatment room in which he speaks his fantasies aloud into a microphone connected with the unseen therapist in another room. Alternately, the client can masturbate to slides or movies under the control of the therapist.

The mechanisms of action of these techniques are not readily apparent, particularly because some seem to head in distinctly opposite directions. Nonetheless, they have been reported to be successful in certain patients and today form an important part of the treatment program for the sexual offender.

BIBLIOGRAPHY

Conrad, S. R., & Wincze, J. P. (1976). Orgasmic reconditioning: A controlled study of its effects upon sexual arousal and behavior of adult male homosexuals. *Behavior Therapy, 7*, 155–166.

Foote, W. E., & Laws, D. R. (1981). A daily alternation procedure for orgasmic reconditioning with a pedophile. *Journal of Behavior Research and Therapy, 12*, 267–273.

Kremsdorf, R. B., Holmen, M. L., & Laws, D. R. (1980). Orgasmic reconditioning without deviant imagery: A case report with a pedophile. *Behaviour Research and Therapy, 18*, 203–207.

Lande, S. D. (1980). A combination of orgasmic reconditioning and covert sensitization in the treatment of a fire fetish. *Journal of Behavior Therapy and Experimental Psychiatry, 11*, 291–296.

Maletzky, B. M. (1983). *The treatment of the sexual offender*. New York: Wiley.

Marquis, J. (1970). Orgasmic reconditioning: Changing sexual object choice through controlling masturbation fantasies. *Journal of Behavior Therapy and Experimental Psychiatry, 1*, 263–271.

Marshall, W. L. (1979). Satiation therapy: A procedure for reducing deviant sexual arousal. *Journal of Applied Behavior Analysis, 12*, 377–389.

See: Assisted Covert Sensitization
     Aversive Conditioning
     Sex Therapy
     Shame Aversion

OVERCORRECTION
Steven A. Hobbs

Overcorrection refers to a diverse set of procedures involving the contingent administration of aversive consequences that are related in form to the inappropriate act they follow. This element of topographical similarity distinguishes overcorrection procedures from other response-contingent punishment techniques. The general rationale underlying the use of overcorrection procedures requires individuals who engage in maladaptive behaviors to: (a) restore the environment (and/or themselves) to a state that is vastly improved relative to its prior condition, or (b) repeatedly practice correct forms of behavior relevant to the context in which the misbehavior occurred.

Consistent with this rationale, overcorrection frequently has been categorized as involving either *restitutional* or *positive practice* procedures. For example, a positive practice overcorrection procedure labeled "functional movement training" has been used to decrease stereotyped head movements. The technique consists of first restraining the client's head and then verbally directing and physically guiding the client through various head movements. Similarly, a restitutional overcorrection procedure labeled "oral hygiene training" has been used to reduce repetitive mouthing, a response that may produce self-infection. Oral hygiene training essentially involves verbal instructions and physical guidance in directing the client to cleanse his/her lips, teeth, and gums with a washcloth or toothbrush dipped in mouthwash. In cases of both restitutional and positive practice overcorrection, physical guidance is used to insure initial client cooperation in the overcorrection sequence. The guidance is then gradually removed as compliance to verbal directions increases.

In addition to oral hygiene training and functional movement training procedures, commonly used restitutional and positive practice overcorrection techniques have included cleanliness training, orderliness training, social apology training, personal appearance training, medical assistance training, and required relaxation/quiet training. Although these labels may be useful as descriptive terms, confusion sometimes arises

as to the specific elements involved in the various overcorrection procedures. However, the major element these techniques have in common involves the active participation of the client in practicing responses that are directly related to the misbehavior. Client participation is primarily accomplished by means of instruction and graduated physical guidance procedures.

Although the majority of clients successfully treated using overcorrection have been mentally retarded children and adults, overcorrection procedures also have been employed in the treatment of autistic and emotionally disturbed individuals as well as clients demonstrating a variety of behavioral disorders. Maladaptive behaviors treated with overcorrection techniques may be classified into general categories of aggressive/disruptive behaviors, stereotyped behaviors of a self-stimulatory or self-injurious nature, toileting problems (e.g., enuresis, encopresis, incontinence), inappropriate oral responses (e.g., vomiting, rumination, pica, coprophagy, drooling), and social-academic responses (e.g., sharing, eye contact, spelling, class attendance).

In general, overcorrection appears to represent an effective response-suppression method. Relatively brief (e.g., less than 10-minute) administrations of overcorrection techniques have produced impressive changes in targeted social-academic and stereotyped behaviors, whereas somewhat lengthier (e.g., 15-minute to 2-hour) administrations have produced decrements in aggressive-disruptive behaviors, inappropriate toileting, and maladaptive oral responses. Such changes have typically occurred within treatment periods of a few days or weeks, although isolated studies have reported the need to administer overcorrection for several months in order to produce desired treatment effects.

As with most punishment procedures,

positive and/or negative side effects have been reported in a majority of studies employing overcorrection. Increased prosocial responses, such as compliance/cooperation, peer interaction, and toy play, as well as generalization of positive treatment effects to new settings have been observed in several reports. Negative side effects such as increases in non-targeted self-stimulatory or self-injurious responses, have been reported when treating aggressive, disruptive behaviors. As yet, valid conclusions cannot be made regarding which subset of overcorrection techniques will yield positive or negative side effects. It has become increasingly apparent, however, that claims regarding the educational value of overcorrection in teaching appropriate responses have limited empirical support. Further, despite its well-documented effectiveness in reducing various targeted responses of a maladaptive nature, caution must be used in administering overcorrection with highly assaultive or combative clients.

BIBLIOGRAPHY

Axelrod, S., Brantner, J. P., & Meddock, T. D. (1978). Overcorrection: A review and critical analysis. *Journal of Special Education, 12*, 367–391.

Foxx, R. M., & Bechtel, D. R. (1982). Overcorrection: A review and analysis. In S. Axelrod & J. Apsche (Eds.), *The effects of punishment on human behavior*. New York: Academic Press.

Hobbs, S. A. (1976). Modifying stereotyped behaviors by overcorrection: A critical review. *Rehabilitation Psychology, 23*, 1–11.

Marholin, D. H., Luiselli, J. K., & Townsend, N. M. (1980). Overcorrection: An examination of its rationale and treatment effectiveness. In M. Hersen, R. M. Eisler, & P. M. Miller (Eds.), *Progress in behavior modification* (Vol. 10). New York: Academic Press.

Ollendick, T. H., & Matson, J. L. (1978). Overcorrection: An overview. *Behavior Therapy, 9*, 830–842.

See: Positive Practice
     Punishment

PARADOXICAL INTENTION
L. Michael Ascher

Paradoxical intention, a technique which was originally developed in the context of logotherapy, derives its name from the fact that the client is instructed by the therapist to perform behavior which appears to be in opposition to (or paradoxical with respect to) the client's therapeutic goals. A common example concerns an individual complaining of an inability to fall asleep within a satisfactory brief interval. The therapist's suggestion, based upon the concept of paradoxical intention, would require the client to remain awake for as long as possible.

Since the client expects techniques that will be of some "help" in falling asleep, the therapist's instruction is seen as being incompatible. The direction of incompatibility is typically toward that of maintaining the behavior as the client initially describes it, or in restraining attempts to change. Thus, the agoraphobic who cannot go into crowded places for fear of suffering cardiac arrest as the result of the experience of panic anxiety is instructed to go into crowded places and try to become anxious. This procedure is paradoxical from the position of the client, not from that of the therapist.

Although there are a number of paradoxical strategies, some of which are quite commonly employed (e.g., symptom prescription), only paradoxical intention has been systematically adopted by behavior therapists. This is possibly due to the requirement of behavior therapists that the clinical efficacy of therapeutic procedures be supported by data derived from appropriately controlled experimental studies. At the present time, such supporting data exist for paradoxical intention to the exclusion of other paradoxical techniques.

ASPECTS OF CLINICAL APPLICATION

Due to the unique background of paradoxical intention, aspects of its application differ with respect to more traditional behavioral techniques; also, components of the paradoxical intention procedure when utilized in a behavioral context appear in contrast to their form in other therapeutic formats. For example, one of the basic tenets of behavior therapy requires that the client be completely informed with respect to the procedures which the therapist plans to employ. It is an assumption that this knowledge will facilitate therapeutic progress. In contrast, paradoxical procedures, as a group, have been associated with a failure to completely inform the client regarding specific significant aspects of the strategy and/or of the therapist's motives in utilizing the technique; again, however, this has generally not been the case when paradoxical intention is employed in the context of behavior therapy. In fact, the scant research that does exist supports the behavioral position of the informed client. The relevant literature has described instructions for providing the client with complete details of the procedure in a manner similar to those which accompany conventional behavioral techniques, yet maintaining the unique characteristics of paradoxical intention.

It has been suggested that one of the most significant of these distinguishing aspects is humor. That is, paradoxical intention, which is inherently humorous, is typically administered within a context which also is humorous. It is hypothesized that a person who complains of a problem perceived as life-threatening (but realistically is not), will rigidly maintain the defensive strategies which they have been employing to protect themselves, and which are probably exacerbating the discomforting symptoms. If the client can be encouraged to adopt a lighter attitude toward his or her presenting complaint, the consequences of greater flexibility and cooperation become more likely.

One of the prime targets of paradoxical intention is that group of anxiety-based disorders which, in some clients, exhibit a recursive component. Thus, as the client attempts to exert greater control over the presenting complaint, the symptoms appear to increase in severity and the client develops a fear of the possible results of high levels of anxiety. In such cases, gaining the clients' cooperation to risk their "disastrous consequence" is perhaps the most difficult aspect of the administration of the technique. One method of assisting clients to follow the paradoxical suggestion in spite of the feared consequences is to attempt to neutralize the potency of the hypothesized disastrous consequence.

A detailed history of individuals complaining of this recursive type of neurosis typically fails to obtain even a single instance of the experience of the disastrous consequence. The absence is particularly noteworthy under circumstances when clients report having experienced conditions optimal for the development of the disaster. This fact must be emphasized on numerous occasions. Another way in which to vitiate the myth is to challenge the individual to experience the unpleasant consequence in the relative safety of the therapist's office. The client is usually unsuccessful in the attempt to exhibit the disaster and thereby adds to evidence which contradicts the facts of the myth.

Additional procedures for assisting clients to utilize paradoxical intention include strengthening their self-esteem. Often individuals are reluctant to employ the technique because they fear the social consequences of risking the hypothesized disasters which the paradoxical instructions typically require. Enhancing self-esteem can serve to reduce the relative imagined negative effects of clients' behavior on their immediate social environment. Improving self-esteem also has the benefit of increasing clients' confidence in the technique and in their ability to successfully use the procedure. In addition, the disruptions caused by setbacks, which invariably occur, are moderated by strengthened self-esteem, enabling clients to more rapidly return to use of paradoxical intention.

SUGGESTED BEHAVIORAL TARGETS

Paradoxical intention, which is a relatively recent addition to the behavior therapist's repertoire, has been associated in the literature with a specific dynamic which seems to represent a significant component of a number of related neurotic complaints. The disorders include, but are not confined to: aspects of primary insomnia, agoraphobia, some forms of social phobia, obsessions and the obsessive-compulsive syndrome, some male and female sexual dysfunctions, fear of blushing and perspiration, and some disruptions of elimination. The common element is reflected in the fact that the above-listed disorders are often complex symptoms of anxiety. If the affected individual attempts to fight anxiety and its symptoms, and failing in this goal of controlling the discomfort experiences additional discomfort, what develops is a pernicious spiral which maintains anxiety at continuously increasing levels of severity. Paradoxical intention is effective because it requires the client to maintain the very behavior which he or she seeks to change under conditions which cannot support the continuation of that behavior. When following the paradoxical directive, the performance anxiety which has maintained the

annoying symptoms is obviated and the symptoms dissipate.

Interactions between personality characteristics and behavioral categories have also been suggested as indicants for effective utilization of paradoxical instructions. Among the most promising of these is the interaction between the "cooperativeness" of the client and the degree to which the behavioral target is perceived by the client to be voluntary vs. involuntary. Paradoxical intention seems to be effective with relatively cooperative clients who complain of behaviors over which they appear to have little control. In fact, this is a good description of the clients discussed in the initial portion of the present section whose presenting problem is anxiety based. Uncooperative clients with responses which they may reluctantly admit are under their control appear in the opposite quadrant of the cooperative-uncooperative voluntary-involuntary interaction, and would seem most effectively approached through the strategy of symptom prescription.

The novel nature of paradoxical intention suggests that it should be cautiously applied with certain groups of individuals, and in the case of those with problems which could pose a health hazard. For example, under most circumstances, a client addicted to controlled substances, prescription or non-prescription medication, or alcohol, should not be induced to give up controls and to increase the intake of the undesired chemicals. (Although there are several reports in the literature suggesting that this strategy when applied by an experienced clinician under optimal circumstances, can be quite effective with the addicted individual.)

BIBLIOGRAPHY

Ascher, L. M. (1980). Paradoxical intention. In A. Goldstein & E. B. Foa (Eds.), *Handbook of behavioral interventions: A clinical guide*. New York: Wiley.

Ascher, L. M. (1981). Employing paradoxical intention in the treatment of agoraphobia. *Behaviour Research and Therapy, 19*, 533–542.

Ascher, L. M., & DiTomasso, R. A. (in press). Paradoxical intention in behavior therapy: A review of the experimental literature. In R. M. Turner & L. M. Ascher (Eds.), *Evaluating behavior therapy.* New York: Springer.

Frankl, V. E. (1955). *The doctor and the soul: From psychotherapy to logotherapy.* New York: Knopf.

Weeks, G. R., & L'Abate, L. (1982). Paradoxical letters. In G. R. Weeks & L. L'Abate (Eds.), *Paradoxical psychotherapy.* New York: Brunner/Mazel.

See: Anxiety Management Training

PARENT MANAGEMENT TRAINING

Steven Beck

Parent management consists of training parents to deal with their children's problematic behaviors through the application of behavioral principles. Several rationales are offered for training parents to deal with their children's behavior problems. First, since parents usually have the primary influence and contact with their children they are in the best position to modify their children's maladaptive behaviors and increase their adaptive behaviors. Second, given the number of children in need of help, the only viable alternative to reach many children appears to be to teach parents how to deal with them more effectively. Third, if appropriate child behaviors are to occur and be maintained, it must take place in the child's natural environment (i.e., in the home). Consequently, behavioral therapists working with children in consulting rooms or offices often do not have the opportunity to either observe or modify a child's problematic behavior. As a result, behavior therapists usually endorse the model of working with the adults who are in the position to be present when the child's target behavior takes place, and who have control over the contingencies of reinforcement when appropriate and inappropriate behaviors occur.

CLINICAL APPLICATION

Perhaps the most striking and impressive fact associated with parent management training is the empirical documentation of the wide range of children's behaviors that have been modified. Parents have been trained to decrease their child's hair-pulling, psychogenic vomiting, stealing, and nightmares, and to increase desirable sibling interaction as well as to increase simultaneously children's compliance and decrease noncompliant behavior.

Skills taught in most parent training programs generally can be categorized as differential attention and time-out techniques. Parents are usually trained to increase appropriate child behaviors by reinforcing their occurrence by attention, verbal praise, or contingency contracting (recording points or tokens for the child which can be later exchanged for agreed-upon tangible rewards, such as toys or family outings). Similarly, parents are often taught to reduce the frequency of competing verbal behaviors, such as number of commands, questions, and criticisms directed at the child. Such management programs typically teach parents to ignore minor inappropriate behaviors. Some management programs also focus on teaching parents to give direct, concise commands. If a child does not eventually comply, the parent is then taught how to implement time-out.

Most parent management programs teach these techniques to parents by incorporating modeling, behavioral rehearsal, and feedback from the therapist. In fact, providing parents with opportunities to observe, practice, and then receive feedback when learning new skills should be basic tenets of any behavioral parent management program. Recent data have shown that parents made aware of social learning principles, as well as the aforementioned training techniques, are more likely to show generalization of treatment from the clinic to the natural environment.

EXPECTED OUTCOME AND TIME FRAME

The parent management literature indicates that treatment ranges from 1 to 106 sessions. However, the modal range of parent training sessions appears to be between 6 and 12, with perhaps some additional booster sessions at monthly or bi-monthly intervals.

There has been a good amount of treatment outcome research conducted on parent management programs. Indeed, there is substantial evidence that behavioral parent training has been demonstrated to be an effective procedure for modifying deviant child behaviors. Not surprisingly, data regarding the generalization of treatment effects have been less impressive. Generality of treatment effects can be divided into four parts: (1) temporal generality, which denotes the maintenance of treatment effects following termination of treatment; (2) setting generality, which includes the occurrence of treatment effects in settings other than the clinic; (3) behavioral generality, which involve changes in behavior not targeted for treatment; and (4) sibling generality, which encompasses changes in the behaviors in the treated child's sibling. Unfortunately, many parent management studies have failed to report such generalization results. Nonetheless, given this limitation, when reported, temporal generality has generally been demonstrated in parent management programs for about 3 months following treatment, and one study has reported stable child behavior changes after parent training 2 ½ years after treatment. Setting generality is infrequently reported, but has been found in a few studies to generalize from the clinic

to the home setting, and even into several community sites, such as shopping centers. Several studies have found that parents successfully trained in decreasing their child's noncompliant behavior display behavioral generalization by similarly decreasing other nontargeted deviant behaviors, such as tantrums, aggressive behaviors, and crying. Only one study reported sibling generality, and found that parents did use their new skills with siblings.

POTENTIAL SIDE EFFECTS AND CONTRAINDICATIONS

There are no documented side effects or contraindications for parent management training to deal with children's deviant behaviors. Therapists, however, should make sure that parents employ frequent positive behavior (i.e., differential attention for desired behavior) and do not just implement punishment procedures (i.e., time-out) once training is completed.

An important issue which is now beginning to receive attention in the parent training literature is whether certain types of parents will be more or less able to complete and benefit from behavioral parent management programs. For example, some family therapists have argued that parent training for extremely ineffectual parents or for chaotic families would only exacerbate the child's problem behavior. This, however, has not been empirically documented. Studies have found that drop-outs from parent training programs differ from participants who complete the program in three important ways: socioeconomic status, parental adjustment, and parental commands. Lower socioeconomic class clients appear more likely to terminate treatment than middle or upper class clients, maternal depression has been related to dropping out, and mothers who terminated treatment prematurely have issued more commands than mothers who have completed treatment. Other investigators underscore the necessity of examining broader family variables which may affect the ability to train parents successfully. One study reported that parents of clinic-referred children were less satisfied with their marriages than those of non-clinic children. Another study tentatively isolated social characteristics that may influence mother-child interactions. In this investigation, a sample of trained mothers did not maintain positive mother-child interactions following the termination of behavioral parent training. These mothers were characterized as having low-income, little contact with friends, and were primarily engaged in aversive exchanges with extended family members and social agencies. Therefore, it would appear that behavior therapists need to assess broad family variables such as maternal depression, marital difficulties, and limited support systems, before embarking on a parent management program with the aim of reducing children's problematic behaviors.

BIBLIOGRAPHY

Becker, W. C. (1971). *Parents are teachers: A child management program*. Champaign, IL: Research Press.

Forehand, R., & Alkerson, B. M. (1977). Generality of treatment effects with parents as therapists: A review of assessment and implementation procedures. *Behavior Therapy, 8*, 575–593.

Forehand, R., & McMahon, R. J. (1982). *Helping the noncompliant child: A clinician's guide to effective parent training*. New York: Guilford Press.

Moreland, J. R., Schwebel, A. I., Beck, S., & Wells, R. (1982). Parents as therapists: A review of the behavior therapy parent training literature — 1975 to 1981. *Behavior Modification, 6*, 250–276.

O'Dell, S. L., Flynn, J. M., & Beuldo, L. A. (1977). A comparison of parent training techniques in child behavior modification. *Journal of Behavior Therapy and Experimental Psychiatry, 8*, 261–268.

See: Home Based Reinforcement
    Operant Conditioning

POSITIVE PRACTICE
Richard M. Foxx

Positive practice is one of the two major components of overcorrection punishment; the other is restitution. The positive practice rationale requires a misbehaving individual to practice overly correct forms of relevant behavior in those situations where the misbehavior commonly occurs. The determination of how positive practice is to be accomplished involves two steps: (a) identifying appropriate behaviors that should be practiced, and (b) requiring the individual to perform these appropriate behaviors whenever the misbehavior occurs. For example, the positive practice for table overturning would involve requiring the misbehaver to perform an appropriate behavior or task while seated at the table. Thus, the purpose of the practice would be to instruct the individual in the appropriate manner in which to behave while at a table. Positive practice also can be used to increase desirable behaviors such as class attendance, spelling achievement, sharing, and eye contact, by using it in an avoidance conditioning program such that the positive practice functions as an aversive stimulus.

See: Overcorrection

POSITIVE PUNISHMENT
Alan Poling

Positive punishment is an operant conditioning procedure in which a response is followed by the onset of a stimulus (positive punisher), and is thereby weakened. The response-weakening effects of positive punishment usually involve a decrease in the future rate or probability of occurrence of the punished response, although other changes in behavior (e.g., an increase in response latency or a decrease in response magnitude) may also be indicative of positive punishment. Positive punishment operations inevitably weaken the response class for which they are arranged, although they may strengthen, weaken, or have no effect on other behaviors.

Using response-dependent electric shocks to reduce the rate and intensity of pernicious self-injurious behavior is an example of positive punishment.

See: Negative Punishment
    Punishment

POSITIVE REINFORCEMENT
Alan Poling

Positive reinforcement is an operant conditioning procedure in which a response is strengthened by the onset of an event (positive reinforcer) which follows the response in time. The response-strengthening effects of positive reinforcement typically involve an increase in the future rate or probability of occurrence of the response, although other changes in behavior (e.g., a decrease in response latency or an increase in response magnitude) may also be indicative of positive reinforcement. It is important to recognize, however, that delivery of a positive reinforcer always strengthens the type of behavior that preceded its delivery, although this process may weaken, strengthen, or have no effect on other response classes.

An example of positive reinforcement is saying "thank you" each time a child passes a dish while dining, as long as the outcome is an increase in the individual's rate of dish-passing.

See: Contingency Management
    Primary Reinforcement
    Premack Principle

PREMACK PRINCIPLE
F. Dudley McGlynn

Experimental psychologist David Premack performed an ingenious series of operant conditioning experiments in which a positively reinforcing contingency was shown to be *any* contingency in which the instrumental or to-be-rewarded behavior occurred with a lower momentary probability than did the contingently available or rewarding behavior. Out of these experiments Premack articulated what Lloyd Homme later termed the Premack Principle: "For any pair of responses the more probable one will reinforce the less probable one." Behavior modifiers sometimes speak of Premack contingencies or Premack reinforcers by which they mean a special class of reinforcing operations in which access to high probability ("desired") behaviors is made contingent upon clinically targeted activities. More accurately, Premack's original idea of "rate differential reinforcement" was offered to explain *all* instances of instrumentally reinforcing contingencies. For example, a child may watch television after (contingent upon) doing his homework.

See: Positive Reinforcement

PRIMARY REINFORCEMENT
Thomas R. Kratochwill

Primary reinforcement is the functional relationship between the primary reinforcer and a behavior which serves to strengthen, increase, or maintain that behavior. Primary reinforcers are stimuli that are necessary for life or for the satisfaction of physiological needs. These stimuli are naturally reinforcing. For example, water, for a thirsty organism, has a type of "inborn capacity" to strengthen behavior. In other words, primary reinforcers are reinforcing without a history to explain how they acquire their reinforcing properties. Examples of primary reinforcers include food, water, sexual release, tactual stimuli, sucking-produced stimulation, taste stimuli, skin temperature, rest and sleep, and the opportunity to breathe.

See: Positive Reinforcement

PRIMING
Michael Milan

Priming was narrowly defined in the early experimental literature (1950s and 1960s) as the brief presentation of a stimulus that results in the initiation of a pattern of responding which continues on after the stimulus is terminated. In its current usage, the definition of priming has broadened and the term now refers in general to the use of antecedent events to instigate behavior. Priming has been described variously as a form of prompting in which the individual is induced to engage in the initial steps of a response sequence, as the process of directly initiating behavior by either verbally describing it or by physically guiding it, and as the provision of a few easily-earned or "free" reinforcers to encourage individuals to begin to engage in activities that then earn those reinforcers. For example, priming is commonly used as a first step in the initiation of a token economy to make subjects aware of the role and value of tokens, and thus stimulate behaviors that will be reinforced.

BIBLIOGRAPHY

Ferster, C. B., & Skinner, B. F. (1957). *Schedules of reinforcement*. New York: Appleton-Century-Crofts.

See: Token Economy

PROBLEM SOLVING TRAINING
Karen Marchione

Problem solving training (PST) is a treatment method through which an individual learns to utilize an effective set of cognitive skills to cope with problematic interpersonal situations. PST emphasizes the importance of cognitive operations in understanding, mediating, and resolving intra- and interpersonal conflicts. Successful coping and adaptation to one's social environment requires a set of interpersonal problem-solving skills that are not measured by either traditional intelligence tests or personality measures. Problem-solving skills have been directly related to adjustment in children, adolescents, and adults. Conversely, deficits in problem-solving skills have been associated with impaired psychological functioning including substance abuse, depression, anxiety, behavioral dysfunctions, marital and child-rearing difficulties, and interpersonal dysfunctions. The association between psychopathological states and deficient problem-solving skills is becoming increasingly evident. As a result of the growing recognition of the importance of problem-solving skills and subsequent adaptation, PST is being applied to diverse target populations.

PST PROCESS

PST involves a complex and inter-related skill-acquisition strategy. While various definitions have been offered, each describing their own relatively unique combination of factors, there are a number of common elements which encompass PST. First, the individual learns *problem sensitivity* and *orientation*. This process includes recognizing and understanding the origin and nature of interpersonal problems and recognizing that they are solvable. The next component, *problem identification, definition,* and *formulation* requires the individual to assess the problem, identify factors resulting in the problematic situation, and set realistic and specific goals. This entails objective, logical thinking and information-seeking. The third component refers to the *generation* of alternative solutions. In this process a multitude of options are identified utilizing brainstorming techniques as a means of identifying potentially viable solutions. The individual draws from a reservoir of ideas and attempts to view the problem from a variety of perspectives, while appreciating how others might feel and respond in the same situation. The fourth component involves *decision-making*. In this phase, the individual chooses a particular solution that may either effectively alter or constructively resolve the problem. The procedure is accomplished by *causal* and *consequential* thinking processes. Each solution is assessed individually in regard to both the short- and long-term consequences and the personal and social effects of acting upon the particular decision. This entails the use of *means-end thinking*, which involves sequentially thinking through the requisite steps involved in resolving the problem. This phase also includes recognizing possible obstacles that may be encountered and/or results that may be expected from the execution of the plan. Finally, the individual is instructed to choose a solution with the most positive overall outcome. Solution generation is followed by the final phase, which includes *implementation of the solution* and *observation* and *evaluation* of the resultant outcome. In this last PST stage, the individual performs the requisite behaviors of the solution and subsequently observes and evaluates the results of utilizing the solution.

CLINICAL APPLICATION

The therapist meets the client in an individual or group format. The sessions can take place in the office or in an external facility such as a school classroom. Each component is presented individually, in conjunction with components previously presented and, finally, in relationship to the skills of problem solving as a whole. The therapist may begin or end by introducing each factor and explaining the importance of utilizing the components. This precedes or follows an exercise to clarify the need for the skill and model its use. This can be accomplished by use of a number of exercises, including games and role play that require the client to be aware of the presenting factor. The amount of time spent on each component may vary depending upon the client's assimilation of the material. Homework assignments promoting generalization of the skill are utilized, with discussion of the client's practice, at the next session. This process is continued until the client demonstrates proficiency both within and outside the treatment setting.

PST has been successfully utilized with normal pre-schoolers; at-risk pre-schoolers; maladjusted children; psychiatric inpatient, as well as outpatient, children; as part of parent training in child management procedures; with normal, at-risk, and delinquent adolescents; test-anxious subjects; agoraphobics; psychiatric inpatients and outpatients; couples with marital dysfunction; substance abusers; alcoholics; smokers; and those with geriatric depression.

While definitive conclusions regarding identification of the most salient elements in PST training awaits further research regarding its content, duration, intensity, and format of presentation, a number of clinical observations can be culled from the literature. First, while wide variations in the number and duration of training sessions have been reported, thus making a consensus difficult, it appears that at least 10 weekly sessions are necessary to insure that PST skills are acquired. This figure represents a minimum and in most cases training encompasses from 20 to 30 sessions to enhance consolidation and generalization effects. Furthermore, PST is frequently employed with spouses, parents, teachers, or significant others to facilitate maintenance and social reinforcement of these fragile, yet vital skills. The use of periodic PST booster sessions may also prove highly beneficial. One of the advantages of PST is that while specific processes of the strategy remain consistent across the diverse client populations to which it has been applied, these procedures are also readily adapted and modified for the specific needs of different clinical groups. In addition, PST is easily disseminated. Indeed, paraprofessionals such as teacher aides and students have been successfully trained to conduct PST modalities. In the majority of studies utilizing PST, both statistically significant and clinically salient results have been obtained, particularly in the area of treating impulsive, maladjusted, and/or antisocial children. A number of studies suggest that PST may also hold much promise in regard to preventing behavioral disorders in childhood, as well as remediating a variety of adolescent and adult dysfunctions.

Several PST advocates have offered suggestions regarding facilatory strategies to enhance its acquisition and utilization. These include: (1) using stimulating formats including audio and video tapes, pictures, and stories; (2) making the PST problematic situations as close to real-life scenarios and events as possible; (3) having clients generate numerous solutions, rather than select solutions offered by others; (4) developing skill acquisition sequentially, instructing clients on how to generate solutions prior to having them examine the consequences of their solutions; (5) providing frequent spotchecks, feedback, and guidance to insure that each step is mastered; (6) facilitating continued use of the skills by instructing significant others in the importance of these processes; (7) utilizing experienced trainers; (8) providing booster sessions where feasible and appropriate; and (9) systematically evaluating the effectiveness of training by assessing *each* of the component PST skills.

CONTRAINDICATIONS

While there are presently few empirically-derived specific contraindications for PST, clinical reports suggest that learning PST may be problematic for acutely disturbed patients, prior to their being stabilized. Overall, the PST strategy is designed to enhance decision-making, problem-solving, and social competency in both individuals and groups. However, due to methodological limitations in the PST literature, its long-term efficacy must await more systematic and longitudinal research. Therefore, it is advisable to monitor the effectiveness of the approach systematically with regard to remediating clinical disorders on both a short- and long-term basis.

BIBLIOGRAPHY

D'Zurilla, T. J., & Nazu, A. (1982). Social problem solving in adults. In P. Kendall & S. Hollon (Eds.), *Advances in cognitive-behavioral research and therapy* (Vol. 1). New York: Academic Press.

Spivack, G., Platt, J., & Shure, M. (1976). *A problem-solving approach to adjustment.* San Francisco: Jossey-Bass.

Spivack, G., & Shure, M. (1974). *Social adjustment of young children: A cognitive approach to solving real-life problems.* San Francisco: Jossey-Bass.

Spivack, G., & Shure, M. (1978). *Problem-solving techniques in child rearing.* San Francisco: Jossey-Bass.

Urbain, E. S., & Kendall, P. C. (1980). Review of social-cognitive problem solving interventions with children. *Psychological Bulletin, 88,* 109–143.

See: Behavioral Marital Therapy

PROGRAMMED PRACTICE
Michael A. Greenwald

Programmed practice is a term used to describe a behaviorally-based bibliotherapeutic treatment for agoraphobic clients. The procedure includes specific and systematic instructions to engage in self-directed graded self-exposure to phobic stimuli. Although this procedure is frequently viewed by its originators as sufficient for the effective treatment of agoraphobia, the majority of clinical researchers employ and view programmed practice as an important adjunctive treatment. While programmed practice may be viewed as a home-based treatment, it is typically administered under the supervision and guidance of an experienced therapist, concurrently with cognitive, behavioral, or pharmacological treatment for agoraphobia.

Graded practice involves the client's graduated exposure to actual phobic situations under the client's control. In some variants of graded practice anxiety is minimized, and clients might be expected to enter phobic situations and remain until they being to experience anxiety. Programmed practice, on the other hand, invites clients to expect and learn to cope with (via calming self-instruction) moderate to high levels of anxiety, in progressively difficult situations. Clients are encouraged to remain in or near the phobic situation for a sufficiently prolonged time so that habituation to phobic stimuli will occur.

CLINICAL APPLICATION

Clients (and often partners) receive programmed practice manuals, which outline the nature of agoraphobia, principles of graded exposure, and methods for coping with anxiety and encouraging regular practice. A conditioning model of phobic avoidance in maintaining fear is presented, and clients are instructed that in order to overcome various fears, it will be necessary to reverse the pattern of habitual avoidance and enter phobic situations, remaining until anxiety decreases and/or the urge to escape disappears. Clients learn that gradual and repeated exposure to phobic situations, with daily practice aimed at specific goals, will help to overcome the disorder. The manual emphasizes that practice is to occur *despite* anxiety; clients are reminded that phobic symptoms are merely unpleasant exaggerations of normal bodily reactions to stress, which are harmless and will pass with time. Clients are taught to notice only what they are experiencing at present, rather than thinking about what they might experience or where it might lead. They are invited to delete frightening thoughts, and notice that when this happens, fear begins to fade. They are encouraged to focus on their progress, instead of on symptoms or difficulties, and on their plans for what to do next rather than on past experiences. Occasional minor "setbacks" occur; clients are reminded that this is quite common, that lost ground can be regained quickly, and that these experiences do not affect their chances for eventual recovery.

THERAPIST ROLE

The therapist serves as advisor and guide in helping the client optimize practice. Client and partner are to be responsible for carrying out the program, and the therapist will be available to review progress, help solve problems (e.g., in targeting appropriate practice objectives), and provide assessment and supervision of the couple's activity. Treatment sessions focus on review of practice during the previous week, particularly on the nature of the practice situation, time in situation, initial and final level of distress, and latency to habituation or obstacles to habituation.

RECORDS

Baseline data include self-ratings of anxiety associated with entering phobic situations, as well as a list of situations presently avoided completely. Ongoing patient records include destination, duration of time in the situation, initial and final anxiety ratings, and annotation as to whether practice is accompanied or independent. Space for comments pertinent to specific situations facilitates trouble-shooting during the programmed practice review sessions.

PARTNER'S ROLE

The partner agrees to attend all meetings with the client and assume an active part in the program. He or she will support client practice despite distress, encourage independence, and praise approximations and achievement of target behavior. During daily conversations, practice is reviewed, help offered in selecting targets, and appreciation expressed for client effort. Some targets will require partner accompaniment, especially in the early stages of practice. The partner avoids excessive concern over panic and encourages the client to remain in the situation until the distress moderates, while respecting the client's right to decide whether to push himself to remain, or to leave and approximate exposure to the situation with additional practice steps.

PRACTICE

At the outset the therapist helps the client target one of the less anxiety-eliciting situations to begin practice, and sets as an initial goal: the smallest possible step beyond the client's current functioning in that area. It is important, particularly at the beginning, to select practice objectives that the client is *likely to attain*, with a moderate level of distress. Equally important is helping the client to view small approximations as mean-

ingful progress towards their longer range objectives.

Clients are directed to practice daily, exposing themselves to a range of target situations, typically in two or three major areas per week, in situations where they are phobic. They are to remain in these situations at least 20–30 minutes or until habituation occurs (or their level of distress drops to a 3 or less on a scale of 0–8). Clients may need to remain in situ for prolonged periods, up to 60–90 minutes or more, especially early in treatment or for difficult steps. They are informed that they should try to avoid running from a situation should panic occur and are advised to simply wait until habituation takes place. Those receiving treatment in an additional cognitive coping strategy (i.e., paradoxical intention, self-statement training, etc.) would employ these procedures as directed by their therapist to moderate anxiety during exposure. Patients should be reminded that their level of subjective distress will fluctuate during the period of exposure. However, as they remain in the phobic situation, their level of anxiety will ultimately drop. The client is to increase the difficulty of practice over time by means of achievable steps or approximations. Regular daily practice in facing increasingly difficult situations is essential to success. Therefore, obstacles to practice must be examined and surmounted by the client, therapist, and partner. These obstacles may take several forms. Scheduling constraints, such as long working hours, need for child care, etc., may be addressed as problems which can be solved through careful planning and rearranging of resources. Occasionally, clients may avoid practice after a particularly difficult outing, and may choose to regard this as a "setback." Helping the client see that occasional difficulty in practice is a normal, common occurrence and encouraging return to practice, perhaps on simpler steps, will prevent a small period of discouragement from becoming a "crisis of confidence" regarding continued programmed practice. Clients are praised for amount of practice, amount of time in situations, and new steps or situations attempted. Level of distress in phobic situations is not considered an important criterion for progress in early treatment; many clients mistakenly focus on level of anxiety alone as a sign of progress. Therapist emphasis is placed on amount of practice and duration of exposure during initial treatment, and on obstacles to practice or difficulty in habituation. As treatment progresses, the therapist will note decreases in latency to habituation and decreased levels of anxiety in practice situations.

TREATMENT RESPONSE

Treatment response to programmed practice is reported in the range of 40%–75%. Variables likely to affect outcome include diagnosis, age of client, severity, presence of secondary depression, marital dysfunction, medical conditions, and client expectations, attributions, and cognitive coping skills.

Those who are likely to show favorable responses manifest noticeable gains during the first 2 to 3 weeks of practice. These gains are, of course, notable in the context of the clients' limitations, and must be viewed in a relative sense. Typically, clients first experience increased time in situations where they were previously avoidant. With continued and repeated exposure, duration and level of distress drop significantly. Over a period of 12 to 15 weeks, anxiety is reduced to negligible levels. Certain clients who do not show initial benefit may show gains with additional therapist intervention to alleviate highly anxiety inducing cognitions interfering with practice or habituation. In unusual cases, anxiolytic medication may be prescribed to permit practice. This would be faded out at the earliest opportunity.

Clients who do not respond to programmed practice should be evaluated for their appropriateness for cognitive, in vivo flooding procedures as primary or adjunctive treatments, or other modalities including marital, individual, family, or pharmacological interventions.

PROGRAMMED PRACTICE AS AN ADJUNCT TO OTHER PROCEDURES

Programmed practice is most often employed in conjunction with other interventions, such as cognitive or in vivo flooding procedures. Indeed, several research centers report only a 40% recovery rate with this technique alone. Clients (sans partners) can be seen in psychoeducational groups, the first portion of which is devoted to weekly diary review, mutual support and problem-solving regarding practice issues. The therapist provides specific feedback on performance, praise for approximation of exposure to target situations, and assistance in specifying subsequent practice objectives for the following week. In addition, the therapist addresses other issues related to practice: fear of setbacks, morale, coping with panic, and the like. During the latter part of the session, the therapist trains clients in procedures for coping with anxiety, which may be used during weekly practice.

CONTRAINDICATIONS

The programmed practice procedure was designed for agoraphobics with a relatively consistent pattern of avoidance of everyday situations. It is not likely to be appropriate for situations which are encountered rarely, or in cases where phobic anxiety exists but avoidance does not. In cases where severe marital disorder exists, the use of spouse as collaborator must be questioned.

Clients who manifest alcohol or drug abuse are poor candidates for treatment prior to detoxification/withdrawal. Those whose reading level is poor or who have significant intellectual deficits may be poor candidates for a principally bibliotherapeutic treatment.

Finally, routine medical clearance and careful psychological/psychiatric screenings to rule out concurrent medical disorder or psychopathology would eliminate any possibility of medical risk or psychiatric deterioration.

TIME FRAME

Several researchers have suggested two visits during the first week and one per week for the following 3 weeks, with 2- and 4-week follow-up. The initial session with the therapist is about 1½ hours in length, and is principally didactic in nature. Subsequent meetings, for practice review, are ½ hour in length. During one of the early practice outings, the therapist accompanies the couple as an observer. Patient practice (45 minutes per session) is to occur on a daily basis during this time and as needed posttreatment.

Other investigators have employed a group protocol in which programmed practice is a major component. They call for 12 visits, of programmed practice review and coping skills training, after baseline assessment. Patients are trained in programmed practice during the first visit (1½ hours) and during successive weeks; half-an-hour is made available for diary review and coaching on programmed practice. Patients continue to practice as needed after formal treatment ends. Follow-up data suggest that with continued programmed practice, patients continue to maintain treatment gains at subsequent assessments.

BIBLIOGRAPHY

Emmelkamp, P. M. G. (1980). Agoraphobic interpersonal problems: Their role in the effects of exposure in vivo theory. *Archives of General Psychiatry, 37*, 1303–1306.

Jannoun, L., Munby, M., Catalan, J., & Gelder, M. (1980). A home-based treatment program for agoraphobia: Replication and controlled evaluation, *Behavior Therapy, 11*, 294–305.

Matthews, A. M., Gelder, M. G., & Johnston, D. W. (1981). *Agoraphobia: Nature and treatment.* New York: Guilford Press.

Matthews, A., Teasdale, J., Munby, M., Johnston, D., & Shaw, P. (1977). A home-based treatment program for agoraphobia. *Behavior Therapy, 8*, 915–924.

Mavissakalian, M., Michelson, L., Greenwald, D., Kornblith, S., & Greenwald, M. (1983). Cognitive-behavioral treatment of agoraphobia: Paradoxical intention vs. self-statement training. *Behaviour Research and Therapy, 21*, 75–86.

See: Homework

PROMPTING
Laura Schreibman

Prompting is a procedure in which an added cue is provided to lead the individual to the correct response in a discrimination procedure. The prompt stimulus is presented with the training stimulus and then is withdrawn, usually gradually, so that control over the response transfers from the prompt to the training stimulus. For example, a teacher may be teaching a child to discriminate between red and green blocks. The teacher may say "red" while simultaneously pointing to the red block. Since pointing is a prompt with which the child is familiar, he/she correctly identifies the color. On subsequent trials, the teacher gradually fades the pointing prompt (by withdrawing the hand gesture). If the prompt is successful, the child should now correctly identify the color without any prompt.

See: Operant Conditioning

PUBLIC POSTING
Joel Hundert

Public posting is a procedure to increase the performance of individuals through the visual display of results in a public place. Typically, the results are presented in the form of a chart, graph, posters, signs, etc., depicting an individual's actual results or personal best scores. Through the feedback provided and increased publicity, individuals change their behavior in desirable directions.

CLINICAL APPLICATION

To date, public posting has had relatively limited clinical application. Most of its use has been as a classroom or staff management procedure for non-clinical populations. In the case of classroom applications, public posting has been used to increase the academic productivity of regular class and special class pupils under a "performance feedback system." Here, a dimension of an academic area is selected to be increased (e.g., number of reading lessons completed, number of words in story writing, number of correctly-answered reading comprehension questions). Pupils complete a standard work assignment in the selected area and their results are displayed on a poster conspicuously located in the classroom. The poster displays each pupil's personal best score and the highest score for the group to date. As pupils surpass their personal or the group's best score, those numbers are changed on the poster. No backup reinforcement is provided. Although mainly used in connection with academic performance, public posting could also be used to change other quantifiable pupil behaviors including conduct behavior, tardiness, and homework completion.

A second major application of public post-ing is for staff management of such problems as absenteeism, lack of completion of job duties, and poor meeting attendance. In these situations, some aspect of staff performance (e.g., percentage of staff arriving at meetings on time, number of therapeutic interactions with clients) is measured and results posted in a public location in the workplace. When used to increase staff therapeutic interaction with clients, the obtained changes in the performance of clients (e.g., number of deaf pupils wearing hearing aids, number of ambulatory clients), rather than staff behavior itself, have been publicly posted as indications of staff action.

In addition to pupil and staff management, public posting has also been used for such diverse problems as reduction of highway speeding and improvement of the tutoring of paraprofessional tutors.

EXPECTED OUTCOME

Public posting has been shown to be an effective and practical behavior change technique. Its effects are immediate and produce a marked improvement in the target behavior. The effects of public posting have been shown not to be due to the feedback and self-scoring which are often associated with the procedure, but related to heightened motivation created by publicizing the individual's performance.

Although public posting increases behaviors, its effects do not generalize to other behaviors nor maintain over time automatically once the procedure is withdrawn. However, there has been demonstration that public posting of pupils' academic performance during one classroom period will increase that same performance during a second classroom period when public posting is not applied. Moreover, the effects of public posting seem to be enhanced when the performance of both the individual and the group are displayed. Here, the individual receives added recognition when he/she improves upon the group's best score.

Public posting has also repeatedly been demonstrated to be effective in increasing staff performance when alternative motivational techniques, such as workshops, memos, and supervisor instructions, were ineffectual. In the case of staff management, public posting seems to serve to both cue staff of the task to be completed and motivate their performance as a result of the increased publicity.

Public posting is certainly a low-cost, simple alternative to other more involved behavior change strategies (e.g., token economy). Its use is restricted by the range of situations for which it can practically or ethically be applied. Obviously, for many clinical problems, an individual's progress is private and confidential and should not be publicly displayed. Therefore, the application of public posting may be limited to everyday problem areas where confidentiality is not so much an issue, and the individual is accountable to others for the behavior in question (e.g., job attendance, academic work, execution of job responsibilities).

Even for these problems, public posting may not work for all individuals. For example, individuals for whom the connection between their actions and the information later displayed on a chart is too delayed or abstract or who are not motivated by public exposure of their performance (e.g., young children, low functioning children and adults) may not react to public posting.

SIDE EFFECTS

As is the case with many effective behavior control techniques, public posting can be abused if applied indiscriminately, in a degrading manner, or used in situations where less intrusive procedures are as effective. For instance, staff have mixed feelings about the public display of information pertaining to their performance. Although public posting is often seen as a helpful procedure in overcoming the problem at hand, it is also viewed as an unpleasant intrusion.

When applied in the classroom, pupils do not seem to have a negative feeling about public posting. On the contrary, teachers have reported an increase in pupils' positive attitudes towards the subject matter when their performance in that area is publicly posted. Moreover, along with the introduction of public posting, is an increase in the frequency of pupils' positive comments while working in the subject area. This is not to say that the public posting is more acceptably used in the classroom. In fact, because of the control exerted by schools, there may be even more need to prevent the misuse of public posting in the classroom.

The intrusiveness of public posting probably depends upon how it is presented. Public posting may be more acceptable when positive behaviors (e.g., best score) rather than negative behaviors (e.g., worst score) are recorded, based on participants' self-scoring rather than scoring by an observer. Moreover, public posting would be more acceptable if introduced as a means to recognize the efforts of individuals rather than to criticize individuals for poor performance.

Although these variables may influence the acceptability of public posting, their actual impact on performance has not been well examined. Moreover, other parameters such as the relative effectiveness of posting of the daily actual performance of individuals versus their personal best scores to date and the superiority of different forms of visual display (e.g., chart, graph, sign) remain unknown.

BIBLIOGRAPHY

Greene, B. F., Willis, B. S., Levy, R., & Bailey, J. S. (1978). Measuring client gains from staff-implemented programs. *Journal of Applied Behavior Analysis, 11*, 395–412.

Quilitch, H. R. (1978). A comparison of three staff management procedures. *Journal of Applied Behavior Analysis, 8*, 59–66.

Van Houten, R. (1979). The performance feedback system: Generalization of effects across time. *Child Behavior Therapy, 1*, 219–236.

Van Houten, R., Nau, P., & Marini, Z. (1980). An analysis of public posting in reducing speeding behavior on an urban highway. *Journal of Applied Behavior Analysis, 13*, 383–396.

Van Houten, R., & Van Houten, J. (1977). The performance feedback system in the special education classroom: An analysis of public posting and peer comments. *Behavior Therapy, 8*, 366–376.

See: Feedback

PUNISHMENT
Alan Poling

Punishment is an operant conditioning procedure in which the future rate or probability of occurrence of a response is reduced as a result of response-dependent delivery (positive punishment) or removal (negative punishment) of a stimulus (punisher). Punishment may weaken, strengthen, or have no effect on other response classes, but the procedure by definition weakens the response class for which it is arranged.

An example of positive punishment is spraying water mist in the face of a self-injurious child each time an instance of self-injurious behavior is observed, thereby reducing the rate of occurrence of such self-injury. Taking an earned token from an individual working in a sheltered workshop each time he or she curses, and thereby reducing the rate of such cursing, is an example of negative punishment.

See: Avoidance Training
     Contingency Management
     Escape Training
     Overcorrection
     Lemon Juice Therapy

RAPID SMOKING
Michael Lowe

Rapid smoking is an aversive conditioning procedure used to help cigarette smokers quit smoking. The technique is based on a classical conditioning paradigm wherein the unpleasant unconditioned responses elicited by the procedure replace the pleasant conditioned responses the smoker has come to associate with smoking. A theoretical advantage of rapid smoking over other aversive conditioning procedures (e.g., electric shock) is that the stimulus used to create aversion (cigarette smoke) is the same as the stimulus which created positive conditioned responses to smoking.

The rapid smoking procedure involves having the smoker smoke a cigarette at the rate of one inhalation every 6 seconds. This concentrated smoking soon produces unpleasant sensory and physiological effects such as dizziness, nausea and an increased heart rate. The smoker is asked to concentrate on these negative sensations during the procedure. Rapid smoking continues (with the client lighting a second cigarette if necessary) until he or she cannot bear to take another puff, or is about to become physically ill. The smoker is then allowed to breathe fresh air until these reactions subside, at which point the rapid smoking procedure is repeated. This cycle continues until the smoker is unable to tolerate another cigarette. Rapid smoking sessions are held daily (usually for 2 or 3 days) until the smoker is able to abstain completely. Clients are urged not to smoke between rapid smoking sessions. In its original form, smokers who relapsed within 6 months were seen for booster sessions of rapid smoking, but subsequent investigators have altered this and other details of the procedure. Early studies of rapid smoking produced impressive results, in the neighborhood of 60% abstinence at 6-month follow-up. However, a number of investigators have been unable to replicate these promising outcomes.

There are at least two possible reasons for the inconsistent findings concerning rapid smoking's efficacy. First, some applications of the procedure have not matched the intensity and frequency of application as described in the original report. Second, it has been shown that rapid smoking is more effective if administered in the context of a warm and supportive therapeutic atmosphere; some of the less impressive outcomes may be partially due to insufficient attention being paid to these "nonspecific factors."

In applied work, rapid smoking is almost always used in conjunction with other behavioral techniques (e.g., contingency contracting, stimulus control). The use of multicomponent cessation strategies is appropriate in light of the multiple determinants of smoking and the well-known difficulty of maintaining initial abstinence. The rapid smoking component of a cessation program requires about an hour a day for 2 or 3 days, at which point most clients are ready to quit completely. Because of possible health risks associated with rapid smoking, clients may need to receive permission from their physician before participating in the procedure and to be monitored for potentially dangerous effects of rapid smoking during and/or just after completing it.

The potential health risks of rapid smoking have been the subject of controversy. Rapid smoking, compared to normal smoking, produces increases in heart rate, carboxyhemoglobin and other blood gases, and blood nicotine levels. Some cardiovascular irregularities have been shown to occur during rapid smoking, but no clinical symptoms have been reported. Based upon the current literature, it appears that rapid smoking is safe in healthy individuals and even in patients with cardiovascular disease if proper screening is done and precautions taken. Well over 35,000 individuals have been reported to have undergone rapid smoking treatment with no known serious consequences or side effects. However, it has been recommended that individuals with a history of heart disease, high blood pressure, diabetes, chronic bronchitis, or emphysema be excluded from rapid smoking treatment and that physician approval be required for all other participants.

BIBLIOGRAPHY

Danaher, B. G. (1977). Research on rapid smoking: Interim summary and recommendations. *Addictive Behaviors, 2*, 151–166.

Lichtenstein, E. (1982). The smoking problem: A behavioral perspective. *Journal of Consulting and Clinical Psychology, 50*, 804–819.

Lichtenstein, E., & Glasgow, R. E. (1977). Rapid smoking: Side effects and safeguards. *Journal of Consulting and Clinical Psychology, 45*, 815–821.

Poole, A. D., Sanson-Fisher, R. W., & German, G. A. (1981). The rapid-smoking technique: Therapeutic effectiveness. *Behaviour Research and Therapy, 19*, 389–397.

Sachs, D. P. L., Hall, R. G., Pechacek, T. F., & Fitzgerald, J. (1979). Clarification of risk-benefit issues in rapid smoking. *Journal of Clinical and Consulting Psychology, 47*, 1053–1060.

Schmahl, D. P., Lichtenstein, E., & Harris, D. E. (1972). Successful treatment of habitual smokers with warm, smoky air and rapid smoking. *Journal of Consulting and Clinical Psychology, 38*, 105–111.

See: Controlled Smoking
Nicotine Fading

RATIONAL-EMOTIVE THERAPY
Albert Ellis

Rational-emotive therapy (RET) is the pioneering form of cognitive-behavior therapy developed by Albert Ellis early in 1955 after he had found psychoanalysis inefficient. General RET is synonymous with cognitive-behavior therapy (CBT). Preferential RET, to be described herewith, has several theories and practices that significantly distinguish it from CBT.

Preferential RET includes the following theories:

1. The ABCD theory of RET holds that people's disturbed emotional and behavioral Consequences (C) stem from the interaction between the Activating Events (A) they experience and their Belief System (B). For therapists to help clients change their disturbed Consequences (C), they had better actively and forcefully Dispute them at point D — and do so by using (and teaching the clients) several cognitive, emotive, and behavioral techniques.

2. While people use many descriptive, inferential, and evaluative cognitions to help create their disturbed feelings and behaviors, they most importantly contribute to them by actively accepting and creating evaluative irrational Beliefs (iBs). Their iBs usually consist of conscious or unconscious (implicit) absolutistic evaluations of what is happening to them at A. They predominantly embody unconditional shoulds, musts, demands, and commands. If as RET holds, people *only* stayed with their wishes and desires and never escalated them into absolutistic necessities, they would feel appropriately sad, concerned, and annoyed when their wishes were frustrated, but they would rarely feel inappropriately anxious, depressed or enraged.

3. Many kinds of unrealistic, antiempirical, and illogical cognitions contribute to emotional disturbance. Thus, when people fail at an important task, they frequently infer or conclude, "I am a *failure*" (labeling), "I will always *fail*" (overgeneralizing), "It was *my* fault that I

failed" (personalizing), and "It is *catastrophic* and *awful* that I failed" (catastrophizing and awfulizing). These antiempirical ideas are largely derived from their absolutistic musts, for if people believe "I *must*, under practically *all* conditions, succeed," and they actually fail, they will *therefore* often conclude, "I am a *failure*," "I will *always* fail," "It was *my* fault that I failed," and "It is *awful* that I failed." Their absolutistic musts are usually (though not necessarily always) basic to their unrealistic inferences.

4. People are born and reared with strong potential to be both rational and irrational — to be self-preserving and self-defeating. Through social learning they acquire self-actualizing and self-sabotaging behaviors. But they also are born with creative tendencies to invent rational and irrational responses to frustrating stimuli, and they *easily* change their rational preferences into irrational commands. Their innate predispositions to be bigoted, dogmatic, perfectionistic, and grandiose sabotage their innate self-actualizing tendencies and make it difficult for them to benefit profoundly from all forms of psychotherapy.

5. What we call thinking, feeling, and behaving notably overlap and are highly interactive. People's environment, the desires and thoughts they bring to stimuli, and their behavioral responses to these stimuli also interact and transact. They have virtually no "pure" thoughts, feelings, or behaviors; and no "monolithic" stimuli, sensations, perceptions, or responses.

6. To help people change their fundamental irrational Beliefs (iBs), therapists had better actively-directively use many cognitive emotive, and behavioral methods; had better be scientific and experimental during therapy sessions; and had

better teach their clients how to use the scientific method in their own lives and to acquire a basic attitude of tolerance, flexibility, skepticism, and openness to change.

7. Because people have strong innate as well as acquired tendencies to behave irrationally, therapists had better vigorously Dispute (D) their irrational Beliefs (iBs) and encourage them to powerfully and persistently push themselves into feeling and acting differently.

8. Clients had better be shown how to acquire three major kinds of insight: (1) Activating Events (A) contribute significantly to emotional and behavioral Consequences (C) but the more direct and more therapeutically important contribution or "cause" comes from B, clients' Belief Systems. (2) No matter where clients' iBs started nor what past events contributed to them, when they are presently disturbed they are still actively holding on to them. (3) There is usually no way but *work and practice* for clients to change their disturbances and keep them changed.

9. Symptom removal is acceptable in therapy; but efficient or "elegant" therapy involves clients making a profound philosophic change that includes: (a) amelioration of their presenting symptoms and other disturbed behaviors, (b) maintenance of symptom removal, (c) reduced likelihood that new or related symptoms will occur, and (d) clients' determination, when disturbed behaviors recur, to quickly find the basic irrational Beliefs that underlie them and to use powerful RET methods of dealing with them.

10. Most disturbed individuals not only have ego anxiety and feelings of inadequacy but also have discomfort anxiety or low frustration tolerance. Effective therapy — such as RET — therefore seeks out *both* these sources of disturbances and tries to minimize them.

11. Disturbed people frequently have secondary as well as primary symptoms and consequently disturb themselves about their disturbances: make themselves anxious about their anxiety, depressed about their depression, and guilty about their hostility. RET actively looks for clients' secondary disturbances, shows them how to alleviate these, and then how to minimize their primary disturbances.

CLINICAL APPLICATIONS

After clients' problems have been properly assessed, RET usually begins with the therapist's showing them how to place one of them — e.g., social anxiety — within the ABCD framework. Thus, a severely shy and inhibited woman will be shown that when she encounters attractive men at A (Activating Event) and reacts with anxiety and withdrawal at C (emotional and behavioral Consequence), she tends to contribute to or "cause" her symptoms (C) by holding important Beliefs or cognitions (B). Her Bs usually consist of, first, a set of rBs (rational Beliefs): "I would like or prefer to socialize adequately and win the approval of men I find attractive" and, second, of iBs (irrational Beliefs), "I *must* socialize adequately and win the approval of men I find attractive. If I don't do as I must, it is awful, I can't stand it, and I am an incompetent and worthless person!"

RET encourages this client to retain (and enhance) her preferences and rational Beliefs and to ameliorate or change her absolutistic irrational Beliefs. To do this, it especially tries to help her go on to D, Disputing her iBs by using the scientific method of challenging them. She then would end up with E, a new Effective Philosophy or new set of rBs. For example: Disputing: "Where is the evidence that I *must* socialize adequately and win the approval of men I find attractive?" Effective Philosophy: "There is no evidence that I *must*, though it would be highly *preferable* if I did." Disputing: "Prove that it is *awful* and *catastrophic* if I fail and get rejected." Effective Philosophy: "It is only inconvenient but hardly the end of the world!" Disputing: "In what way can't I *stand* being socially inept and disapproved?" Effective Philosophy: "I *can* stand it and still be happy, though I'll never like it!" Disputing: "Where is it written that I am an incompetent and worthless person if I fail socially and get rejected?" Effective Philosophy: "Only in my nutty head! I am just a person *who* has failed and got rejected this time, *who* does well in many other respects, and *who* can keep trying till I finally succeed and get approved."

In addition to its main method of Disputing, RET would usually employ several other cognitive methods to help this client change her iBs and her disturbed Cs. These include: (a) Rational and coping self-statements — For example: "Even though I have failed socially before, that is no reason why I cannot succeed in the future." "Social anxiety is handicapping but it is not the end of the world and I can work at overcoming it."; (b) Problem-solving techniques — For example: Plans to approach attractive males and speak to them in an interesting manner; (c) Modeling — Observing socially adept people and following their methods; (d) Referenting — Reviewing the advantages of trying to socialize and being rejected and the disadvantages of withdrawal; (e) Imagery — The client's imaging herself succeeding at socializing; (f) Semantic precision — Her changing her overgeneralized statements, such as "I *should always* succeed socially and *never* be rejected" to "*It would be preferable* if I *sometimes* succeeded socially and were *seldom* rejected."; and (g) Psychoeducational methods — Read-

ing RET books and pamphlets (such as Ellis & Harper, *A New Guide to Rational Living* and Ellis & Becker, *A Guide to Personal Happiness*) or listening to recordings (such as Ellis, *How to Stubbornly Refuse to Be Ashamed of Anything*), and attending talks and workshops that teach RET-oriented philosophies and techniques.

In addition to these cognitive techniques of helping this client change her self-debating Beliefs, emotions, and behaviors, RET would usually employ several emotive methods, such as: (a) Rational emotive imagery: having her imagine one of the worst possible social situations and making herself feel only appropriately sorry, regretful, and frustrated rather than inappropriately anxious, depressed and self-pitying; (b) Unconditional acceptance: having the therapist show the client that he or she unconditionally accepts her, in spite of her failures and handicaps, and also show her how she can fully accept herself with her failings; (c) Forceful self-statements: teaching the client to *vigorously* and *forcefully* say to herself rational self-statements, such as: "I do *not* need what I want but only *desire* it!" "I am a *fallible* human who has the right *often* to fail!"; and (d) Role-playing: having the client role-play an assertive, un-shy person in a social situation, and having the therapist (or therapeutic group) critique her presentation and help her to see the irrational Beliefs she tells herself while she does the role-playing.

Finally, RET would use a number of behavioral methods with this socially shy client, such as: (a) In vivo homework assignments: encouraging her to take social risks, no matter how uncomfortable she at first feels in taking them; (b) Implosive assignments: having her, if feasible, do many risk-taking acts in a short period of time, until she overcomes her fear of doing them; (c) Reinforcement and penalization: showing her how to reinforce herself when doing "dangerous" socializing and, possibly, how to penalize herself when she refuses to do what she promises herself to do; and (d) Skill training: teaching the client certain social skills, such as skills in encountering others, in communicating with people, and in asserting herself in social situations.

EXPECTED OUTCOMES AND TIME FRAMES

Although clients can learn cognitive, emotive, and behavioral procedures of RET and can start using them in relatively few sessions (from 10 to 20), they had better keep employing them for some period of time until they become "second nature." Most "neurotics" who work at RET, therefore, can look forward to significant improvement, and sometimes overcome their major presenting symptoms, in about a year of individual RET (which may comprise about 20 to 25 sessions) or a year of once-a-week group therapy.

It is hypothesized that almost all clients who work hard at using RET can benefit from its use — including those diagnosed as borderline, schizophrenic, manic depressive, and mildly mentally deficient. These severely disturbed individuals can be especially helped to unconditionally accept themselves *with* their disturbances. While doing so, they may also be able to ameliorate their disturbed feelings and behaviors to some degree — but hardly to effect a complete cure. Clients with severe character disorders and with low frustration tolerance can be expected to benefit minimally, though RET practitioners can sometimes, by active-directive methods, induce them to make significant changes. Severely depressed, anxious, obsessive-compulsive, borderline, and psychotic clients are often treated, in or out of mental institutions, with RET plus appropriate medication.

POTENTIAL SIDE EFFECTS AND CONTRAINDICATIONS

Side effects of RET may include: (1) Clients make quick and dramatic improvement, wrongly think that they are "cured," and quit therapy prematurely before they habituate themselves to improved ways of thinking, feeling, and behaving. (2) Clients become overenthusiastic about finding their absolutistic shoulds and musts and irrationally conclude, "I *should* be rational!" or "I *must* use RET well and it's *awful* if I don't!" (3) Severely depressed clients, especially those who have had a passive and warmly accepting therapist for a period of time, are sometimes put off by RET's confrontation and homework assigning, and may make themselves temporarily feel more depressed. (4) Clients with abysmal low frustration tolerance may rebel against active-directive RET and insist that the therapist should change them rather than that they should work at changing themselves. A more subtle and sometimes paradoxical mode of RET may therefore be advisable with these clients.

BIBLIOGRAPHY

Ellis, A. (1962). *Reason and emotion in psychotherapy.* Secaucus, NJ: Lyle Stuart and Citadel Press.

Ellis, A. (1973). *Humanistic psychotherapy: The rational-emotive approach.* New York: Crown Publishers and McGraw-Hill.

Ellis, A. (1984). *Rational-emotive therapy and cognitive-behavior therapy.* New York: Springer.

Ellis, A., & Grieger, R. (Eds.). (1977). *Handbook of rational-emotive therapy.* New York: Springer.

Ellis, A., & Whiteley, J. M. (Eds.). (1979). *Theoretical and empirical foundations of rational-emotive therapy.* Monterey, CA: Brooks/Cole.

See: Cognitive Therapy

REHEARSAL
Arnold A. Lazarus

Behavior *rehearsal* is the term used to describe "a specific procedure which aims to replace deficient or inadequate social or interpersonal responses by efficient and effective behavior patterns. The patient achieves this by practicing the desired forms of behavior under the direction of the therapist." Unlike other forms of role-playing such as "psychodrama," behavior rehearsal aims primarily to modify current maladaptive patterns of behavior rather than "working through" early symbolic conflicts. In applying rehearsal, the therapist assumes the role of significant people in the patient's life, and in a progressive stepwise fashion, more difficult encounters are enacted.

Role-reversal is an important component wherein the therapist acts the part of the patient and models the desired verbal and nonverbal behaviors, while the patient assumes the role of the person(s) with whom he/she has (or anticipates having) a problem. The use of videotapes is helpful in monitoring the patient's tone of voice, inflection, hesitations, querulous undertones, posture, gait, and eye contact.

BIBLIOGRAPHY

Lazarus, A. A. (1966). Behavior rehearsal vs. nondirective therapy vs. advice in effecting behavior change. *Behaviour Research and Therapy, 4,* 209–212.

See: Homework

REINFORCED PRACTICE
Edward J. Barton

Reinforced practice is a facilitative procedure whereby an individual is reinforced for emitting repeatedly the behavior of a model. Thus, following the emission of each practice (or on an intermittent basis), the rehearsed behavior is consequated with a stimulus which has a positive valence (e.g., praise or a hug). Use of reinforcement is important in the development and maintenance of practice behaviors. In most instances, reinforced practice produces rapid long-lasting effects. Reinforced practice typically is used in combination with instruction, modeling, and/or feedback. The procedure of rehearsal offers suggestions related to its use with young, mentally retarded or non-compliant individuals.

See: Contingency Management
    Homework
    Operant Conditioning

REINFORCEMENT OF INCOMPATIBLE BEHAVIOR
Diane E. D. Deitz

Reinforcement of incompatible behavior is a procedure which involves the reinforcement of a specific behavior which is topographically incompatible with (or prevents the occurrence of) an unwanted behavior. As incompatible behaviors cannot be performed at the same time, the inappropriate component of the incompatible behaviors should decrease as the appropriate component is increased. For example, a student who exhibits unwanted out-of-seat behavior could be reinforced for in-seat behavior. As in-seat behavior increases, out-of-seat behavior will decrease. Other examples include: reinforcing a person who chews with mouth open when he/she chews with mouth closed and reinforcing a person who is usually late for appointments when he/she arrives on time.

See: Differential Reinforcement of Low Rate
        Behavior
    Differential Reinforcement of Other
        Behavior

REINFORCER SAMPLING
John T. Neisworth

Reinforcer sampling is a procedure whereby individuals are noncontingently provided with items or events that are potential reinforcers in order to: (a) evaluate from an array of items or events those that may be most effective as reinforcers, or (b) initiate or establish particular items or events as reinforcers.

Sampling usually involves a structured situation that promotes actual consumption of, or engagement in, several reinforcer options. Reinforcer preferences and potency can then be evaluated once the client has come into contact with the options. Besides evaluation of options, *sampling* can sometimes acquaint the client with an item or event and thus create a reinforcer. Some populations (e.g., low functioning) exhibit few reinforcer preferences; *required* sampling can sometimes "prime" or establish a reinforcer in these cases.

The technique has been employed on words to increase walking outside as a preferred activity, church attendance (after a required 5-minute sample), and to increase attendance at scheduled meals. Commercial illustrations of reinforcer sampling include such things as free food samples in supermarkets, gift items in the mail, and a bonus product attached to an item that is purchased.

See: Operant Conditioning

RESPIRATORY RELIEF

See: Aversion Relief
     Negative Reinforcement

RESPONSE COST
Saul Axelrod

Response cost is a punishment procedure in which an individual or group loses a positive reinforcer contingent upon a specified behavior. The positive reinforcer is often a conditioned reinforcer within the context of a token economy. Thus, response cost might involve the removal of a token from a client's possession, where the token was exchangeable for an hour of off-grounds privileges. A traffic citation involving the payment of a fine is a common example of response cost. Response cost is distinguishable from extinction in that extinction consists of the failure to deliver reinforcers, whereas response cost involves the removal of reinforcers in one's possession. Response cost is distinguishable from time out, in that time out specifies a time period in a less reinforcing environment, whereas response cost need involve no temporal component. Response cost derives from the notion that the probability of the occurrence of a behavior is related to its physical or monetary cost. That is, the greater the cost of performing a behavior, the less likely it is that the behavior will be performed.

CLINICAL APPLICATION

Response cost is a much researched and widely applied punishment procedure. The technique has been applied to a diversity of behaviors, including inappropriate and disfluent speech, inappropriate classroom behavior, incidents of violence, cigarette smoking, failure to lose weight, self-abuse, facial tics, poor posture, absenteeism, tardiness, incorrect answers on standardized tests, failure to obey housekeeping rules, and requesting telephone directory assistance. One application of response cost might be to charge clients an extra fee each time they come to a therapy session without a demonstrated loss in weight. The program could be supplemented with a negative reinforcement procedure in which clients paid a reduced fee for a demonstrated weight loss. Another example of response cost would be to offer students an extra 10 minutes of free time, but to deduct one minute of free time each time a student violated a stated classroom rule. Three variations of response cost have appeared. In the first, individuals receive tokens noncontingently and then lose them for inappropriate behavior. In the second, individuals start without tokens, but gain them for performing inappropriate behaviors. The third variation consists of group contingencies in which individuals lose points, at least in part, according to their group's performance.

EXPECTED OUTCOMES, TIME FRAMES, AND DIFFERENTIAL DIAGNOSTIC CHARACTERISTICS

Response cost often is a remarkably effective behavior reduction procedure, both in terms of the degree of suppression and the onset of the effect. Thus, it is not unusual to experience a large-scale reduction in the level of a behavior after a few sessions of applying response cost. The procedure can be applied to numerous behavior problems and across a wide variety of populations, both handicapped and nonhandicapped. Diagnostic restrictions on the application of response are minimal, with the exception that clients must be able to comprehend the notion of quantification associated with many response cost procedures. Thus, response cost involving the loss of points depicted in descending order, would often be inappropriate with a severely retarded client, simply because of the cognitive limitations of the individual.

POTENTIAL SIDE EFFECTS AND CONTRAINDICATIONS

Response cost is typically not associated with a large number of adverse side effects. In addition, public reaction to the use of response cost is usually that of acceptance, particularly in comparison to most other punishment procedures. Thus, in many cases Human Rights Committee approval for the use of response cost is not required. Nevertheless, there are instances of undesirable side effects resulting from response cost. Included are verbal objections to the removal of tokens and occasional avoidance of the environment in which tokens are removed. Side effects can sometimes be suppressed by exposing such behaviors to the same response-cost procedure that is being applied to the target behavior. Another problem that can occur is that staff who successfully apply response cost to a serious misbehavior will later apply it to minor infractions. Overall, the advantages of effectiveness, ease of implementation, and the nonnecessity to intervene physically, far outweigh the disadvantages of response cost.

BIBLIOGRAPHY

Kazdin, A. (1972). Response cost: The removal of conditioned reinforcers for therapeutic change. *Behavior Therapy, 3,* 533–546.

Pazulinec, R., Meyerrose, M., & Sajwaj, T. (1983). Punishment via response cost. In S. Axelrod & J. Apsche (Eds.), *The effects of punishment on human behavior.* New York: Academic Press.

Reisinger, J. J. (1972). The treatment of "anxiety depression" via positive reinforcement and response cost. *Journal of Applied Behavior Analysis, 2,* 125–130.

Sweeny, A. J. (1978). The effects of response cost on the behavior of a million persons: Charging for directory assistance in Cincinnati. *Journal of Applied Behavior Analysis, 11,* 47–51.

Weiner, H. (1962). Some effects of response cost upon human operant behavior. *Journal of the Experimental Analysis of Behavior, 5,* 201–208.

See: Contingency Management
Punishment

RESPONSE PREVENTION
Donald A. Williamson

Response prevention is a technique which has been used primarily in the treatment of obsessive-compulsive disorder (neurosis). Recently, it has also been used in the treatment of bulimia. Response prevention usually involves exposing the patient to the stimuli which cause obsessional thinking, anxiety, and compulsive behavior. However, when response prevention is used, the patient is prevented from engaging in the ritualistic behavior which initially causes an increase of obsessional thinking and anxiety. After repeated sessions, the anxiety and obsessions usually gradually reduce to subclinical levels. This procedure is based upon an extinction model. In cases of obsessive-compulsive disorder, the patient is exposed to stimuli such as dirt, "contaminated objects," disordered objects, etc. Exposure must be given for stimuli which are central to the patient's obsessions. Therefore, an individualized approach must be used. Response prevention of rituals must be prolonged. In many cases this treatment can only be conducted in an inpatient setting where close supervision of the patient can be accomplished. For less severe cases, outpatient treatment can be attempted. However, involvement of family members or friends is usually required for successful outpatient treatment. For bulimia, exposure involves having the patient eat a meal. Response prevention involves preventing the bulimic from purging for at least 3 hours after eating. This procedure induces reactions of increased obsessional thinking about weight gain and anxiety. Response prevention as a treatment of bulimia should be combined with a program for modification of eating and exercise habits in order to prevent weight gain. Clinical research has firmly established response prevention as an effective treatment procedure for obsessive-compulsive disorder. Treatment of this disorder usually requires at least 3 to 4 weeks of hospitalization and several additional months of outpatient treatment. Treatment of bulimia can often be accomplished on an outpatient basis. Outpatient treatment is often done in small groups. Duration of treatment is usually 3 months of two sessions per week.

Response prevention is one of the few behavioral techniques with significant negative side affects. Practically all patients treated with this technique experience considerable anxiety and emotional distress. This distress is most acute during the initial stages of treatment. Careful discussion of these adverse reactions is required in order to prepare the patient for treatment. Because of these adverse reactions, withdrawal from treatment is a common problem for response prevention. One method of dealing with this problem is to use a hierarchy for exposure such that less-anxiety-provoking stimuli are used initially so that the patient can learn to cope with lower degrees of anxiety before going on to stimuli which are central to the problem.

BIBLIOGRAPHY

Foa, F. B., & Goldstein, A. (1978). Continuous exposure and complete response prevention in the treatment of obsessive-compulsive neuroses. *Behavior Therapy, 9*, 821–829.

Marks, I. (1975). Behavioral treatments of phobic and obsessive-compulsive disorders: A critical appraisal. In M. Hersen, R. M. Eisler, & P. M. Miller (Eds.), *Progress in behavior modification* (Vol. 1). New York: Academic Press.

Meyer, V., Robertson, J., & Tatlow, A. (1975). Home treatment of an obsessive-compulsive disorder by response prevention. *Journal of Behavior Therapy and Experimental Psychiatry, 6*, 37–38.

Rosen, S. C., & Leitenberg, H. (1982). Bulimia nervosa: Treatment with exposure and response prevention. *Behavior Therapy, 13*, 117–124.

Turner, S. M., Hersen, M., Bellack, A. S., & Wells, K. C. (1979). Behavioral treatment of obsessive-compulsive neurosis. *Behaviour Research and Therapy, 17*, 95–106.

See: Flooding

RETENTION CONTROL TRAINING
Daniel M. Doleys

Retention control training (or bladder expansion exercises) is defined by a procedure which requires the individual to refrain from voiding for progressively longer periods of time. The goal of the procedure is to increase the functional bladder capacity as measured by the average and maximum urine output over a specified period of time. Retention control training (RCT) has been applied in the treatment of a variety of urological problems, including daytime and nighttime enuresis.

There are several parameters to RCT which vary. First is liquid intake. In some instances, the patient is required to maximize liquid intake so as to increase the number of retention trials during any given 24-hour period. The second parameter is the rate of increase of retention time. Some clinicians have begun retention intervals at 2 minutes, and gradually increased them, by 1 or 2 blocks, based upon the patient's success at retaining. Other therapists have had the individual retain for as long a period as they can without imposing any gradation of retention time on the process. Third is maximum retention time. The maximum amount of time that the individual is asked to retain varies considerably. The variation usually extends from approximately 20 to 85 minutes. The interval is somewhat difficult to accurately measure as after a brief period of time, perhaps 15 minutes, many individuals lose the urge to void only to have it reappear some time later. In this instance, an individual may actually retain

for several hours without difficulty. This can be understood easily by the data suggesting that under ordinary circumstances, most older children and adults void from 4 to 6 times a day. A fourth parameter is the presence of the therapist or clinician. In some cases, the therapist is present and the procedure is carried out in the office or in a home setting. Under the most usual circumstances, however, parents are given written instructions and the procedure is carried out at home.

Obtaining a baseline is critical to the use of RCT. This can be accomplished by having the client utilize some type of graduated container as a voiding receptacle, monitoring the volume of each voiding episode for a 2-week period of time. The average, calculated over all episodes, is considered the typical bladder capacity, while the largest amount recorded is considered the maximum bladder capacity. The maximum bladder capacity may also be assessed by using the "water loading" procedure. In this instance, the individual is asked to drink up to 16 ounces of liquid, usually water, tea, etc. Voiding is inhibited until a moderate degree of discomfort is reached on the next two occasions. The magnitude of the void is determined, and the largest is considered the maximum functional bladder capacity.

There has been some attempt to establish normative data regarding functional bladder capacities. Retention control is most frequently applied to those children who, upon assessment, are found to have a small functional bladder capacity and urinary frequency. This has been most frequently utilized in the treatment of nighttime enuresis, but also has found application to the daytime enuretic. On occasion, it has been applied to individuals demonstrating the "bashful bladder syndrome," characterized by inability to void in any type of public setting. In such cases, patients tend to void at very small amounts of bladder volume, thus finding it extremely difficult because of minimal intravesical pressure. Training such patients to retain until the urge is significant usually is beneficial.

The greatest amount of research with RCT appears to have been done with nighttime enuretics. It was once thought that improving the functional bladder capacity of enuretics would naturally result in a reduction of frequency of bed wetting. This, however, has not been borne out. Several studies have shown a lack of correspondence between increased bladder capacity and frequency of nocturnal enuresis. Similarly, children who become continent at night through other procedures, such as the Bell and Pad, often show dryness in the absence of any change in functional bladder capacity. There does seem to be some potentially positive application for the use of retention control training with daytime enuretics. The mechanism of action is not entirely clear, though the combined use of RCT with full cleanliness training (a type of over-correction) has been found quite useful.

There are some potential side effects and contraindications to the use of retention control training. The urological consultation to rule out any structural or functional abnormality should be considered in those children who describe any dysuria, uncontrolled post-voiding dribbling, unusually broad stream of urine, and/or recurrent infections. Chronic expansion of the bladder can result in hypertrophy. Children unaccustomed to retaining will often experience the sensation as painful. Focusing attention of this degree on bladder functioning may be embarrassing for the individual and contribute to noncompliance. Inadequate instructions and/or monitoring may result in the utilization of protracted retention time. Parents of children who experience and dramatically present their discomfort may become upset and withdraw from treatment.

Although not frequently described as part of the retention control training, sphincter exercises can be helpful. Sphincter exercises require the individual to practice voluntarily starting and stopping the flow of urine during a single voiding episode. This exercise helps to improve voluntary control of external sphincter muscles which, in the intact urinary system, are primarily involved in the voluntary inhibition and subsequent voiding process. Anxiety-based urological disorders may be influenced, at least in part, by reduced voluntary control over external sphincters as a function of anxiety. Sphincter exercise combined with RCT and relaxation procedure, can facilitate control over bladder functioning.

BIBLIOGRAPHY

Doleys, D. M., Ciminero, A. R., Tollison, J. W., Williams, C. L., & Wells, K. C. (1975). Dry bed training and retention control training. *Behavior Therapy, 6*, 685–688.

Doleys, D. M., & Meredith, R. L. (1982). Urological disorders. In D. M. Doleys, R. L. Meredith, & A. R. Ciminero (Eds.), *Behavioral medicine: Assessment and treatment strategies.* New York: Plenum Press.

Harris, L. S., & Parohit, A. P. (1977). Bladder training and enuresis: A controlled trial. *Behaviour Research and Therapy, 15*, 485–490.

Starfield, B., & Mellits, E. D. (1968). Increase in functional bladder capacity and improvements in enuresis. *Journal of Pediatrics, 72*, 483–487.

Zaleski, A., Gerrard, J. W., & Shokier, M. H. K. (1973). Nocturnal enuresis: The importance of a small bladder capacity. In I. Kolvin, R. C. Mac-Keith, & S. R. Meadow (Eds.), *Bladder control and enuresis.* Philadelphia: W. B. Saunders.

See: Bell and Pad Conditioning
Dry Bed Training

ROLE PLAYING
Steven Beck

Role playing is a very common strategy to assess and train clients in social skills training. Role playing involves having a subject or client perform in a contrived interpersonal situation assuming that his or her responses are parallel to those which would occur in the natural environment. Numerous studies indicate that role playing may be moderately valid, although validity is affected by the type and content of role playing procedure. Role playing can allow the assessment and training of molecular skills (e.g., gaze) or molar skills (assertiveness). Role playing usually involves having a subject or client interact with an individual (a confederate or therapist) who will respond to a contrived interpersonal situation in a specific manner. For example, to assess or train a client in assertiveness, the client can be told to imagine he is in a restaurant and has ordered a very rare steak. The confederate or therapist then acts as if he is bringing a steak to the table that is so well done it looks burned. The verbal and nonverbal responses made by the client will assess his assertiveness skills to that situation. Recent data suggest that clients may perform better in role plays compared to more naturalistic situations since client role playing may exhibit more behaviors in these contrived situations which may result in more favorable ratings.

See: Rehearsal
      Social Skills Training

ROLE REVERSAL
Steven Beck

Role reversal refers to a role playing situation whereby the client role plays or practices the role of his or her antagonist. For example, if a client is role playing a discussion of finances with his wife, he is asked to assume the role and point of view of his wife while the therapist assumes his role. Role reversal is typically performed after the client first role plays the scene playing himself or herself with another person playing the antagonist. Role reversal helps the client to take the point of view of the counterpart and understand how that person may view the situation. This technique can aid the client in formulating effective interpersonal approaches to the situation.

See: Role Playing

SATIATION TRAINING
Cynthia G. Last

Satiation training is a cognitive-behavioral technique that is intended to reduce subjective and psychophysiological distress accompanying obsessional thoughts or images. The treatment procedure essentially consists of prompting or instructing clients to "form" or imagine the obsession for prolonged periods of time. Often, clients are asked to verbalize the disturbing thought continuously while focusing on the image representing the thought. Treatment sessions generally last for one hour each. The satiation technique may be applied while the client is under relaxation, although the benefits of including this component is unknown at this time. The treatment is thought to work by effecting habituation of the anxiety response elicited by obsessional material. In this regard, the technique more recently has been re-labeled *habituation training*.

Satiation or habituation training is useful clinically for treating obsessions. When obsessions are followed by avoidance responses, that is, compulsive rituals (e.g., cleaning, checking, etc.) or "neutralizing activities" (e.g., "counter-thoughts," requests for reassurance, distraction, etc.), treatment also should include response prevention of such behavior. Response prevention instructions usually entail instructing the client to refrain from carrying out any rituals or neutralizing acts during exposure to obsessional material. The two treatment techniques — satiation training and response prevention — can be, and should be, applied concurrently. In addition to therapist-guided treatment sessions, homework sessions, where clients undertake increasing amounts of practice alone, may increase the efficacy of intervention.

Treatment with satiation training should decrease the duration and frequency of obsessions, as well as the distress (subjective and psychophysiological) elicited by them. In addition, the technique may increase the "acceptability" of the obsessional thought or theme. The number of sessions required for optimal outcome varies amongst clients; however, between 4 and 12 sessions can be anticipated for most individuals. The relative benefit of "massed" versus "spaced" sessions is unknown.

Preliminary evidence suggests that satiation training may be particularly helpful for the "horror-disgust" type of obsessions (e.g., sexual thoughts, thoughts depicting contamination, etc.). In addition, when marked subjective and psychophysiological distress dominate the clinical picture, such symptoms may indicate this treatment technique to be the treatment of choice. Alternatively, when duration of obsessions presents as the primary complaint, other treatments may be more efficacious (e.g., thought-stopping, distraction training, etc.). Clients who present with compulsive ritualizing as a primary complaint, rather than the obsession itself, may benefit more from live (in vivo) exposure to objects/situations that elicit ritualistic behavior, rather than imaginal exposure. Severely depressed clients who present with concurrent obsessions should be treated for depression first since: (1) treatment of depression may simultaneously alleviate ob-

sessional problems, and (2) habituation to obsessions (through satiation training) may not be possible during dysphoric states.

Clients undergoing this treatment are likely to experience anxiety/distress, especially during the early stages of treatment. However, such reactions should be attenuated or eliminated as treatment progresses. No contraindications to using satiation training are known at this time.

BIBLIOGRAPHY

Rachman, S. (1971). Obsessional ruminations. *Behaviour Research and Therapy, 9,* 229–235.
Rachman, S. (1976). The modification of obsessions: A new formulation. *Behaviour Research and Therapy, 14,* 437–443.
Rachman, S., & Hodgson, R. J. (1980). *Obsessions and compulsions.* Englewood Cliffs, NJ: Prentice-Hall.

See: Extinction
     Massed Practice
     Paradoxical Intention

SCHEDULES OF REINFORCEMENT
Samuel M. Deitz

Schedules of reinforcement specify which of many instances of the same behavior will produce reinforcement. It is possible that every occurrence of the behavior will be reinforced and that situation is referred to as *continuous reinforcement* schedule (CRF). In the natural environment, however, CRF is probably rare. In most cases, some, but not all, instances of behavior are reinforced. Any such case is referred to as *intermittent* reinforcement. Intermittent reinforcement can occur based on the number of behaviors required for reinforcement (ratio schedules), or an amount of time which must elapse before a behavior is reinforced (interval schedules), or the length of time between behaviors (Differential Reinforcement of Low Rate, Differential Reinforcement of High Rate), or various combinations of any of those possibilities. Intermittent schedules of reinforcement have been found to have important effects on the frequency and patterning of behavior and on its resistance to extinction conditions. These effects of reinforcement schedules show them to be, perhaps, the central influence on the control of behavior.

Continuous schedules of reinforcement are usually most appropriate for teaching a new behavior to a student or client. When first introducing new information or skills, such as history facts or thought stopping, all student or client behavior correctly relating to the new material should be reinforced. Once those behaviors have been learned, however, the teacher or therapist should arrange intermittent reinforcement. Reinforcing every third or fourth correct behavior, for example, will serve to better maintain them than will continued use of CRF.

See: Operant Conditioning

SELF-CONTROL DESENSITIZATION

E. Thomas Dowd and Kathryn Govaerts

Self-control desensitization is a technique used in the treatment of specific, circumscribed phobias, as well as more generalized anxiety disorders, in which the client assumes a major responsibility for planning and implementation. It is a variation of systematic desensitization, but involves a different theoretical rationale and minimal therapist contact.

The therapeutic process of systematic desensitization involves teaching a relaxation strategy and constructing a hierarchy of events that produce small, but increasing, amounts of anxiety. The hierarchy culminates with the target situation. In the re-

laxed state the client visualizes the first item on the hierarchy. If the image can be maintained for three presentations without the subjective experience of anxiety, the next item is introduced. When anxiety accompanies an item, that image is abandoned and the client returns to the previous, non-anxiety-producing visualization. The goal of treatment is to imagine the item designated as most anxiety-producing while still remaining relaxed.

Self-control desensitization differs in two ways from the traditional approach. First, its theoretical rationale is different. Self-control desensitization states that the effects derived from desensitization can be attributed to active use of muscular relaxation and cognitive relabeling of the feared stimulus, rather than reciprocal inhibition. What the client learns is an active coping technique, rather than a passive and automatic inhibition. Second, self-control desensitization typically involves one or more forms of self-directed stimulus presentation that, at least in part, replace therapist-client contact.

CLINICAL APPLICATION

Self-control desensitization has been described in the treatment of speech anxiety, acrophobia, snake phobia, social anxiety, test anxiety, and math anxiety.

The scope of self-control desensitization has been extended from the treatment of one specific anxiety-producing stimulus, to desensitization combined with the cognitive skills necessary to recognize unrealistic and self-defeating thoughts that lead to increased anxiety at different times and under varying conditions.

Self-control desensitization differs from the standard technique in several ways. One way is in the preparation of treatment tools. For example, the client can make audio recordings of the instructions for relaxation and desensitization to be used in the treatment endeavor. In other cases, the client may utilize a recording made by the therapist, or one that is commercially prepared. Between relaxation and desensitization the client may be encouraged to keep homework records, summarize treatment instructions and goals, and practice at home, and in new anxiety-producing situations.

A second difference is in the preparation of the hierarchy, which often is not as formally structured as in traditional desensitization. A third difference is in the amount of client and therapist interaction. For example, after an initial screening interview clients may receive the desensitization materials (a manual explaining the procedures and a record of relaxation instructions) in the mail and have no further contact with the therapist until the hierarchy is completed. Another variation, with slightly more therapist contact, consists of an initial explanatory interview plus weekly phone calls from the therapist. In yet another variation, the client reports to the therapist's office to use the taped relaxation and desensitization instructions, and meets with a therapist briefly after every second session.

The majority of treatment programs are based on individual sessions. However, some therapists have utilized a group treatment setting. During desensitization, clients are taught to use their anxiety as a cue to initiate the relaxation response. They are instructed to record the relaxation experience, paying attention to the tension levels before and after imagining the hierarchy item. A group discussion follows the third presentation of each hierarchy scene. Several authors report that treatment can reasonably be expected to last about seven sessions. However, some have stated that three or four sessions were devoted to relaxation training and 5 to 14 were needed for the desensitization process. Hierarchies included a range of 12 to 20 items. Currently there are no data to suggest that these varieties of self-control de-

sensitization procedures lead to differential results.

EXPECTED OUTCOMES

Systematic desensitization is known to be highly effective for decreasing fears and phobias. The self-control variations seem to be no less effective. Reports of their use consistently demonstrate that treated clients improve significantly more than do the nontreated controls.

Several studies have evaluated different levels of therapist control. The results are equivocal, although they tend to suggest that both high and low control are about equally effective. Some studies have found the totally self-administered programs to be most effective, while one study treatment demonstrated that completely self-administered clients attempted more specific target behaviors (60.5%) than did the clients in the therapist-directed situation (40%). The self-control clients also showed greater gains on self-report measures. Other reports indicate that there is a slight, but not statistically significant, edge for those clients who had the therapist present. One study found therapist-administered desensitization to be more effective and postulated that this may have occurred because interaction with the therapist more closely resembled an in vivo desensitization process. Systematic desensitization, as well as its self-control variant, has been most commonly employed in the treatment of anxiety-related disorders and phobias. Self-control desensitization appears to be equally useful in treatment of anxiety, although there is some evidence that it may not be as successful as therapist-administered desensitization for severe clinical phobias.

POTENTIAL SIDE EFFECTS OR CONTRAINDICATIONS

There are no reports of any symptom substitution or other untoward side effects in cases where self-control desensitization has eliminated the target anxiety. In fact, many clients report a positive generalization of anxiety control to other tension generating events. An obvious positive effect is economy of therapist time and resources. Additionally when the client is able to attribute positive changes to personal efforts, the effects of the treatment may be more permanent and generalizable.

Since high attrition is a frequently reported problem with this treatment strategy, the principal contraindication would be its use with the poorly motivated client. For example, one study reported that only 8 of 17 clients in the two self-sensitization treatment groups completed at least one-half of the hierarchy items. Six failed to get beyond the relaxation phase. These results compare quite favorably with six of nine clients in the therapist-administered program who completed the entire program in an average of 10 sessions. Because continued client participation is a critical factor in the success or failure of this treatment strategy, the therapist will want to consider ways to increase that involvement. Such techniques as contracting, refundable cash deposits, or some other program for reinforcement of participation have been suggested.

BIBLIOGRAPHY

Baker, B. L., Cohen, D. C., & Saunders, J. T. (1973). Self-desensitization for acrophobics. *Behaviour Research and Therapy, 11,* 79–89.

Goldfried, M. R., & Goldfried, A. P. (1977). Importance of hierarchy content in the self-control of anxiety. *Journal of Consulting and Clinical Psychology, 45,* 124–134.

Morris, R. J. (1980). Fear reduction methods. In F. H. Kanfer & A. P. Goldstein (Eds.), *Helping people change.* New York: Pergamon Press.

Phillips, R. E., Johnson, G. D., & Geyer, A. (1972). Self-administered systematic desensitization. *Behaviour Research and Therapy, 10,* 93–96.

Rosen, G. M., Glasgow, R. E., & Barrera, M., Jr. (1976). A controlled study to assess the clinical efficacy of totally self-administered systematic desensitization. *Journal of Consulting and Clinical Psychology, 44,* 208–217.

See: Bibliotherapy
Systematic Desensitization

SELF CONTROL THERAPY
Alan M. Gross

Self-control therapy involves training patients to control their own behavior through the systematic use of behavior technology. This goal is achieved by teaching individuals the technical aspects of the various behavior modification procedures such that they may apply them to themselves to modify their own responding. A critical component of this therapy is education regarding the principles of behavior. It is believed that in order to successfully use behavior therapy procedures people must understand the nature of the relationship between responding and environmental conditions. This understanding will facilitate a person's ability to identify the events supporting both desirable and undesirable behavior, hence leading to the selection and appropriate self-administration of the behavior change strategy.

In general, training begins with instruction in behavioral assessment. Patients are taught the importance of operationally defining target behaviors. When this aspect of training has been completed the individual is told to monitor the occurrence of the target response. Self-monitoring not only provides an indication of the frequency of the specific behavior, but by noting the conditions in which the behavior occurs, important data are provided regarding variables that support and maintain the response.

As baseline data are gathered the patient is taught how to analyze this type of information. This aspect of training provides the therapist the opportunity to begin teaching the individual about the principles of behavior. The focus here is to identify the functional relationships existing between appropriate and/or inappropriate behavior and environmental events. Analysis of baseline data is also intended to produce a specific response performance criterion.

Following assessment, behavior modification techniques are discussed. The therapist educates the patient regarding the technical aspects of various behavior change procedures. From these discussions and the analysis of baseline data the method most appropriate to the individual and his/her situation will be selected for use. While almost any behavioral method used to alter responding in mediator-directed programs is a possibility, the majority of self-directed behavior change programs employ reinforcement procedures.

In a self-reinforcement program, patients are taught to administer consequences to themselves contingent on the performance of the target behavior. For example, in a weight-loss program patients might monitor their daily caloric intake. Following baseline, a reinforcement contingency would be established in which rewards would be earned for consuming less than a specific number of calories each day. Patients would continue to monitor their eating, evaluate their performance, and self-deliver a self-selected reward each day they met their performance criterion. Similarly, someone suffering from a phobia might observe his/her behavior and with the help of a therapist, develop a stimulus hierarchy consisting of a series of responses that resulted in graduated exposure to the phobic stimulus. The individual could then establish a reinforcement contingency in which each time he/she completed one step on the hierarchy he/she rewarded himself/herself for the performance of that behavior.

It is clear that in its most common form

self-control therapy involves self-monitoring, self-evaluation (to determine whether a criterion has been achieved), and self-delivered rewards. However, various other techniques have been included in self-control programs. People have been taught to self-administer desensitization and punishment as well as to use stimulus control techniques to effectively manage their own behavior (rearrange their environment to eliminate cues associated with undesirable responses).

Similar to behavioral interventions in which the contingencies are applied by an external treatment mediator, self-control therapy requires regular direct patient-therapist contact. The time course for therapy is similar to externally controlled treatments. That is, 10–20 sessions provide a general time frame. However, it is suggested that once the patient has learned the basic principles and procedures of behavior management he/she assumes the majority of treatment responsibility and therapist contact becomes more supervisory.

A case illustration of the use of self-control therapy can be seen in the treatment of an 11-year-old boy with an eye blink tic of 3-year duration. The child emitted the tic behavior (rapid multiple [3–5] opening and closing of both eyes accompanied by bunching up of the cheeks) throughout the day. It was a source of embarrassment and resulted in the child being teased by peers. Treatment began by teaching the child to identify when he emitted the behavior. He was taught to do this by having him observe himself performing the response in front of a mirror. When he could reliably identify the occurrence of the tic he was instructed to collect baseline data using a frequency count measure. Treatment consisted of self-administered overcorrection. The youth was told that every time he emitted the target behavior to bring his hand to his forehead and shield his eyes. He then held his eyes open and counted to 10. This was followed by holding his eyes closed and counting to 10. This procedure of counting to 10 with his eyes open and closed was repeated three times. The procedure resulted in a rapid decline and elimination of the tic, which was maintained at the 3-month follow-up.

Self-control therapy has been used to treat a wide array of disorders. An example is problem behavior (both academic and social) of children in classrooms. These applications have generally involved teaching youngsters to monitor their behavior and self-deliver rewards when they have met a specific response criterion. The use of self-control training with children, however, requires a large amount of adult supervision. In the absence of adult surveillance, the youngsters tend to self-reward noncontingently.

Self-control therapy has been applied to various adult disorders. Smoking, alcohol abuse, obesity, dating skills, study skills, anxiety, phobias, marital difficulties, tics, insomnia, headaches, and medication compliance have been successfully treated using this approach. However, it is important to note that the majority of these demonstrations have not included long term follow-up. Before definitive statements can be made regarding the maintenance of treatment effects resulting from self-control programs, further research must be conducted.

A number of potential benefits from teaching patients self-control, rather than using external agents to administer treatment contingencies, have been suggested. When parents, teachers, or other individuals are in control of the contingencies, a great deal of target behavior will go unconsequented. The individuals who administer the contingencies may also become discriminative stimuli for the target behaviors. Because of their association with reinforcement, patients may learn only to perform the desired behavior when these agents are present. Or, in the case of punishment programs, patients may refrain from emitting inappropriate behaviors only when treatment agents are present. Moreover, self-control therapy allocates a great deal of responsibility to patients. Including patients in the development and actual administration of the treatment program may serve to increase their interest in therapy and, as such, enhance their performance.

Another area in which self-control therapy may offer advantages over traditional treatment approaches involves behavior problems which are not readily accessible to therapists. Insomnia or obsessive thoughts, for example, are not easily observed by therapists. In situations such as these, having patients administer their own contingencies may be the most reasonable treatment strategy. Lastly, it has been suggested that teaching individuals to be their own therapist will contribute to generalization of treatment effects because patients will be able to continue to administer the program or develop new treatments following the formal termination of therapy. While this suggestion appears reasonable, as noted earlier, substantiating data are lacking at this time.

Although there are a number of potential benefits associated with self-control therapy, problems with the procedures have been reported. In particular, difficulties with adherence to treatment are not uncommon. Patients frequently self-deliver consequences in the absence of performing target behaviors. This results in reinforcement for inappropriate behavior. Noncontingent self-administration of rewards has been most problematic in programs concerning children. Noncontingent self-reward and the failure to self-deliver punishers have also been reported in adult self-control therapy programs. Creating an externally controlled contingency for adherence to treatment can reduce the magnitude of this problem. However, the increased involvement of treatment mediators raises questions regarding how much personal control patients are exhibiting over their behavior.

Criteria for selecting patients appropriate for self-control therapy have not been developed. Problems of adherence to treatment suggest that these procedures will be most effective with individuals who demonstrate a high level of motivation. Research also demonstrates that self-control therapy should only be applied to children in situations in which adult surveillance of the youngster's use of the procedures is possible. While there are clearly a number of potential benefits that may result from teaching patients self-control techniques, the lack of data on the long term effectiveness of these procedures, as well as the absence of clearly defined prerequisites for choosing patients appropriate for this type of therapy, indicate that this technique should be applied cautiously.

BIBLIOGRAPHY

Gross, A. M. (1983). Self-management and medication compliance in children with diabetes. *Child and Family Behavior Therapy, 4,* 47–55.

Gross, A. M., & Mendelson, A. N. (1982). Elimination of an eyeblink tic using self-administered overcorrection. *Behavioral Engineering, 8,* 1–4.

Kanfer, F. H. (1980). Self-management methods. In F. H. Kanfer & A. P. Goldstein (Eds.), *Helping people change.* New York: Pergamon Press.

Karoly, P., & Kanfer, F. H. (1982). *Self-management and behavior change.* New York: Pergamon Press.

Kazdin, A. E. (1980). *Behavior modification in applied settings.* Homewood, IL: Dorsey Press.

Rosenbaum, N. S., & Drabman, R. S. (1979). Self-central training in the classroom: A review and critique. *Journal of Applied Behavior Analysis, 12,* 467–485.

See: Overcorrection
      Self-Control Triad
      Self-Monitoring
      Self-Punishment
      Self-Reinforcement

SELF-CONTROL TRIAD
Joseph R. Cautela

The self-control triad is a covert conditioning procedure that is employed to reduce the probability of the occurrence of undesirable behavior such as negative thinking, fear of loss of control, or overeating. The client is instructed to say the word "stop" to him/herself when performing the undesirable covert or overt behavior, take a deep breath, relax while exhaling, and then imagine a pleasant scene.

The self-control triad fulfills the definition of covert conditioning since the pleasant scene is assumed to reinforce the operant "stop" and the relaxation breathing after the maladaptive behavior is performed.

See: Cognitive Therapy
      Self-Reinforcement

SELF-INSTRUCTIONAL TRAINING
Donald H. Meichenbaum

Self-instructional training is a multifaceted training regimen that is designed to teach clients to interrupt their maladaptive behavior and to produce task-relevant and situation-appropriate strategies and behaviors. The training regimen consists of cognitive modeling, overt and covert rehearsal, graded practice on carefully selected training tasks, and performance feedback. Such training is conducted only after adequate preparation which ensures that the client: (a) understands the reasons why he or she is being seen and perceives that he or she has a problem, (b) collaborates in the selection of the skills to be targeted, and (c) appreciates how the skills that will be worked on in training sessions will be helpful in changing behaviors in the criterion situations. In short, clinical skill is required in teaching the client how to self-monitor, self-interrogate, and self-evaluate his or her behavior.

In order to teach clients to "think before they act" and to influence the content and style of such thoughts, self-instructional training entails the following steps:

(a) the trainer performs a task while talking out loud (or one can use a voice overplay when using a videotape) (cognitive modeling),

(b) the client performs the same task under the direction of the model's instruction (overt, external guidance),

(c) the client performs the task while instructing himself/herself aloud (covert self-guidance),

(d) the client whispers the instructions to himself/herself (faded overt self-guidance), and finally,

(e) the client performs the task while guiding performance via private speech (covert self-instruction).

Over a number of training sessions, the package of self-statements modeled by the trainer and rehearsed by the client (initially aloud and then covertly) is enlarged by means of response chaining and successive approximation procedures. For example, in the work with hyperactive children the cognitive strategies included stopping to define a problem and the various steps within it, considering and evaluating several possible solutions before acting on any one, checking one's work throughout and calmly correcting errors, sticking with a problem until everything has been tried to solve it correctly, and giving oneself a pat on the back for having tried. The following example illustrates the modeled cognitive strategies that were taught to hyperactive children.

"I must stop and think before I begin." "What plans can I try?" "How would it work out if I did that?" "What shall I try next?" "Have I got it right so far?" "See,

I made a mistake there—I'll just erase it." "Now let's see have I tried everything I can think of?" "I've done a pretty good job!" (Douglas, Parry, Marton, & Garson, 1976, p. 408)

The cognitive modeling and overt and covert rehearsal procedures can be tailored to each target problem and can be adapted to the specific client's abilities. It is a flexible training procedure and some clients may be able to skip certain steps (e.g., follow modeling with covert rehearsal and omit overt rehearsal).

Training tasks are tailored to the specific population. Such behaviors as anger control, reduced distractibility, altruism, reading comprehension, solving arithmetic problems, social problem solving and so forth have been successfully taught by means of self-instructional training.

A number of clinical techniques can be used to enhance the training procedures. For example, in the case of children these include (1) using the child's own medium of play to initiate and model self-talk, (2) selecting tasks that have a high "pull" for the use of sequential cognitive strategies, (3) using peer teaching, (4) guarding against the client using the self-statements in a mechanical non-involved fashion by using discovery procedures, (5) using a trainer who is animated and responsive to the client, and (6) supplementing the training with imagery techniques such as the Turtle Technique and response cost procedures.

Closely related to the work on self-instructional training are recent attempts at meta-cognitive training and social skills training. Social problem-solving training programs use several teaching modes including videotapes, group discussion, cartoon-workbooks, poster-pictorial and flash card activities, behavioral rehearsal and role playing, and in vivo assignments. The clients are taught to identify problems, generate alternatives, collect information, recognize personal values, make a decision, and then review that decision at a later time.

At this point there are some encouraging data that the self-instructional training approach is a useful addition to the clinical armamentarium, but more comprehensive long-term evaluation is needed in order to assess its potential and limitations.

BIBLIOGRAPHY

Brown, A., & Campione, J. (1978). Permissible inference from the outcome of training studies in cognitive development research. *Quarterly Newsletter of the Institute for Comparative Human Development, 2,* 46–53.
Douglas, V., Parry, P., Marton, P., & Garson, C. (1976). Assessment of a cognitive training program for hyperactive children. *Journal of Abnormal Child Psychology, 4,* 389–410.
Kendall, P., & Finch, A. (1976). A cognitive-behavioral treatment for impulse control: A case study. *Journal of Consulting and Clinical Psychology, 44,* 852–857.
Meichenbaum, D. (1977). *Cognitive-behavior modification: An integrative approach.* New York: Plenum Press.
Meichenbaum, D. (1983). Teaching thinking: A cognitive-behavioral perspective. In J. Segal, S. Chapman, & R. Glaser (Eds.), *Thinking and learning skills* (Vol. 2). Hillsdale, NJ: Erlbaum.
Meyers, A., & Craighead, E. (Eds.). (1984). *Cognitive behavior modification with children.* New York: Plenum Press.
Schneider, M. (1974). Turtle technique in the classroom. *Teaching exceptional children, 7,* 22–24.
Spivack, G., Platt, J., & Shure, M. (1976). *The problem-solving approach to adjustment.* San Francisco: Jossey-Bass.

See: Self-Statement Modification
Self-Verbalization

SELF-MONITORING
Steven Beck

Self-monitoring involves observing, recording, and evaluating one's own behavior. While proponents of most forms of therapy and personal growth acknowledge that their intervention involves some form of self-monitoring or awareness, in behavior therapy self-monitoring is carried out in a systematic, deliberate manner. Self-monitoring involves three steps: (1) discriminating when overt (e.g., smoking a cigarette, swearing) or covert (e.g., thoughts, hunger) responses occur, (2) the systematic recording of the response, and (3) examination or evaluation of one's self-observation data. Self-monitoring is the cornerstone of most behavioral change techniques. Self-monitoring is an invaluable technique because it is inexpensive, portable, and allows information about the entire range of behaviors an individual performs (often not accessible to outside observers).

CLINICAL APPLICATION

Self-monitoring has been used extensively as an assessment or intervention technique with a wide range of target behaviors and populations. Accurate self-monitoring can and has been carried out by children, adolescents, college students, parents, marital couples, retarded and institutionalized patients, and adult outpatients. The following target behaviors have been monitored: social behaviors such as assertive responses, addictive and consummatory behaviors such as alcoholic and caloric intake, classroom behaviors, psychotic behaviors, covert behaviors such as thoughts and feelings, psychophysiological events such as headaches or backaches, and habits such as nail biting or back pulling. As encompassing as the above-listed target behaviors seem to be, these only include a partial survey of the types of target behaviors that have been observed and recorded in the behavioral treatment literature.

Self-monitoring serves three primary functions in behavioral assessment and treatment. First, self-monitoring is often employed as a pretreatment technique to identify antecedents and consequences of specific target behaviors. Second, self-monitoring of target behaviors is used to assess the effectiveness of treatment. Third, self-monitoring can be used as a means to facilitate behavior change.

There are numerous ways to record the occurrence of self-monitored target behaviors. One of the most popular self-observing devices is the wrist counter. The most common method to record responses and pertinent information about the target responses is the 3″ × 5″ index card, which can be kept conveniently in a pocket.

EXPECTED OUTCOMES, TIME FRAMES, AND DIFFERENTIAL DIAGNOSTIC CHARACTERISTICS

Therapists must train clients how to self-monitor. Clients need to be informed of the importance and relevancy of accurate self-monitoring, and probably should be given an initial assignment which is not exceedingly demanding. Therapists need to give explicit instructions with illustrative examples of self-monitoring so that clients will understand how to implement this technique. As mentioned earlier, self-monitoring is a critical component in successfully assessing and facilitating behavior change. Consequently, when target behaviors are not being accurately recorded or not recorded at all by the client, the therapist needs to explore why this assignment fails to be carried out. The therapist may discover, for example, that the client does not know how to self-monitor, or may not understand the importance of accurate self-monitoring, or believes that the response(s) being monitored is (are) not clinically relevant.

Self-monitoring, like any other observational procedure, may affect change in the rate or topography of the monitored behavior. That is, when an individual begins to self-observe his or her own behavior, there is a change in the usual stimulus situation. The nature of the target behavior may also influence the degree of reactivity.

Several other factors may influence the reactivity or accuracy of self-monitoring. It has been empirically documented that self-monitoring of positive behaviors is likely to cause an increase in frequency, whereas the self-observation of negative behaviors will likely result in a decrease in frequency of the behaviors targeted for observation. It has also been shown that low frequency behaviors which are easily discriminable (e.g., sexual contacts, seizures, physical aggression) may be more accurate, while high frequency behaviors (e.g., verbal behaviors) or responses whose onset may be difficult to identify (e.g., feelings of sadness) may not be as accurately monitored. How each target should be recorded can influence its accuracy and uility as an assessment or therapeutic aid. For example, are target behaviors counted over the course of a day or during very specific times? Clients should also be instructed to make their recordings immediately after the occurrence of the target behavior, since the time between the occurrence of the target behavior and its recording appears to affect the accuracy of self-monitoring. The continuous, excessive, or recording of too many concurrent behaviors may result in failure of self-monitoring or inaccurate self-observations. It also appears to be more useful to record occurrences of behavior rather than non-occurrences. Finally, adults may be more accurate self-recorders than children.

POTENTIAL SIDE EFFECTS OR CONTRAINDICATIONS

Many studies have reported low aggreement between self-monitoring of individuals and that of independent observers. Hence, self-monitored data should be viewed with caution, but can be considered more valid if the above-mentioned factors influencing the accuracy of self-recorded behavior are recognized and dealt with by the therapist. For some, clients' self-monitoring of negative target behaviors (such as depressive thoughts or feelings) or more specific target behaviors (such as daily weight) can lead to further feelings of hopelessness and failure. In these situations, self-monitoring should be discontinued.

BIBLIOGRAPHY

Ciminero, A. R., Nelson, R. O., & Lipinski, D. P. (1977). Self-monitoring procedures, In A. R. Ciminero, K. S. Calhoun, & H. E. Adams (Eds.). *Handbook of behavioral assessment*. New York: Wiley.

Haynes, S. N. (1978). *Principles of behavioral assessment*. New York: Gardner Press.

Kanfer, F. (1970). Self-monitoring: Methodological limitations and clinical applications. *Journal of Consulting and Clinical Psychology, 35*, 148–152.

Kazdin, A. E. (1974). Self-monitoring and behavior change. In M. J. Mahoney, & C. E. Thoresen (Eds.). *Self-control: Power to the person*. Monterey, CA: Brooks-Cole.

Thoresen, C. E., & Mahoney, M. J. (1974). *Behavioral self-control*. New York: Holt, Rinehart, & Winston.

See: Controlled Drinking
Controlled Smoking

SELF-PUNISHMENT
Alan S. Bellack

Self-punishment is a self-control procedure in which the client attempts to decrease undesirable behaviors by administering aversive consequences contingent upon occurrence of the response. Any form of externally administered punishment can be converted to a self-administered format. Examples of response cost include: self-imposed fines (e.g., money sent to a disliked organization) and depriving oneself of privileges (e.g., no shower or no television). Time out can include temporarily turning off the television, shutting a book, or leaving the dining table. Aversive stimuli include self-critical thoughts and images (e.g., picturing oneself in a larger clothing size), and snapping a rubber band on one's wrist. Self-punishment has primarily been used with outpatient adults who are plagued with high frequency undesirable behaviors, including: cigarette smoking, obsessions, compulsions, sexual fantasies, overeating, tics, and mild alcohol and drug abuse. The literature on the effectiveness of these procedures is equivocal, especially in regard to durability of effects. Self-reinforcement (self-reward) is preferred when possible, and self-punishment is probably not effective with severe problems.

See: Punishment
Self Control
Self-Reinforcement

SELF-REINFORCEMENT
Thomas R. Kratochwill

As with other forms of reinforcement, self-reinforcement serves to strengthen, maintain, or increase behavior. However, in self-reinforcement, the individual determines the responses that will be followed by the reinforcer and is free to reinforce himself/herself at any time. Self-reinforcement is typically employed as a component of a complete self-control program. Self-reinforcement can be overt or covert. In overt self-reinforcement the individual manipulates observable aspects of the environment to provide reinforcing consequences. In the covert type, self-reinforcing stimuli are typically in the form of images, thoughts, and recalled experiences which elicit positive feelings. Such self-reinforcing stimuli are usually evoked when one's behavior compares favorably to the observed standards of behavior of significant socializing agents (e.g., parents, teachers, peers). Thus, self-reinforcement is a process that involves evaluating one's own behavior in terms of perceived standards and permitting oneself to experience certain positive overt consequences or covert images, thoughts, or recalled experiences if behavior is consistent with these standards. For example, an individual on a diet might self-reinforce himself by attending a movie contingent upon losing two pounds in a week.

See: Controlled Drinking
    Self-Control Therapy
    Self-Control Triad

SELF-STATEMENT MODIFICATION
E. Thomas Dowd

Self-statements are overt or covert statements that individuals say to themselves regarding an event and/or its meaning. They are lower-order examples of cognitive phenomena in that they are situation-specific and conceptually restricted. Self-statements are considered to be a form of automatic thought in which originally overtly verbalized statements have become covertly verbalized and then often emitted without conscious awareness. For example, upon entering a party, a socially anxious individual might think, "I'm going to say something stupid," or "No one will want to talk to someone as ugly as me." Self-statement modification occurs in three stages: (1) Self-observation, in which individuals become aware of their own self-statements; (2) The deliberate production of self-statements incompatible to those whose elimination is desired, as well as the production of alternative self-statements; and (3) The individual's assessment of and reaction to the new self-statements and their subsequent modification. Self-statement modification has been applied to a wide variety of emotional disorders, including anxiety, depression, stress, and impulsivity.

See: Cognitive Restructuring
    Cognitive Therapy

SELF-VERBALIZATION
Donald H. Meichenbaum

Subsumed under the heading of self-verbalization are a variety of techniques which include the ability to notice (self-monitor), interrupt and evaluate one's maladaptive behavior, set appropriate standards, develop and implement appropriate cognitive and behavioral strategies, and produce coping and reinforcing self-statements. Self-verbalization procedures (including both problem-solving self-statements and images) have been applied to many clinical populations (for example, teaching attention-focusing to schizophrenics, anxiety control to phobics, and self-control to hyperactive and aggressive children).

See: Self-Statement Modification

SENSATE FOCUS

See: Sex Therapy

SETTING EVENTS
Sandra Twardosz

Setting events are antecedent social and environmental conditions that facilitate or inhibit the occurrence of behavior that is already in an individual's repertoire. They are more complex and temporally removed from behavior than discriminative stimuli. One type of setting event consists of the immediate circumstances in the environment that precede and overlap behavior, such as food deprivation and the presence or absence of specific objects or people. For example, the availability of planned activities in a residential setting may facilitate participation and social interaction among the residents. A second type of setting even occurs separately in space and time from the behavior it influences and includes the individual's response to the event. For example, children's active play outdoors may set the occasion for disruptive behavior when they return to a quiet indoor activity. Unpleasant interactions at work may increase the probability of later unpleasant interactions at home. Setting events are important for both the prevention and remediation of behavior problems because they facilitate incompatible behavior and may enhance the probability of generalization from treatment to natural settings.

See: Operant Conditioning

SEX THERAPY
R. M. Turner and *Blanche Freund*

Sex therapy is the directive, short-term, symptom-focused, rapid behavioral treatment of sexual dysfunction. It is a psychotherapeutic specialty practiced by many disciplines in the health professions and clergy.

Dysfunctions or disorders in the psychosexual area that respond to sex therapy are classified as follows: orgasmic dysfunction, erectile failure, premature ejaculation, inhibited ejaculation, inhibited sexual arousal and desire, dyspareunia, and vaginismus.

DESCRIPTION

Broadly described, sexual dysfunctions cause physiological, cognitive, behavioral, and interpersonal problems that can prevent satisfactory sexual enjoyment (intercourse and orgasm) in intimate relationships. Sexual

dysfunction is considered a marital-unit (or couple) dysfunction. Skills are usually needed in marital and communication areas, as well as specialized training in sexual technique.

Most couples (estimated at 50%) experience some sexual performance deficits at one time or another but are not stressed because of it. Typically, couples or individuals stressed by performance deficits initially complain to their physician, who may refer them to a sex therapist. However, other cases are self-referred and usually have self-labelled themselves dysfunctional.

Sometimes, sexual problems can be ameliorated through sex education, bibliotherapy, or the simple sharing of sexual anxieties and fears. Others require more than educative procedures. The symptom-focused rapid treatment can be remarkably successful in such cases. Central to this treatment is the systematic desensitization of sexual anxiety by prescribed, graded, in vivo couple exercises. In sex therapy terms this is called *sensate focus* (to be discussed more fully later). Imbedded in successive steps directed toward the greater experience of pleasure, specific tactics are introduced to reduce the symptom (e.g., lack of erection, early ejaculation, no orgasm). For instance, in the treatment of premature ejaculation, graduated training in experiencing pleasure would be implemented; then the behavioral tactics to learn to delay ejaculation via the "squeeze technique" would be gradually incorporated into pleasuring sessions. When ejaculation is successfully delayed using the squeeze technique, the successive steps of sensate focus would be continued through the predetermined goal of penis-vagina intercourse without early ejaculation.

CLINICAL APPLICATION — ASSESSMENT

Sex therapy begins with a comprehensive behavioral assessment that occurs over several sessions and often is ongoing during therapy. The first two sessions, however, necessarily involve taking a thorough sex history. This is often a slow, progressive task due to the sensitivity of the topic. Sharing sexual traumas, beliefs, and the intimate details of one's sex life generally is anxiety-producing and needs to be pursued at the client's own comfort. It is generally the practice to begin with an open-ended session where each partner relates how they view the problem; then gradually the therapist guides the session towards greater specificity. Clients' expectations and goals in seeking therapy are addressed here as well. Before assessment is considered complete, a developmental, social, sexual, and dating history should be obtained from both partners. At least in one of these assessment sessions, time should be spent with each individual alone. This is necessary to complete a history of abuse, extramarital affairs, or "secrets" of which the therapist needs to be aware. Confidentiality issues associated with "secrets" are discussed. In addition, a microanalysis of the current sexual and marital interaction is important to clarify the learning integration of past with present data.

In general, and particularly in a male dysfunction, a recent medical workup should be completed before sex therapy interventions are initiated. A non-medical sex therapist is advised to have a close working relationship with appropriate medical colleagues who practice sexual medicine. Sexual medicine has developed into an important subspecialty, particularly in endocrinology, obstetrics and gynecology, urology, and vascular surgery. Also, knowledge of a reliable sleep laboratory to be used in evaluating male organic dysfunction is crucial. In addition to the medical history and contact with necessary referral agents, a sex therapist should conduct an assessment of pre-scribed medications and alcohol and illicit drug usage. A dysfunction may no longer be a problem if it can be alleviated by reduction or change in medication, particularly in the area of side effects with the use of hypertensive drugs, antipsychotics, or antidepressants. On the other hand, many non-retractable medical conditions or necessary medications can cause permanent or long-term dysfunction, which in itself requires the help of a sex therapist to re-educate the couple about alternate methods of sexual technique.

In some cases, the assessment can effect a one or two-session cure. Having a third ear evaluate the problem can, when conducted by a therapist in an educative manner, relieve isolation, uniqueness, misinformation, and inhibitory beliefs. Normative information during assessment may cause the patient to reframe the problem and see that there is no dysfunction, and hence achieve a solution. However, these cures are seen less and less in clinical practice because of the proliferation of self-help books, open-medical discussion, and sex education/human sexuality courses. It is also important to note that the reverse can happen and some people misconstrue and erroneously diagnose themselves as dysfunctional. Problems can occur if persons compare their sex lives with the sexual prowess of X-rated movie stars or what friends say they do. In summary, the aim of a comprehensive assessment is to identify inhibitions, deficits, excesses, and traumas from the past that may have set the stage for performance anxieties.

The next step is for the therapist to discuss the assessment findings with the couple or individual. This session is called a *round table discussion* and should generate a clear statement of how the therapist views the clients' problem. It is the time to establish motivation and commitment to make necessary changes, establish the treatment plan, and set long-term goals. In addition, a contract specifying the number of therapeutic sessions over an approximated amount of time, as well as ground rules for treatment, is worked out. Once the couple or individual has agreed to the contract, therapeutic tactics can commence.

TREATMENT TECHNIQUES AND TACTICS

Sex therapy involves educative therapeutic sessions in conjunction with the prescribed individualized behavioral assignments which are carried out in the privacy of the home. Most techniques are applicable with individuals, couples, or groups. For the most part, both partners are involved in the clinic sessions and the at-home treatment components. On occasion, at-home assignments may involve one partner (e.g., pre-orgasmic women learning to masturbate).

Sessions with the couple focus on assignments, performance feedback, communication training, resolving relationship issues (i.e., power struggles), sexual repertoire, frequency discrepancies, intimacy, privacy, and assertiveness. The thrust is to decrease the symptomatic partner's performance anxiety. Also interspersed in these sessions is sex education to correct myths and misconceptions.

Behavioral assignments are integral to the learning theorist approach to treatment, and include successive or graded, imaginal, and in vivo exposure to fear-provoking stimuli, as well as anxiety reduction techniques. Assignments for specific dysfunctions are numerous. For example:

Sensate Focus. This exercise is one of the basic assignments used in sex therapy (Masters & Johnson, 1970). It involves weekly assignments in graded body touching. There is no genital contact at first. Usually there is a ban on genital sex to prevent concern about performance (i.e., no orgasm, ejaculation, or erection). Relearning pleasure associated with body contact and reducing performance anxiety are the purposes of sensate focus. The partners practice massaging and touching each other with an emphasis upon learning to recognize what feels good. In addition, the couple learns to slow down and not rush the sexual encounter.

Squeeze Technique/Stop/Start. This is a basic sex therapy technique and is used widely for treatment of premature ejaculation. The technique requires the partner to stimulate the erect penis to the point where the male experiences premonitory sensation of ejaculatory inevitability. Stimulation at this point is interrupted and the partner squeezes the coronal ridge of the penis and awaits reduction in arousal. The process is repeated until longer and longer periods of control of ejaculatory reflex are reported. A variation of this technique is the stop/start method. This is accomplished on premonition not by squeezing, but with the cessation of erectile stimulation. This exercise is useful for a partner who cannot squeeze, or persons without partners and persons who wish to practice alone during masturbation. Good textbook descriptions of these techniques are numerous.

Masturbation Exercises. The procedure to reduce anxiety associated with genital self-stimulation and orgasm involves progressive but specific exercises. At first, the individual attends to body imagery (nude, genital, and body examination with mirrors). After comfort is established in this area, tactile and visual location of pleasurable areas are self-stimulated. Self-stimulation continues in increasing duration and intensity toward the goal of orgasm. Manual or vibrator simulation may be paired with fantasy and erotic images. For females, pubo-coccygeus (PC) muscle training is assigned to increase awareness of vaginal feelings. Finally, once orgasm is experienced and practiced, graded partner exercises are incorporated to promote generalization of this new behavior. Several reference books are available for more elaboration of these specific exercises.

TIME FRAME AND EXPECTED OUTCOME

In an uncomplicated case, where the couple is functional in its basic marital communication and intimacy skills, treatment could be effective in as few as 4–6 weeks of 1-hour sessions. This same couple would also have to be committed to prioritize sexual skill building with daily, at-home practice. The more typical time commitment for sex therapy, however, is 15–20 consecutive weekly sessions. Contracts built around the time constraints of therapy are helpful to: (1) prevent dropouts during discouraging or resistant weeks, (2) prioritize the sexual aspects of the relationship for a sustained period, and (3) insure a sufficient dosage of treatment.

Unfortunately, many individuals presenting with sexual dysfunction involve marital trauma and the threat of separation or divorce. Under such circumstances, the task of restoring sexual interaction is secondary to marital therapy. When this is the case, the overall duration of therapy is increased. For some couples, sex has been avoided for a long period of time and the issues underlying this avoidance may need to be the focus of treatment. For instance, lack of trust in the relationship may have been precipitated by an extramarital affair. Therapy would first have to focus on the trust issues before proceeding to reduce avoidance and restore sexual stability. A longstanding, dysfunctional marital system that has caused cessation of caring, intimacy, desire, and

initiation behaviors complicates the treatment plan still further. Under these circumstances, the rapid treatment model must be modified appropriately.

Resistant sex therapy cases have been reported extensively in the literature but each has its own characteristics. There has been no way to predict success. Despite this lack of specificity, many complicated marital/sex cases have been amenable to treatment. Some literature suggests that it is possible to bypass interpersonal psychodynamics and proceed with sex therapy interventions in the hope that success in restoring sexual functioning will restore marital harmony.

Successful outcome typically occurs with motivated couples who prioritize homework practice, comply with assignments, and are reliable in keeping weekly appointments. As smooth as this sounds, there are weeks that couple assignments go well with much resultant progress, and weeks that produce less progress. Even unproductive weeks can be utilized for therapeutic purposes. Making mistakes, avoiding assignments, and not complying to behavioral prescription can be salient events to concentrate on during the therapeutic session. Discussion and resolution of power issues, attempts at sabotage, and resistance can redefine a marital relationship and generate new sexual behavior gains.

In summary, the time frame for sex therapy is dependent on complications in marital interactions, compliance with homework assignments, compliance with attending consecutive sessions, sustained motivation, realistic goals, and the desire of the couple to work together for long-term improvement.

The success rate of first reports seemed high but credible. Masters and Johnson (1970) reported a success rate of around 80%. Treatment of premature ejaculation and vaginismus continues with high success. The high rate of failure first reported for primary cases of erectile dysfunction has been reduced by the work of medical and surgical specialists. Clinicians agree these are the more difficult cases in which to predict success. However, desire phase dysfunction has been resistant to treatment. Marital and psychodynamic issues are seemingly the causes for lack of desire. However, incorporating more strategies associated with interactional skills and intimacy skills will hopefully generate increased success in the treatment of desire phase dysfunction.

CONTRAINDICATIONS AND SIDE EFFECTS

Therapy should only be begun when there is reasonable evidence that the couple (or individual) is well-motivated. In addition, the public sector has many misconceptions of what sex therapy is about, what sex therapists do, and what the task of sex surrogates are.

Therefore, it is important to screen out:

1. Patients who present with a "dysfunction" and think sex therapists do the work of sex surrogates and/or need to increase their prowess by sex therapy treatment.
2. Patients with severe psychopathology that is in need of individual psychotherapy.
3. Patients who are severely depressed, since sexual dysfunction or lack of desire can be the result of depression.
4. Last-ditch effort by one partner to save the marriage with sex therapy while the other partner is not committed to sustain the relationship with any therapy.
5. One member of the couple is involved in individual psychotherapy.
6. A couple where one partner refuses to be part of the therapy.
7. The lack of maturity or intelligence of one partner, which would make it difficult to accept therapeutic direction and to carry out at-home assignments.
8. If the individuals' goals seem unrealistic

for sex therapy and cannot be comfortably reformulated to realistic goals.
9. One partner's involvement in an ongoing clandestine affair, especially when he/she will neither disclose the relationship to his/her spouse nor disrupt the outside relationship during the course of therapy.

BIBLIOGRAPHY

Masters, W. H., & Johnson, V. E. (1970). *Human sexual inadequacy*. Boston: Little Brown & Co.

See: Orgasmic Reconditioning
     Shame Aversion
     Squeeze Technique

SHAME AVERSION

See: Aversive Conditioning
     Punishment
     Sex Therapy

SHAPING
Robert E. Becker

Shaping is the process of gradually changing the quality of a response. Usually, a simple response is required initially and criteria for reinforcement are gradually made more stringent so as to produce more complex or refined responses. Initially, a simple response would be sufficient to receive reinforcement. After this behavior is performed reliably, reinforcement is given only for a more complex or difficult response. Once again, after this new, more complex, response has been acquired, reinforcement shifts to the next slightly more complex response. This pattern continues until the final desired behavior is achieved regularly. Shaping can be aided by demonstrating the new skill to be learned before shifting the reinforcement.

See: Forward Chaining
     Operant Conditioning
     Successive Approximation

SOCIAL SKILLS TRAINING
Randall L. Morrison

Social skills training is a collection of techniques which are used in the treatment of persons whose social functioning is inadequate in some respect. The purpose of social skills training is to increase the social competence and/or skill repertoire of the target individual(s). Social skill is a broad construct that incorporates a variety of interpersonal response dimensions such as assertiveness, friendliness, warmth, conversational facility, and empathy. Each of these dimensions involves an extensive set of verbal and non-verbal response elements. For example, in order to be assertive, an individual must emit certain critical response components such as speaking in a loud voice, and maintaining eye contact. Social skills training impacts on any of the above response dimensions (e.g., conversational facility) by teaching the patient how to effectively perform the specific component elements which comprise that dimension.

Some of the most important components of social skill are listed in Table 1. *Expressive elements* are those parameters responsible for sending messages to others. *Receptive elements* involve the ability to attend to and decode the cues provided by the interpersonal partner. *Interactive balance* refers to the skills involved in timing and turn-taking during interactions. These distinct behavioral components of social skill comprise the focus for social skills training. Ideally, training begins with a comprehensive assessment of the target individual's competencies with regard to each of these component areas. However, it is more commonly the case that emphasis is placed on one or another component area to the relative exclusion of others.

The great majority of the social skills training studies that have been reported in

Table 1. Components of Social Skill

(A) Expressive Elements
   (1) Speech Content
   (2) Paralinguistic Elements
      (a) Voice
      (b) Pace
      (c) Pitch
      (d) Tone
   (3) Nonverbal Behavior
      (a) Proxemics
      (b) Kinesics
      (c) "Eye Contact"
      (d) Facial Expression
(B) Receptive Elements (Social Perception)
   (1) Attention
   (2) Decoding
   (3) Knowledge of Context Factors and Cultural Mores
(C) Interactive Balance
   (1) Response Timing
   (2) Turn Talking
   (3) Social Reinforcement

the literature have been based on the skills deficit model. According to this model, the individual who evidences poor social skills lacks certain specific motor response from his/her behavioral repertoire and/or uses inappropriate responses. Given this orientation, the most commonly employed assessment (and treatment) strategies have emphasized expressive response components.

TRAINING

Based on the skills deficit model, training is implemented according to the response acquisition approach. The treatment proceeds by training on each deficit response element using a series of social problem situations which provide the content material for role playing. The situations are derived from the assessment process, in which areas of difficulty are identified. The situations are dealt with sequentially in training, in order of increasing difficulty. The training consists of the five techniques outlined below:

Instructions. The patient is first given specific instructions about the response at issue, including why and how it should be performed.

Role Play. After instructions are given, the patient role plays a scenario with a therapist or a role model assistant. The format for a role play includes a description of the situation and a prompt (or a series of prompts in an extended interaction).

Feedback and Social Reinforcement. Following the role play, the patient is given feedback about his/her performance. Regardless of the success of any given role play attempt, the feedback should emphasize positive aspects of the patient's performance, and include positive social reinforcement.

Modeling. Rather than simply instructing the patient regarding how to respond, the therapist actually performs (models) the appropriate response. The modeling display focuses on the particular response element at issue. It should be prefaced by a description of the relevant aspects of the display, in order for the patient to be alerted to behaviors to which to pay particular attention.

This sequence of instructions, role play, feedback, and modeling is repeated until a response is mastered. Training then shifts to the next response or, if the target situation has been mastered, to the next situation.

Practice. Practice is encouraged both by giving general instructions to "try things out" and by giving specific homework assignments at the conclusion of each session. The assignment should be relatively specific and should be geared to a level of difficulty and a situation that will maximize the probability of success (and reinforcement by the environment).

Training is typically conducted in hour-long sessions, several times per week. Either an individual or group format can be used. Often, the group format is advantageous in that it presents additional opportunities for modeling and practice. When used with a group, training is best conducted by co-therapists, who can share responsibilities for explanation and modeling of various target social behaviors. Optimal group size for training is six to eight patients. Homework and in vivo practice are critical to facilitate the effects of training.

An effective procedure to be used with patients who evidence severe deficits is therapist-assisted practice. The therapist can accompany one or possibly two patients into the natural environment to supervise their practicing responses which have been taught as part of the training.

TIME FRAME AND EXPECTED OUTCOME

Duration of training varies with the nature of the clinical deficit. The technique is appropriate with patients from almost any diagnostic classification. Typically, schizophrenic patients evidence global social skills deficits, requiring extensive remediative efforts. In such cases, training may be conducted for 8 weeks or even longer. Patients with affective disorders often are recalcitrant to practice newly acquired skills, and so they may require rather extensive interventions. Patients with more circumscribed deficits typically require treatment of a much more limited duration.

Most patients show noticeable increases in interpersonal competence. These increases are especially apparent in terms of the patient's responses to role-played practice material presented within the context of training. Special effort should be directed toward assuring generalization and maintenance. As indicated, strategies which have been shown to be useful in this regard include in vivo practice during training sessions (i.e., therapist-assisted practice in the natural environment) and the assignment of homework. Reinforcing contingencies should be established to promote the completion of homework assignments.

Patients whose attentional or learning abilities are limited due to the nature of their disorder or psychotropic medication are not likely to do as well in treatment. Such patients may be disruptive to training efforts conducted in a group format. While training is best conducted according to a structured training curriculum, therapists should be trained clinicians and should remain alert with regard to clinical issues which may affect the patient(s). The fact that treatment is proceeding according to a standardized format should not preclude modifications to the treatment protocol in response to clinical necessity.

The reader should be aware that the skills deficit model is but one of four prevailing viewpoints regarding the etiology and maintenance of social disability. As implied, each model emphasizes one or another component area of social skill. Other models are the *conditioned-anxiety* model, the *cognitive-evaluative* model, and the *faulty discrimination* model. Each of the four conceptualizations has given rise to differing social-skills training protocols. The conditioned-anxiety model assumes that the individual has the requisite skills in his/her repertoire but is inhibited from responding in a socially appropriate fashion because of conditioned-anxiety responses. Anxiety reduction techniques are treatments of choice for social dysfunction considered to be due to such anxiety.

The cognitive-evaluative model of social disability posits that the source of an individual's social inadequacy is faulty cognitive appraisal of social performance and the expectation of aversive consequences. Negative self-appraisals and negative self-statements are seen as mediating poor social functioning. The social skills training procedures that follow from this model typically approximate the cognitive restructuring techniques which are described elsewhere in this volume.

Finally, the faulty discrimination model assumes that the social disability is due to the individual's not knowing how to match specific social behaviors with specific social situations. Socially inappropriate or inadequate behavior may be the result of a failure on the part of the individual to adequately discriminate the situations in which a response already in the repertoire is likely to be effective. This model suggests a therapy concerned with teaching the individual to discriminate which situations call for which behaviors. Training of this sort is typically conducted using a role play format in which matching of appropriate response alternatives to various types of social situations is demonstrated to patients. However, empirical evidence regarding the efficacy of such response discrimination training is limited. Further research is needed to identify and evaluate the most effective strategies for training more appropriate response discrimination skills. Similar recommendations regarding applicability, outcomes, and potential contraindications are relevant to the use of these latter three models of social skills training.

Of course, patients may manifest social deficits involving abilities and responses from each of the four models of social functioning. Hence, comprehensive skills training interventions will often incorporate techniques drawn from several of the models. Determination regarding which of the various techniques to include in the training protocol should be based on a comprehensive assessment of all of the relevant parameters of social functioning.

BIBLIOGRAPHY

Bellack, A. S., & Hersen, M. (1977). *Behavior modification: An introductory textbook*. Baltimore: Wilkins & Wilkins.

Bellack, A. S., & Hersen, M. (Eds.). (1979). *Research and practice in social skills training*. New York: Plenum Press.

Bellack, A. S., & Morrison, R. L. (1982). Interpersonal dysfunction. In A. S. Bellack, M. Hersen, & A. E. Kazdin (Eds.), *International handbook of behavior modification and therapy*. New York: Plenum Press.

Curran, J. P., & Monti, P. M. (Eds.). (1983) *Social skills training: A practical handbook for assessment and treatment*. New York: Guilford Press.

Morrison, R. L., & Bellack, A. S. (in press). Social skills training. In A. S. Bellack (Ed.), *Treatment and care for schizophrenia*. New York: Grune and Stratton.

See: Assertiveness Training
     Conversational Skills Training
     Heterosocial Skill Training
     Homework
     Instructions
     Modeling
     Role Playing

SPEECH SHADOWING

See: Delayed Auditory Feedback

SQUEEZE TECHNIQUE
Michael E. Thase

This procedure and its variants are the best-established treatments for premature ejaculation. Treatment is initiated by having either the man or his partner provide manual penile stimulation until premonitory sensations of impending ejaculation are noted. The penis is then firmly squeezed at a point just below the coronal ridge for 15–30 seconds, resulting in diminished sense of ejaculatory inevitability. The procedure is then repeated a number of times until the ability to anticipate and forestall impending ejaculation is established. In the stop/start variation, cessation of manual stimulation is used instead of the actual squeeze technique itself. Using either approach, therapy advances through application of such procedures in progressively more demanding sexual activities. Over several weeks of practice and graded exposure, the ability to attend to premonitory urges and delay ejaculation generally become well-established in intercourse positions. When conducted within the context of short-term psychoeducational treatment programs, improvement rates using these techniques approach 100%.

See: Sex Therapy

STIMULUS CONTROL
Laura Schreibman

Stimulus control refers to the differential effects of various stimulus conditions on our behavior as a result of discrimination learning. Thus, if we are reinforced for Response A in the presence of Stimulus A and not in the presence of Stimulus B, then we will perform the behavior in one situation (A) and not in the other (B). Our behavior is under stimulus control; we are discriminating. For example, a ringing telephone is a stimulus associated with reinforcement for picking up the receiver and saying "Hello." The reinforcement is the response of another person. However, a silent telephone is a stimulus that is associated with no reinforcement for picking up the receiver. Therefore, we answer a ringing telephone and ignore a silent one.

See: Cueing

STRESS INOCULATION
Patricia A. Resick

Stress inoculation is a general treatment paradigm which combines physiological arousal management, behavioral rehearsal, and cognitive coping strategies for the prevention and treatment of a wide variety of stress-related problems. The paradigm includes three treatment phases: an educational phase, a skills-building phase, and an application phase. The length of these phases has varied from one session to many months.

During the educational phase, the client is presented with a conceptualization of his/her responses to stress; including physiological, cognitive, affective, and behavioral response channels. The conceptual model presented during this phase varies depending upon the presenting problem. Schacter's cognitive-physiological model of emotion, or Lang's tripartite model of fear have been presented to anxious and fearful clients, while Melzack and Wall's gate-control model of pain has been used with pain clients. Clients are taught to conceptualize their reactions as a series of stages, or manageable units rather than one automatic, overwhelming response. Suggested temporal stages are: preparing for a stressor, confronting and handling the stressor, coping with arousal and feelings of being overwhelmed, and reinforcing self-statements for coping or reflection on how stress was not resolved. The educational phase may also include training in self-monitoring and response analysis.

A variety of techniques may be introduced during the skills acquisition phase. Physical coping skills may include progressive muscular relaxation, deep breathing, autogenic training (mental relaxation), or other brief relaxation techniques. Cognitive strategies consist of thought stopping, cognitive restructuring and guided self-dialogue, covert modeling and rehearsal, or problem solving. Other cognitive techniques that have been used in the management of pain also include attention diversion strategies such as focusing on the environment, imaginative inattention or imaginative transformation of pain. Behavioral skills such as social skills training or behavioral rehearsal have also been trained within the skills acquisition phase.

The application phase usually begins with covert rehearsal of skills and behavioral rehearsal within therapy sessions in a graded fashion before moving to in vivo implementation of skills.

The stress inoculation paradigm has been implemented with a variety of target populations with a range of problems. Appropriate target problems include pain management, stress management of health problems and medical procedures, social anxiety, multiple phobias, and control of anger. Among others, stress inoculation has been implemented with burn patients, aggressive adolescents, abusive parents, military recruits, rape victims, police and probation officers, and socially anxious college students. In other words, the clinical application may extend to anyone who is experiencing or anticipates needing to cope with stressors.

Outcome research is difficult to assess for the paradigm as a whole since the components, range of problems, and length of treatment have varied extensively. However, there have been a number of successful clinical applications of stress inoculation reported in the literature. Generalization of treatment skills to untreated stressors has been limited in analogue studies but has not been reported to be a problem in clinical applications. No side effects or contraindications have been reported in the literature.

BIBLIOGRAPHY

Jaremko, M. E. (1979). A component analysis of stress inoculation: Review and prospectus. *Cognitive Therapy and Research, 3*, 35–48.

Meichenbaum, D. (1975). A self-instructional approach to stress management: A proposal for stress inoculation training. In C. Speilberger & J. Sarason (Eds.), *Stress and anxiety* (Vol. 2). New York: Wiley.

Meichenbaum, D. & Jaremko, M. E. (Eds.). (1983). *Stress reduction and prevention.* New York: Plenum Press.

Novaco, R. W. (1975). *Anger control: The development and evaluation of an experimental treatment.* Lexington, MA: D. C. Heath.

Turk, D., Meichenbaum, D., & Genest, M. (1979). *Pain and behavior medicine.* New York: Guilford Press.

See: Anxiety Management Training
 Anger Control Therapy
 Stress Inoculation

STRESS MANAGEMENT TRAINING
Donald A. Williamson

Stress management training refers to a package of techniques which have been used for assisting patients to cope with stress more effectively. This treatment package commonly includes: (a) self-monitoring of stressors and stress reactions, (b) relaxation training, (c) biofeedback training (usually either skin temperature or EMG biofeedback), and (d) cognitive-behavior therapy approaches for modifying maladaptive cognitions. Stress management training can be conducted in groups as well as individual sessions. Generally, the patient will have been referred for a specific stress-related disorder. Typical disorders which have been successfully treated using stress-management are: headache, irritable bowel syndrome, tempero-mandibular joint dysfunction, essential hypertension, and Raynaud's Disease. A common protocol for conducting stress-management training is to first educate the patient in the effects of stress upon behavior and health. The sec-

ond step is self-monitoring of stressors, physical symptoms, behavioral reactions, and cognitions. From such self-monitoring the therapist may learn more about the individual's stressors and his/her method of coping prior to treatment. Self-monitoring is commonly used throughout treatment. The third step is training in relaxation. The most commonly used relaxation procedure is progressive muscle relaxation. Home practice of relaxation is usually prescribed. Biofeedback training is also commonly used, especially if the patient has been referred for a specific stress-related disorder. The final stage of stress management training is cognitive-behavior therapy. The most common techniques employed are cognitive restructuring and self-instructional training. This phase of treatment requires identification of faulty cognitions and beliefs and systematically assisting the patient to replace these faulty cognitions with thoughts and beliefs which are more effective for coping with stress. For example, instead of catastrophizing (e.g., "Oh no, this is the worst possible thing that can happen!"), the patient may be trained to adopt coping thoughts (e.g., "I can cope with this . . . Now what can I do? . . . relax, you can handle it. Sure it's not what you wanted to happen, but you can handle it.").

Stress management training usually requires 8 to 16 sessions. The length of treatment is usually dictated by the severity of the patient's problem(s). Stress management is most successful when there is an obvious relationship between stress and physiological disorder. Self-monitoring is especially helpful for establishing this association. For most cases with a clear relationship between stress and the identified problem, stress management training is very successful. In many cases, continuation of medications on a lower dosage is required for long-term maintenance of therapeutic gains. No significant negative side effects have been reported for stress-management training.

BIBLIOGRAPHY

Suinn, R. M. (1982). Intervention with Type A behaviors. *Journal of Consulting and Clinical Psychology, 50*, 933–949.

Turk, D. C. (1982). Cognitive learning approaches: Applications in health care. In D. M. Doleys, R. L. Meredith, & A. R. Ciminero (Eds.). *Behavioral medicine: Assessment and treatment strategies.* New York: Plenum Press.

Whitehead, W. E., & Bosmajian, L. S. (1982). Behavioral medicine approaches to gastrointestinal disorders. *Journal of Consulting and Clinical Psychology, 50*, 972–983.

Williamson, D. A., Labbé, E. E., & Gransberry, S. W. (in press). Outpatient treatment of somatic disorders in adults. In M. Hersen (Ed.). *Outpatient behavior therapy: A clinical guide.* New York: Grune & Stratton.

Williamson, D. A. (in press). Behavioral and pharmacological treatment of physiological disorders. In M. Hersen & S. E. Breuning (Eds.). *Pharmacological and behavioral treatment: An integrative approach.* New York: Wiley.

See: Anger Control Therapy
　　　Anxiety Management Training
　　　Stress Inoculation

SUCCESSIVE APPROXIMATION
Patricia Wisocki

Successive approximation is one of the key concepts in the operant process for shaping new responses in a behavioral repertoire. In the course of shaping, successive approximation to the desired end behavior is systematically reinforced.

The process of successive approximation is also evidenced in the technique of systematic desensitization. In the building of a desensitization hierarchy, the anxiety-provoking scenes are ordered along a continuum from least- to most-fearful.

See: Forward Chaining
　　　Shaping

SYMBOLIC MODELING
Michael Milan

All forms of modeling in which a human model is observed "live" by the client are considered to be symbolic modeling. Symbolic modeling therefore includes such diverse forms of modeling as films or videotapes of individuals engaging in behaviors that are to be imitated; the use of puppets, dolls, cartoon figures, or animated objects that perform live, on film, or on videotape; specific instructions that are listened to by the client, read by the client, or memorized by the client and then repeated overtly or covertly to guide behavior; and descriptions of behaviors that are embedded in stories that are listened to by the client, read by the client, or learned by the client and then repeated aloud or in imagination. It has long been recognized that much, if not most, of what is learned in the natural environment is learned from models, and many, if not most, of those models are symbolic rather than live. Only recently, however, has symbolic modeling been studied carefully by psychologists, and what has been learned been applied to the development of new and effective psychotherapeutic techniques.

CLINICAL APPLICATIONS

The clinical applications of symbolic modeling are numerous and varied, and it has been successfully employed to treat problems occurring in the three major psychological domains of affect, behavior, and cognition. The use of symbolic modeling in the affective domain is exemplified by Melamed and Siegel's (1975) treatment of anxiety experienced by children facing hospitalization and surgery. In that study, 60 children between the ages of 4 and 12 years who were about to undergo elective surgery were shown either a film of a relevant peer being hospitalized and receiving surgery, or an unrelated control film. The 16-minute modeling film consisted of 15 events that most children encounter when hospitalized for surgery from the time of admission to discharge, with various scenes narrated by the male patient who described his feelings, concerns, and coping responses at each stage of the hospital experience. The 12-minute control film presented the experiences of a relevant male who was followed on a nature trip in the country. Stated measures of anxiety revealed a significant reduction of pre- and post-operative fear arousal in the children who viewed the modeling film in comparison to the children who viewed the control film. Moreover, parental reports of behavior following return to the home indicated an increase of behavioral problems in the children who viewed the control film but not in the children who viewed the modeling film.

Undoubtedly, most symbolic modeling research and practice is directed at the modification of inappropriate behavior. An early and remarkably sophisticated example of this strategy is provided by Chittenden (cited in Bandura, 1969) who sought to decrease the aggressive and domineering behavior of preschool children and replace it with cooperative solutions to interpersonal conflicts. To do so, Chittenden constructed 11 brief plays featuring dolls who modeled aggressive or cooperative solutions to realistic interpersonal conflicts common to the preschool setting, with the aggressive solutions resulting in unpleasant outcomes for the models and cooperative solutions producing desirable outcomes for the models. In comparison to a no-treatment control group, children who viewed and discussed the 11 plays showed a decrease in dominative aggressiveness in a situational test. In addition, pre-, post-, and 1-month followup analysis of the treated children revealed a decrease in domination and an increase in cooperativeness during naturalistic obser-

vations in preschool. More recently, Mitchell and Milan (1983) utilized comic strip drawings for four popular "super-hero" cartoon characters to symbolize and encourage four different pre-school skills deemed necessary for the continued educational development of children who showed deficiencies in those areas. Once each week intensive symbolic modeling was conducted by the teacher who directed the children's attention to a large and prominently-placed drawing of a super-hero displaying one of the four skills and told a story about the super-hero which incorporated the performance of the skill and ended in a desirable outcome. On the remaining days of the week the teacher merely referred to the model and reminded the children of the skill and its importance. The symbolic modeling procedure produced a small but durable improvement in behavior. The subsequent addition of tangible reinforcement for imitation then produced a larger, clinically-significant improvement in behavior. Moreover, the effect of reinforcing the imitation of some skills generalized to the imitation of other skills and produced correlated, clinically-significant improvements in behaviors which were never directly reinforced.

The impact of symbolic modeling procedures upon the cognitive domain is exemplified by the thorough work of Sarason and Sarason (1981) who combined live or videotape modeling with role playing in preventative efforts that involved the teaching of both cognitive and social skills to students in a high school with high dropout and delinquency rates. The models portrayed adaptive, problem-solving cognitive processes and social skills in problematic situations common to the student population, such as resisting peer pressure, asking questions in class, and getting along with parents. The modeled enactments were then followed by group discussions and role plays in each of the 11 class sessions devoted to the training portion of the program. A control group received routine health instruction while the live and symbolic modeling groups participated in the prevention program. Comparisons among the pre-, post-, and follow-up data for the three groups revealed that the students in the prevention programs increased their skill at thinking of more adaptive ways of approaching problematic situations, performed more effectively in problematic situations and, at 1-year follow-up, showed lower rates of tardiness, absenteeism, and behavior referrals relative to the students in the control group. The two treatment groups did not differ from each other on these measures.

EXPECTED OUTCOMES

The expected outcomes of symbolic modeling are excellent, and the time frames in which these outcomes may be achieved are relatively brief. The studies cited herein document that when symbolic modeling is properly utilized, it can serve as a key ingredient in therapeutic efforts directed towards the remediation of a wide range of affective, behavioral, and cognitive difficulties; the effects of these procedures have considerable generality; the results can be long-enduring; and the improvements in levels of functioning can be achieved in a relatively small number of sessions, often ten or less.

CONTRAINDICATIONS OR UNTOWARD SIDE EFFECTS

Symbolic modeling has few contraindications or untoward side effects and in large part is more dependent upon the characteristics of the client and the form of symbolic modeling employed than upon the general effectiveness of symbolic modeling itself. It would be unwise, for example, to use any form of symbolic modeling with clients who

had not yet learned imitation, or to employ symbolic modeling through literature with clients who were poor readers. Similarly, symbolic modeling has been found to be less effective than live modeling with retarded persons and young children. Additional factors bearing upon the applicability of symbolic modeling have also been identified. In the treatment of irrational fears, for example, researchers found that children with a wide variety of fears benefited less from symbolic modeling than did children with few fears. Also, ability to generate clear mental imagery appears to be a necessary ingredient of covert symbolic modeling procedures. Continued research will undoubtedly generate additional knowledge about the conditions under which symbolic modeling should and should not be employed as a treatment of choice.

Several guidelines that should be followed in order to maximize the benefits of symbolic modeling have also been established. Among these, three are deserving of note. First, symbolic modeling that is supplemented with actual exposure to and contact with feared situations is more effective in the treatment of irrational fears than is modeling alone. Second, the opportunity to practice skills that have been modeled symbolically is more effective in teaching these skills than is modeling alone. Finally, symbolic modeling that is supplemented with reinforcement for imitation is more effective in the fostering of appropriate behavior than is modeling alone.

BIBLIOGRAPHY

Bandura, A. (1969). *Principles of behavior modification.* New York: Holt, Rinehart & Winston.

Lazarus, A. A., & Abramovitz, A. (1962). The use of "emotive imagery" in the treatment of children's phobias. *Journal of Mental Science, 108*, 191–195.

Melamed, B. G., & Siegel, L. J. (1975). Reduction of anxiety in children facing hospitalization and surgery by use of filmed modeling. *Journal of Consulting and Clinical Psychology, 43*, 511–521.

Mitchell, Z. P., & Milan, M. A. (1983). Imitation of high-interest comic strip models' appropriate classroom behavior: Acquisition and generalization. *Child and Family Behavior Therapy, 5*, 25–30.

Rosenthal, T. L., & Bandura, A. (1978). Psychological modeling: Theory and practice. In S. L. Garfield & A. E. Bergin (Eds.), *Handbook of psychotherapy and behavior change: An empirical analysis*. New York: Wiley.

Sarason, I. G., & Sarason, B. R. (1981). Teaching cognitive and social skills to high school students. *Journal of Consulting and Clinical Psychology, 49*, 908–918.

See: Modeling

SYSTEMATIC DESENSITIZATION
Joseph Wolpe

Systematic desensitization is a term applied to a class of methods used for gradually weakening unadaptive anxiety-response habits through the use of responses competitive with anxiety. In the commonest routine, a physiological state inhibitory of anxiety is produced in the patient by means of muscle relaxation, and he/she is then exposed for a few seconds at a time to a stimulus arousing weak anxiety. With repetition of the exposure, the stimulus progressively loses its ability to evoke anxiety. Then successively "stronger" stimuli are treated in the same way.

EXPERIMENTAL BACKGROUND

The physiological process on which desensitizing procedures are based is counterconditioning (reciprocal inhibition). Its use in the context of anxiety was first proposed by Watson and Rayner after they had conditioned fear of a white rat in an 11-month-old child. Of four treatment strategies they suggested, one was to enable feeding to occur in the presence of the feared object. The successful implementation of this suggestion by Jones (1924) in the treatment of a variety of childhood fears marked the formal inception of behavior therapy. Her method was the progressive approximation of the feared object while the child was enjoying candy, keeping the object always far enough away not to interfere with the eating.

The weakening of anxiety response habits by a competing response was studied in detail by Wolpe (1958) using cats as experimental subjects. High levels of anxiety response to an experimental cage were conditioned in the animals by high-voltage low-amperage shocks applied to their feet. The response was not decreased by prolonged and repeated exposure of the animal to the cage — an observation in contrast to modern day therapeutic flooding. The anxiety inhibited the eating of fresh meat in the experimental cage, or even on the floor of the experimental laboratory. Other rooms elicited anxiety by generalization — according to their similarity to the laboratory. In a room where the anxiety was not great enough to inhibit feeding, the animal ate successive pellets of meat with increasing readiness, while the anxiety receded, finally to extinction. The same train of events occurred in rooms successively more similar to the experimental laboratory. Eating behavior was thus eventually re-established in the experimental cage, and by its repetition all anxiety was eliminated.

Informal trials with human adults revealed feeding to be of very little value for overcoming their unadaptive anxiety response habits. Assertive expressiveness was successfully employed as an inhibitor of the anxiety associated with timidity; but no formal clinical parallel to the experimental therapy could be developed until a clinically viable anxiety-inhibiting response was found. The response that eventually proved usable was progressive relaxation, which Jacobson had for some years been advocating to combat "nervous hypertension." A great many patients benefited from his program of intensive training and assiduous daily practice. But this method was very time-consuming and gave the therapist very little control of the process of change. Wolpe (1958) experimented with programs of exposure to graded phobic stimuli in patients who had acquired modest ability to calm themselves by 6–10 sessions of relaxation training. Finding it difficult to grade real-life situations, he explored the use of imaginary situations and found that felt anxiety diminished progressively through the repeated presentation of imaginary situations that were weakly anxiety-arousing. Increasingly fear-invested situations could thus be deconditioned of anxiety. Of great significance was the observation of transfer of the deconditioning to the corresponding real situations.

In the conduct of desensitization the autonomic effects of relaxation can ordinarily counteract only relatively weak anxiety responses. A stimulus that evokes a *strong* anxiety response may be presented many times to the relaxed patient without the anxiety diminishing (Wolpe, 1958). This of course is generally true only of *brief* stimuli. Many observations indicate that response decrement often does occur if relatively strong stimuli are administered for long periods.

STANDARD DESENSITIZATION TECHNIQUE

Before attempting behavior therapy, a thorough assessment of the requirements of the patient must be made, based upon a careful anamnesis and appropriate questionnaires. When systematic desensitization is indicated, it is begun as soon as possible, and may take place in parallel with measures aimed at other areas of disturbance. It is important

to note that systematic desensitization is effective not only in classical phobias, but also in many social anxieties, as well as less obvious and often complex sources of neurotic disturbance, which may involve ideas, bodily sensations, or extrinsic situations. The most common extrinsic sources of anxiety relate to people in contexts that make irrelevant the use of direct action, such as assertion. As examples, one patient reacts with anxiety to the mere presence of particular persons, another to definable categories of people, a third to being the center of attention, a fourth to people in groups, a fifth to inferred criticism or rejection.

However, in every instance for which systematic desensitization is appropriate, the anxiety is a *conditioned response*—i.e., it is elicited by a triggering stimulus, though the subject perceives no danger. These cases must be clearly distinguished from those with unadaptive anxiety responses that are based on the *belief* that danger exists where objectively it does not, and whose treatment calls for cognitive correction.

Three separate sets of operations are involved in the technique: (1) introduction to the subjective anxiety scale, (2) training in deep muscle relaxation, (3) construction of anxiety hierarchies, and (4) counterposing relaxation and anxiety-evoking stimuli from the hierarchies.

THE SUBJECTIVE ANXIETY (SUD) SCALE

Quantification of the patient's anxiety responses is useful to the therapist for judging the efficacy of relaxation training, and for indicating how much anxiety different stimuli arouse. The subjective scale is introduced thus: "Think of the worst anxiety you have ever experienced, and assign to this the number 100. Now think of being absolutely calm and call this zero. Now you have a scale to communicate how much anxiety you feel at any time."

TRAINING IN RELAXATION

The method of relaxation usually taught is essentially an abridged version of Jacobson's—taking up 10 to 15 minutes of each of four to six sessions, with 15 to 20 minutes' homework practice required daily. Many people achieve adequate calming from relaxing only the upper half of the body and no further training need be given them.

Attention is first drawn to the sensations that tension produces in individual muscles, starting in the arms, then moving in turn to face, jaws, tongue, neck, shoulders, trunk, and lower limbs. At each site the patient is told, after locating the tension, to let go and to "keep trying to go further and further in the negative direction." Particular attention is given to relaxing the muscles of the head and neck, since these appear often to produce the most marked calming, indicated by the *sud scale*.

If the patient has previously learned to calm himself by another method, such as autogenic training or transcendental meditation training, relaxation training is usually unnecessary.

CONSTRUCTION OF ANXIETY HIERARCHIES

The stimuli to anxiety almost always belong to a limited number of themes. Most are either classically phobic like fear of heights, or social, like fear of rejection. Hierarchies are usually constructed at the same sessions as relaxation training, but they can be altered or added to at any time. It is important to note that this operation is carried out in an ordinary conversational way and not under relaxation, drawing on information from three main sources: (1) the patient's history, (2) his responses to the Willoughby and Fear Survey Schedules (Wolpe, 1982), and (3) special probings about particular fear areas. The patient ranks the items of each area in order of intensity of fear arousal; and this ranked list is the hierarchy.

The construction of a hierarchy may be straightforward, as in many classical phobias, but may also be very difficult, because, for example, the sources of anxiety are not directly revealed by the patient's listing of what he avoids. For example, one person's fears of trains, heights, and other situations turned out to be secondary to a phobia about losing control of urination.

Fear and avoidance of social occasions is in some cases based on fear of criticism or of rejection; and in others it is a function of the number of people to whom the patient is exposed. One patient's fear of social situations was really a conditioned anxiety response to certain food odors in public places. Social hierarchies are invariably outwardly variegated in content, as the following example illustrates:

Guilt Series
1. "The Dean wants to see you."
2. Thinks: "I only did 10 minutes' work today."
3. Thinks: "I only did an hour's work today."
4. Thinks: "I only did 6 hours' work today."
5. Sitting at the movies.
6. Reading an enjoyable novel.
7. Going on a casual stroll.
8. Staying in bed during the day (even though ill).

Most hierarchies vary in a single dimension, but many have two or more. Bi-dimensional hierarchies are the rule in fears of the attitudes and opinions of other people. The fear's intensity varies with the character of the disparagement (selfish, lazy, etc.) and also with the person who expresses it. The hierarchy is set out in the form of a grid instead of the customary list.

DESENSITIZATION PROCEDURE

In the standard procedure, progressively "stronger" anxiety-arousing stimulus situations are presented to the imagination of the deeply relaxed patient. While he sits or lies with his eyes closed, the therapist calms him by having him relax in systematic order, from the head downwards, the muscle groups in which he has been trained.

The presentation of scenes at the first session is to some extent exploratory. The first scene is always a neutral one — to which a patient is not expected to have any anxiety reaction. This is followed by the presentation of the mildest item from one of the hierarchies. The patient raises an index finger when an image is clear. When, after a few seconds, the therapist terminates the scene, he elicits from the patient by how much his *sud* level was raised by it. After a pause of 20–30 seconds during which relaxation is renewed, the scene is presented again, and the sequence is repeated until the scene ceases to evoke any anxiety, at which point the next scene up the hierarchy is introduced. Three or four presentations of a scene are usual for extinction of anxiety, but 10 or more may be needed.

There is great variation in how many themes, how many scenes from each, and how many presentations are employed at a session.

THE RESULTS OF SYSTEMATIC DESENSITIZATION

Of 68 anxiety-response habits in 39 patients treated by systematic desensitization in a 1962 study, 45 were apparently eliminated and 17 more markedly improved (Wolpe, 1982, p. 173). Numerous later reports showed similar results. Among controlled studies, two early ones are noteworthy. Paul (1966) found that psychoanalytically trained therapists obtained, in subjects with severe public speaking fears, significantly better results with systematic desensitization than with their own insight-based techniques or a placebo treatment. Lang, Lazovik, and Reynolds (1965), comparing systematic desensitization with a "pseudotherapy" in the treatment of snake phobias, found the former superior at the .001 level. All of eight well-controlled experiments surveyed by Paul (1969) produced "solid evidence of the effectiveness of systematic desensitization."

VARIANTS OF SYSTEMATIC DESENSITIZATION

More than a score of variants of systematic desensitization have been reported. Real stimuli or their pictorial substitutes are necessary for patients in whom imagined scenes cannot be used effectively. Most of the other variants involve responses that can replace relaxation as anxiety-competitors. These include emotional responses evoked by verbally induced imagery, responses to weak electrical stimulation, electromyographic biofeedback, and conditioned "anxiety-relief" responses.

CONTRAINDICATIONS

In general, systematic desensitization is not appropriate for unadaptive fears aroused by situations that require motor skills on the part of the patient. Treatment of the fearfulness of timidity, for example, also calls for the development of new modes of motor and verbal behavior, which is achieved at the same time as deconditioning of anxiety by assertiveness training.

Systematic desensitization is also inappropriate for fears based upon misconceptions (which require cognitive correction) and for realistic fears, which are understandably unresponsive to all efforts to remove them. Furthermore, it should not be used, except in special circumstances, in syndromes in which other methods have been notably more effective — as in the fears of contamination that are the basis of handwashing compulsions.

COMMENTS ON CRITICISMS

In recent years, the view that countercondi-tioning is the basis of the change that follows systematic desensitization has been called in question. Some researchers, for example, perceive its true basis to be non-specific effects of "expectancy." However, the experiments they quote do not show expectancy to be much of a factor. Nonspecific emotional events are indeed the presumptive basis of most of the effects of therapies other than behavior therapy apparently through pro-viding an unplanned source of response competition, and doubtless contribute to the success of behavior therapy, too. The existence of non-specific effects was indicated by the positive results found in Paul's (1966) attention-placebo group. But the significantly greater success he noted with systematic desensitization clearly showed that that pro-cedure produced *additional* effects.

It has also of late been stated that relax-ation makes no contribution to the efficacy of systematic desensitization. A great deal of the research supposedly showing this has been summarized by Kazdin and Wilcoxon (1976). Most of this research is of dubious significance, since it studies analogue popu-lations with weak fears that are known to be susceptible to elimination by minimal procedures that apparently depend on non-specific effects, and some studies have em-ployed hopelessly inadequate relaxation. Borkovec and Sides (1979) showed that in

studies where relaxation was a factor in recovery, there had been an average of 4.57 relaxation training sessions, in contrast to 2.30 sessions in studies where it had been found to make no difference.

BIBLIOGRAPHY

Borkovec, T. D., & Sides, J. K. (1979). Critical procedural variables related to the physiological effects of progressive relaxations: A review. *Behaviour Research and Therapy, 17*, 119.

Jones, M. C. (1924). Elimination of children's fears. *Journal of Experimental Psychology, 7*, 382.

Kazdin, A. E., & Wilcoxon, L. A. (1976). Systematic desensitization and non-specific treatment effects: A methodological evaluation. *Psychological Bulletin, 23*, 729.

Lang, P. J., Lazovik, A. D., & Reynolds, D. (1965). Desensitization, suggestibility and pseudo therapy. *Journal of Abnormal Psychology, 70*, 395.

Paul, G. L. (1966). *Insight versus desensitization in psychotherapy*. Stanford, CA: Stanford University Press.

Paul, G. L. (1969). Outcome of systematic desensi-tization. In C. M. Franks (Ed.), *Behavior therapy: Appraisal and status*. New York: McGraw-Hill.

Wolpe, J. (1958). *Psychotherapy by reciprocal inhibition*. Stanford, CA: Stanford University Press.

Wolpe, J. (1982). *The practice of behavior therapy* (3rd Ed.). New York: Pergamon Press.

See: Autogenic Training
    Deep Muscle Relaxation
    In-Vivo Desensitization
    Self-Control Desensitization

THOUGHT STOPPING
Patricia Wisocki

Thought stopping is a self-control procedure developed for the elimination of persevera-tive thought patterns which are unrealistic, unproductive, and/or anxiety-arousing, and either inhibit the performance of a desired behavior or serve to initiate a sequence of undesirable behaviors.

As part of the behavioral analysis, the therapist asks the client to list any disturb-ing thoughts which s/he feels are out of her/his control including those which may have harmful social consequences, as thinking about robbery or rape, and those which contribute to a negative self-image. Each item on the list is translated into a concrete statement in the client's own vocabulary. The Thought Stopping Survey Schedule, a list of 51 statements commonly repeated by clients, may also be administered to provide some focus to the interview. The client is also asked to estimate the frequency of occurrence of each self-statement selected.

Once the target thoughts are agreed upon, the therapist and client discuss the rationale for eliminating them. This discussion is all-important. It usually centers around the idea that such self-statements have no value to the client and in fact are detrimental to constructive action, often leading to maladaptive overt behaviors, such as withdrawal from social events, derogatory self-statements, and negative verbal behavior. If the client's complaint is in the area of maladaptive approach behaviors, such as overeating, smoking, or excessive alcoholic intake, the therapist inquires about anticipatory thoughts antecedent to the behavior (e.g., saying to oneself, "I'd love to have a drink") and explains that the elimination of such thoughts should correspondingly reduce the frequency of the target behavior. Finally, the therapist discusses the self-control aspects of the thought stopping (TS) procedure, indicating to the client that once s/he has learned TS, it will be available to him/her at any future time as needed.

The following are the verbatim instructions given to a client as a demonstration of the TS technique.

"Now sit back, relax, and close your eyes. In a few seconds, I'm going to say the word 'go.' As soon as I say the word 'go,' I want you to deliberately think this thought: (example: "The future is hopeless"). As soon as you begin the thought with the words, 'The future,' signal me by raising your right index finger. Do you understand the instructions? Okay. Lean back. Relax. Are you ready? Go."

As soon as the client raises his finger, the therapist loudly shouts, "STOP," an event which usually produces a startle response. The client then opens his/her eyes and the therapist asks about the experience. The client may respond in a number of ways. Some typical responses are: "Well, you startled me"; "I got scared"; or "You interrupted the thought." If the client does not mention that the thought itself disappeared, the therapist prompts for that specific response and then goes on to explain that a person cannot think of two things at the same time. A second trial is given during which the therapist does not shout "stop" immediately upon the client's signal, but waits about one second before evoking the startle response again. Again, inquiry is made about the experience and the client usually responds that the thought disappeared.

In explaining the need for the client to learn the technique for his/her own use, the therapist gives the following instructions:

"I'm going to ask you to close your eyes again, but this time I'm not going to shout 'stop.' Try to imagine as well as you can, or try to hear yourself shouting 'stop' very loudly. Keep practicing until you can get it as clear and as loud as possible. Then open your eyes." When the client opens his/her eyes he/she is asked if the imagery was sufficiently clear and loud and able to evoke a jolt. If the client reports some problem he/she is asked to practice again. If there is still a problem the client is encouraged to yell "stop" out loud several times and then to rehearse the technique once more with the particular target thought. If after some repetition, good auditory imagery still has not been obtained, the patient may be asked to imagine he/she sees the word "stop" in red letters, while saying the word to himself/ herself or to image a brick wall or a policeman holding up his hand. Generally, however, after some practice, clients do not report any problems with imagery.

In ensuing trials, client and therapist alternate interruptions of the thought for approximately 10 minutes (amounting to about 20 trials) until the client indicates that he has learned the procedure. At the end of the session, the client is instructed to rehearse the procedure at specified times during the day (two or three blocks of 10 to 20 trials apiece) and whenever there is any spontaneous occurrence of the thoughts discussed during the assessment phase. In order to prevent some discouragement when the thoughts may recur, the therapist points out that there is more value in repeating "stop" than in entertaining the thought. Clients are reminded that, with the use of TS, the target thought will eventually occur less and less frequently, until finally it disappears altogether. A weekly check is made of the frequency of practice, the specific thought that occurred, and any failures experienced with the TS practice.

During each subsequent therapy session 5 to 10 minutes a week are given over to rehearsal of the TS procedure. This time allotment may be increased or decreased, depending on the amount of practice engaged in by the client and on the progress he/she is making. When the client is first learning the procedure, he/she is told to interrupt the thought only at its initiation (e.g., "Signal when you *begin* to think the thought "). Later trials deal with the thought in various stages nearing completion (e.g., "Signal when you arrive at the word _____ "). Finally, other trials are presented in which the thought sequence is interrupted on a random basis, instead of at each occurrence.

OTHER CONSIDERATIONS

1. Although it has sometimes been helpful to follow the "stop" image with a pleasant or distracting thought, it is not generally recommended in the initial stages of learning TS. Usually clients have enough difficulty remembering to say "stop" without asking them to search for another response.

2. If clients express fear that the use of TS will submerge important thoughts which will surface again or that such thoughts are true indications of problems which need resolution, they are reminded of the obsessive and ruminative nature of the thought patterns which interfere with constructive action and generate further anxiety. Clients are told that the elimination of non-constructive worrying should enable them to deal effectively with their specific problem.

3. It appears important to eliminate each link in a particular thought chain. Taylor, however, has presented an example in which successful results were obtained by the interruption of the incipient thought alone.

4. Wolpe has described a modification of the TS procedure in which shock is applied concomitantly with the "stop" signals. He has suggested the use of this method especially for clients who do not respond well to the regular TS procedure. He has also reported successful results in instructing clients to think pleasant thoughts and then to activate a buzzer as soon as any disturbing thoughts intrude. When the buzzer sounds, the therapist shouts "stop."

5. The TS technique is not only useful for thought patterns, but may be employed with "feelings" and "images" as well as several overtly observable behaviors. The TS technique is used with behaviors characterized as "obsessive" or anxiety-

evoking, with avoidance behaviors and with approach behaviors.

6. TS is rarely used alone. It is easily adaptable for use with other behavioral procedures and has been used in conjunction with covert reinforcement, desensitization, relaxation, and covert sensitization.

7. The only cautionary note in the literature occurs in descriptions of the use of TS with clients for whom the unexpected shouting of "stop" may be physically disturbing, such as for people with heart problems or with the elderly infirm. With appropriate preparation and discussion of the procedure, there should not be a problem with these clients. Also, auditory stimuli may be replaced by other sensory stimuli.

BIBLIOGRAPHY

Cautela, J. R. (1975). *Thought stopping survey schedule.* Unpublished form. Chestnut Hill, MA: Boston College.

Cautela, J. R., & Wisocki, P. A. (1977). The thought-stopping procedure: Description, application, and learning theory interpretations. *Psychological Record, 1*, 255–264.

Taylor, J. (1963). A behavioral interpretation of obsessive-compulsive neurosis. *Behaviour Research and Therapy, 1*, 237–244.

Wisocki, P. A. (1976). A behavioral treatment program for social inadequacy: Multiple methods for a complex problem. In J. Krumboltz & C. Thoresen (Eds.), *Counseling methods.* New York: Holt, Rinehart, & Winston.

Wolpe, J. (1969). *The practice of behavior therapy.* New York: Pergamon Press.

See: Covert Rehearsal

TIME-OUT
Rex Forehand

Time-out (TO) is a procedure whereby positive reinforcement is not available to an individual for a period of time. Implementation of the procedure is contingent upon the emission of a response (typically an un-

desirable one by an individual), and it is designed to decrease such behavior. TO primarily is utilized with children but can be used with adults, typically institutionalized retarded or psychotic persons.

TO is a complex procedure consisting of a number of parameters.

1. *Duration:* Length of TO can vary from a few seconds to several hours. The duration typically has been from 3 to 15 minutes.

2. *Location:* TO can be imposed either in the same environment in which the undesirable behavior occurred or by removing the individual to another environment in which reinforcement is not available (e.g., placement in an empty room). When the same environment is used, TO can occur by simply ignoring the individual (e.g., removing attention) or by restricting the individual's movement within that setting (e.g., sitting in a chair or standing in a corner). The primary advantage of the separate area location is an increase in the probability that all positive reinforcement will be effectively removed during TO. However, a separate area may not always be available.

3. *Reinforcing value of the natural environment:* The natural environment from which an individual is "timed-out" can vary in its reinforcing value. For example, a child could be in a classroom which is highly reinforcing (e.g., substantial teacher praise for appropriate behavior) or one which is not reinforcing (e.g., little teacher praise).

4. *Verbalized reason:* TO may or may not be accompanied by a reason (e.g., "You have to sit in the TO chair because you did not pick up your toys.") for why the procedure is being implemented.

5. *Release:* The individual can be released from TO either contingently or noncontingently upon his/her behavior. Contin-

gent release typically involves the individual not displaying disruptive behavior (e.g., screaming, physical disturbance of the environment) for a prescribed period of time (e.g., 30 seconds) prior to removal from TO. With noncontingent release the individual's behavior in TO does not affect his/her release.

6. *Schedule:* TO can be administered on a continuous or intermittent (variable or fixed ratio) schedule.

7. *Warning:* TO can be preceded by a warning (e.g., "If you yell again, you will go to TO.") or implemented without a warning.

Research data are available at this time to *suggest* the following conclusions regarding the various TO parameters.

1. TO durations of medium length (e.g., 3 to 15 minutes) are more effective than shorter durations, particularly if the shorter durations are preceded by longer durations. Ethical concerns exist when longer durations (e.g., 1 hour) of TO are utilized.

2. Removal of the individual to a separate environment where reinforcement is not available is more efficient (i.e., reduces the number of TOs required) than leaving the individual in the same environment and removing reinforcement.

3. If the natural environment is low in reinforcement value, TO will be less effective than in a natural environment that is high in reinforcement value.

4. The presence/absence of a reason does not influence the effectiveness or efficiency of TO.

5. Contingent release from TO is more effective than noncontingent release in decreasing the undesirable behavior for which TO was implemented and for decreasing disruptive behavior during TO.

6. High ratio intermittent schedules (e.g., FR 5), when not preceded by low ratio schedules, are variable in effectiveness. However, such intermittent schedules of TO can be effective when applied to a behavior that has already been reduced to a low frequency by a low ratio or continuous use of TO.

7. The use of a warning prior to TO increases its efficiency (i.e., reduces the number of TOs required).

As is evident from the above parameters, TO can vary substantially in how it is administered. One sequence will be presented as an example:

1. A male child is instructed to pick up his clothes.

2. If he does not comply, a warning is issued ("If you do not pick up your clothes, you will have to go to TO.").

3. If the child again fails to comply, the parent leads him to the bathroom (devoid of all dangerous items) without verbalizations and in an unemotional manner, places him in the room, and states "You did not pick up your clothes so you have to stay in time-out until I tell you that you can come out." The parent then closes the door.

4. Yelling and crying are ignored.

5. After 5 minutes, including the final 30 seconds being void of yelling, the child is released from TO.

6. The original command is repeated.

7. Compliance is followed by praise and noncompliance by a repetition of steps 1–6.

TO has been used in homes, day care centers, pre-schools, schools, institutions, and public facilities (e.g., grocery & department stores). The procedure has been found to be effective in reducing a wide range of maladaptive behaviors, including, but certainly not limited to, noncompliance, aggression, stealing, disruptive verbalization, property destruction, and tantrums.

In order to maximize the effectiveness of TO, several procedures should be followed. First, TO for undesirable behavior should be utilized in conjunction with positive reinforcement for desirable behavior. Second, TO should be administered in a non-emotional manner. Third, during TO all sources of reinforcement should be removed. Fourth, TO should be used consistently, particularly when initially being implemented with a particular behavior.

There are several advantages to using TO as a procedure to decrease undesirable behavior. First, there is substantial research to indicate that the procedure is effective. Second, research is available (as reviewed above) to indicate the most effective parameters of TO and, how it should be implemented. Third, use of TO allows both parties (e.g., the parent and the child) the opportunity to "cool down" rather than undesirable child behavior being handled by yelling, screaming, or use of physical punishment.

There are a number of potential difficulties with the use of TO. These include the following: some settings (e.g., institutions) have banned the use of TO, an individual can potentially injure himself/herself in TO, the procedure may be difficult to implement and to enforce with large individuals, TO is designed to decrease an undesirable response rather than teach an appropriate behavior, and a backup for TO (e.g., physical restraint, removal of a privilege) may be necessary when an individual is not isolated behind a physical barrier (e.g., a closed door). Finally, it is important to note that public reaction to procedures that have been called TO has been negative in some cases.

Ethical issues also must be considered when using TO. When time-out is used in a public institution (e.g., school), consent from the appropriate person should be ob-tained to insure that the individual's rights are not violated. The treatment plan for the individual should also specify the parameters of TO (e.g., duration) and provide mechanisms for data collection and for monitoring him or her while in TO.

BIBLIOGRAPHY

Forehand, R. L., & McMahon, R. J. (1981). *Helping the noncomplaint child: A clinician's guide to parent training.* New York: Guilford.

Gelfand, D. M., & Hartmann, D. P. (1975). *Child behavior analysis and therapy.* New York: Pergamon Press.

Hobbs, S. A., & Forehand, R. (1977). Important parameters in the use of time-out with children: A re-examination. *Journal of Behavior Therapy and Experimental Psychiatry, 8,* 365–370.

MacDonough, T. S., & Forehand, R. (1973). Response-contingent time-out: Important parameters in behavior modification with children. *Journal of Behavior Therapy and Experimental Psychiatry, 4,* 231–236.

Ollendick, T. H., & Cerny, J. A. (1981). *Clinical behavior therapy with children.* New York: Plenum Press.

See: Contingency Management
Punishment

TOKEN ECONOMY
Alan E. Kazdin

The token economy is an intervention based on the delivery of positive reinforcement for specific target behaviors. The reinforcers that are delivered consist of tokens (e.g., tickets, coins, stars, points) that can be exchanged for a variety of other rewards that vary with the particular clientele. Essentially, three ingredients define a token economy: (1) the tokens or medium of exchange, (2) the rewards or back-up reinforcers that can be purchased with the tokens, and (3) the set of rules that define the interrelationships among the specific behaviors that earn tokens and the back-up reinforcers for which tokens are exchanged. The notion of an "economy" reflects the fact that tokens operate in a similar fashion to money in an ordinary economy. In fact, many concepts from economics such as earnings, expenditures, and savings, all have important counterparts in a token economy in a treatment environment.

Any event can serve as a token as long as it is feasible to administer. The tokens must only be obtainable by performance of desired behaviors. Once earned, the tokens can be spent for privileges and other rewards such as consumable items (e.g., food, gum), special activities (e.g., free time, watching television), money, clothes, and others. A wide range of back-up reinforcers is provided from which clients may select. The range of back-up reinforcers imbues the tokens with their generalized reinforcing properties.

The use of tokens offers several advantages. First, tokens are potent reinforcers and can often maintain behavior at a higher level than other reinforcers such as praise, approval, or feedback. Second, tokens help bridge the delay between client performance of a desired behavior and delivery of a reward (back-up reinforcer). Third, tokens are less subject to satiation than many other reinforcers, because they can be used to purchase a variety of back-up events. Fourth, tokens permit conducting a large-scale incentive program using a single system of reinforcement. All clients can receive a common reinforcer (the tokens) and exert their individual reward preferences in exchange for tokens for back-up events.

CLINICAL APPLICATIONS

The token economy has been applied to a wide range of clients including psychiatric patients, the mentally retarded, children, adolescents, and adults in school settings, delinquents, prisoners, substance abusers, autistic children, geriatric patients, and others. Within a particular population, the diversity of applications has been broad. For example, among psychiatric populations, token economies have been applied to acute, chronic, organic brain syndrome, psychosomatic, and neurotic patients. Although the bulk of applications has been in traditional treatment, educational, and rehabilitation facilities, extensions of the token economy have increased in the last decade. For example, token economies have been used on a community-wide basis to address important social problems (e.g., energy conservation), in business and industry to improve employee performance, and by the armed services to enhance basic training of soldiers. The token economy has also been used extensively for outpatient treatment of assorted problems for individual clients including the management of oppositional child behavior at home or at school and adherence to diet, exercise, or medication regimens. There probably is no other psychosocial intervention that has been applied as broadly to diverse populations and settings and at the same time has been so well evaluated empirically.

EXPECTED OUTCOMES

The token economy has been evaluated in hundreds of outcome studies. The evidence has indicated that the token economy can be extremely effective in producing change in specific target behaviors while the program is in effect. Also, changes in specific target behaviors (e.g., self-care behaviors of psychiatric patients) often are associated with broader improvements (e.g., reduction in psychotic symptoms, community adjustment).

The bulk of the research has evaluated the effects of the token economy over relatively short periods and while the reinforcement contingencies remain in effect. Typically, temporary suspension or termination of the progam has led to decreases in the target behaviors to a level at or near pretreatment performance. This has led to concern about the extent to which the token economy can produce long-term changes. Relatively few reports have evaluated the long-term effects of the token economy. However, available evidence suggests that the treatment gains produced by token economies are not inevitably lost. Extended studies with psychiatric patients and disadvantaged youths in educational settings have shown that gains can be maintained up to several years after the program has been terminated and clients enter new settings where the program has not been in effect. Maintenance of treatment effects can be enhanced by a variety of treatment procedures that are introduced into treatment while the token program is in effect. These techniques include such procedures as gradually removing (fading) the reinforcement contingencies, altering schedules of administering the reinforcers, permitting persons to earn themselves off the token economy by showing protracted high level performance, and others.

POTENTIAL SIDE EFFECTS OR CONTRAINDICATIONS

Few deleterious side effects or contraindications have been noted in token economies. Problems that emerge in selected programs usually appear to result from how the particular program has been designed and implemented and hence may be controverted by changes in the contingencies. In a few reports, client resistance (i.e., expressions of anger, complaints) has been noted. Complaints usually stem from the requirement to earn reinforcers that may previously have been provided noncontingently. Consulting with clients during the planning and development of a program and involv-

ing them in the implementation of the economy usually helps to overcome such resistance.

Client resistance is less likely to be a problem than is the finding that a small number of persons fail to respond to the program. Such persons may show little or no change in performance, change in only some of the target behaviors, or evince only transient changes. Rarely is deterioration in performance actually found. In instances where clients show little or no change during the program, various changes in the contingencies such as the alteration of back-up reinforcers, and the use of group or peer-based contingencies can enhance performance.

Although the token economy has been applied widely to different populations, little evidence is available about the differential responsiveness of persons as a function of diagnostic, subject, or demographic variables. For example, among psychiatric patients, no consistent pattern has emerged about the type of patient, chronicity of the disorder, age, gender, or other characteristics that are associated with responsiveness to the intervention. Indeed, one of the attractive features of the token economy is that it can be adapted to a wide range of populations and treatment conditions. Selection of target behaviors, back-up rewards, and tokens can be varied to meet the requirements of special populations.

In institutional settings, special care needs to be invoked to ensure that back-up reinforcers are selected that do not interfere with the legal rights of involuntarily confined persons. Many rewards (e.g., access to exercise, visitors, interaction with others) have been ruled by the courts as rights to which involuntarily confined persons are entitled rather than privileges that need to be earned. In practice, this has not interfered with designing effective programs.

Reinforcement programs for involuntarily confined persons provide back-up events beyond those in the setting to which individuals are normally entitled. Additional activities, privileges, opportunities for free time, and rental and purchase of small commodities are often used in such cases.

BIBLIOGRAPHY

Ayllon, T., & Azrin, N. H. (1968). *The token economy: A motivational system for therapy and rehabilitation.* New York: Appleton-Century-Crofts.

Bushell, D., Jr. (1978). An engineering approach to the elementary classroom: The Behavior Analysis Follow Through Project. In A. C. Catania & T. A. Brigham (Eds.), *Handbook of applied behavior analysis: Social and instructional processes.* New York: Irvington.

Kazdin, A. E. (1977). *The token economy: A review and evaluation.* New York: Plenum Press.

Kirigin, K. A., Braukmann, C. J., Atwater, J. D., & Wolf, M. M. (1982). An evaluation of teaching-family (Achievement Place) group homes for juvenile offenders. *Journal of Applied Behavior Analysis, 15,* 1–16.

Paul, G. L., & Lentz, R. J. (1977). *Psychosocial treatment of chronic mental patients: Milieu versus social-learning programs.* Cambridge, MA: Harvard University Press.

See: Behavioral Family Therapy
  Classroom Management
  Contingency Management
  Operant Conditioning
  Parent Management Training
  Positive Reinforcement

VERBAL AVERSION

See: Covert Sensitization

VICARIOUS CONDITIONING

E. Thomas Dowd

Vicarious conditioning is a social learning procedure in which behavior or emotional reactions are altered by observation of modeling diplays, rather than by direct, in vivo performance. All *direct* conditioning paradigms have vicarious counterparts. In vicarious *operant* conditioning, the model is observed being reinforced (or punished) for performance of the target. In vicarious *classical* conditioning, the model experiences close temporal pairing of the conditioned and unconditioned stimulus followed by the unconditioned response. Research has shown that a coping model, who demonstrates imperfect but improving performance is more effective in vicarious conditioning than a mastery model, who demonstrates perfect behavior from the start. The principles of vicarious conditioning have been applied to explain how individuals can learn from experiences that they do not personally undergo.

See: Classical Conditioning
  Modeling

VICARIOUS EXTINCTION

E. Thomas Dowd

This is a procedure for elimination of fears and behavioral inhibitions by having individuals observe models performing fear-provoking behavior without experiencing negative consequences. Based on social learning theory, vicarious extinction is analogous to overt extinction, except that the individual does not have to be directly exposed to the conditioned stimulus. Rather, he/she learns by observing a model perform. Research has shown that live modeling is more effective in fear reduction than is symbolic modeling (e.g., films), and that multiple models are more effective than a single model. Participant modeling, in which the model first demonstrates the desired behavior, then personally guides the subject through progressively more feared responses until the fear is eliminated has been found to be especially efficacious. Vicarious extinction has been utilized to eliminate a wide variety of fears and behavioral inhibitions.

See: Extinction
    Modeling

VIDEOTAPE FEEDBACK
Michel Hersen

Videotape feedback is a moderately confrontational approach that has been used as an adjunct in individual, family, and group therapy. In addition, it is frequently used during the course of behavioral supervision of graduate level clinicians. As the term implies, the individual client, family, or group is videotaped during treatment. Subsequently, selected sections of the tape or entire tapes will be played back, with a target goal of changing the behavior in question. However, with rare exceptions, videotape feedback is not administered without the addition of therapeutic instructions, verbal feedback, and social reinforcement.

Empirical data do not support the use of videotape feedback, except as one facet of a multi-component treatment program. Also, use of videotape feedback is contraindicated for alcoholics videotaped while drinking and intoxicated. This only serves to increase subsequent alcohol consumption. In contrast, videotape feedback combined with instructions and verbal feedback from a supervisor appears to have potential as a teaching device for improving the therapeutic techniques of graduate level clinicians.

BIBLIOGRAPHY

Hung, H. H., & Rosenthal, T. L. (1978). Therapeutic videotaped playback: A critical review. *Advances in Behavioural Research and Therapy, 1*, 103–135.

Suess, J. F. (1970). Self-confrontation of videotaped psychotherapy as a teaching device for psychiatric students. *Journal of Medical Education, 45*, 271–282.

Eisler, R. M., & Hersen, M. (1973). Effects of videotape and instructional feedback on nonverbal and marital interaction: An analog study. *Behavior Therapy, 4*, 551–558.

See: Feedback

VISUAL SCREENING

See: Facial Screening

AUTHOR INDEX

Aasland, O. G. 66
Abel, G. G. 116, 142
Abramovitz, A. 117, 214
Adams, G. L. 57
Adams, H. E. 199
Adkins, J. A. 151
Agras, W. S. 100, 104, 142, 145
Alberti, R. F. 10
Alexander, J. 29
Alford, H. 145
Alkerson, B. M. 165
Allen, L. M. 14
Andrasik, F. 53
Apsche, J. 184
Argyle, M. 34
Arkowitz, H. 137
Armor, D. J. 82
Arnkoff, D. 60
Ascher, L. M. 160, 162, 163
Atwater, J. D. 227
Axelrod, S. 160, 183, 184
Axelroth, E.
Ayllon, T. 95, 135, 227
Azrin, N. H. 22, 64, 66, 95, 105, 113, 114, 135, 143, 144, 227

Baer, D. M. 77, 108
Bailey, J. S. 138, 140, 175
Baker, B. L. 192
Baker, T. B. 54, 56
Ballard, J. 48
Bandura, A. 68, 151, 213, 214, 215
Barker, J. C. 116
Barlow, D. H. 100, 142
Barmann, B. C. 113, 125
Baron, M. G. 91
Barrera, M., Jr. 147, 192
Barrett, R. P. 125
Barrish, H. H. 132
Barton, E. J. 21, 22, 182
Barton, E. S. 138, 140
Beale, L. L. 125
Bean, A. W. 108
Beauchamp, K. L. 113
Bechtel, D. R. 144, 160
Beck, A. T. 59, 60, 61, 63
Beck, Steven 134, 135, 163, 165, 188, 197
Becker, J. V. 125, 144, 180
Becker, Robert E. 142, 205
Becker, W. C. Jr. 108, 165
Bellack, Alan S. 10, 14, 34, 46, 95, 101, 137, 151, 185, 199, 209
Bennett, A. K. 91
Bergan, J. R. 23, 24
Bergin, A. E. 60, 215
Berman, P. A. 150
Berman, J. S. 63
Besalel, V. A. 143, 144
Beuldo, L. A. 165
Bichajian, C. 101

Bijou, S. W. 57, 77
Blakemore, C. B. 116
Blanchard, E. B. 53
Blenkran, M. M. 48
Borkovec, T. D. 104, 219
Bornstein, P. H. 30
Bosmajian, L. S. 212
Brady, John Paul 148, 150
Braiker, H. B. 82
Brantner, J. P. 160
Braukmann, C. J. 227
Breuning, S. E. 212
Brigham, T. A. 227
Bristol, M. M. 71, 138, 140
Bristow, A. 125
Broughton, S. F. 138, 140
Brown, R. A. 197
Brown, D. A. 53
Brownell, K. D. 46, 100
Broz, W. B. 56
Brunell, L. F. 155
Budd, K. S. 108
Burchard, J. D. 112
Burchard, S. N. 112
Burns, D. 150
Bushell, D. Jr. 227
Butler, J. E. 114
Butz, G. 71

Calhoun, K. S. 199
Campione, J. 197
Cannon, D. S. 54, 56
Carrigan, W. F. 117
Catalan, J. 173
Cataldo, M. F. 45
Catania, A. C. 227
Cautela, J. R. 86, 91, 94, 95, 96, 100, 101, 195, 222
Center, D. B. 121
Cermak, L. S. 147
Cerny, J. A. 224
Chambless, D. C. 130
Chapin, H. N. 142
Chaplin, T. C. 117
Chapman, S. 197
Chappel, L. 110
Chesney, M. 4
Chittenden 213
Ciminero, A. R. 46, 48, 53, 187, 199, 212
Cinciripini, Paul M. 39, 41, 44, 45
Clancy, J. 116
Clement, P. W. 21
Coates, T. J. 46
Cohen, D. C. 192
Coleman, A. D. 53, 118, 119
Conrad, S. R. 158
Conway, C. G. 116
Cordisco, L. 125
Cordua, G. 108
Corsini, R. 155

229

ABOUT THE EDITORS

Alan S. Bellack is Professor of Psychiatry at the Medical College of Pennsylvania and was formerly Professor of Psychology and Psychiatry and Director of Clinical Psychiatry Training at the University of Pittsburgh. He is President of the Association for Advancement of Behavior Therapy, and a Fellow of Division 12 of APA. He is co-author and co-editor of 12 books including: *The Clinical Psychology Handbook, Behavioral Assessment: A Practical Handbook*, Second Edition and *Research Methods in Clinical Psychology*. He has published numerous journal articles and has received several NIMH research grants on social skills, behavioral assessment, and schizophrenia. With Michel Hersen, he is editor and founder of the journals *Behavior Modification* and *Clinical Psychology Review*.

Michel Hersen is Professor of Psychiatry and Psychology at the University of Pittsburgh. He is a Past President of the Association for Advancement of Behavior Therapy. He has co-authored and co-edited 33 books including: *Single Case Experimental Designs: Strategies for Studying Behavior Change* (First and Second Editions), *Handbook of Psychological Assessment* and *The Clinical Psychology Handbook*. With Alan S. Bellack, he is editor and founder of *Behavior Modification* and *Clinical Psychology Review*. He is Associate Editor of *Addictive Behaviors* and Editor of *Progress in Behavior Modification*.

Pergamon General Psychology Series

Editors: Arnold P. Goldstein, Syracuse University
Leonard Krasner, SUNY at Stony Brook